Kirsty
Very Best Wishes,
Sue 19.V.08

The Contempo
Astrologer'
Handbook

an in-depth guide to interpreting your horoscope

Sue Tompkins

Flare Publications
The London School of Astrology

First published in 2006 by Flare Publications
in conjunction with the London School of Astrology
BCM Planets, London WC1N 3XX, England, UK
Tel: 0700 2 33 44 55
www.flareuk.com and www.londonschoolofastrology.co.uk
email: admin@londonschoolofastrology.co.uk

A CIP catalogue record for this book is available from the British Library

ISBN: 978-1-903353-02-8

To contact the author, please email her at sue@suetompkins.com
www.suetompkins.com

Astrological charts drawn by Sue Tompkins
Cover and layout: Tamara Stamenkovic
Editor: Jane Struthers

Series Editor: Frank C. Clifford

To Maureen Barker with love

Acknowledgements

Many people have helped directly and indirectly in the writing of this book. The true list might include every student I have ever taught and every client I have ever had a conversation with, but this much shortened version focuses on some of my closest buddies in the astrological world. Firstly thanks to Frank Clifford for agreeing to publish the book in the first place and for making such a good job of it, and to Jane Struthers for her editing skills and for her input generally. To Tamara Stamenkovic for her artwork and to Deana Necic for her ideas and expertise. Huge thanks too to Jane Hastings for being such a good friend; to Melanie Reinhart for Chironic and other conversations; and to Barbara Norris for negotiating with *Metro*. More generally, my long-term appreciation goes to Kim Farley, Babs Kirby, Lindsay Radermacher, and to members of maybe the oldest astrological group in town: Victoria Harper, Laura Thoresby and Gill Young. Also to all my friends at 60° North, especially Nan Lemaréchal (Oslo), Marit Dahl (Stockholm), Iris Hallankukka and Marita Hölttä (Helsinki). Also to Marja-Liisa Niemi Mattila for her professional generosity when I was working in Finland.

Sue Tompkins, August 2006

Contents

Chapter 1

First Things First – Philosophical Underpinnings

To every thing there is a season,
and a time to every purpose under the heaven ...

Ecclesiastes, 3:1

Some form of astrology has probably been practised in all cultures since civilization began. Seemingly, the roots of Western astrology date back at least several thousand years before Christ and to an area which embraces modern-day Iraq and parts of Syria and Turkey. While the history of astrology is rich and complex, the philosophical implications of the subject are arguably even greater.

Anyone who studies astrology seriously for a while will discover for themselves that it does *work* and, having made that discovery, questions such as '*How* can it work?' start to exercise the imagination. Then those other, sometimes dormant, often nagging, questions such as 'Why am I here?', 'Who is God?' also re-assert themselves. As with any rich and exciting subject, astrology can present us with as many questions as it answers. Regrettably many of the wider philosophical ramifications of astrology, and speculations as to how it might work, have to be largely set aside here.[1] What follows are a few, fairly standard, philosophical principles which underpin my particular way of viewing and practising astrology.

Fate and Free Will

One of the issues that astrologers and would-be astrologers alike grapple with is the issue of fate and free will. One question is: If astrology is true does it mean that our lives are fated? For me, the answer to this question is to be found in the Yes and No universal box of answers. Undoubtedly we must take full responsibility for our lives and for both our successes and failures, and to some extent we are also responsible for much that happens around us. Equally, there is nothing that happens to us, and nothing that we do, which is not reflected as a possibility or likelihood in our horoscope. The natal chart is basically a map of potential. Like a picture on a packet of garden seeds, it shows what we *might* become. Perhaps the best way of viewing the fate and free will question is to turn to the subject of maps. After all, the birth chart *is* quite literally a map for a particular moment. Talking metaphorically, imagine that you were born with a map of the Kalahari Desert and that I was born with a map of Birmingham. One might say that the Kalahari is your fate and that Birmingham is my fate. Our choices and potential are different. I have roads and canals that I can go up and down, and shops I can frequent but just because I have all the various features in my map it doesn't mean that I will visit them or, if I do, that I will do so *consciously*. In your map of the Kalahari you have different choices: choices of country, choices of game park, choices of whether to keep cattle or hunt wild game, choices as to whether you listen to the weaver birds or notice the acacias. So we both have at least some degree of free will but our choices are circumscribed by the perimeters of our particular map. Such perimeters might be described as our fate.

Of course the individual and their horoscope do not exist in a vacuum. We are all also at the mercy of a much larger fate – the destiny of our country, for instance. The fate of the individual is, to an extent, eclipsed by the fate of the greater whole. Similarly, the fate of one's country is secondary to the fate of the continent or the planet itself. Astrology offers an opportunity for glimpsing the potential of both destinies and, in so doing, increasing the opportunity for the exercise of free will. Governments, businesses, events – anything that has a beginning has a horoscope and will be caught up in the particular planetary cycles of the time of its inception.

Macrocosm and Microcosm

The idea that the cosmos is a unity and that all parts of it are interdependent is basic to most subjects under the occult, New Age and healing umbrella; in fact, it is central to the alchemists of yesterday and the quantum physicists of today. The ramifications of this way of thinking are vast, for if the universe is a whole and everything in it is a part of that whole, then hurting one small portion of it (even treading on an ant) means we also hurt the whole, including ourselves. Allied to the idea of unity and interdependence is the concept of macrocosm and microcosm. Stated simply this means that all happenings, all manifestations in and by the universe (macrocosm) are also reflected inside every individual (microcosm). Science confirms that all of nature can be broken down into the 118 elements that comprise the periodic table, so each human being actually contains all aspects of the world around them – all the plants, animals, minerals and celestial bodies.

The Hermetic Doctrine

Alchemy is often known as hermetic philosophy after Hermes Trismegistus, who, if he existed as a single individual, did so around 1900 BC. He is often thought of as the father of the alphabet, astronomy and mathematics as well as astrology and alchemy. His secret doctrine was only revealed to the few who came from far and wide to study at the mystery schools of Egypt. The term 'hermetically sealed' reveals how secret the doctrine was. The compilation of basic hermetic doctrines, passed on from teacher to student, was known as 'The Kybalion', and from it come the seven hermetic principles, all of which are confirmed by astrological practice.

i) The principle of *mentalism*. This first principle is perhaps the most difficult to grasp and perhaps should be set aside for the moment. Briefly the principle states that the universe is a mental creation of All That Is. This principle is basically concerning itself with God, infinity and eternity, which for most of us are unknowable.

ii) The principle of *correspondence* which states As Above, So Below, As Below, So Above. One might add, As Within, So Without. In other words, as it is in the heavens, so it is on earth. As it is on the physical plane, so it is on the mental and spiritual planes. As it is in the body, so it is in the mind. Each is a reflection of the other. The already mentioned notion of macrocosm and microcosm is one example of the principle of correspondence. There will be more on this subject later.

iii) The principle of *vibration*, which states that nothing rests, everything is in a state of flux, in constant and never-ending motion. Even the Earth, which we experience as being pretty fixed, is rotating on its axis and revolving around the Sun. Philosophers and scientists since time immemorial have said much the same thing: Aristotle (384-322 BC) said that all things are in motion all of the time, but this fact escapes our perception; Heraclitus (535-475 BC) held that the world is like a flowing river and that you cannot step into the same river twice. So all things vibrate, or they could be said to have a vibration *rate*. By changing the vibration, one changes the manifestation. Water at a high vibration is steam and at a lower vibration is ice. By changing its vibration, water manifests itself differently.

iv) The principle of *polarity* or duality, which states that everything has an opposite pole. All opposites are identical in nature but different in degree. Up and down are opposite to each other, as are light and dark. There is no such place as 'up' and no such place as 'down' – each is relative to the other. As with everything else on the list, the idea of polarity applies to emotional states, too. Love and hate, joy and despair are just two examples.

v) The principle of *rhythm*, which states that all things have their cycles, their tides; an ebb tide and a flood tide. All things flow in and out, all things rise and fall. All things go through the process of birth, growth, deterioration and death, and death can be taken to be a beginning, as well as an end point. There are thousands of such cycles – each day being one of them, each breath being another. Some cycles may last only seconds, others millions of years. If one accepts this (to me) self-evident truth that everything goes through the process of birth, growth, deterioration and death, then that must also apply to the Earth itself. Indeed, it seems to me that the Earth, or Western society at any rate, has reached middle age, even late middle age. The reason for this conclusion is the observation that the speed of life has increased substantially, especially in the inner cities. This can be taken as analogous to the fact that, as they get older, people report that time seems to go so much faster and, towards the end of life, that it goes very fast indeed. For the child, on the other hand, everything seems to go very slowly.

vi) The principle of *cause and effect*, which states that every cause has its effect and every effect has its cause. According to this principle, *everything* happens according to this law and there is no such thing as 'coincidence'. There are many layers of causation and what seems to be chance has really been caused by something or, usually, several things. The cause and effect principle might also be defined as the law of *consequences* because every thought, action or event has repercussions. Thought, however fleeting, comes before action. Everything we say or do, however trivial, has a consequence – it affects *something*. And whatever is affected, in turn, affects something else. From physics we learn that for every action there is an equal and opposite *reaction*. Not only does every act – mental, emotional or physical – project outwards and have a consequence, the same energy also rebounds back upon us, rather like a boomerang. In the East, the principle of cause and effect is known as karma[2] and isn't usually thought to be limited to the one life; if taken to its logical conclusion, it leads on to the notion of reincarnation. Astrologers don't necessarily believe in reincarnation (I am open-minded on this issue) and it is not necessary to believe in it in order to accept the principle of cause and effect. Whatever the reader's personal beliefs, the subject might as well be touched on at this point. The reincarnationist world view suggests that the physical body is but a vessel and, when it dies, the soul is reborn again and again.[3] The body is viewed as being merely a tool to enable the individual to live out their soul's purpose(s). In each life the individual reaps what they have sown in previous lives and also sows the seeds that can be harvested in a future life. Thus, according to the law of karma, our thoughts and actions may rebound upon us either in this life or in a future one. In each and every moment, we are creating both the next stage of our current life and also a future life, or so the theory goes. Thus, while the legacy of what we have set in motion in previous lives limits, at least to some extent, our current freedoms (and such limits might be defined as our fate), it can be seen that we can also change our future to some extent. While we cannot change what has already happened, we can certainly change our *attitude* to events and, given that action follows thought, by changing our attitudes we can change our destiny.

vii) The principle of *gender*, which states that all things have a yin and yang (or masculine and feminine) principle. The yang force is outgoing, positive and instigating, while the yin force is receptive and incoming. This again works on physical, emotional and spiritual levels. Even when having a conversation with someone, one can see the yin-yang principle at work. The person who is talking is in yang mode (giving out) and the person listening is in yin mode (receiving). In astrology, the fire and air signs are dubbed positive (or masculine), while the earth and water signs are negative (or feminine). Similarly, with the planets, the Sun and Mars are obviously yang and the Moon and Venus obviously yin.

More on Correspondences
While we live in a heliocentric (Sun-centred) universe, due to the Earth's rotation, as we go about our daily business we appear to live in a geocentric (Earth-centred) world: the Sun and all the planets *appear* to revolve around us. While the horoscope can be, and sometimes is, drawn from the heliocentric perspective, it is more commonly drawn from the point of view of human experience and thus depicted geocentrically.

Imagine yourself walking on the Earth. You have no buildings around you to obscure your view. The land under your feet is your horizon. You can look to the east and look to the west and watch sunrise and sunset. At lunchtime the Sun is overhead, and after sunset the Sun disappears altogether. Bear in mind that your particular horizon will be different to everyone else's horizon, unless they happen to be standing on the same spot of land as you. This is basically the start of a horoscope. The upper part represents daylight and the lower part night-time.

A Map of Life: a Starting Point for Correspondences
In fact, we can go further with our circle for it can be viewed as a map depicting a day, a year or a life. Assuming that it doesn't rain, what is the wettest time of day? The answer has to be the morning when there is dew on the ground. During the day, the Sun rises in the sky, creating heat and a drying effect, thus sunset is the dry time of day. It is hot at noon but actually hotter in the middle of the afternoon. Similarly the air is at its coldest some time after midnight, in the early hours. The year is similar: roughly speaking, spring is wet, autumn is dry, summer is hot and winter is cold. The

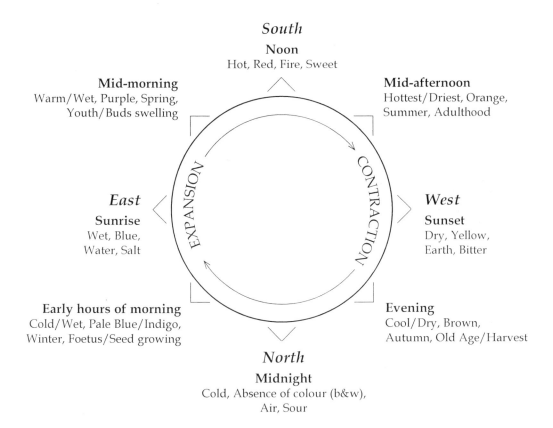

South

Noon
Hot, Red, Fire, Sweet

Mid-morning
Warm/Wet, Purple, Spring,
Youth/Buds swelling

Mid-afternoon
Hottest/Driest, Orange,
Summer, Adulthood

EXPANSION

CONTRACTION

East

Sunrise
Wet, Blue,
Water, Salt

West

Sunset
Dry, Yellow,
Earth, Bitter

Early hours of morning
Cold/Wet, Pale Blue/Indigo,
Winter, Foetus/Seed growing

Evening
Cool/Dry, Brown,
Autumn, Old Age/Harvest

North

Midnight
Cold, Absence of colour (b&w),
Air, Sour

individual's life is no different. We are at our wettest as a baby but dry out with advancing age. Old age is often referred to as the autumn years; a dry time when leaves go crisp underfoot and bones crack, skin dries out and wrinkles appear.

We can easily add the elements of fire, earth, air and water and also add colours and tastes to our circular map of life. Hopefully these are self-explanatory. Water has surely to be associated with blue, and do not salt and water always go together? Fire goes with red. As foods ripen in the sun they grow sweeter. When onions or any vegetables are fried, they become sweet. We grow bitter as we grow older and bitter foods tend to grow closer to the earth. Air can be associated with cold – if our food is hot, we blow air on it to cool it. If we leave milk out in the air it goes sour. We use the refrigerator or a fan – both systems of moving air – when we wish to bring down temperatures. The monthly Moon phases can also be added to the diagram, as can the equinoxes and solstices, and obviously the intermediary compass points.

Note that this illustration is offered as a way of understanding how some correspondences *might* arise – it is a map of life in general, and shouldn't be confused with actual horoscopes. Among different cultures, there are various versions of the elements and seasons. This particular model differs from that used by many astrologers and herbalists who, following the ideas of Plato, have ascribed a warm and moist quality to air. The model presented here accords more with my personal experience. It may have some historical credibility as the 4th-century physician Philistion seems to have favoured it. However, it is not necessary for the astrologer to adopt this diagram or even for the beginning student to understand it. Neither can I confidently assert that it is absolutely true. It is presented simply to illustrate that a day, a year and a life all reflect each other, and to suggest how seemingly unrelated things can reasonably be associated with each other.

The idea of correspondences has been embraced by alchemists and astrologers for centuries, and I doubt if there is an astrologer on the planet who wouldn't, for example, connect all kinds of inflammatory situations with Mars. Indeed, astrology might be described as the study of correspondences. The exciting thing about making these kinds of connections is that there is plenty of room for making more of them. All one has to be is observant and confirm one's observations time and time again to be sure that the ascriptions arrived at are the correct ones. Over the years, I have been able to ascribe different planets, signs and aspects to various members of the animal kingdom. For instance, in my observation (and this might accord with tradition also) the bird kingdom as a whole comes under Aquarius (see pages 64-7). To hone in on individual bird species, you should use all the zodiac signs: poultry may come under the sub-division of Cancer; swans (royal birds), peacocks and the like, under Leo; small birds such as sparrows under Virgo, and so on. One can do the same with insects, reptiles and all flora and fauna. Indeed, one can do it with all of life: notice how news stories concerning the police often 'coincide' with times when there are several planets in the sky in Taurus; how golfers will often have a Capricorn emphasis or Mercury-Saturn aspects in their charts; how Europeans visit Australia under Uranus transits, and countless other examples. With a little thought, one can usually work out *why* the given activity or place can be linked to the relevant symbolism.

One can make such connections without stepping outside one's front door just by observing what is happening in the world and in the sky. On page 15 is the front page for the London newspaper, *Metro*, on 28 June 2000. A casual glance will reveal little, but look a little more closely and notice that, at the top, the reader is advised of a review inside the paper of the then newly released film *Chicken Run*. The activities of the British tennis player Tim *Hen*man are promised on the back page and the cook Nigella Lawson is writing on *fowl* on page 10. All this poultry imagery is rather jokey, but watching the cosmos at work *is* jokey. The headline runs: 'Family backs Dando suspect.' At the risk of stretching things a little too far, a similar word to Dando in French – *dindon* – means *turkey*! With the allusion to family and all the references to chickens, it will not surprise any astrologer to learn that on that day the Sun, Mercury, Venus, Mars and North Node were all in the sign of Cancer – a sign to associate with family matters, food and *poultry*. The other sign that is most concerned with food is Taurus, and the Moon, Jupiter and Saturn were in that sign. The observant astrologer will be able to find yet more Cancerian imagery on this front page, should they choose.

All news items inevitably reflect whatever is going on in the sky at a given time and one doesn't have to confine one's observations to news items; even something as trivial as light entertainment will reflect the heavens. Turn on the TV and be prepared to channel-hop. Or turn to a TV listings magazine (the *Radio Times* is best in the UK because it gives more detail and also includes radio programmes). It doesn't matter which day you choose, or which medium you use (TV just happens to be easy), you will find subject matters that are clustered around a given theme. Of course, the most profound astrological deductions can often be gleaned from watching happenings in our own life and through observing the lives of the people around us.

FREE

METRO

Wednesday, June 28, 2000   www.metro.co.uk

First review of Chicken Run
Page 3

Family backs Dando suspect

Police inspect the wrecked car lying at the foot of the cliffs

Five survive as car falls 150ft down cliff

FIVE teenagers were injured but alive after their car fell 150ft down a cliff yesterday. Two girls and one boy were on the critical list in hospital last night. Two other boys have serious injuries.

The blue Ford Fiesta crashed over the cliff at a beauty spot called Sugar Loaf, a mile east of Beachy Head at Eastbourne, East Sussex at 4.45pm. The car

landed bonnet-first on chalk boulders before skidding on its roof to the water edge.

The 17-year-old driver and four passengers were all thrown clear.

Witness Ian Slothron, 38, from Brighton, said: 'The car seemed to come from nowhere. As it came down I could hear screaming. It was quite frightening.'

BY DAVID FISHER

THE family of the man charged with murdering TV presenter Jill Dando last night broke their silence to insist he was innocent.

In their first public statement on the charges, the relatives of Barry Bulsara said they were 'shocked and devastated' that he had been linked to the crime.

They added they would 'stand by him without reservation'.

Jobless Bulsara, 40, is accused of shooting 37-year-old Miss Dando outside her home in Fulham, West London, in April last year.

The statement, signed The Family of Barry George – his original name – read: 'Barry has been charged with a terrible crime and we are shocked and

devastated by the allegation. We wish to state that we love Barry, support him and stand by him without reservation.

'Despite publications to the contrary, we know Barry to be well-mannered and considerate by nature.

'Barry has good and close friends and we, as his family, love him very much.

'We believe in Barry's innocence and continue to do so. We will seek justice on his behalf and we place our faith in God and in the judicial system at this difficult time.'

The family went on to voice their worries about Bulsara's treatment at top-security Belmarsh prison in South-

East London, where he is being held on remand.

They said: 'We would all like to take this opportunity to register our concerns as to Barry's treatment since he has been in prison. We hope and pray that the prison will respect Barry's basic human rights.'

The statement continued with a request for the media to respect the privacy of Bulsara's family in England and that of his wife Itsako, and her family, in Japan.

Bulsara, who lived a few yards away from Miss Dando in Fulham, was remanded in custody by Bow Street magistrates on Monday to reappear at a committal hearing on July 28.

There was no immediate response from Miss Dando's family.

Although the empirical approach to science is not popular at the current time, for me, as long as one is rigorous in checking one's observations, it is still a very valid approach to employ. Consider astrologer/alchemist Paracelsus (1493-1541), the father of modern medicine, physiology, biochemistry, pharmacy as well as many complementary medicines. He was taught by his father, Wilhelmus, not to rely simply on books or the opinions of other authorities, but to observe nature directly and to learn from personal experience.[4] This he did. However much our knowledge has increased since the time of Paracelsus, there is still much that we don't know and also much knowledge that has been lost. Wilhelmus's advice holds as true today as it did in the 16th century: there is nothing wrong with having an empirical approach to science. Nothing happens randomly. As Jung puts it: 'Whatever is born or done at a particular moment of time has the quality of that moment of time.' In watching this process at work, the astrologer is able to have fun and potentially to make discoveries.

We are not all exposed to the same world and, even when we are, there are different ways of looking at that world and interpreting it. Arguably, it is the job of the astrologer to look at things from a wider perspective, perhaps from an inner, magical or soul perspective – rather as a priest, shaman or psychotherapist might. Or if that sounds too esoteric, one might just say that the horoscope is a map and the astrologer is a map-reader. Maps draw our attention to things that we might not otherwise notice (e.g. the remains of the Stone Age fort over yonder), maps help to give us a sense of perspective – we can see where we are in relation to everything else – and, finally, maps help us find our way. The astrologer's job includes making the whole process of navigating through life that bit easier.

That doesn't mean that the professional astrologer should be telling their clients *where* to go; the astrologer's job includes looking at the map and helping clients to find out where they are now. An example may help. Mrs Bloggs consults an astrologer about her work situation. She is unhappy at work because she feels her boss is being overly dictatorial and 'getting at her'. She reports feeling crushed and frightened. Mrs Bloggs wants her astrologer to tell her whether she should leave her job and try to find another one. Undoubtedly the astrologer would be able to assess whether now is a good time for finding a new job/going self-employed/changing her line of work/retirement, and so on. Indeed, the odds may be so stacked in the sky that the astrologer may even be able to guess pretty much what will happen. However, it is also the case that Mrs Bloggs is responsible for her life and needs to make her own decisions. *Also things change by the simple expedient of looking at them* – as always, energy follows thought.

The astrologer's job may actually be less about predicting what will happen *next* and more about interpreting what is happening *now*. For example, Mrs Bloggs may have a Tenth House Pluto, and Saturn in the sky may be conjuncting it, describing her current feelings and situation. The Tenth House refers to all authority figures including parents. The astrologer, knowing this, might ask Mrs Bloggs if her boss reminds her of anyone from her past, or if she has ever experienced feelings before which are similar to the ones she is experiencing now. The chances are that Mrs Bloggs will say something like: 'It's funny you should say that, my boss reminds me of my mother, who terrified me. I used to feel I was being criticized all the time. I feel now like I did when I was five.' The astrologer might then suggest that Mrs Bloggs is transferring her early feelings of impotence on to her current situation. As a child, Mrs Bloggs *was* powerless in the face of her parent but she is no longer a child. Now she is in a much stronger position to talk to her boss than she ever would have been with her mother. So she is being offered an opportunity. After the conversation, Mrs Bloggs may be able to view her situation differently. She might also speculate that, if she doesn't deal with the issues of feeling criticized and powerless now, she is likely to meet up with them again some time in the future. After all, when we travel, most of us take our baggage with us. It may be that changing her work situation and her boss is entirely appropriate for Mrs Bloggs. What *is* important is that whatever she chooses to do, she does so with as much awareness as possible, and that she makes her own decisions and is able to take responsibility for doing so.

Of course there remains the question of the degree to which her mother (and boss) *was* overly critical of her, and the degree to which she has projected her own criticism of herself on to these authority figures, but that kind of discussion can be left for another time.

The point is that the astrologer's job is, in my view, to discover the inner truth of a situation, in as far as that is possible. Astrology has almost limitless potential to increase consciousness and to shed light on endless situations. En route to being able to do this, the astrology student needs to become fluent in the basic language of the horoscope – the elements, signs, planets, houses and aspects.

Chapter 2

Elements and Modes

The Elements (or Triplicities)

Since the discovery of the periodic table and its 118 elements, the word 'elements' nowadays conjures up something much more complex than merely air, earth, fire and water. Even so, these basic four elements still provide a construct upon which it is possible to view both the natural world and human behaviour.

The four elements represent four basic ways of perceiving and processing stimuli.[1] These four ways can be summarized as:
- The impulse to make something happen or, if already in existence, the need to establish where it may be coming from or going to, and what it might *mean*. (Fire)
- The urge to make the fiery impulse a tangible reality or, if in existence already, the need to touch it and smell it. (Earth)
- The urge to communicate with or about 'it', possibly to name 'it' or establish what 'it' is. (Air)
- The need to emotionally connect with 'it' and to decide whether 'it' is agreeable or not. (Water)

In combination with the qualities, the elements are major building blocks of the zodiac and therefore provide an aid to understanding each of the twelve signs. Individuals and all horoscopes are made up of *all* the elements and qualities but some birth charts will have an obvious emphasis on some and an under-emphasis on others. Thus, an understanding of the elements and modes does more than foster an understanding of the signs: it can provide a starting point towards understanding the whole horoscope. While what follows concentrates on the elements in terms of human experience, it is no less relevant to consider what a preponderance or lack of an element might mean in a horoscope set for a company, country or event. For example, it is not uncommon for horoscopes set for the time of accidents to be weak in the earth element.

Fire – Aries, Leo, Sagittarius

Fire provides warmth and light and, just as heat always rises, the fire signs are characterized by their **upbeat** quality, their **enthusiasm**, their innate **faith** in life and, often, in themselves. Frequently there is an **infectious optimism** and a **joy** in living; sometimes even a Tigger-like bounce. As with a fire in the grate which becomes temporarily subdued for a time when logs are placed on it, the fiery type isn't crushed for long. Neither does classic fire hold grudges. Having said that, if there is a stronger presence of earth or water in a horoscope, these elements can do much to dampen the planets that are in fire, while planets in air will fan the flames.

The fire signs have a **vision** of how things could be and a gift for **inspiration**; each fire sign in differing ways can ignite others into enthusiasm and action. Aries ignites with the idea of a cause or of being a pioneer or warrior; Leo inspires others through appealing to honour, loyalty or the noble spirit; while Sagittarius gets others going through its quest for meaning and desire 'to go further', whether this be physically, emotionally or spiritually. Thus, the purpose of fire is to lead, inspire and imbue others with confidence. The fire signs are **positive** and tend towards extroversion and spontaneity. Fire is **stimulating** and good at just 'making things happen'. However, the classic fiery type has a dislike of any kind of passive situation and undervalues the quality of just 'being'. Fire has a speedy quality, it provides the impulse to do something and also the vision of what the completed thing might be like. The fiery type can sniff future possibilities and believe that they will become reality, and convince others that they will, too.

Overdeveloped, the fire signs periodically suffer from momentary collapse, they can burn themselves out by doing too much. They can also exhaust others, particularly more pragmatic types, by waxing enthusiastically over matters about which there is very little to enthuse.

Idealism rather than realism is the gift of fire – with one's head on the ceiling it follows naturally that one's feet can't touch the floor. Calmness, poise, sensitivity, empathy and subtlety are traits that don't come easily to the fiery type but may of course be found in other parts of the chart.

Earth – Taurus, Virgo, Capricorn

Our planet – the Earth – supports all life; we walk on it and we grow things in it. Not surprisingly, the earthy type of person tends to be **reliable** and **dependable**. **Practical**, **thorough**, **realistic** and **'down-to-earth'**, those who vibrate strongly to this element are usually comfortable with life's responsibilities, with earning a living, and with caring for and maintaining the body. The earthy type understands and works in accord with the limitations of the material world. They understand money and possessions and are aware of their own and others' reliance on these things. Earth is concerned with the 'real' world and, unlike fire, is not that interested in future possibilities. Each of the earth signs has an appreciation for what is real and tangible, a concern for what 'is', not for what 'might be'. Taurus and Capricorn especially want to produce something in tangible form, ideally something that can be seen and measured. Earth is at home with *matter* and feels quite insecure without it. This can apply to Virgo too, but Virgo with its mutable quality and Mercury rulership is perhaps the least earthy of the earth signs, feeling as it does slightly airy or more like *sand*.

The earth signs tend to be concerned with **security** in financial and material terms. Some earthy types will be acquisitive and ambitious to have a 'good life', but, for many, being secure materially doesn't necessarily mean being rich. The needs of the earth signs (whose goals in life may be narrower than their fiery counterparts) may be comparatively few, and many an earthy type feels comfortable as long as they have just enough, plus a little bit more. Classically, the earthy type has a fairly even and calm temperament. A dry sense of humour may also be in evidence.

If overdeveloped in the birth chart, earth can get bogged down by material considerations, reluctant to let anything threaten their material security. Unable to take risks, even if making life changes may be just what is required. At worst, overdeveloped earth can be narrow, overly cautious, conventional and conservative, perhaps even a plodder and a slave to routine. The presence of fire or the strength of fiery planets can do much to offset some of these tendencies.

Air – Gemini, Libra, Aquarius

Air has no form: it moves more from side to side than up and down, although air can and does go everywhere. Air ensures that there is no such thing as empty space. The right/left movement of air symbolizes the basically even temperament of the airy type. All sound, including speech and music, is dependent on air as all sound is produced by some kind of *vibration*.

Fire envisioned something, earth produced it and now air has to inform everyone about it. It is also the task of air to consider the *implications* of what has been produced and to generally decide where it falls in the general scheme of things.

The strong need of those with an emphasis on the air signs is to **communicate** and to feel communicated with, so relationships are essential to the airy type. While not necessarily warm or involved, typically airy people have strong **social skills**; they understand about give and take and don't get easily ruffled or take offence unnecessarily. In many ways the social skills arise out of the airy ability to keep things in **perspective** and **proportion**. The airy quality adds **rationality**, **objectivity** and an ability to take **the long view**. The strongly airy type may be interested in your point of view and able to understand it, even without necessarily agreeing with you. Not one of the air signs is depicted by animals and this also gives a clue to the very **civilized** nature of these signs.

At best, the airy type is refined, humane and courteous, with an awareness of the rights of others and a true sense of fair play. At worst, and if overdeveloped, the airy type can be unrealistic and overly rational, 'heady' and theoretical. Air tends to see life in patterns and formulas and then coerce all of life experience into those formulas. The problem is that things in practice can often be very different to how they are in theory. At worst, air is a slave to theory and principles, and the overly airy type can become out of touch with the real world and their own more personal needs. Excess air can also produce an indecisive, anxious and scattered quality.

Water – Cancer, Scorpio, Pisces

In nature, the water element can take on many forms: the babbling brook, a drizzle of rain, a stagnant pond and the raging sea are a few images. Undoubtedly water is wet; it lubricates, it cleanses, things can get dissolved in it, and without it there would be no life. Water has no form of its own and takes on the shape and colour of its container and, even more important, water always goes to the lowest point.

The water signs tend to be more **introverted** and **downbeat** than the other elements. The water signs are concerned with **emotional security** and belonging. With Cancer it is the family that provides a feeling of belonging, with Scorpio an intense intimate relationship, and with Pisces it is nothing less than a feeling of oneness with the universe, a spiritual belonging. As a glass of water needs the glass in order to feel contained, so the water signs can reflect whoever they are with. The water signs tend to be **impressionable** (Scorpio is less so) and absorbent. Watery types tend to be **sensitive**. They take on board all the feelings, subtleties and nuances around them and ideally assimilate what needs to be assimilated and let the rest flow away. At worst the watery type can get waterlogged and overwhelmed by all that they have picked up. With all this sensitivity it is not surprising that strongly watery types tend to feel **vulnerable** and exposed and thus tend to be **protective**, often self-protective, and rather **secretive**. With all the water signs there is a feeling of **'still waters run deep'**, a feeling that what you see is most definitely *not* what you get, that so much more is submerged.

Working well, water is the most **empathetic** of the elements and also the most **responsive**. At best, water can feel as you feel. The difficulty is that the overly- watery type may not be able to separate and may not know where you leave off and they begin. Overdeveloped, water can be clingy, needy, dependent, irrational, manipulative, unable to separate themselves from others and therefore over-identified with all that happens around them.

Elements in Combination

From an understanding of individual elements it is only a short step to understanding what they will be like in combination. Much could be written here, but I will put it briefly. While the **Fire/Earth** type may lack subtlety, they are likely to be dynamic; a visionary who gets things done, whatever the obstacle. **Fire/Air** may be an idealist full of big ideas (hot air), whereas steamy **Fire/Water**, a real creative type, will tend towards emotionality and mood swings. **Earth/Water** is the nurturer and burden-carrier of the zodiac and usually very concerned with their own and others' security. **Earth/Air** is a dry, pragmatic combination, often with a marked sense of humour and a very practical intelligence. For the rather sedentary **Air/Water** type, relationship is everything and a good understanding of people may be in evidence.

Elemental Lacks

As every horoscope embraces all twelve signs, no element can be truly said to be missing in any horoscope, nor in an individual's make-up. However, an element can be untenanted, i.e. there may be no planets falling in that element. Or there may simply be fewer planets in the given element. When this happens, the characteristics of the weak or missing element may manifest very strongly but operate from what appears to be an unconscious and less accessible standpoint. The individual seems to have no control over, and difficulty processing, whatever the given element signifies. Often the element takes on a pessimistic or negative cast. For example, fire is the element most at home with intuition, so a lack of fire can manifest as someone whose intuitions tend to be negative; in other words they are prone to a world view that expects dreadful things to happen. It is ideal for the writer of lurid horror and crime stories.

Perhaps it is because we humans are all struggling towards wholeness, but we tend to either 'marry' or work with any strong elemental (or other) lacks in our horoscope. Thus, the person who lacks air may choose partners whose charts are dominated by the air element, or they may work as counsellors or librarians. These are the individuals who endlessly collect books and maps. Whatever the so-called 'missing' element, we access it from *somewhere*. It is not only the number of planets in a given element which has to be considered but *where* the planets are falling. One might, for instance, have four planets in water in the Seventh House (the house of partners) but not seem watery at all. In that instance, it is the *partner* who will carry and manifest the water element.

In practice, a lack of an element can manifest in a vast number of different ways, depending to a marked degree on which factors *are* strong in the horoscope. Many charts will not have any obvious elemental imbalance at all, in which case the elements are not going to be a way into understanding those horoscopes. Listed below are some of the psychological principles to associate with missing elements, followed by common manifestations of elemental lacks.

• As a rule the individual has *less control* over what the given element represents. For example, a lack of water person may have less control over their feelings. Basically, the missing element just functions more *slowly*.

• As already noted, they often become obsessed with what the missing element signifies – they 'marry' it or do 'it' for a living. Sometimes an under-emphasis and an over-emphasis on a sign can *seem* to manifest very similarly, even if it is only at first glance.

• Individuals often express the missing element in quite a childlike, unsophisticated and innocent way. For example, a lack of earth person may have no embarrassment about revealing their body, and may be seemingly unaware of the effect their semi-naked body is having on others.

• Individuals can be very sensitive and 'touchy' with respect to what their missing element signifies. So, those with air under-emphasized may think others underestimate their brainpower, missing water may have a horror of being considered insensitive, and so on.

• Because of this sensitivity, the individual often seeks to overcompensate; the lack of water person may send more flowers and thank-you cards, for instance, and the lack of air person may be a great collector of qualifications or books.

• On another level, they tend to *undervalue* what the given element signifies and there is often an emotional charge around the difficult area, or a negative interpretation of others who appear to be sophisticated in that area. Thus, the lack of air person may have a dislike of 'intellectuals', the lack of water a suspicion concerning anyone who is 'too emotional' or 'sweet'. The lack of earth may accuse others of being too materialistic or dislike what they consider to be undue vanity in others. Finally, a person who lacks fire may dislike the world's gamblers or those who appear to get through life just trusting to luck.

What Constitutes an Elemental Lack?

There are no hard and fast rules as to what constitutes an elemental lack. Basically if something is not obvious then it is probably better to ignore it. Vast swathes of the population do not have strong elemental imbalances and, when looking at such horoscopes, the best bet is to move on and concentrate on other chart factors that are obvious. The important point to bear in mind, however, is that all planets are not created equal when it comes to assessing elemental strength in the chart. *Much* less emphasis should be given to the element in which the outer planets are found, for instance. After all, Pluto may be in a sign for thirty years and Uranus and Neptune are each in a sign for seven and fourteen years respectively. Similarly, Jupiter and Saturn need to be given much less weight than the personal planets.

What about Angles and Houses?

Like the other personal planets, and especially the Sun, Moon and Ascendant ruler, the Ascendant sign itself can be weighted fairly strongly in terms of assessing elemental preponderance, whereas the MC should probably be ignored from an elemental point of view, as it is not really such a personal point in the chart. However, it sometimes occurs that an individual has no planets in a particular element although that element is found on the Ascendant or MC. In my view, when an element is found on the Ascendant but scarcely anywhere else, the issue is that the individual *still* lacks the element but has some awareness of the lack and often accesses the element through the medium of the sign which is rising. Or someone may have no earthy planets, for instance, but have packed earth houses (Second, Sixth, Tenth). In this example, the individual will usually work with the earthy lack in their professional activities. The same would apply if the 'missing' element is found on the MC but nowhere else, an example of this being the horoscope for Marilyn Monroe.[2] Marilyn had no planets in earth, other than Chiron, but did have Taurus on her MC. Her career featured her looks and body a great deal, and to an extent her physicality is what she is famous for. However, her psychological make-up had all the hallmarks of an earthy lack.

Absence of Planets in Fire

While a lack of fire can sometimes manifest as a lack of drive and 'oomph' (depending on what the fiery planets – Sun, Mars and Jupiter – are up to in the chart), the more common difficulties concern accessing trust and faith. Faith and confidence in oneself, and in life itself, can be elusive. It is not easy for those who lack fire to access the childlike knowledge that things will 'turn out all right in the end'. The intuitions and hunches of the individual lacking fire tend to be negative. This may manifest as frequent feelings that something terrible is going to happen, such as dramatic 'something is out to get me' imaginings of assaults, robberies, murders and road traffic accidents. Superstition is another common manifestation. Many people consult the church, astrologers and clairvoyants (or take up these subjects) because of a lack of fire; they think if they know the worst, they can prepare for it! They can be slow too to realize that their fate, to a large extent, lies in their own hands. Subjects that defy easy explanation are ideal for the individual lacking fire. Subjects such as astrology and tarot can be beneficial because they open up the notion of *possibility*. Any kind of play and fun situations are also ideal as the ability to 'let go' can be elusive for some with the fire signs untenanted.

Absence of Planets in Earth

Difficulty with the earth element often manifests as an individual being out of touch with their body, with money or with 'things'. Equally the individual may be over-delighted with the earthy world and many have a strong, if naïve, appreciation of nature and the natural world. There can be fascination with the body and a childlike need to exhibit it, thus models, people who wear little or too tight clothing, even people who frequent nudist colonies, may all have a lack of planets in earth. Hypochondria can be another manifestation; the individual wonders if they have a terminal illness with each passing pain, whereas it is more likely that they simply forgot to stop for lunch! A lack of earth can also sometimes contribute to addictive personality types, as those with a weakness here often have difficulty in appreciating when enough is enough or knowing when to stop. An emphasized Saturn in the chart will decrease the chance of any addictive tendency, while a strong Neptune may increase it. Clumsiness, losing things or getting into debt are other possibilities with a lack of earth. Suggested therapy for those lacking earth can be anything physical such as gardening, yoga, massage or simple, physical exercises; anything that will help the individual to realize that the body isn't alien or separate.

Absence of Planets in Air

The main problem here can be in seeing the implications of one's actions and the actions of others. Being able to take an overview of a situation can be elusive too, and this can be problematic because glimpsing the larger picture enables us to keep things in perspective. Seeing our own needs in the context of the needs of others is another offshoot of being able to grasp the wider picture. Thus, individuals lacking in air may have difficulty in co-operating and compromising with others, and with behaving in a *reasonable* way. They may not be able to distance themselves from their problems and may be prone to wallowing (especially if the chart is watery) in their pain. For some, the prospect of meeting new people and adjusting to new situations can be anxiety-making, so much so that making life changes may not come easily. There may be a tendency to think the worst and to be something of an Eeyore or 'voice of doom'. A tendency to worry is the norm here. As a rule, a lack of air by no means diminishes the intellectual capacity or ability to think (for example, Einstein lacked air), but it can give rise to a lack of confidence in communicative and learning situations. Some will be easily influenced by the opinions of others. Missing air people often like maps and subjects that provide some kind of map for living; subjects such as psychology or astrology are ideal here as they can help increase a sense of objectivity and perspective.

Absence of Planets in Water

The main difficulty in having a lack of water can be in *processing* feelings. A minority who lack water or who have difficulty with the element may be completely out of touch with their feelings to the point of being downright lacking in empathy. In these instances, the feeling realm is felt to be so painful that feelings have become well and truly suppressed, usually due to early traumatic experiences. More frequently, though, the difficulty is not that the feelings aren't there – they may exist in abundance – but the individual has a less sophisticated relationship with them and less control over them. Rather like a tap when the washer needs replacing, feelings come and go willy-nilly. A lack of water can manifest as someone who is super-sensitive: after an argument with a loved one, for instance, they might believe that the spat spells the end of the relationship, rather than just the fact they have had a tiff. Thus, mismanaged water can be touchy and' defensive and feel emotionally raw. There is often a proneness to what might be called the 'grand passion' – periodically becoming so emotionally attached to someone that the individual feels as if they are drowning in feelings. People who lack water often express feelings in a sentimental way and are attracted to the more sloppy or childish expression of feelings. Various art forms such as music and painting are useful to those lacking water as they provide an outlet for the expression of feelings. And almost any situations involving people have the same potential.

The Modes (or Qualities or Quadruplicities)

As well as being divided into the four elements, the signs of the zodiac are also classified into three groups of four signs, known as the quadruplicities, modes or qualities.

	FIRE	EARTH	AIR	WATER
CARDINAL	Aries	Capricorn	Libra	Cancer
FIXED	Leo	Taurus	Aquarius	Scorpio
MUTABLE	Sagittarius	Virgo	Gemini	Pisces

As with the elements, an understanding of the quadruplicities is central to a good understanding of the horoscope. As well as helping us to understand the zodiac signs, any imbalances in terms of the modes usually gives clues as to how the individual both *views* and *deals with conflict*. Given that life itself is about conflict, we may as well say that the modes have much to tell us about *how we deal with life itself*. All twelve signs exist in each chart and most horoscopes will seem to have a fair balance between the modes, but some will obviously show a significant preponderance or lack, which, when it occurs, can be central to an understanding of the chart overall. More to the point, it is estimated that 40% of charts will have at least one T-square configuration (see page 228) and 5% of charts will have a Grand Cross (see page 229).¹ The way into the first steps of understanding how a given T-square or Grand Cross will operate is through careful consideration of the mode in which the configuration falls.

Cardinality – Aries, Cancer, Libra, Capricorn

The Sun's entry into each of the cardinal signs marks the beginning of the seasons for both Northern and Southern Hemispheres (albeit with different seasons), and the qualities of **beginnings, fresh starts** and **change** are strongly associated with cardinality. Having said that, this initiatory quality may sometimes be less obvious where the individual signs themselves are concerned. Aries is certainly concerned with pushing forward but Cancer can appear timid and Libra is characterized by indecision. However, each sign *can* be initiatory in its own particular fields. The word 'cardinal' comes from the Latin word *cardo* meaning 'upon which life hinges'. In the same way the cardinal signs concern themselves with the **central conflicts and issues of life**. The conflicts are those everyday pulls upon our time, interests and resources on which, for many people, life does indeed hinge: how to forge ahead, be a pioneer, do one's own thing (Aries), while honouring the need to co-operate and unite with another (Libra), and at the same time acknowledging the need to be established and respected in the world, to have status and a career (Capricorn), versus the need for home, familiarity, protection (Cancer), or even the needs and demands of our parents or of being a parent (Cancer and Capricorn).

People who vibrate strongly to cardinality tend to see conflict as being something external to themselves rather than as a reflection of something which is going on within them. Their energies are taken up with meeting the challenges presented by the outer world and perhaps by seeking to conquer them. The cardinal type doesn't stick in ruts;

if unhappy with a situation they go on to pastures new. Keen for action, people who vibrate strongly to cardinality (especially Aries) are not afraid to get things going and to roll up their sleeves. The problem with an overdose of cardinality can be the tendency to create a crisis if one doesn't already exist. **Initiatory**, **pro-active** and **opportunistic**, there can be a lot of **drive** and **dynamism** here with a corresponding dislike of restriction. A strongly cardinal type will not like to be hampered by restraints imposed by others or by circumstance, and often they will feel more comfortable being in charge. Cardinal types like to run things, to be in the driving seat – even before they have learned to drive. This is especially obvious in those with cardinal T-squares, and more especially Grand Crosses, who can suffer greatly from frustration, so urgent is the need to do their own thing in their own way. Suffering from overdrive and often an over-the-top **competitive spirit**, they will often be anti-establishment and anti the usual way of doing things. Poor planning is another feature of this action-at-any-price type. Thus, direct **head-on confrontations with others** are likely. Poise, calmness and some ability to accept the limitations both of oneself and others need to be cultivated.

From the health/body perspective, the cardinal signs can be associated with the onset of illness and acute conditions which invite swift intervention from health care practitioners. Acute situations left unattended are self-limiting; the organism will either recover (usually) and grow stronger, or will die. Acute disease is less observable in Western society these days as symptoms tend to be suppressed with antibiotics, rather than allowed to work their way through the system.

Well developed	Overdeveloped	Underdeveloped
• Able to start things	• Always starting things – possibly a difficulty in completing	• Lacks initiative – needs others to 'kick-start'
• Self-motivated • Goal-orientated	• Finds co-operating with others difficult, because so bent on the given goal	• May stick in ruts (if fixed) or avoid challenge (if mutable)
• Good in crisis	• Creates crisis and stirs up problems	• Avoids crisis at all costs
• In touch with the 'here and now'	• Concerned only with 'here and now' issues	• Avoids 'real' life

Fixity – Taurus, Leo, Scorpio, Aquarius

The notion of **attachment** is central to an understanding of the fixed perspective: Taurus can be overly attached to the material world and to trusting only what is tangible, Leo's attachment is to pride, Scorpio's to feelings and Aquarius's to ideas.

Fixity provides **persistence**, **stability**, **constancy**, **reliability** and thus the capacity for **endurance**. Endurance because the fixed type can put up with situations that cardinal or mutable types would find intolerable. Fixed types are the ones you want with you over the long haul, the concentrated kind of energy which is more akin to a cart-horse than a thoroughbred, highly-strung racehorse. On the down side, fixity tends to get stuck in ruts or stalemate situations. Letting go, whether of people, feelings, things or ideas, does not come easily to those overly developed in this area.

Fixity has great **resistance to change** and to being pushed, pulled or coerced. The meaning is akin to those times which mark the middle of the seasons, when change seems far off, for example, in high summer when spring is long gone and before there is even a hint of autumn in the air. The fixed time is a time for **establishing**, for making secure and building upon what cardinality started. The energy is concentrated, intense and prolonged. To fix something is to mend it and the fixed types are the great sustainers and **preservers of the status quo**. There is also the notion of being 'in a fix' where it seems as if movement in any direction is impossible. Those with a fixed T-square or more especially a Grand Cross can be especially unyielding and stubborn or particularly determined and persistent, depending on one's point of view. A 'might makes right' attitude can be the downfall of this type, who needs to learn to cultivate flexibility.

From the health/body perspective, fixity can be associated with chronic disease: diseases that take years to develop, which will slow the individual down, go on forever and simply have to be endured. Slow poisoning of the body and a holding on to pain are also fixed characteristics.

Well developed	Overdeveloped	Underdeveloped
• Determined and persistent	• Stubborn, obstinate and inflexible	• Lacking strength and staying power
• Self-willed	• Overly wilful	• Lack of willpower
• Constant, reliable and loyal	• Rigid, implacable and unable to adapt	• Inconstant and irresolute
• Sticks at it • Resistant to change	• Sticks in ruts • Inert, stuck	• Sticks at nothing
• Enormous energy ... once it gets going	• Tends to conserve energy (a pressure cooker)	• Blown every which way (especially if mutable)

Mutability - Gemini, Virgo, Sagittarius, Pisces

The mutable signs equate with the end of the seasons, for example when summer is turning to autumn. Not surprisingly, therefore, those people who vibrate strongly to this mode are good at coping with uncertainty and **shifting goalposts**. They are able to live in a **state of flux** and **transition**, always ready to respond to whatever is required of them. Not expecting (or even necessarily wanting) anything to be permanent, the mutable signs all have some tendency towards **restlessness**.

All the mutable signs are concerned with **ideas** (Gemini and Virgo) or **beliefs** (Sagittarius and Pisces), and since each has some tendency to experience life vicariously, to read about it, to talk about it or to philosophize about it, the challenge of the mutable type can sometimes be to actually live life. These are the signs that are concerned with their relationship to life itself, and are neither goal-orientated nor into power. Thus, although **commitment-shy**, the mutable type can be the easiest to get along with, as they don't tread so much on others' toes. The mutable types can hang on in there if they are interested; otherwise, forever restless, they move on. And when faced with conflict, discord or confrontation, there is a strong tendency to avoid it by simply changing direction. The establishment of goals and the achievement of them can therefore be particularly elusive, especially if a T-square or Grand Cross is involved. And those with mutable T-squares and Grand Crosses are particularly prone to anxiety, restlessness and inconsistency. To be productive, a modicum of self-discipline is essential here, as is the ability to set and keep to realistic goals. With mutable types there is not the urge to get to the root of things or put up with them (as with fixity), or to get on top of them (cardinality), but mutability is very gifted at adapting to circumstance. The mutable signs are sometimes called the 'common' signs and surely the reason for this is that the usual or common way of dealing with life is for us to adapt to it. The uncommon person is the person who gets the world to bend to them.

From a health perspective, as elsewhere, the main problem with the mutable signs can be a lack of resistance. These are the types who pick up every sneeze that is going and get anxious whenever a decision or commitment is required of them.

Well developed	Overdeveloped	Underdeveloped
• Adaptable and flexible	• Overly yielding and malleable	• Unable to bend or accommodate
• Able to co-exist with each and every circumstance	• Too easily side-tracked	
• Inclusive in orientation	• Unable to exclude	
• Ability to adjust	• Adjusts inappropriately – shifts when should hold firm	• Unable to adjust
• Curious, searching	• Without a goal, directionless	• Uncomfortable with moving goalposts
	• Scattered. Anxious	• Narrow

Chapter 3

The Zodiac Signs

The twelve signs of the zodiac can be described as 'ways of being' or types of energy. Most people are familiar with their Sun sign, but actually each planet is modified in its expression by the zodiac sign in which it is found. Similarly the activities of each house in a horoscope are modified by the sign on its cusp.

It is important to remember that the signs are not as important as Sun sign books and newspaper columns would have us believe. The planets, and the relationships between the planets and angles, are far more important in chart interpretation than signs. The signs are like adjectives, the words that describe, whereas the planets are the nouns.

Symbols and Glyphs

Each of the twelve signs has a symbol attached to it: e.g. Aries is the Ram, Taurus is the Bull, and so on. Basically, symbols are compressed and concentrated carriers of meaning. Each sign, like each planet, has a glyph, a pictorial representation to convey quickly the given symbol and a whole host of shorthand meanings and associations. Society as a whole is full of logos – instantly recognizable images – which convey information and feelings quickly and efficiently to people whose language may not even be the same. In the same way that we learn the common language of road signs, we can learn the astrological symbols (or glyphs) and use them as a shorthand.

The Signs as Developmental Phases

The signs can be read as a developmental story. For instance, one common story goes along the lines that Aries pioneered the land, Taurus built on it, Gemini went to meet the neighbours, Cancer started a family, and so on. In fact, one could come up with a range of stories while travelling through the zodiac. The signs grow more complex as one travels through them. At Aries we are simply at the embryonic 'I' stage of development, but travelling through all twelve we learn about ourselves, about relating to others, and about society and the universe as a whole. By the time we arrive at Pisces, more spiritual dimensions are in the frame.

Another significant point about the order of the signs is that each sign reacts against its predecessor, attempting to compensate for any lacks or extremes that the previous sign brought with it.

Sign Groupings

As we have already seen, the signs can be grouped in terms of their element or mode. Dividing signs in other ways can also be helpful to their understanding and, as with elemental or modal imbalances, can sometimes provide an important 'in' into understanding a horoscope.

The twelve signs neatly fall into three sectors of four signs. The first sector, comprising the first four signs (Aries, Taurus, Gemini and Cancer), is concerned with the basics of life, what might be termed fundamental or survival needs. The next four signs (Leo, Virgo, Libra and Scorpio) venture into more social and relationship issues, while the last four signs (Sagittarius, Capricorn, Aquarius and Pisces) concern themselves with collective or universal matters and, in the case of Pisces, the spiritual realm. Sometimes a horoscope has an emphasis or under-emphasis on one of these three groupings and this can provide the all-important entry into understanding what the chart and individual are about. For instance, where there are no planets in the first four signs (or, if one is using this idea with the houses, the first four houses), the individual may put their own personal needs aside or be out of touch with them. Where there are no planets in the last four signs (or houses), the person may ignore some of the larger questions of life or the wider world. The meanings of the various permutations should be fairly obvious. Not too much stress should be laid on this idea, unless, as usual, it is also borne out by other factors. For instance, if the houses tenanted *also* reflect similar ideas to the signs that are tenanted (e.g. no planets situated in the last four signs and no planets in the last four houses either), this could be taken as being significant.

Sections on the Body

Health comments must not be taken too seriously as all twelve signs do appear in every horoscope and, as with everything, the *whole* chart has to be considered and each individual factor appropriately weighted to assess its importance (or lack of). In general terms, though, health comments based on signs (which can only ever be vague) apply not only to your Sun sign but also to the sign on your Sixth House cusp and possibly your ascending sign, too. Note that the sign position of Saturn is often a weak area of the body.

Points to Consider When Using this Section

• Learning about the signs should help you to interpret the various planets and angles in a horoscope from the point of view of their sign. The cookbook sections under each planet will also help you do this.
• As there has been so much written on Sun signs, they have not been emphasized in this book but this section should help you to understand the main Sun sign characteristics. Just remember that Sun signs are hugely over-emphasized in the press, and that our Sun describes more *what we are striving to become* than a set of characteristics that are already completely ours.
• Every sign is contained within each horoscope somewhere; you can tell in which area(s) of life you are at your most Taurean or Geminian, for instance, by looking for the houses (and cusps) where those signs are to be found. Don't forget that the ruler of the house cusp is crucial and will give you more information. This is explained in more detail on pages 300-1.

Aries ♈

Element: Fire
Mode: Cardinal
Ruler: Mars

The Symbol and Glyph

The Ram is the symbol for Aries and the glyph of the sign can be interpreted as being the horns and nose of the male sheep; the so-called battering ram. The beginning of Aries starts with the first day of spring (in the Northern Hemisphere), *the* time of new beginnings. Aries rules the head and the glyph also resembles the eyebrows and nose.

General Characteristics

As the first sign of the zodiac, Aries is concerned with **new beginnings**. Being first is a key to much of the psychological traits of the sign and also to its vulnerability and naïveté. Any planet in Aries is usually affected with this '**being first**' and **competitive** quality. But despite the theme of being first, many an Aries type, in my experience, appears to be the great **copier** of the zodiac: if you have got it then Aries wants it. Aries will pick up an idea, run with it and become famous for it as if no one had ever thought of it before. Aries can be like a child revelling enthusiastically in the discovery of something, joyfully unaware that countless others have previously made the same discovery.

Pioneers have **courage** in embarking into the unknown. However, doing things for the first time (or, never having asked, *believing* them to be for the first time) usually means that one is ill-prepared. Little wonder that the sign is associated with traits such as **fervour, enthusiasm, immaturity** and **naïveté** and also with **impetuosity, foolhardiness** and **recklessness**. These are qualities that go with youth, vitality and the pioneering spirit. They also on occasion go with mischief-making and generally getting oneself into hot water. Mythical stories of swashbuckling heroes and knights on white chargers rescuing damsels in distress (e.g. Robin Hood) all have an Arien ring to them. Having said that, it should be added that planets in Aries can represent either the rescuer (Robin) or the rescued (Maid Marian), and not necessarily along gender lines.

Aries needs **action**; a pro-active sign, it isn't Aries' style to idly sit around waiting for something to happen. Aries meets life head-on. **Having a cause** of some kind brings out the best of the sign, and by that I mean **something or someone to fight for** or, at least, something to *do*. Aries is good in situations which require quick decision-making or have a trouble-shooting aspect to them. Anything which has the aspect of chase or conquest is also ideal. Activities that require reflection, self-doubt or compromise, on the other hand, will often fall way outside the typical Arien league.

The Aries quality can be arrogant, **impulsive, impatient** and sometimes downright reckless, but the **vitality** and enthusiasm of the sign can do much to spur others into action. Planets in Aries can also spur other parts of the horoscope into action. On the other hand, those who vibrate strongly to the sign can be overly self-centred and opportunistic, and the often seemingly naïve way of pushing themselves forward can be **antisocial** and may offend more subtle types. The ram is **honest** and **direct** in its dealings – there is no going round the houses. It may not be easy for the strongly Arien person to see another's point of view; co-operation doesn't come easily to those who vibrate to Aries, but the real weakness of the sign stems from the inability to separate oneself from what is going on and thus a tendency to take everything personally.

Sun and Moon Ariens are often accused, sometimes quite justifiably, of being bossy, but the sign is not really into power or even into leadership for its own sake. It is just that Aries is **self-motivated** and doesn't need or seek the approval, permission or co-operation of others. Typically, planets in Aries (and the Arien type generally) just want to do things in their own way; that is, not to be hampered, constrained or fettered by anyone or even by the energies described by other chart factors. Planets in Aries (in hard aspect) will often give rise to a feeling of frustration. This is sometimes because there can be a 'taking over' quality and a **tendency to butt in uninvited** in those with this sign strong. Others may not take kindly to such interference and may make efforts to block it. This pushiness is largely because of the need for action and the general impatience at the perceived slow pace of life and the slow pace of others. Aries hates sitting round while others are making decisions or spending too much time in preparing to act. Thus, Aries types make bad subordinates and are not usually good as team players either for, again, they tend to find others far too slow. Aries is wonderful at just doing, getting on with it, whatever the project in hand actually is, but the type tends to lack staying power. The purpose of Aries is to initiate, not necessarily to complete.

Aries thrives best on challenge but some degree of preparedness will always increase the chances of success in any undertaking. And understanding that results cannot always be quick will limit the feelings of frustration when obstacles do occur. As with Mars, the ruler of Aries, those with the Sun or Moon in Aries can be prone in particular to **whining** when things do not go as they want. Indeed, the phrase 'I want' is traditionally a key phrase of this sign. 'I want it now' might be more accurate. I am indebted to the astrologer John Alexander for his very accurate observation that the Sun in Aries person often reports feeling abandoned or, at least, left out of things. This can of course result from the difficulty that Aries can have in co-operating. For instance, imagine the Arien whose choice of dinner is a Mexican take-out while all his friends want to dine at the local Chinese. He is then nonplussed when they all leave him for noodles and sweet and sour! But the feeling of being left out can also be a reflection of how much Aries wants to be in the thick of whatever is going on. It is not that he is left out any more than anyone else, merely that he wants to be included more.

The Wider World

Countries who have historically been aggressors and colonizers often vibrate to Aries. England would be one example (but see also Capricorn). I have noted that people from overseas who settle in England often have Aries strong in their charts. In the animal world, male sheep and any animals that tend to 'lock horns' over matters of territory or courtship can be viewed as Arien. The robin with its territorial attitude, cheeky ways (always bravely waiting while the bird table is being restocked) and red breast also has a touch of the Ram about it.

Colours/Taste/Style

Red for 'go' is the classic Aries colour. But black and white also belong here, for those who vibrate strongly to this sign tend to see things in black and white terms. Typically, Aries makes strong statements in matters of taste: perhaps the wearing of bold colours, the latest hairstyle or the shortest hem-lines. Flamboyant or not, Aries is the sign that likes hats. This can even be seen in non-Aries types when their progressed Sun or Moon enters the sign. More specifically, those with natal Sun conjunct natal Mercury in Aries particularly like wearing hats.

The Body

Aries holds dominion over the **head**, and not only has a propensity for many head-related disorders (headaches, migraine, concussion, neuralgia) but many 'head' words can be appropriate for the sign. The Arien principle can be impulsive and reckless; success only comes about when the thinking process is engaged first. In short, Aries needs to 'use its head'. Failure to think first can make those who vibrate strongly to this sign rather accident-prone. On a physical level, injuries to the head and eyes are likely. Many Ariens have a prominent nose (or eyebrows and nose) or some kind of facial scar. Those with Sun in Aries, especially, are often well-known among their friends for gazing very directly at you or, in shyer types, for not being able to look you in the eye when talking.

Planets in Aries

Planets here are usually **speeded up** and operate in a more impulsive, adventurous, impetuous, decisive or courageous way, but the action associated with the planet may only be short-lived. The quality of **daring** can be added to the psychological traits associated with the given planet. Any planets here will also take on a competitive edge. (Note that Saturn in Aries may be frightened of competition, both fearful of coming first and fearful of not coming first.)

Aries on a House Cusp

This shows the area of life where we may show **daring**. Where we may be **willing to bravely start anew**. Where we may be competitive. Here, we may be eager for action – and possibly able to spur others into action. This area could be where we may be able to say 'I'm going do what I want to do, when I want to do it' – an area where we act first and think later. The Aries house may act as a launch pad or starting point for many of the individual's activities. For instance, Aries on the Seventh House cusp may imply that it is one's partner, or the requirements of partnership, that spurs one into action.

Taurus ♉

Element: Earth
Mode: Fixed
Ruler: Venus

The Symbol and Glyph

The glyph can be taken to represent the head and horns of the Bull, the Taurean symbol. The bull conjures up a picture of enormous strength: an animal slow to move but a force to be reckoned with when aroused. The bull is a living bulwark, a rampart, a barricade, simply by virtue of its size and strength. The bull is a fertile animal but the 'reined in bull', the Ox (a mature castrated male), is capable of carrying the heaviest of loads without buckling. Baseball teams often call themselves 'Bulls' (e.g. the Chicago Bulls) to indicate the strength and endurance of the team. Bulls are also taken to symbolize **fertility** and some have even viewed the Taurean glyph as depicting fallopian tubes leading into the uterus.

General Characteristics

If it was the job of Aries to start things, then the tasks of sustaining, taking root and accumulating fall to Taurus. Whereas Aries wanted 'to do', Taurus doesn't particularly want to do, or want to reflect or want to speculate. The Taurean impulse is just to be and to have. Taurus seeks to create or acquire something and then **hold on to it**. Little wonder therefore that the sign has a reputation for being **possessive**.

As well as being **patient**, **placid** and **calm**, Taurus is the most **enduring**, **persistent**, and **steadfast** of all the signs: an oak tree rather than a willow. Oak trees are not as good at bending as willows but it has to be acknowledged that oak trees are much more satisfying to lean against. And you can lean against and rely on those whose chart vibrates strongly to Taurus. **Persevering** and **determined**, if not stubborn and obstinate, the Bull is **deliberate** and cannot easily be pulled, pushed or coerced into anything against its will. With some planets in Taurus (e.g. Mars), resistance to movement and change can sometimes give rise to 'bullying' behaviour, especially in people who have not learned how to get their needs met in healthier, more conscious ways. As any farmer will testify, under stress ('stress' here might be defined as undue disturbance) even normally placid cattle can become aggressive, although on the whole one might associate Taurus with more passive aggression.

While not the most imaginative sign, Taurus is blessed with **realism** and **common sense**. Those with many planets here want an unchanging life and seek to preserve the status quo and stability in almost all areas. Many decisions, whether or not to do something, stem consciously or unconsciously from this **desire to have a quiet life** and basically from a strong instinct for **self-preservation**. Taurean philosophy dictates that they leave well alone – permanently if possible, or at least until, in true bovine style, they have had the chance to chew things over slowly and carefully. Thus, all else in the horoscope being equal, the Taurean type doesn't interfere with (or even have an opinion about) the affairs of others. Equally, Taurus doesn't like to be interfered with themselves.

Practical in orientation and disliking of the purely theoretical, Taurus doesn't easily believe in anything that can't be seen or touched. Taurus likes the simple life and, indeed, in most matters prefers **simplicity**. Taurus doesn't cope well with complexity or complex types of people. **Pragmatic** and down-to-earth, those who vibrate strongly to this sign don't like things unnecessarily 'wrapped up'. They can see through *bull*shit. Indeed, this is typical Taurean language, so very often appreciative of lavatory humour.

The concern of Taurus is with **producing and building something tangible**. Building is undoubtedly a keyword to use with respect to any planet found in this sign. There can be a capacity for building slowly upon previous efforts and the building-block approach to life has a slow-but-steady aspect to it which is distinctly Taurean. This considered approach can often bring in real wealth in the longer term. An educational role is not the most obvious one for the typical Bull but if there is a need to teach it will be done in a clear, step-by-step, keep-it-simple, building blocks kind of way.

The Bull is also very concerned with **security** and **stability**. For those with a Taurean emphasis in the chart, it is the basics of life – home, food and physical security – that must not be endangered. Thus, Taurus will not easily do anything that might threaten their physical or material security and can appear to be rather plodding and stick-in-the-mud to more carefree, adventurous types.

Basically, Taurus is **stoical**. Not easily ruffled, those with an emphasis here may seem to be unaffected by grief or joy, pain or pleasure. This is because of an ability to calmly accept everything that happens as the unavoidable result of the natural order of things. Thus, Taurus, perhaps more than any other sign, is in touch with nature. There is usually also an **appreciation of nature's bounty**, an appreciation of the beauty and riches of the land and of the food it produces. In life and in art, this contributes to a sense of proportion. Fundamentally, the rhythms of nature are unchanging, which may be another reason why Taurus feels so at home with the natural world. Being in touch with nature also includes being in touch with the body: its needs and its skills. As well as being a very earthy and **sensual** sign, the senses tend to be highly developed – taste, smell and touch in particular. The strong sense of **touch**, **texture** and **form** found with a variety of placements in Taurus are ideal for those who work in occupations dealing with textiles. Ideal too for anyone whose life involves **tactile** skills – massage, aromatherapy or healing, for instance. Construction, musical, agricultural and horticultural trades are also potentially Taurean. Music is applicable because Taurus is so good with all things oral – singing as well as eating! The vulnerability of some with Taurus emphasized in their chart can lie in the tendency to be addicted to physical comforts and the good life. Taurus can be a **self-indulgent** and lazy sign, prone to **inertia** and **stagnation**, to conserving energy rather than using it.

With its realistic two (four?) feet on the ground and strong sense of proportion, Taurus is perhaps one of the sanest signs of the zodiac. Emotionally, sexually and in matters requiring anger management, the type is characterized by quiet resistance, slow arousal and considerable endurance. The down-to-earth quality of the sign also contributes to its sense of humour as much laughter is gleaned from the more basic attributes of human nature. Thus, Taurean humour tends to be simple and earthy unless other parts of the horoscope predominate.

Staunch might be another keyword for the sign. Like the Bull, Taurus is so **firm** and steadfast, it checks the flow of whatever comes into its path. Therefore, Taurean energy can allay anxiety and protect, but equally it can block change and progress.

The Wider World

Although Sagittarius is traditionally associated with Spain, I associate that country with Taurus. This is partly through experience with clients and Spanish news stories but also because Spain is a country that is fertile, dry and famed as the land of bullfighting. The country is home to many an earthy peasant who, when you get to know them, is often surprisingly well-off. Cattle (especially bulls!) and potentially all farm animals including pigs are reminiscent of Taurus. In other words, they are animals that get converted to food! Note that the police (which I believe comes under this sign) are often referred to as 'pigs'. Taurus would also apply to PC Plod. Detectives come under the umbrella of the opposite sign, Scorpio. Ireland is another country that has traditionally been associated with Taurus, an attribution that I can neither confirm or deny but which seems reasonable given the highly rural nature of that country.

Colours/Taste/Style

Taurus is usually associated with pastel shades or colours associated with nature. Pale pink, green and blue-green sometimes feature. There can be a liking for floral patterns and those who vibrate strongly to the sign may be quite traditional in their tastes. Whatever the preferred colours, Taurus is always very hot on texture – there will invariably be a liking for fabrics that feel good (e.g. velvet or silk) in those with this sign strongly emphasized.

The Body

The Taurean bodily terrain is the **neck**, including the larynx and thyroid. The neck of the Taurus type is often noticeable for its long, slender beauty or, conversely, its thickness. Taurus is *the* sign to be associated with a beautiful voice, and in terms of health may be prone to sore throats, and pain and stiffness in the neck.

Planets in Taurus

Planets in Taurus tend to operate more slowly, simply and often more cautiously than in other signs. Taurus will add a traditional and usually a stable quality to the psychology of the given planet, the affairs of which may also be tinged by matters of money or beauty. Or at least tinged with the notion of ownership.

Taurus on a House Cusp

In this house, one might want **value for money**. For example, one woman with Taurus on the Second House cusp told me she bought designer clothes but only in the sales! In our Taurean house we may **stick to what is tried and tested**, be more traditional, be down-to-earth or motivated by matters of self-preservation. Here, perhaps, we may be known for being realistic and reliable. Sometimes we may be possessive in this area of life. For example, Taurus on the Seventh House cusp might imply either that one may have a tendency to attract possessive partners or that one might be possessive of one's own partner.

Gemini ♊

Element: Air
Mode: Mutable
Ruler: Mercury

The Symbol and Glyph

Two twin pillars depicted by vertical lines joined at top and bottom signify the Twins, and also the notion of duality. In common parlance, we have the expression 'from pillar to post' which captures the spirit of Gemini, meaning moving hither and thither; going to and fro; from one place or predicament to another; travelling backwards and forwards.

General Characteristics

One of the key principles of Gemini is that of **connection**. This super-networking sign is concerned with connecting people, places, ideas and all else; its purpose is concerned with **association** and **communication**. Gemini's job is to gather information and then process and distribute it. It is left to Sagittarius (Gemini's opposite sign) to consider what the information might *mean* and to the other Mercury-ruled sign, Virgo, to decide whether the information is useful or not and to discard it if it isn't. Gemini's task is merely to **gather information** and disseminate it. Hence Gemini is the sign of both the scholar and the gossip. Each gathers information and each conveys it to others. Gathering facts requires an open attitude. Any kind of censorship on information will stop it moving freely. Basically, too strong a sense of right or wrong limits where one can go. Little wonder, then, that Gemini is essentially an **amoral** sign and those who vibrate strongly to it are mentally agile, curious and flexible. **Curiosity** is perhaps the dominant trait here.

Versatile, flexible and **adaptable** and very much liking **variety** and **diversity**, Gemini seeks an infinite variety of tasks and as many different ways as possible of carrying out the given assignment (unlike Taurus, its predecessor, which liked to do the same things and in the same way). Thus, there is an **experimental** attitude to life with this sign, a tendency to **live life provisionally** and to not take things too seriously. **Commitment-shy**, whatever the situation, Gemini will choose to keep all possible options open.

In common with the other mutable signs, Gemini is not goal-orientated. Goals imply the commitment to cover a long distance, whereas Gemini prefers **short distances** and revels in the little deviations and digressions along the given path. Gemini *does* cover a lot of ground (perhaps more than any other sign) but the ground covered is not found in a simple linear direction, it is more accidental than that. Arguably, true satisfaction in life comes from experiencing what is to be experienced *deeply*. One tastes the flavours more when one chews slowly and carefully, but Gemini's style is to hop from flower to flower. This butterfly existence has not only **restlessness** but also, very often, **dissat-isfaction** as part of its package. For this reason, those with a strong emphasis on this dilettante sign can easily feel that they are missing out in some way, even while actually being at the very centre of all that is going on.

Gemini is the great cosmic agent, always able to put A in touch with B. Gemini is able to make a phenomenal number of connections – this is *the* sign of **networking**. There is a need to be 'in' on whatever is going on, a dislike of being excluded, but always the requirement to be able to move freely within the hub of activity, remaining uncommitted and able to move or exit if things become too restrictive or heavy. The Gemini type is essentially a **juggler**: forever juggling people, time, places and ideas.

A preponderance of planets in Gemini will often lead to a **talent with language** and languages. Often too there is a liking and aptitude for games, especially card games. Cycling, tennis and skateboarding are also often Geminian pursuits, as are all matters concerned with knowledge or communication. Intelligence is not something that can be measured in the horoscope but commonly those who vibrate strongly to this sign are **clever**.

At worst, those who vibrate strongly to this easily bored sign may be flighty, fidgety and **fickle**. Lacking in both concentration and conviction, some will appear tricksterish, **vacillating** and **changeable**. A strong Saturn or the presence of fixity in the chart can do much to offset such tendencies. Both scepticism and gullibility can also be part of the Gemini package, for arriving at a depth of understanding can be hard. The openness to everything and inability to exclude information can also lead to difficulties in decision-making. The typical Gemini is invariably 'in two minds' about most things. Like Janus, the Roman god of gates and doorways, Gemini can face two ways simultaneously.

At best though, strongly Geminian types are **skilful** and **versatile** and able to turn their hand to anything. Contemporary, always ahead of the game, **sociable** and **busy**, Gemini is an **interesting** sign. Planets in Gemini may seek novelty but they may also produce individuals who provide it. It is also the sign most associated with **youth**, as typically youngsters want and need variety and perhaps shouldn't commit themselves until they have sufficiently experimented with life. Lifetime youthfulness and a Peter Pan quality can be especially associated with individuals who have both sides of the Gemini-Sagittarius polarity emphasized in their horoscopes, especially where the fire element is also strong and/or the earth element weak.

Although the Third House and Mercury are much stronger indicators, the part of the horoscope where Gemini is to be found (and planets placed in the sign) often also contributes information about an individual's siblings: the people they are or were, and the nature of the relationship with them.

The Wider World

The insect world in general can be associated with Gemini, especially flying insects, moths and butterflies. I have noted that transits from, or to, Mars in Gemini, for instance, often equate with insects that bite or sting, such as bees and wasps. The monkey family may also owe something to the sign. Birds renowned for mimicry such as parrots, the crow family and mocking birds may also vibrate to Gemini. London, city of commerce and infinite variety in all things, has for centuries been associated with this sign. William Lilly's famous prediction of the Great Fire of London in September 1666 was depicted in a woodcut of the Twins surrounded by flames.

Colours/Taste/Style

This is a contemporary and fashionable sign. The colour associated with Mercury, the ruler of Gemini, is yellow – a stimulating colour, long connected with communication and intellectual matters. For this reason the walls of mental hospitals used to be painted yellow. More importantly, yellow is a cheerful colour, and certainly Geminian taste veers towards the bright and the cheerful. Patterns with lines rather than curves may be favoured. In matters of taste, as elsewhere, Gemini cannot be pinned down, though there is usually a liking for variety in colours and styles.

The Body

The **agility** of Gemini can also be physical: Gemini has rulership over the **lungs, arms** and **hands** but, in my experience, also has a connection with all the **limbs** in the body. People who have difficulty getting around, for whatever reason, will usually have this fact partially shown by planets in the Third House or in Gemini. Gemini is a nervous, worrying sign and this may be in evidence in those who have a preponderance of planets here. This is especially the case when something is expected of them. Mercurial types, including those who vibrate strongly to Gemini, may be more predisposed to smoking (for starters, there is a need to do something with one's hands) or sometimes more ill-disposed to smoking than others. The respiratory system is a key area for this sign.

Planets in Gemini

Gemini **lightens** up – seems to almost add air – to any planet found in the sign. The qualities of the given planet will not only seem to become lighter and less serious but also more scattered and difficult to get hold of. With the exception of Saturn, the attention of the given planet may more easily stray. Often the issues associated with the planet will be verbalized more. The individual may want to **understand** the aspect of themselves described by the particular planet. **Youth** will also be added to the equation: for instance, Venus, and especially Mars, in Gemini can suggest age differences between lovers.

Gemini on a House Cusp

Gemini on a house cusp always implies **dualism**: for instance, two marriages when on the Seventh House, two jobs on the Sixth or Tenth, two parents sometimes on the Fourth or Tenth, and so on. Siblings will also often feature in the activities of the given house and there may be links to schooldays. Activities associated with the given house may become more diverse and the individual will approach the activities associated with that house with curiosity and from a rational and cerebral point of view.

Cancer ♋

Element: Water
Mode: Cardinal
Ruler: Moon

The Symbol and Glyph

The symbol for Cancer is the Crab. The glyph can be taken to depict the crab's claws encircling each other in a protective posture. Curiously it also looks like the number 69 turned on its side. The crab has a hard shell to protect a soft body and the Cancerian person can also be like this: crusty and defensive on the outside but soft and squidgy within. The glyph can also be interpreted as being representative of breasts (a Cancerian part of the body), or cradling arms, both images reminiscent of the nurturing and maternal nature of the sign.

General Characteristics

The emphasis for Cancer is on the **home**, the **family** and the **past** – the key principle being **a need to feel safe** and a strong **urge to belong**. Those who vibrate strongly to the sign often have a great liking for **history** and sometimes for antiques. Both history and family provide a feeling of continuity with all that has gone before. This sense of having a past affords the individual a feeling of **emotional security**. The knowledge that they belong to a family also provides a sense of security, as an important role of the family unit is to provide a cushion against outside dangers.

Although a cardinal sign, the Cancerian method of initiation is not a straightforward one. Like the crab, the movement of Cancer tends to be oblique, sideways and manoeuvring; Cancer can be skilled at 'going round the houses'. Going sideways or retreating into one's shell can be useful defensive measures to take when a degree of protection is required, but can also be ways of avoiding issues that need to be dealt with. And as the crab has very large claws to hold on tightly when necessary, so too does the Cancerian type have a tenacious grip.

The oblique, sideways quality associated with this sign can be a way of dealing with **shyness** and **timidity**. Sidling up can feel easier than a head-on confrontation. Those with a preponderance of planets in Cancer may be **defensive** and cagey but can often be very **shrewd**, too. The shrewdness, conservative attitude and tendency to let go of nothing often makes for skills with money and what might be termed 'good husbandry'. Sometimes hoarding and penny-pinching go with the territory.

Cancer is noted for its characteristic traits of **imagination**, **sensitivity** and **sympathetic understanding**. Its energy is soft and yielding and yet surprisingly defensive. The Cancerian type is very **protective**; not only self-protective and protective of their clan but even of their country. Cancer can be **patriotic**. Those who vibrate strongly to this sign often feel easily threatened. There are various ways that might be used to respond to a supposed threat but often the response is to become touchy, sulky or huffy. Cancer is a **moody** sign although, more positively, one might say that it is in touch with the changeability of the feeling realm. Be that as it may, there can be a great **sensitivity to slights** whether these are imagined or real.

The protective, sympathetic quality of the sign goes alongside the strong urge to mother, to **nurture**, to care for. Planets here can be useful in both kinds of nursery: those that are child-based and the horticultural variety. And there is a strong nest-building propensity with Cancer. Home, the ultimate place of retreat and safety, is everything. The house position of any planet in Cancer can show where the individual creates some kind of home-from-home.

Whereas in many ways Gemini was the sign of the child, being youthful and innocent and either oblivious to, or not frightened by, the horrors of life, Cancer is the sign of the **mother**, who, almost by definition, is always alive to danger and takes little that happens in life lightly. Hence, in the same way that the crab has a tough shell to protect a sensitive body, those whose charts have a Cancerian emphasis can be rather crusty. In other words they can be moody, negative and pessimistic. For all that, it should be added that **humour** is very much part of the Cancerian picture, partly because laughter increases a sense of belonging. Aldous Huxley's theory of in-group/out-group hostility may be relevant in a discussion of both the sign of Cancer and a discussion of the nature of humour. Cancer will do anything for *their* group; usually jokes are targeted at people who are not perceived as belonging to their own group. Potentially, therefore, Cancer is the sign more likely to find it difficult to accommodate foreigners and foreignness.

Tenacity is another keyword and, reminiscent of the claws of the crab, this is indeed the most tenacious and potentially **clingy** of the signs. It is not easy for Cancer to let go of the past or of family members, or indeed of anything that provides any kind of support system. Cancer can cling to people and to things, no matter how old. In some with the sign emphasized, their tendency to cling to people can result in possessiveness, a smothering propensity and needlessly fussing over them.

The sign has an association with **memory**; not for having a memory for facts so much as a memory for feelings, such as what happened on holiday thirty years before. Cancer is a **sentimental** sign and some with planets here will have a tendency to collect and hoard. The typical Cancerian type does not want to forget the past and does not want you to forget it either. Not only might they cling to you and not let you go, they might actually want you to cling to them. The need to be needed is very great and, again, provides a feeling of security. Still on the theme of tenacity, those whose charts are dominated by the sign are probably, statistically speaking, the longest living. And this is despite the fact that the disease called cancer has undoubtedly (in my experience) a strong link with the sign. Readers with planets in Cancer need not panic when they read this. There are few of us, in Western society particularly, whose lives have not been touched by the disease. The area in your chart where the zodiacal sign falls may simply show through whom and where you come face to face with it. Note that a study of crustaceans (including crabs) is called carcinology and that the disease was probably named after the crab because of the tenacious way in which it can cling. The Latin word *cancer* literally means 'crab'.

The Wider World

Countries with a rich history and heritage often vibrate to the sign. So do lands which are family-orientated or downright clannish; examples might include Italy with its Mafia and Scotland with its clans. In the animal kingdom the sign connects with crustaceans, e.g. crabs, molluscs and other sea creatures that aren't exactly fish. Turtles and tortoises seem to belong to the Cancer/Capricorn axis (or maybe Saturn in Cancer).

Many chicken stories have been triggered by planets moving through Cancer. Perhaps jointly with Taurus, cows may resonate to the sign, too. Elephants also may belong here (or at least with the Cancer/Capricorn polarity) as they are renowned for their memory and their strong familial ties. A curative remedy for a homœopathic patient of mine with four planets in Cancer turned out to be made from that most clinging of plants, clematis!

Colours/Taste/Style

White, silvery and pearly colours. Often the first thing one notices upon meeting someone with an emphasis on Cancer, and with a Cancer Ascendant particularly, is their white or pale-coloured clothes. There may also be a liking for soft pastel, watery shades. The clothes are often loose and flowing. The preferred styles of furniture tend to be soft and yielding. Some who vibrate strongly to this sign favour antiques and most will be traditional in their orientation. Others have a liking for knick-knacks and for keeping hold of things that have sentimental value.

The Body

The **stomach, gall bladder, digestive organs** (but not the bowels) generally, or at least partially, come under the jurisdiction of Cancer, as do the **breasts**. Many with this sign on the Ascendant (particularly) or with a predominance of personal planets in Cancer have prominent breasts. The rulership of the sign by the Moon may increase catarrhal tendencies and above-average vulnerability to the cold and the damp. A minority with the sign emphasized will have a crab-like walk, for any number of physical reasons.

Planets in Cancer

Any planets in Cancer will tend to take on a **maternal, nurturing** or **protecting** edge. Depending on the planet and the house in which it falls, the nurturing quality may be what is given or what is received from others. Any planets in Cancer – even outer planets (also the Cancerian house cusp) – will always invoke something of the experience of the individual's **mother**, even though it is not usually the major statement in the chart that describes her. Planets in Cancer provide information not only about our experience of the biological mother but also our experience of all subsequent caretakers.

Cancer on a House Cusp

This will show areas of life where we may be **protective** and **nurturing**. For example, Cancer on the Eighth House cusp suggests taking care of other people's money. When found on the Sixth or Tenth House Cusps it suggests work or a career which is involved with nurturance, security or protection. Cancer on the Seventh House cusp indicates that a maternal flavour will feature in one-to-one relationships. If on the Eleventh, perhaps our friends provide a sense of home and family; perhaps we mother our friends or they mother us.

Leo ♌

Element: Fire
Mode: Fixed
Ruler: Sun

The Symbol and Glyph

The symbol for Leo is the Lion, a beast long honoured and respected by humans for its beauty, sense of nobility and seeming courage. In fact, the story is one of bluff. It seems that lions are not so courageous: they choose the weakest prey and attack from behind. The males often steal the kill of the females! The glyph itself is sometimes interpreted as signifying the lion's mane and sometimes the tail.

General Characteristics

The old-fashioned images of kings and queens beloved of fairy stories are well suited to Leo, as is our image of the big cat itself: **majestic**, **proud**, at best having a sense of their own **dignity**, at worst seeming rather **self-important**, haughty and proud. Just as a king can only be a king if he is recognized as such by loyal and faithful subjects, achieving some kind of recognition from others is key to the Leonine psychology. The quest of Leo seems to be self-discovery, to discover in which ways the self is unique and important. Planets in Leo describe facets of the individual that demand to be noticed, to be considered important and generally appreciated. Individuals with Leo strong in their charts similarly hate to be ignored. Being a bystander is not an option for those who vibrate strongly to this sign, but the problem with being centre stage is that inevitably everyone else has to have a much smaller role.

While a monarch and others in authority do usually have genuinely loyal and admiring subjects, they also attract sycophantic followers ever hopeful of rising up a rung or two on the social ladder. The weakness of Leo lies in its capacity for naïvely **believing its own publicity**; the type can be vain and easily flattered. And, as everyone knows, fairy-tale monarchs are notoriously prone to favouritism. Often they choose to consort with people beneath them. Perhaps this is to better show off their own superiority, or to simply bask in flattery. Leo, like most cats, appreciates being stroked. Perhaps loyal underlings are necessary to help ward off any threat of their position being usurped. Anyone who has ever kept a domestic cat (note that cats seem to vibrate strongly to the sign Virgo, too) will know that cats often find safety in high vantage points. Similarly the Leo type likes to stay high. High not only in terms of social prestige (though that too) but high in terms of feeling upbeat and confident. Heat always rises and, in common with the other fire signs, Leo likes to stay a little above what lies beneath.

The image of a monarch (or any kind of leader really) can never be far away from any discussion of Leo. At best, we have an image of a wise, benevolent and charitable ruler. Of course, rulers can be despotic, too. Being a ruler implies a superiority over everyone else and perhaps a condescending attitude towards lesser mortals. But a truly confident and successful leader has a realistic attitude as to their own importance in the overall scheme of things and will have sufficient confidence in themselves and their place in the world to be able to recognize, acknowledge, give attention to and generally illuminate others. These people can then bask in the warmth of their leader. It is only under the stress of doubt, when their self-esteem is uncertain, that Leo may have to be the centre of attention. If you know you are great, you don't need people to tell you so all the time.

Warmth, **loyalty**, **generosity** and **magnanimity** are key Leonine traits. Magnanimity because, unlike its predecessor Cancer, Leo doesn't bear a grudge. With Leo there is a certain buoyancy and, as with all fire signs, **enthusiasm**. Leo isn't easily crushed or defeated. And the generosity of the sign goes further than the use of their credit card, for Leo is a sign that is generous in spirit as well as in deed. At best, it is large-hearted and warm-hearted.

Confident and ready for the task (whatever that task may be), the Leonine type is in many ways fitted for the role of leader. They may not be fitted for the actual implementation of what needs to be done but, if they have truly recognized the worth of others, will be suited for the task of appropriate **delegation**. To be in power, one must exude confidence, **faith** and **enthusiasm**. One must also be able to be positive and to skate over both real and imagined shortcomings and problems. One has to be loyal to the project in hand and be able to inspire a similar loyalty in others.

Closer inspection can reveal that it is all show with Leo; their trick is to be good at bluffing it out. This is rather like what happens on the stock market: prices of shares take a dive when confidence in a commodity is lost. The rise and fall of prices need have very little to do with the reality of a situation: it is the shareholders' *perception* of the situation which is key. The trick is always to keep others' confidence high. And here lies the skill of Leo: the **ability to inspire confidence**. Leo is good at show. Hence another reason for the (probably unconscious) Leonine penchant for choosing less able or confident companions: the ruler or banker (Leo rules banking) cannot afford for those companions to shout to the crowd that the emperor isn't wearing any clothes or that they need to sell their shares in a particular company.

The capacity for 'show' and bluff, and the need for recognition, makes Leo a prime sign for the entertainment industry and especially for acting. An emphasis on both Leo and Pisces in a chart will frequently point to **drama** as being a major activity in the life. Leo is a creative sign generally because, among other reasons, creativity implies the **wholehearted** throwing of oneself into what one is doing, and this sign has a gift for that.

Planets in Leo work best where the individual has some measure of self-esteem, for then the generosity and magnanimity can shine in a very positive way. An emphasis on Leo can be descriptive of a person who commands as well as demands respect. Leonine **integrity** can make for a pride that is appropriate. However, on the flip side, **pride** can be at the root of many Leonine problems. A too-high sense of their own personal dignity, coupled with a dislike of not meeting their own high standards of behaviour, can sometimes make the Leonine type reluctant to try anything at all. For classically, Leo hates being laughed at and will not risk appearing a fool. Sometimes planets in Leo seem to confer too high an opinion of oneself, and boastfulness and conceit can result.

The Wider World

In the animal kingdom, Leo is most obviously reminiscent of the large wild cats (especially lions) but can also be associated with animals that are linked to royalty, e.g. swans are definitely Leonine. The peacock may also belong here. A good friend of mine who has a home in *Swan*age in Dorset has three planets in Leo in her Fourth House of home.

Colours/Taste/Style

This is the person who may *pride* themselves on their taste, appearance or home. There may be a liking for strong statements in colour (*royal* blue and bright, strong or warm colours) and sometimes a liking for gold, glitz and show. Frequently there is a need to create a personal and distinctive style. Not every Leo type will like a palatial home but there may well be a need to impress, even in more introvert, understated types. Sometimes the more over-the-top Leonine style can be traced to planets such as Saturn in Leo: the individual may, unconsciously, be fearful of being ignored.

The Body

The **heart** is the major organ to be associated with Leo but the **spine** and **upper back** particularly may also come under its umbrella. Given that Leo is so concerned with honour and pride and being upright, this traditional linkage with the back should come as no surprise. Over-indulgence and rich living can often prove to be the downfall of the Leonine type. Huge kids themselves, Leo types are usually very fond of children but seldom have many themselves.

Planets in Leo

With the possible exception of Saturn, planets expressed through Leo usually want to be **noticed** and **appreciated**. They may express themselves with drama, show and confidence. For instance, one can never doubt that individuals with Mercury in Leo are very sure of their opinions. Those with Venus or Mars in Leo may choose partners whom they can show off or at least feel proud of. Similarly they may put in plenty of effort themselves so their partner may feel proud of them.

Leo on a House Cusp

The house where Leo is found can show where an individual feels at their **most illuminated** or **alive**. The area of life indicated may be one where it is possible to be **generous** in both spirit and deed. Pride may also be an issue with respect to the activities of this house. The activities of the Leo house will be closely connected to the house and sign in which the Sun is placed, and is therefore a house that is always worthy of investigation.

Virgo ♍

Element: Earth
Mode: Mutable
*Ruler: Mercury**

The Symbol and Glyph

The symbol for Virgo is the Maiden or Virgin. She is usually depicted as wearing flowing robes and carrying an ear of corn. Exactly what the glyph depicts is debatable but it may be a shaft of corn. In Northern latitudes the Virgo time is the time of the harvest, when the produce is fully ripe and packed with nutrition. At this time, crops are sorted and the harvest is weighed and measured and categorized. Similarly, the maiden is ripe, she is endowed with all the fruits of womanhood but can remain independent and whole if she wishes. She has to discriminate carefully with respect to potential suitors. Whole grain is, of course, more **wholesome** than the refined variety and the maiden also has the virtue of not having been tampered with. Vesta and the vestal virgins are often associated with the sign. The hearth and home were the backdrop of society in Ancient Rome. Vesta and her nuns, the vestal virgins, were charged with the job of ensuring that Rome's sacred fire would never go out. If it did, then it was thought that Rome would fall prey to the most terrible omens and bad luck. Thus, it could be said that the vestal virgins were entrusted with ensuring that the city continued to function.

General Characteristics

Virgo's prime concern is with 'sorting out the wheat from the chaff', in other words deciding what is and isn't useful and, ideally, eliminating the latter. (In practice, frequently the eliminatory part of the proceedings gets left to Scorpio and Virgo ends up with indigestible chaos.) Virgo is concerned with ensuring that things function, so there is a need to prioritize, to decide what needs to be done now and what can be left until later.

Like Gemini, the other Mercury-ruled sign, Virgo wants information but, whereas Gemini is inclusive in orientation in that it gathers *all* information, Virgo is more *exclusive*: it only wants information if it is **useful**. Thus, Virgo has a gift for **discrimination** and **prioritizing**. There is a capacity for **selection**, an ability to sift. To be able to discriminate between X and Y, to be able to decide that this is 'good' and this is 'bad', requires a critical faculty and also an analytical one, so it should come as no surprise that **criticism** and **analysis** are key Virgo skills. Virgo is ideally suited for any quality-control role. The sign is, arguably, **striving for perfection**, and if perfection is not possible then Virgo's concern is that everything **functions** and that things work. Virgo's problem can lie in the fact that it can miss the overall beauty of something by concentrating on a small flaw. In keeping with the succeeding sign, Libra (but less so and for different reasons), Virgo can get paralysed by indecision. The anxiety underlying this indecision can stem from the fear that things will go wrong, or will become even more flawed, if a wrong decision is made. The average Virgo type comes unstuck since, having no appetite for positions of responsibility or authority themselves, they then have to suffer the shoddiness of more confident but less painstaking superiors.

Virgo is the antithesis of its predecessor, Leo, in that Virgo tends to be embarrassed by show or pretence and can see through bluff at a hundred paces. Virgo's role in the zodiacal pantheon is to **serve** and to serve quietly. Virgo prefers false modesty to showy ostentation. The Virgo type goes in for understatement and usually wants to do things properly rather than bluff their way through. In every way, shape and context, Virgo is concerned with **small things**. Indeed, the secret of Virgoan success lies in the **attention paid to detail** and in noticing things that others overlook. Basically, Virgo is **observant**. Those who vibrate strongly to the sign can get bogged down by detail and lose sight of the larger picture. By getting so caught up in analysing a part (or criticizing a minor detail), Virgo can miss the gist and the spirit of something. However, the sign is not only critical of the outside world: Virgo is the most **self-critical** sign, too. It is also the most **modest**, **unassuming** and **humble** of signs. Planets expressing themselves through Virgo may similarly be dwarfed by more extrovert energies in the horoscope. Those who vibrate strongly to the sign are frequently **discreet** and **reserved** and, being unconcerned with power and getting ahead, are often **kind** and well-meaning.

Virgo may not, of itself, be as creative as its predecessor, Leo, but it tends to be more **skilled**. The sign can be associated with **technique** and craft. This is not surprising because most crafts require qualities that come easily to Virgo: a capacity for practice, the honing of a skill, a continual striving for improvement, a capacity for criticism, and an ability to recognize what is good and what isn't.

Images of the Virgo type will include anyone involved in a **craft**, such as the carpenter, clock-maker or some other kind of artisan. The maiden aunt and the fussy bachelor are also caricatures of Virgo the Virgin and are immortalized in the fictional characters of Miss Marple and Hercules Poirot respectively (both invented by Agatha Christie, who had the Sun and Ascendant in Virgo).

One of the more independent signs of the zodiac, part of Virgo's well-known concern about the physical body (sometimes bordering on hypochondria where the sign is emphasized in a chart) stems from a horror of being dependent. Virgo likes to serve but finds it difficult *being* served; among other things, being ill implies being served by others.

Much has been written about Virgo and tidiness in Sun sign books but actually Virgo tends to be more than usually **untidy** (unless Libra is also strong in the chart), often veering towards the chaos associated with its opposite sign, Pisces. Virgo does tend to be **fastidious** in certain matters, and planets expressing themselves through the sign can be rather **exacting**, **scrupulous** and **meticulous**. Virgo is an earth sign, and while perhaps being the least earthy (more like sand), it is still concerned with being practical and productive. Being practical and realistic and often bogged down by little things, Virgo, at best, knows it cannot attend to everything and is thus concerned with **prioritizing** (this often manifests as list-making). People who vibrate strongly to this sign may well be concerned with cleanliness but rarely prioritize tidiness.

The Wider World

Historically, domestic pets were animals that in some way 'served', thus many pets such as cats (especially the moggy variety) and sheep-dogs are particularly reminiscent of the sign. Rodents, especially grain-eaters such as mice, also have an undoubted affinity with this sign which, through its connection with the Sixth House, has a resonance with small animals. With its clean image and connection with watch-making and cuckoo clocks, Switzerland may vibrate to the sign. Vietnam certainly does. In addition, icons characterized by their **smallness** – the mini skirt and the Mini car – can be associated with Virgo.

Colours/Taste/Style

In keeping with the other earth signs, Virgo values **simplicity** in design and, in terms of clothes, has a tendency to dress down. It often also likes colours that are fairly neutral. There may be a dislike of designs that are too busy, although a liking for small patterns such spots, checks and small stripes is common. There is usually an appreciation of natural materials. The Virgo type values ordinary, useful things (e.g. kitchen utensils) which are beautifully designed and made.

The Body

Traditionally, Virgo is associated with the small intestine (and therefore embraces the duodenum, jejunum and ileum) and possibly with the spleen. The job of the small intestine is typically Virgoan, for its task is to facilitate transportation and absorption of the food we eat by breaking down foodstuffs from large aggregates into small molecules. The exact role of the spleen is controversial but it is thought that it plays a crucial role in protecting us from bacterial infections and sepsis. Apart from the 'keeping us clean' role, the spleen is typically Virgoan in that its role in the body tends to be ignored or undervalued by the medical fraternity. Virgo is a fairly delicate sign but tends to fare surprisingly well in health matters, due no doubt to the Virgoan propensity for clean living, fastidiousness and moderation in most things. A tendency to worry may be the trait most prone to undermining the health.

Planets in Virgo

Some degree of **discrimination, discernment** or **criticism** will rub off on any planets found in the sign. Those with the Moon or Venus placed here, for instance, may be critical of people they are involved with and are prone to analysing their relationships. Smallness also will often enter into the psychological equation of the matters concerning the given planet.

Virgo on a House Cusp

This is where the individual's **critical faculties** may be most utilized. The person may also be particularly self-critical with reference to the activities associated with the house and may tend to be **undervalued** in this area as a result. Or the Virgo house may be where the person **seeks to serve** others.

---

* Note: Some of the main asteroids – Ceres, Vesta, Pallas and perhaps Hygeia – also have some kinship with Virgo and may even be Virgo's true rulers. More information concerning the asteroids can be found on page 312.

Libra ☋

Element: Air
Mode: Cardinal
Ruler: Venus

'... tact and diplomacy run to seed are uncommonly like insincerity and moral
cowardice and when contemplating the sons and daughters of Aphrodite ... we are
reminded that foam is only another name for froth, and that one of its characteristics is
that it spreads itself very lightly over the surface and is never found at the greatest depths.'
Isabelle Pagan, *From Pioneer to Poet*

The Symbol and Glyph

The glyph is reminiscent of its symbol, the scales; an appropriate symbol since a main concern of the sign is that of balance. The Sun enters Libra each year around 22 September at the time of the Autumnal Equinox in the Northern Hemisphere (and the Vernal Equinox in the Southern Hemisphere), when the length of night and day are equally balanced, each being roughly of the same duration.

General Characteristics

Libra is the only sign of the zodiac symbolized by an inanimate object. The lack of the animal element gives a clue to the strongly **civilized** nature of the sign, which is both its blessing and its curse. When people are overly civilized they run the risk of being removed from more human, *un*civilized feelings, even though these feelings (for instance, rage and jealousy) are part of the human condition. On the other hand, the Libran attitude is precisely what is required to achieve a peaceful and ordered existence and a civilized society. Those who vibrate strongly to this sign can often 'rub along' with anyone.

The symbol of the scales also reveals a major concern of Libra: that of **weighing things up**. **Justice** belongs here, as a just decision can only be arrived at when the viewpoints of opposing factions have been carefully weighed. An ability to **compromise** is also part of Libra's armoury, as is **conciliation**. Perhaps no other sign has such good potential for helping parties in a dispute to reach an agreement, a particularly useful skill not only in diplomatic fields but also for helping separating or divorcing couples. Virgo, in its orientation towards service and humility, tends towards the servile and therefore can create relationships with a servant/served feeling to them. Libra rectifies this imbalance by being concerned with **equality** and **partnership** where, at best, no one holds the upper hand. Libra meets the 'other' as an equal and is the first sign to do so.

Libra is the sign of the **bridge-builder**. As well as the capacity for building bridges between people and nations, physical bridges and the card game of bridge come under its umbrella. Bridges allow connections to occur; they make the inaccessible accessible. The game of bridge is ideal for Libra because it is played in couples and requires a capacity for **strategy** and **persuasion**. Libra is skilful at strategy and at manoeuvring situations and people. In a number of different ways, Libra is one to keep its cards up its sleeve. Revealing all (in relationships, anyhow) can often risk toppling a harmonious situation.

Individuals who vibrate strongly to this sign will often find themselves in anything but peaceful situations. The battlefield and warring marriage have more than their share of people with the Sun or Ascendant in Libra. This is not so surprising when one considers that a peacemaker needs war in order to fulfil the purpose of making peace and achieving harmony. Also it is the Libran type who wails 'it's not fair!' – a viewpoint often used to justify court proceedings or military action.

Grace is another strongly Libran characteristic and by that I mean an effortless expression of **beauty**, **courtesy**, **elegance**, **refinement** or **charm**. Such qualities may potentially be expressed both physically and socially. Libra has a sense of **propriety** and, with its Venusian rulership, a dislike of anything coarse, rough, harsh or crass. The sign has a reputation for **laziness** and this is undoubtedly because the Libran type dislikes getting their hands dirty – a phrase that can be interpreted on a number of levels. With a dislike of anything ugly or sordid, Libra runs the risk of avoiding huge segments of life and of getting other people to do its dirty work. And while extremely concerned with relationship and also being a very social and even affectionate sign, Libra can find passion and the experience and expression of deeper feelings (indeed any kind of confrontation) rather difficult. Many students of astrology consider that Libra is about love; it isn't really. Feelings of love are much more tumultuous. Libra's concern is with mutuality, reciprocity, harmony, unity and **compromise** – major building blocks of **marriage**, with which Libra *is* concerned.

Like the other Venus-ruled sign, Taurus, Libra doesn't like rocking the boat because boat-rocking invokes disharmony. Those with this sign strong also very much want approval, and fear that upsetting apple-carts can jeopardize relationships. In fact, it can have the reverse effect. The dislike of confrontation may be a reason why those with planets in Libra so often find themselves caught up in battle zones, because potentially it means that problems are not dealt with as they crop up. When pushed under the carpet, unresolved issues gain momentum. In marital types of setting, many individuals will do anything to keep the peace and, in so doing, avoid the open communication that, while sometimes difficult, actually increases intimacy, understanding and closeness.

Libra basically doesn't like spoiling things. Thus, it is a rather conservative sign. It is **conservative** in attitude and also in taste. Libra also has a liking for **order** (order makes for harmony!) and **symmetry**. The sign is much tidier than Virgo, whose concern is more with cleanliness. Libra's liking for order can express itself in a number of different contexts; it has been noted that Libra doesn't like its relationships to be messy, for instance. There can also be a dislike of things and situations which are mixed in some way.

The preoccupation with **harmony** is the basis of Libran creativity. If a Libran person happens not to be artistic themselves, there will still normally be a need for an aesthetic environment. If they are musical, the orientation will tend toward the melodic and harmonious.

Interestingly, the weakness of Libra also lies in its need for harmony and fairness, because it can give rise to **indecision**. Constantly weighing things up can be paralysing to the decision-making process, especially if this is coupled with being somewhat out of touch with the deeper realities of their feelings, and what they want on a deeper level. But, in a sense, the choice for Libra is already made. Those with this sign emphasized do know what they want: they want not to make a decision, they want the harmonious and least-messy option. Indecision occurs while one is weighing up which choice will deliver maximum **co-operation**, order, **companionship** and **peace**. Libra needs relationship because it needs someone to tip the scales, someone to bounce ideas off, someone to act as a sounding board. However, the occasional inability to arrive at their own viewpoint, the tendency to sit on the fence, can give rise to dependency (the stereotypical Libran doesn't like to do or decide anything on their own) and to insincerity.

Libra is a sign that is good with appearances and first impressions, and is therefore well utilized in any reception or front of house situation. (This is especially true when Libra is the ascending sign in the horoscope, as this part of the chart is also concerned with one's initial impact.) Many different branches of the beauty industry also owe much to the sign.

The Wider World

Greece, considered to be the cradle of Western civilization, is a popular destination for the civilized Libran type. In the animal kingdom, Libra can be associated with animals that are decorative. There is a tradition that Libra rules small reptiles such as lizards but I can neither confirm nor deny this.

Colours/Taste/Style

Classic styles of dress, decor and music – styles which don't date and therefore don't have to be changed too often – are frequently favoured by those with this sign emphasized. Harmony is always key to Libran taste. Returning to the notion of civilization and Greece being the home of Western civilization, when you find yourself in a home filled with busts of the classical Greek gods and goddesses, you can almost guarantee that Libra is emphasized in the host's horoscope.

The Body

The **loins** are the area traditionally associated with Libra, and therefore the sign embraces the **kidneys**, **adrenals** and the lower or **lumbar part of the back**. In Chinese medicine, the kidneys are associated with the emotion of fear, a feeling common to the Libran type when having to deal with confrontation.

Planets in Libra

Libra adds a quality of **refinement** to any planet. Seeking some kind of balance will inevitably be an issue. While other chart factors will predominate (e.g. the Descendant and Descendant ruler), any planets in Libra may also play the role of minor co-significator in marital types of relationship; either describing facets of the partner or of the relationship itself.

Libra on a House Cusp

Partners and **partnership matters** may be affected by the activities of this house. Sometimes the house is indicative of where partners are found, although the house placements of Venus or Mars or the ruler of the Seventh are stronger indicators. The Libran house cusp may be indicative of a life area where the individual may be keen to share and may like to do things in partnership with another.

Scorpio ♏

Element: Water
Mode: Fixed
Ruler: Pluto (modern ruler) and Mars (traditional ruler)

'Technically, the only way water can be fixed is when it is ice. Certainly the iceberg, like Scorpio, reveals little of itself, the greatest part being submerged and treacherous.'
Martin Freeman, *How to Interpret a Birth Chart*

The Symbol and Glyph

The symbol is the scorpion. It is a creature that generates a good deal of fear but, of roughly 1300 different species, only about 20 types are dangerous to humans. These animals are very old and can be found in most types of habitat. Many can survive for months without eating. They are nocturnal and seek dark, isolated places in which to live. The glyph for the sign is not dissimilar to the one for Virgo, except that the 'tail' points outwards, seemingly on alert to suddenly release its sting if threatened. As well as the Scorpion, Scorpio has other images strongly associated with it: the eagle, the phoenix and the dove are the most common and reflect the psychological complexity that characterizes the sign.

General Characteristics

Scorpio is a sign characterized by its enormous strength. The strength is emotional and psychological but often there is physical toughness, too. Scorpio's strength lies in its capacity for **self-mastery** and **self-control**, and also in its stamina. Those who resonate strongly to this sign have difficulty in accepting weakness and inadequacy in themselves or in others. There is a refusal to be dominated by other people or by circumstance. This not only makes for great **fortitude**, self-discipline and **willpower** but it also helps to explain why Scorpio has such a reputation for healing. Scorpio's strength, it has to be said, also can make the type rather **controlling**. But domination over others can sometimes be useful in terms of pulling people through times of great crisis, pulling them past what they thought they were capable of, past the seeming limits of their endurance.

It could be said that Scorpio **thrives on crisis**. Whereas Libra is scared of anything sordid or of upsetting the apple-cart, to Scorpio there is only one reason to have apple-carts and that is to push them over. For the Scorpio type, *everything must be experienced*, all aspects of human life. In this respect Scorpio is **unflinching**, **courageous** and shrinks from nothing.

Scorpio is a sign of **colour**, **passion** and **intensity**; after all, neutrality is not possible in times of crisis. Whereas Libra tries to avoid extremes, Scorpio revels in them. With the twin rulers of Mars and Pluto, it should not be surprising perhaps that **survival** is a huge theme here. At worst, those with this sign emphasized in their chart have a tendency to turn everything into a battle for survival, whether such a battleground really exists or not. There is a tendency to feel easily threatened – the threat also may be real or imagined, but the great sensitivity of the sign means that the Scorpio type can easily feel persecuted. On the plus side, there is often an above-average capacity to empathize with people prone to experiencing feelings of persecution or paranoia. Scorpio is a sign capable of great compassion and, at best, the person who vibrates strongly to this sign can truly understand the whole gamut of human emotions and reactions.

Taking nothing at face value can make for a **suspicious** attitude and a certain amount of cynicism ('There is no such thing as a free lunch'). The major problem that individuals who are strongly Scorpionic often have to battle with is that of **trust and mistrust**. There is a need sometimes to loosen up a little, to accept their mistakes, to learn to forgive both themselves and others, and to learn to share. As with its opposite sign Taurus, Scorpio has a reputation for being **possessive**. There is also often a difficulty in accepting second place. Like Aries, Scorpio wants to be first but here the need to be first surfaces mostly in relationships and sexual matters. At the Virgo stage of the zodiac story there is the maiden ripe for plucking, and with Libra there is marriage and partnership, so it is hardly surprising therefore that Scorpio, the next sign along, is associated with sex itself. But in practice, many who vibrate strongly to this sign can and do live celibate lives. As always, Scorpio can be associated with extremes.

While the Eighth House and various planets (Saturn, Pluto and Chiron) are associated with death, the only *sign* to have a **strong awareness of death** and all transformative experiences is Scorpio. No less a warrior than Aries, the difference between these Mars-ruled signs is that, whereas Aries is direct and overt, Scorpio operates in a much more covert way. While not shrinking from death, Scorpio is more concerned with survival, whereas Aries is too devil-may-care and naïve to think about the possibility of being vanquished. Perhaps because on some level the Scorpio type has come to terms with death, many with this sign emphasized choose to live life intensely. They can appear to be crisis junkies and they like getting things over and done with, hoping to come through the other side transformed and transmuted. To live life to the heights and depths, to live on the edge and to have some experience of being in extremis is part of the Scorpionic experience. To feel pain, to intensely feel anything, is better than feeling nothing.

In common with all the water signs, but much more so than Cancer or Pisces, Scorpio is **secretive** and has a sophisticated understanding of all matters requiring **subterfuge**, **sabotage** and **subtlety**. People who vibrate strongly to Scorpio may hold on to their possessions but almost certainly will hold on to their feelings and also on to pain. The sign can be quite unbending and unforgiving emotionally. As with all the fixed signs, attachment is a key element to this determined and stubborn sign and here the attachment can be to pain, drama and crisis. However, whichever undercurrents or storms may be brewing inside, usually they won't be obvious to the casual observer: Scorpionic energy is like an iceberg in that very little is actually visible.

Whereas Libra is the most compromising sign of the zodiac, Scorpio is perhaps the most **uncompromising** and also, with perhaps Leo, the most **loyal**. There is nothing nicey-nicey about Scorpio but it is an emotionally honest sign. Those with major planets here may be **insightful**, **penetrating** and canny, finding it easier to trust their feelings than their airy Libran counterpart. **Irrationality, ruthlessness** and an **unforgiving** streak may also go with the territory but it is not that Scorpio has a monopoly over **jealousy** or vengeful feelings. Far from it. It is more the case that Scorpio is not frightened of such feelings and believes that they have to be experienced before they can be transmuted.

Having a liking for depth, it is perhaps not surprising that the Scorpio type is often drawn to the mysteries of life, whether these are matters of an occult nature, psychology, detection or archaeology. This is a great sign for subjects that require research and probing.

The Wider World

The sign is associated with scorpions and other creatures which, even if harmless, generate fear. Other arachnids such as spiders and mites may belong here. Birds of prey, too: eagles, buzzards, falcons and probably crows and rooks, etc. Bloodsuckers and scavengers (such as leeches and vultures respectively) in general are connected to Scorpio, and animals that clean up the natural world by removing carcasses and excrement. From a correspondence point of view, Japan with its raw fish and custom of hara-kiri is reminiscent of this sign.

Colours/Taste/Style

The Scorpio type often has a liking for strong flavours, colours and tastes, and won't like anything that they perceive as wishy-washy. As with most things where Scorpio is concerned, there is often an appreciation of strong, bold statements. Black and deep reds (the colour of congealed blood!) may be favoured.

The Body

Scorpio governs the **reproductive** and **excretory organs**: the genitals, rectum and bladder. To preserve good health it is important that feelings are not bottled up and nowhere is this more the case than in those who have this sign emphasized.

Planets in Scorpio

Any planet here will tend to react **intensely**, **passionately** and **secretively**. Whatever the message of the planet, **all may not be revealed** to the casual onlooker. Scorpio adds **depth** and sometimes death or near-death experiences to the planetary equation, although there will always be other horoscopic factors pointing in the same direction for this to be true.

Scorpio on a House Cusp

In this area of life, the individual insists upon, or is fated to meet, a degree of **depth** and **passion**. Here the individual cannot live lightly on life. When found on the Third, Ninth or Eleventh House cusps, it suggests an interest in psychology or the occult and perhaps a gift for research. When found on the cusp of a relationship house (the Third, Fifth, Seventh, Eighth or Eleventh), complicated emotional ties are suggested with respect to the type of relationship.

Sagittarius ♐

Element: Fire
Mode: Mutable
Ruler: Jupiter

The Symbol and Glyph

The symbol for Sagittarius is the Centaur, a being who is half-man, half-horse, and often depicted carrying a bow and arrow. The glyph is that of an arrow pointing upwards. Sagittarius always urges **upwards** – whether to the heavens, to God, or merely beyond the here and now.

General Characteristics

Whereas Scorpio is always deeply involved, passionate and very attached to whatever and whoever the involvement is with, Sagittarius prefers to keep things more casual, needing the space and freedom required in order to rove, roam and explore. **Exploration** and **questing** are key issues for Sagittarius, who always wants to go *further* and take things *farther*. The sign has a **nomadic, wandering** feel to it and can be associated with having the most **wide-ranging interests** of all the signs.

Sagittarius exudes all the **faith, optimism** and **trust** that Scorpio found so elusive. The more extrovert, jovial Sagittarian type will often have a Tigger-like quality, being bouncy and boisterous and prone to exaggerated gestures and responses. At best, there can be an appreciation of fun and an ability to spread joy. Ruled by Jupiter and gamblers at heart (and often in practice), the Sagittarian type is allergic to taking things too seriously. **Enterprising, energetic** and **adventurous**, hopes are rarely dashed for long and the temperament is well-meaning, **generous** and **forgiving**. After being dealt one of life's blows, the typical Sagittarius has the gift of being able to pick themselves up and start all over again. However, the exaggerated responses mean that this is not the most subtle of signs. People who resonate strongly to this sign may lack subtlety and be downright clumsy; Sagittarius has a **careless, slapdash** and **undisciplined** quality. Indeed, the sign can be associated with both types of cowboy: the adventurous cattle-herder beloved of the Wild West and the unreliable, slipshod builder full of empty promises. D-I-Y shops are populated by amateurs who underestimate the skills required for a particular project, and are consumed by enthusiasm and belief in the project in hand. Only the Sagittarian type can believe that a project is as easy as the sales pitch suggests.

Honest, open, sincere and **candid**, Sagittarius is also well-known for suffering from 'foot and mouth' disease. In other words, the sign is famed for another type of clumsiness – its sometimes quite extreme **tactlessness**.

Whereas Scorpio was concerned with depth, Sagittarius is more drawn to **breadth**. Breadth of understanding and breadth of interest are the gifts of the Sagittarian way of being. Sagittarius is always drawn to the **big picture** and hates anything small, including people or anything that it finds small-minded or mean. The gift of Sagittarius is for the *spirit* of something. Those with the sign emphasized are usually gifted at getting the gist of a subject but there is no liking for the more limited task of getting involved in the finer detail. Sagittarius dislikes any kind of limit because limits are not conducive to the process of exploration. The worst kind of limits for Sagittarius can be linked to the notion of maturity: emotional ties, responsibilities and duties. In common with its opposite sign of Gemini, Sagittarius hates to grow up.

The Sagittarian concerns are with the **future**, **growth** and **morality**. The future orientation may manifest as an interest in fashion and other trends in society, and perhaps with being trendy. Additionally, many Sagittarians are attracted to novelty. In common with their opposite number, Gemini, the type can get hooked, albeit temporarily, on every passing whim or phase. Or the future orientation may manifest as a concern with **education** and youth (the makers of the future). The sign is also concerned with what is right and what is wrong. Some with the sign emphasized can be prone to moralizing and self-righteousness, while most will be interested in what is right, ethical and moral.

The future orientation and capacity to catch the gist of a subject, coupled with enthusiasm, gives Sagittarius a **flair for teaching**, **education**, **sales**, **travel**, **politics** and **religion**. The final two subjects apply because, at the Sagittarian level of development in the zodiac, there is an interest in how society functions and in the beliefs of that society.

Mentally, the Sagittarian type may be very active. Certainly there is **a need to cover long distances** both physically and mentally. Sagittarius is *the* sign associated with **travel**. It is often credited with participating in sport but this does not meet with my own experience unless Mars is also prominently placed. However, it is a sign to associate with walking. Often there is a liking for the open air and, both physically and mentally, an appreciation of **space**, **freedom** and **wide open places**. Physically, the typical Sagittarian is less comfortable in over-populated homes and countries. In just about every context, Sagittarius likes things to be **open**. Emotionally, the type also enjoys space, doesn't like ties and, in common with the other mutable signs, tends to be commitment-shy.

The typical Sagittarian type is not interested in the now but always interested in the long-distance goal, for anything near is considered boring and will often be overlooked. Psychologically, Sagittarius is **long-sighted**, being able to see into the distance but unable (or unwilling) to see what is close at hand. Not seeing what is in front of you can make you clumsy and there can, indeed, be a clown-like quality to many who vibrate strongly to this sign.

Another instance of Sagittarian **clumsiness** is that the sign can seem remarkably off-hand and naïve when it comes to emotional matters. This is perhaps because they will tend to avoid too much involvement in areas of life that run the risk of bringing them down; this is the sign that would prefer to stay up, if at all possible. Other people's motives (or even their own) can seem like a foreign country. Their own particular orientation to life will often mean that they find other people's worries and preoccupations to be too small to be worthy of so much angst. On the other hand, Sagittarius is a sign prone to **exaggerating**, and the part of the horoscope where it is to be found will often offer information as to where an individual may blow matters out of proportion. In the way that Virgo can be associated with all things small, minimum and mini, Sagittarius embraces all that is large or maxi.

Sagittarius is perhaps *the* sign to associate with **lateness**. It is difficult for the typical Sun Sagittarius, at any rate, to meet deadlines: they over-optimistically believe they can fit much more into their lives than is realistically possible. So often they will arrive late for appointments and end up leaving until tomorrow those things they hoped would be completed today. Basically, those who resonate strongly to this sign **over-extend** themselves. In keeping with its fiery nature and lofty Jupiterian rulership, Sagittarius is an **idealistic**, rather than a realistic, sign. Even the more introverted Sagittarian type is usually blessed with great enthusiasm about *something*. Such enthusiasm can be very inspirational and uplifting or can feel inappropriately placed, depending on the circumstance or world view of the non-Sagittarian observer.

The Wider World

Horses (along with Jupiter and Neptune) and possibly large dogs owe something to a Sagittarian rulership. Animals over which people gamble (horses and greyhounds) and migratory animals all resonate at least partially to the sign. Sagittarius has a strong affinity with hunting and the sign can be linked with animals that the hunter employs (e.g. the horse and the dog) and perhaps also the animals that are hunted. The birth-time for the USA is somewhat controversial but, with the wide-open spaces, cowboys, the Statue of Liberty and the proliferation of religious sects, few would doubt that the USA Cancer Sun horoscope also has a Sagittarian Ascendant.

Colours/Taste/Style

Sagittarius can feel more at home with the abstract and theoretical than some other signs. Little wonder, then, that some Sagittarian types like designs with abstract patterns. Some with the sign emphasized feel quite at home with clashing colours and mixed patterns. Some will have a clown-like quality to their appearance. Dressing outrageously (from the point of view of more traditional types) can come easily to a minority in whom this sign is strong. There is something of the Boy Scout/Girl Guide to Sagittarius, and some who vibrate to this sign may be often seen in khaki!

The Body

The **hips** and **thighs** come under the Sagittarian umbrella. For some this will be a vulnerable area (e.g. a proneness to sciatica or to rheumatism and arthritis here), while others will be noticeable physically for their strength or for the ample proportions (!) of this part of the body.

Planets in Sagittarius

At best, any planets in Sagittarius are infected with joy, **enthusiasm** and **generosity**, even if there is a tendency to manifest in an exaggerated and **over-the-top** way. At worst, Sagittarius lends a careless, slapdash, **undisciplined** quality to the psychology of the given planet. Mercury, Mars and even Saturn can sometimes operate in a high-minded and high-handed, even self-righteous, manner.

Sagittarius on a House Cusp

Travel, **foreigners** or **foreign countries** will often come into the life through the activities of the given house. Therefore, if Sagittarius is on the Fourth House cusp, the individual might live abroad; on the Eighth House they may invest abroad; on the Eleventh House cusp they might enjoy foreign friends, and so on. Perhaps because of the Jupiterian rulership, often one is fairly fortunate with respect to the activities of the Sagittarian house. It can also be an area ripe for **exaggeration** or largesse, in which case the placement and condition of Jupiter can be the key to clarifying the situation.

Capricorn ♑

Element: Earth
Mode: Cardinal
Ruler: Saturn

The Symbol and Glyph

The word *Capricornus* comes from the Latin for 'horned goat', and the glyph can be taken as a diagram of the face and horns of the animal. In Northern latitudes, when the Sun enters Capricorn each year it marks the point farthest South where the Sun is overhead at noon; after this point (the Winter Solstice), the Sun begins to steadily climb – like the sure-footed goat – higher and higher in the sky. A more ancient symbol for the sign is the mythical sea-goat, a creature with the head of the goat and the tail of a fish. Perhaps both the goat and the fish tail can be seen in the Capricornian glyph. The so-called 'southern gate' of the Sun was thought to be a place where the souls of the dead passed and the fish tail may allude to dissolution.

General Characteristics

Capricorn checks the enthusiasm, irresponsibility, optimism and general bounciness of Sagittarius by injecting a more **sober** and **responsible** way of being into the zodiac story. Whereas a stereotypical Sagittarian might earn a reputation for their dislike of limits and love of various types of excess, a Capricornian is more likely to be known for their **temperance**.

Capricorn is the sign most concerned with the **structure, fabric** and **backbone of society** and thus is at home with the **Establishment**. There is a respect for age and experience and for all that has stood the test of time. Physically, there is an appreciation of stone and rock, and some with this sign emphasized will be involved with working with or on the Earth's crust itself, perhaps in mining, farming or digging roads. Those with the sign emphasized often have a strong appreciation of the land. The temperament of those who vibrate strongly to the sign may be **unswerving, persistent** and **rock-like**. The purpose of the sign is to uphold **tradition** and **authority** and to follow, or possibly shape, society's conventions and rules. The Capricorn type has a capacity for self-discipline and, with its respect for age and experience, is capable of obedience. Feeling at home with hierarchy comes with the territory; obeying their seniors and expecting a similar deference from their juniors comes naturally. Even if the chart overall suggests a person who dislikes hierarchy and has trouble obeying rules, the individual will usually be very aware that **class, rank** and a **pecking order** are realities of society.

Renowned for being **dignified, careful** and **industrious**, Capricorn is also perhaps the most **worldly** sign of the zodiac. An earth sign, one Capricorn concern is with the material world. Ruled by Saturn, other concerns are with **reality** and the **ageing process**. These features combine to create individuals intent on ensuring their material security in old age; the thought of financial dependence is often abhorrent. Traditionally, Capricorn is considered to blossom, improve and even grow to look and feel younger with age, while seeming much older than its peers in early life.

The Capricornian type feels most at home when achieving measurable and tangible results. Those with the Sun placed here will often be **ambitious**, but the ambition is not for celebrity or show (as with Leo) but to achieve something that will stand the test of time. Capricorn is **classy** rather than flashy. **Patience** is another characteristic; those with the sign emphasized are not usually in a hurry (unless Mars is also very strong). They are happy to serve their apprenticeship. This focused sign is also very skilled at organization and **planning**. **Time-management**, that attribute so elusive to the Sagittarian type, comes easily to Capricorn; this can be time-management on a daily or lifetime basis. Having a strong sense of **order**, management generally comes easily to this **efficient, organized** and **disciplined** sign. In a managerial role or not, the Capricorn type is well suited to being in **control**. Self-control comes easily as does the ability to control matter, people and situations, although planets in this sign do not usually operate in a particularly bossy or domineering kind of way. Another key issue with Capricorn is that of **respect**. The Capricorn type can respect those who they think deserve it, and they don't easily do anything that is beneath their considerable sense of **dignity**. Capricorn behaviour tends to be appropriate (if a little stiff and old-fashioned) and thus commanding of respect. Whatever the actual occupation, the Capricorn way of doing things is to be **professional**. This can be difficult for some planets placed in the sign as professionalism isn't a trait required in more intimate situations.

Pondering on the nature of the goat can do much to illuminate the characteristics of this sign. Out in all weathers, the stoical and **hardy** goat is cheap to keep, as it will eat almost anything and has a particular fondness for weeds. The mountain goat climbs to the top of the mountain without putting a foot wrong and this mirrors the way that the Capricorn type tends take the suitable, sensible and **prudent** path. The goat may jump from crag to crag but does so cautiously. Like those who vibrate strongly to this sign, the goat is good at shrewdly assessing situations and knowing which way to jump. Cashmere, the ultra-fine but extremely strong wool of the Kashmir goat, has been sought as a luxury fibre since before Roman times. Whether Kashmir goat or farmyard variety, the goat is a useful, profitable animal.

Not only is Capricorn **industrious** by nature, it is also the sign most concerned with the manufacturing industry. In society, the stereotypical Capricorn type comes in two distinct forms. One is the industrious worker whose low income and dignified temperament inclines to **self-denial** and a **spartan** lifestyle. This type of person is the **backbone** of many a society; a scapegoat, perhaps, one who carries society's burdens and creates its wealth, but doesn't share equally in that wealth or become dependent on the State. (The goat has been a popular sacrificial animal both in mythology and in real life.) The other stereotype comes from the upper or upper-middle classes, perhaps through the government or landed gentry, and has a family that can be traced back generations (the traceable ancestry applies to both stereotypes). This type (often representing 'old wealth') upholds the traditions of society and keeps within, and perhaps moulds, its laws and structures.

Despite the seeming conservatism of the sign, people with many a planet in Capricorn are often interested in occult matters. This is principally because Capricorn is concerned with the **rules** and **laws** governing the world we live in, and occult subjects are basically concerned with cosmic law.

The Wider World

In terms of countries, and from a correspondence point of view, India with its caste system seems to resonate at least partially to this sign. The 1066 and 1801 UK charts each have the Sun in Capricorn, and the UK is famous for its class consciousness. In the UK, images of the dry-stone walls of Yorkshire and Derbyshire are reminiscent of the sign. As for the animal kingdom, goats obviously belong here but perhaps so do mules, donkeys, camels and other beasts of burden. Possibly all cloven-footed animals come under this sign. Morocco seems to have a particularly Capricornian, or possibly Saturnian, feel to it because of the donkeys, camels, architecture and the Atlas mountains.

The Body

The body part associated with this sign is the **knees** and, through their rulership by Saturn, the **skin**, **joints** and the **skeleton** in its entirety may be implicated. Skin difficulties, sometimes allied to feelings of insecurity or anxiety, can feature. Hearing comes under the umbrella of Saturn and may also be a Capricornian issue. Those with the sign strongly tenanted, or perhaps with Capricorn on the Ascendant, will often be angular or bony in appearance with perhaps either splendid teeth or obvious tooth problems (depending on the aspects).

Colours/Taste/Style

A love of natural materials such as stone and wood will influence architectural and domestic tastes. An appreciation of form, structure and age inclines to a liking for traditional styles of dress, music and taste generally. Darker earth colours are favoured, as are those associated with work in the city or in roles where one has to look professional, such as brown, grey, charcoal, navy blue and black.

Planets in Capricorn

Any planet in Capricorn will tend to express itself cautiously and in a **restrained** and **controlled** manner. It will also say something about an individual's experience of their **father**. Venus and Mars in this sign may invoke paternal images in romantic matters. Certainly, there will often be marked age differences (in either direction) between lovers.

Capricorn on a House Cusp

This may be an area of life that is taken **very seriously** but also where a certain amount of discipline or austerity is invoked. The house will often have links with the individual's experience of their father. The house position of Saturn and the aspects it is receiving will provide additional information.

Aquarius ≈

Element: Air
Mode: Fixed
Ruler: Uranus (modern ruler) and Saturn (traditional ruler)

The Symbol and Glyph

The symbol for Aquarius is the water-bearer, usually shown as a man or, in olden times, as a woman on one knee pouring out water from an urn or jug. The contents of the jug turn into two wavy lines to produce the Aquarian glyph. The time of the year is February, the month the Romans set aside for cleaning their homes and outhouses. Indeed, the word *februarius* literally means 'month of purification'. Thus, the water-bearer can be interpreted as washing away the past and making ready for a fresh, clean start. This is appropriate imagery for this forward-looking, progressive, reforming sign. The wavy-lined Aquarian glyph has also been taken to symbolize the sea (from which all life comes, perhaps), electrical waves (Aquarius is associated with electricity and electronics) and electromagnetic and earth energies. The water is usually interpreted as a universal fount of knowledge which is to be circulated among all of humanity, as in the peculiarly Aquarian World Wide Web.

General Characteristics

Two main concerns of Aquarius are with **freedom** and **equality**. And, as with fellow air sign, Libra, Aquarius is concerned with **fairness**. To the Aquarian ideal, the class structure so beloved, or at least respected, by Capricorn clearly does not lead to fairness and equality for all. Aquarius is the sign of the ordinary person in the street, the sign of Tom, Dick and Harry. The Aquarian ideal (which shouldn't be confused with ordinary Sun in Aquarius mortals) believes that everyone is special and also that no one is. Aquarius has no time for hero-worship and is less impressed than most by celebrity. Basically, there is a dislike of hierarchy and privilege.

As with the other air signs, Aquarius has curiosity as a characteristic. Perhaps 'detached interest' would be more accurate. The sign is characterized by its **objective**, **impartial** and **detached** standpoint. Even Aquarius knows that there is no such thing as true objectivity, but the sign comes nearer than most to this state. Aquarius is also known for being rational, **humane** and logical; for the typical Aquarian type, if a law (scientific or societal) applies to one person, then it must apply to all. And if it applies to the human species then surely it should apply to the animal kingdom as well? At best, Aquarius refuses to recognize borders between nations and boundaries between people (and imposed by people) which are based on, for instance, race, class, gender, sexual orientation. Depending on one's point of view, this can make some who resonate to this sign either progressive and broad-minded visionaries or out-of-step with the masses and unrealistic.

The detached attitude can be both the good news and the bad news for people involved with the Aquarian type, for often what one wants from a friend or loved one *is* some show of partiality. One wants a buddy who is on one's side, no matter what, but Aquarius tends to be on the side of **truth**, as they see it. The typical Aquarian is good at seeing *everyone's* point of view and may not go overboard in supporting you if they feel that your position is not fully truthful. The stereotypical Aquarian doesn't believe in duty or in the idea that blood is thicker than water. What Aquarius does believe in is **principle** and the type has a strong **social conscience** to boot. The Aquarian ideal replaces duty with the notion that both relationships and organizations should be based on free choice and on co-operation between individuals. The individual whose chart resonates strongly to the sign may find themselves struggling to make this ideal a reality; many Aquarian types can be dogmatic and, rather as with the old USSR's enforcement of Communism, they are prone to forcing their co-operative principles on the uninterested and unwilling.

The concern with truth leads naturally on to **tactlessness**, **outspokenness** and also to the notion of sincerity. Authenticity might be an alternative word here, since authentic means 'one who acts independently'.

Those with this sign strong tend to say what they mean and mean what they say; or at least do so at the time. This is a sign characterized by **conviction**. In the realm of Sun sign astrology, Aquarius is often labelled as cold and **aloof** but the reality may have more to do with a desire to be **sincere**. The typical Aquarian is very **interested in people** and in what makes them tick, and is also concerned with humanity as a whole. You can throw a typical Aquarian type into any social situation and they will be quite **friendly**, **open** and seemingly interested. Aquarius is probably the friendliest sign of the zodiac. Nevertheless, they may not like very many individuals on a more personal level and only wish to fraternize with the few. Hence the people who think Aquarians are cold don't realize that they have actually just been rejected. The typical Aquarian would see themselves as being truthful and sincere, not pretending to like you if they don't, not starting relationships which they know they don't want to pursue. Having said that, Aquarius is an air sign and needs people. Family no, friends yes. It was probably an Aquarian who said that you can't choose your family but you can choose your friends. Companionship and **friendship** – having a pal and a buddy – are essential to the typical Aquarian and sometimes lay them open to charges of cronyism (from the Greek *chronios* and originally meaning 'long-standing friend'). Nevertheless, many Aquarians, while friendly to all, won't become closely involved with just anybody. This is perhaps the most **tolerant** but also the most **intolerant** sign of the zodiac. Intellectually, Aquarius may be 100% on the side of every living thing but emotionally will reject a huge percentage of the human race. The Aquarian type will reject others for a variety of reasons but insincerity, snobbery, trivial conversation and what they interpret as narrow-mindedness feature highly on the hit list.

Aquarius has a justifiable reputation for **unconventionality** and for **unorthodoxy**, but those who vibrate strongly to the sign are rarely that radical or revolutionary unless Uranus is also strongly configured in the chart. On its own, the type is not that keen on change at all and is often quite mild in temperament, though the more extrovert type can be dominating and opinionated. But if the introverts are frequently mild, they are also often as **wilful** and know-it-all as their louder counterparts.

The Aquarian type is **self-willed** with a strong **independent** spirit. Typically the type will not be interfered with or told what to think or what to do. The individual who resonates strongly with this sign is one who insists on the freedom to make up their own mind on just about everything. They may be interested in what others say but will arrive at their own judgements independently. You may like or dislike someone or something intensely but that won't prevent your strongly Aquarian friend feeling completely differently. Their independence runs through everything; those who vibrate strongly to the sign simply don't care what others think. They don't choose lifestyles to please others or, outside adolescence anyway, dress to fit in with the dictates of fashion. The adherence to their own principles and judgement can make the typical Aquarian seem rather arrogant and superior, trusting as they do in no one else's judgement half as much as they do in their own.

Aquarius is the sign to associate with **technology** and **science**. This is partly because the Aquarian is concerned with progress, as they see it. Setting people free through the use of robots so they don't have to do mind-numbing tasks, or setting people free from disease are two examples. (The reality is, of course, that machinery makes people redundant and they might prefer to have their jobs, however monotonous, and also what often seems like a cure for a disease is merely a suppression of its symptoms.)

The Wider World

Many with this sign accentuated in the horoscope have a strong appreciation of nature, wildlife and wilderness. In the animal kingdom, Aquarius ought definitely to be associated with birds, partly because they can be taken to symbolize freedom, but also because it is suspected that many migrating birds navigate themselves by detecting electromagnetic signals en route. Not surprisingly, many bird-watchers have an emphasis on this sign as do those who are drawn to the sky generally, including astronomers, astrologers, and those in the aviation industry (air stewards, pilots and air-traffic controllers, etc.).

Colours/Taste/Style

There can be a liking for the very old and the very contemporary, and often an inclination to mix the two. Usually there is a dislike of fripperies and a preference for plainer, starker styles. Electric blue, aquamarine and turquoise are the colours most associated with the sign, and occasional flashes of vibrant colours generally may be appreciated. The dress sense of the typical Aquarian will often be ethnic or, at any rate, somewhat individual, often mixing the very latest fashions with Granny's cast-offs and Oxfam's best. As has often been noted, there is frequently an **androgynous** quality to the Aquarian type and this can sometimes be reflected in the personal style. The androgynous quality offers another take on the mythological fact that Ouranos (Uranus), the contemporary Aquarian planetary ruler, was castrated.

The Body

The **ankles** are the main part of the body traditionally associated with Aquarius, but this area can be taken to embrace the legs from the knees down to the feet. Whereas Leo, the opposite sign, has jurisdiction over the heart, Aquarius governs the whole **circulatory system**. Frequently, of course, myocardial infarctions (heart attacks) and strokes start with blood clots in the legs. The Sun is in its detriment in Aquarius (see page 217) and certainly this may not be the most robust of signs. Uranus, the sign's ruler, seems to have an association with the nervous system and a certain nervy or high-strung quality can sometimes be observed.

Planets in Aquarius

Personal planets tend to operate in a more **unorthodox**, atypical, **independent** and **unconventional** manner when found in Aquarius. With respect to what the given planet signifies, the individual will tend to go their own way regardless of the approval or otherwise of the rest of society.

Aquarius on a House Cusp

Friends will usually feature strongly in the activities associated with the given house. For instance, on the Seventh House cusp, friends can become life-partners and vice versa, while on the Third House cusp, pen pals are implied.

Pisces ♓

Element: Water
Mode: Mutable
Ruler: Neptune (modern ruler) and Jupiter (traditional ruler)

The Symbol and Glyph

The glyph is a pictogram of two fish swimming in opposite directions. Fish don't swim in any particular direction, and perhaps like the typical Piscean they have to choose between swimming upstream or drifting downstream.

General Characteristics

One can usually hear the strong presence of Pisces in a horoscope when the individual uses words like 'soul', 'bliss' or 'blessing'. It has often been observed that the qualities and life areas connected with Pisces are very similar to those associated with Christianity. Christians, seeing themselves as 'fishers of men', even use the fish as their symbol. **Sacrifice**, the notion of a saviour, martyrdom and redemption are all central Christian motifs, as are stories of fish-sharing and feet-washing. Jesus associated with Jews and gentiles alike, with prostitutes, beggars, lepers and criminals. Similarly, operating at its highest level, Pisces recognizes **no boundaries between people**. There is no assumption of superiority over someone who is mentally ill, poor, uneducated or belonging to the criminal underclass. Pisces is concerned with **wholeness** and **universality**. Although this may not apply to Piscean individuals (who are, let's face it, merely mortal), the Pisces developmental stage of the zodiac teaches that we are all interdependent parts of the same universe, the same oneness. How, then, can any member of that universe be superior to any other? At the Piscean phase of evolution, external factors are not so important (and whether someone is a leper or a beggar is merely external labelling). What *is* important is spiritual development. And spiritual development probably (I say 'probably' because it is perhaps unprovable) involves balancing the karmic scales of what happened in past lives and possibly earlier in this life. Arguably, humans do this by helping to heal the suffering of others, by carrying (as opposed to displacing) their own burden of suffering, and by putting right the damage of what went before. In other words, by paying off outstanding debts. Both Pisces and the Twelfth House can be associated with slavery in a number of different contexts and there is a connection between slavery and debt, for when are in debt we are enslaved to our debtors.

Rather as when painting with watercolours, where each colour bleeds into its neighbour, it can be difficult to isolate a pure Piscean quality in the horoscope because planets in Pisces easily get contaminated by other planets in aspect to them. Pisces is not only the most **unworldly** zodiacal sign but is the one with the **weakest sense of self**. Similarly, planets in Pisces also rarely dominate in a horoscope. If anything, they get victimized by the energies of other planets plugging into them.

As with the other mutable signs, Pisces is **commitment-shy**. Individuals with the sign strong can be elusive; they hate to be confined in any way and, similarly, the meanings of various Piscean placements are not easy to define, classify or pin down. I understand that Richard Ideman, the late American astrologer, gave a lecture in which he described Pisces as '**Not Me, Not Here and Not Now**', and that is a perfect summing up of Piscean energy. Thus, there is often a **wistful, elusive** quality to those who resonate strongly to Pisces. Just when some kind of definition seems possible, some clear goal perhaps is reached, our typical Pisces type somehow slips and slithers away.

Whereas Aquarius is so confident in its views, so full of conviction and so intent on finding the truth, Pisces knows that the truth is relative and rarely what it seems. Pisces' orientation to life is to embrace rather than reject. The blessing and the curse of Pisces is that it doesn't judge but seeks to accept. On the plus side, the **capacity to embrace, accept** and **understand** can make Pisces the most **compassionate** and truly loving sign of the zodiac. Like its opposite number Virgo, Pisces tends towards **humility** and **kindness**. Not having a strong sense of self (what some might describe as a weak ego) means that people who resonate strongly to Pisces are **receptive** and very **impressionable**. On the down side, those with Pisces accentuated in their chart may not only lack conviction but may be **weak-willed, easily influenced** and perhaps **easily led**.

The lack of a strong identity can make for a fine actor, because classically Pisces can **bend, blend** and generally **contort** themselves to whatever is required. The **ego-less** quality also makes it easy for the Pisces type to sacrifice themselves. This capacity for selflessness and the **sacrificial** quality are positive manifestations of the sign if they are done consciously. Basically, devoting the self to something or someone brings out the best in the type. The 'other' (whether the 'other' be a person or project) can provide anchorage, shape and a goal to the otherwise **goalless, drifting** fish. For all that, Pisces may not always over-contort themselves, not by choice anyway, as the type often avoids anything that is too taxing, difficult, crass or irksome. Pisces always tends towards **indolence** and while the Piscean type of person might mean well, a **vague, dreamy** quality may prevent them from actually rolling their sleeves up and being of any real help. At worst, the Piscean type can persuade themselves towards any point of view and this can easily undermine their impulse to act, to actually *do* something.

With Neptune as its contemporary ruler, perhaps it is not surprising that Pisces is famous for its strong **escapist** tendencies. At best, this can be described as the desire to transcend ordinary reality, to rise above the crass and merely worldly. However, their sensitivity to suffering can mean that the Pisces type will merely do anything to avoid unpleasantness. At worst, these traits, coupled with an urge to escape, can lead to addictive behaviour. Additionally, the tendency to identify with the **victim** and often to cast themselves in that role can make the Pisces type something of a user in non-drug as well as in drug-related terms. When this trait is very pronounced, those who vibrate strongly to Pisces ensure that, whatever the project in hand, someone will do it for them, someone will rescue them. That is because the typical Pisces type has no compunction in admitting to weakness or inadequacy.

The sign is **idealistic** rather than realistic. It is not that Pisces is incapable of being realistic – containing as it does the seeds of all preceding signs, Pisces is capable of being just about anything at all – it is more that Pisces will tend to ask 'What is so good about reality?' Feelings of **longing** and **yearning** are part of the Piscean package, as are **dissatisfaction, disillusionment** and **self-pity**. Those who vibrate strongly to the sign may be the most open-minded as to whether fairies exist at the bottom of their garden, and be more than willing to pretend that they do. For Pisces, the **fantasy** is worth tossing about a bit. Being mutable, the orientation as always is inclusive, so a typical response to the fairy question might be: 'How are we to know?' or 'Who are we to say there aren't?'

Thus, the **open-mindedness** of the sign is one of its greatest gifts but often leads to charges of **gullibility** or woolly-mindedness by more pragmatic types, who miss the joy to be gained and truth to be gleaned from **make-believe** and fantasy.

It could be argued that all the zodiac signs are creative in their way, but Pisces is **artistic**, bearing in mind that the artist is one who **mirrors** the world for the rest of us. Mirroring – the capacity to reflect back what is received – is perhaps Pisces' greatest skill. With Pisces, tremendous **imagination** may be coupled with the need to be enchanted, to be magnetized by others or by circumstance. Dance and poetry are the arts that Pisces can be drawn to, or at which they are skilled. Both art forms have an **expressive, free-flowing** quality.

The Wider World

In the animal kingdom, Pisces obviously has jurisdiction over the fish kingdom as a whole and also perhaps to mammals that live in the sea, such as dolphins, seals and whales. Parasitical animals and plants probably also come, at least partially, under its umbrella. I have noticed individuals with transits or progressions to or from planets in Pisces have often chosen Cuba as a holiday destination. Arabic countries may also be favoured and I have noticed that Westerners who are drawn to Arabic dancing often have a strong Piscean or Twelfth House emphasis, especially with respect to Mars.

Colours/Taste/Style

Flowing and comfortable styles are the norm here but sometimes Pisces doesn't seem to have any specific taste, with the choice of clothes and household furnishings being nondescript and able to fit in anywhere. On other occasions, Pisces goes for the rich and exotic, and certainly the bohemian or cosmopolitan. There is often a very marked propensity for amassing (but not necessarily wearing) vast quantities of footwear. Frequently the onlooker is told of the difficulty in getting shoes to fit comfortably. Very often, the typically Pisces type is characterized by having a mass of hair.

The Body

The Piscean body part is the **feet**, that area of the body which connects us to the Earth and all the Earth's ley lines and subtle energies. Thus, in a sense, our feet connect us with spiritual dimensions. The feet are also a symbol of humility, as can be seen with the disciples washing the feet of Jesus. In any event, the feet are often a vulnerable area for those who vibrate strongly to this sign. The weaker sense of self can make the Piscean type peculiarly prone to depression and addiction to drink or drugs but, as always, the whole chart must be studied and Pisces by no means has the monopoly over such problems.

Planets in Pisces

As stated earlier, Piscean planets rarely dominate a horoscope and will tend to take on the colouring of other energies plugging into them. Planets such as the Moon and Venus benefit from the **imaginative** and **empathetic** qualities of the sign, while Mars and Saturn can lose some direction. The sign reduces the 'oomph' factor of many planets while increasing a feeling of **fluidity** and **romanticism**.

Pisces on a House Cusp

Activities associated with this house may be those where the individual's **empathy** and **compassion** are aroused. For instance, Pisces on the Fifth House cusp may suggest an individual who feels sorry for children and has some tendency to rescue them. Or if the Fifth shows an individual's method of creative self-expression, then watercolour painting, drama, music and, more especially, dance are possibilities (as always the whole chart must be studied). As with planets in Pisces, the house cusp where the sign is to be found may be an area where a certain amount of **sacrifice** or **suffering** is implied, or at least an area where one's more egotistical needs count for little.

More on the Signs: the Six Pairs

Arguably there are not so much twelve zodiacal signs as six pairs of opposing ones, each dealing with a particular kind of continuum. What each side of a given pair represents cannot exist without the associated characteristics of its opposite number. For example, a teacher (Sagittarius) cannot teach without a pupil (Gemini). Each sign can learn much from the sign that opposes it. Similarly, the more extreme characteristics of a sign are tempered by the influence of the opposite sign. Again, sometimes a chart will have a strong emphasis across a particular polarity and due attention needs to be paid to this. Such oppositions can describe either-or conflicts in the life but also usually describe strong traits in the personality.

Aries and Libra

This is the duo to associate with the **competition** versus **co-operation** continuum, with the **battle of the sexes**, with **war and peace**, with **'I' versus 'we'** and with social (Libra) and antisocial (Aries) behaviour. Aries insists upon personal choice and autonomy whereas Libra favours mutual choice, reciprocal arrangements and social contracts. Aries acts alone, Libra operates jointly and through compromise and consensus. Aries opts for selfhood, Libra for partnership. Aries is honest, frank and outspoken, whereas socially-skilled Libra, who may be unaware of their true feelings or gifted at hiding them, opts for diplomacy and appeasement. Aries is direct and Libra circuitous. Aries puts their cards on the table (and is often therefore unsuccessful in battle), while Libra, a much better strategist, keeps things close to their chest. Disliking being hindered or thwarted, Aries wants to be free, unimpeded and uncluttered. Libra's closest concern is with order, both socially and physically. Aries is decisive, whereas Libra gets others to make decisions (Libra can be very indecisive and vacillating). Aries is passionate, may be unable to see another's point of view and will often be keen to fight. Libra, being usually much less personally involved, tries to build bridges and arrive at compromise and consensus at best, or, at worst, simply to duck the issue. Libra is concerned with fairness, rights and obligations, while Aries wants to be honest and just get things done. Aries can be dominating, Libra is more likely to be dominated. Possibly unsophisticated and naïve, Aries is usually keen to try something new, whereas Libra, not wanting to make waves or exert itself too much, dithers on the sidelines. Aries likes to be active, whereas Libra prefers taking things easy.

Taurus and Scorpio

This fixed pair are concerned with **sex, desire** and **ownership**. Here they come together while the opposing ends of this continuum deal with **building** (Taurus) and **destroying** (Scorpio). Both signs grapple with issues concerned with the acquiring and keeping of money, possessions and lovers. Both can be very possessive of people and resources, but whereas Taurus inclines more to the accumulation of things, Scorpio inclines more to emotional ownership. Typically, the strongly Scorpio type tries to possess those with whom they are emotionally involved. For Taurus, the body is a source of pleasure and something to be revelled in, whereas the Scorpionic view of the sexual act is linked with its desire for a psychic emotional merging with another. While Taurus wants to gather possessions, Scorpio seeks to notch up intense life experiences. The average Taurean may be possessive and want to enjoy nature's bounty but is satisfied if their basic needs for food, shelter and sex are met. Taurus, seeking familiarity and stability as it does, stoically accepts what is and builds upon it unquestioningly. Scorpio, on the other hand, having much more complex desires, cannot leave well alone. The type is easily dissatisfied and compulsively wants to experience more and more of life (and to analyse it), however painful that process may be. Thus, Scorpio will be tempted by the unfamiliar, even if that means destroying what already exists. Taurus can teach Scorpio acceptance and patience, while Scorpio can introduce Taurus to passion and living life more deeply.

Gemini and Sagittarius

Both signs are concerned with **gathering** and **spreading knowledge** and, between them, all matters concerned with **education** and **travel**. The duo are the **Peter Pan** pair and, if both feature strongly in a chart, then a disinclination to grow up is likely to be a strong factor in the person's psychological make-up. Although both signs 'spread the word', Gemini is more the reporter while Sagittarius is the broadcaster and publisher. Whereas Sagittarius sets itself up as teacher, preacher and advice-giver, Gemini is the pupil. Gemini gathers and shares facts, wants to know everything and can miss the overview. Gemini learns and forgets easily. Sagittarius, on the other hand, seeks overall comprehension and can remember the gist of a subject, but may be slapdash with details. Gemini takes things apart to see how they work; Sagittarius, seeking an overall philosophy, puts things together (even if they don't fit!). Gemini lives in the moment, Sagittarius lives in the future. Gemini asks 'Why?'; Sagittarius asks 'Why not?' Gemini covers a lot of ground (although generally close at hand) and Sagittarius covers long distances. Gemini is a sceptical sign and is also essentially amoral (morality can interfere with information-gathering), whereas Sagittarius is concerned with Church and State and matters of morality. Gemini loves game-playing and tricks, whereas Sagittarius is the clown.

Cancer and Capricorn

This is the traditional **parenting** duo, Cancer being maternal in nature and Capricorn paternal. Any planets found in Cancer and Capricorn usually speak very literally about a person's experience of mother and father respectively. If this pair is highly focal in a chart, the experience of having parents and being parents is likely to be paramount. Whereas Cancer will look after the family because they belong to it and feel nourished and protected by it, Capricorn does so because it is their duty to look after kith and kin, and perhaps the law of the land to do so, too. Thus, both signs uphold the status quo of **family** and **State**, and both have a preservative and conservative role in society. Cancer has a strong association with the sea and Capricorn with the land (specifically the Earth's crust). Cancer is soft, yielding and fluid, while Capricorn is rigid, hard, obeys the rules and can discipline those who don't. Cancer is associated with home and family and Capricorn with society, which is made up of families. Cancer tends towards sentimentalism and Capricorn towards realism. Cancer holds on to the past, whereas Capricorn, while venerating age and tradition, assesses the present and makes plans for the future. Cancer goes back and Capricorn moves cautiously forward. Cancer tends towards dependency while Capricorn seeks to rely on no one and is therefore independent.

Leo and Aquarius

The Leo/Aquarius polarity deals with **personal** and **collective authority** and also with **art** (Leo) and **science** (Aquarius). When this sometimes wilful pair feature strongly in an individual's horoscope, that person will often find it difficult to accept the advice or authority of another. While Leo is concerned with self-expression, Aquarius focuses on the larger group having the freedom to express and rule itself. Aquarius can be associated with science and technology which, at its best, can free people from disease and drudgery, although often at the expense of seeing people as individuals. Leo is the sign of the leader, ruler and monarch, while Aquarius is associated with Joe and Josephine Bloggs, the so-called ordinary or common people. Or, one might say, Leo is the king, while Aquarius is concerned with the kingdom. There is a centre (Leo) to circumference (Aquarius) feeling about this pair. For instance, Leo is always personally involved with whatever is going on, whereas Aquarius is the detached bystander. Leo is concerned with uniqueness, personal glory and specialness, while Aquarius tends to reject personal advantage and celebrity, seeing it as being at the expense of the many. Just as there is a danger of dictatorship at the Leo extreme of this continuum, at the extreme Aquarian end comes a society where the individual counts for nothing. Creativity (Leo) becomes stifled when people lose their sense of personal identity and significance. Both signs are concerned with socialization. Leo is the sign of play, creativity and fun, and play always increases social skills. Aquarius is the sign to associate with friends – what one might call playmates.

Virgo and Pisces

Both signs are concerned with **service**. Where these two signs feature strongly in a chart, one can expect the behavioural traits of humility, modesty and self-effacement to be noticeable. However, Virgo, being critical and discriminating, is *exclusive* in orientation, whereas Pisces, seeking wholeness and totality and therefore embracing everything and everyone, is *inclusive*. Virgo judges, whereas Pisces accepts. Virgo seeS foibles while Pisces overlooks them. Virgo is fairly worldly and Pisces is *the* most unworldly sign. Virgo seeks out the reality of a situation and feels safest knowing what the perameters of a given situation are. Pisces, disliking perameters of all kinds, is usually hell-bent on escaping from what it sees as the limitations, and often squalidness, of reality. Virgo likes things to be categorized and thus, even if untidy at times, can be associated with efficiency and putting information into some kind of order, whereas Pisces is the sign of chaos. Virgo, ever gifted at differentiation, views life through a microscope, whereas Pisces, only concerned with the larger whole, and disliking finite distinctions, favours a telescope. Virgo is concerned with maintaining the body and, in medical terms, with taking it apart to diagnose and treat ailments. Pisces is concerned with the body's dissolution and with viewing it holistically, embracing mind and spirit along with the body. Virgo seeks to get the 'right' answer whereas Pisces considers right answers to be elusive or misleading (for Pisces everything is relative). Virgo is often a craftsperson and is good with matter, whereas Pisces is more the artist, skilled with colour. Virgo may be scholarly but Pisces inclines to the experiential and imaginative. Virgo may be the humble servant but Pisces doesn't so much serve as surrender.

Chapter 4

The Planets and Other Essential Bodies

Influenced by tabloid newspapers perhaps, the lay public in the West generally believe that the subject of astrology is primarily concerned with the signs of the zodiac. However, this is far from the case. Concentrating on the signs is analogous to waxing lyrical about the paper in which a gift is wrapped. Usually the gift is reckoned to be more important than the packaging! While most astrologers like using the signs and many have come to 'real' astrology through an initial passion for Sun-sign astrology, it is perfectly possible to practise meaningful and accurate astrology without any recourse to the signs whatsoever. Of course the signs do have some significance but their given meaning can often be gleaned elsewhere. Of all the symbolism that can be included in the horoscope, just about the only factors that cannot be omitted are the planets and their relationship to each other and to the angles. So deep and significant is the material offered by the planets that whole books have been written about each of them. Indeed, one could spend a lifetime studying any planet and still leave much to be discovered.

In days gone by, this section would have simply been entitled 'The Planets', but the demotion of Pluto to that of dwarf planet renders this title increasingly inappropriate, especially since the Sun is actually a star and the Moon is a satellite of the Earth.

The Sun ☉

'We are all worms, but I do believe I am a glow-worm.'

Sir Winston Churchill

Astronomy

The Sun is *the* star at the centre of our solar system, providing us with heat and light and making life possible.
• Mean distance from the Earth: approximately 93 million miles/150 million kilometres (the distance is known as 1 astronomical mile).
• Diameter: approximately 865,000 miles/1.4 million kilometres. This is 100 times greater than our Earth and 40 times larger than the Earth's Moon: the Sun is huge!
• Period of rotation of the Earth around Sun: 365.25 days.

Mythology

The mythology associated with the Sun is extensive in all cultures. To ancient peoples, the Sun was a symbol of heroism, disappearing each night to battle with the forces of nature and then returning valiant each dawn. In Greek mythology, the Sun is associated with the archer Apollo, Zeus's favourite son, a golden boy of whom his father was proud. Apollo had a difficult birth. For a start, his mother Leto couldn't find anywhere she could deliver him. This was because Leto was one of Zeus's 'other' women and everyone feared the wrath of Zeus's jealous wife, Hera, if they helped Leto out. When she did give birth on the barren island of Delos, she had an awful labour because Hera had prevented the goddess of childbirth coming to her aid. The story goes that it took nine days and nine nights for Apollo to be born, that his twin sister, Artemis, helped at his birth, and that he was born on the seventh day of the month and under a palm tree. Similarly, when we do something difficult and unfamiliar, or when we strive to go somewhere or achieve something (we are in hero mode – see below), it can indeed feel like a difficult birth.

As he grew into manhood, it is clear that, while Apollo looked good, he was less successful in his relationships. Perhaps this was because he had such a poor start with the females in his life (he was very much his *father's* son) or because he was not deep enough, or maybe it was because he pursued lovers in the manner of an archer, in a goal-orientated way. This is analogous to the fact that when we are set on a goal, most other areas of life, of necessity, become somewhat neglected.

Modern Mythology – the Hollywood Hero

An image of the modern-day Apollo can be found in the all-American clean-cut boy beloved of Hollywood movies; he is some kind of super-hero who does something wonderful. For all that, he is usually rather like a cardboard cut-out or comic-book hero figure and gets by pretty much on appearances. He is usually popular with the guys, a star in any team, and in the marriage stakes is considered to be a very good catch. He isn't usually gay or ugly or short. He doesn't wear glasses, he isn't clumsy or misguided or rebellious. He isn't fully like a real human being but he invites hero-worship, he looks how young people often want to look. He is an image of something to aspire to for young people. His character is unblemished (a hero always has integrity) and he achieves something great, such as saving civilization. Significantly, the film always ends well before the viewer can see how he fares over time.

As we get older, most thinking adults come to appreciate the complexity of the human condition. We recognize the value of pragmatism, and learn that most things are relative and that every decision has a consequence. In the fully matured state, the individual is no longer able to be so sure about anything. The Hollywood hero is two-dimensional and youthful but sincere and principled, too. The truly mature human being is inevitably somewhat tarnished by life and the mistakes they have made. They may have acquired maturity, wisdom and compassion – qualities provided by other planetary energies – but they are no longer fully the hero. The hero is a necessary construct of youth, an image to aspire to and identify with.

Ego and Identity

The Sun is merely one of a billion stars in space that produce heat and light so, on one level, there is nothing special about it. But on another, of course, it is crucial, for without the Sun there would be no life on Earth. Similarly, each individual is one of billions of other human beings, but nevertheless each manages to feel important. This is because in Western culture, at any rate, the individual is decidedly egocentric; their world revolves around themselves. Similarly, while sitting on Earth, it seems as if the Sun revolves around us rather than the other way round. In contrast to this egocentric way of thinking, in Hindu astrology the Sun is viewed as malefic in nature. This is because the traditional Indian world view emphasizes the value of community and views the overly Western obsession with individual ego as spiritually moribund and potentially injurious to the welfare of the world as a whole.

Although in many ways the easiest energy to interpret in the horoscope (at least on a superficial level), it is difficult to define exactly what the Sun signifies in personal terms. Sometimes it is described as the significator of 'the self' but that rather depends on what is meant by the term 'the self'. If interpreted in the Jungian sense as meaning one's *whole* self, then the Sun is not appropriate, for the whole self must surely be the whole birth chart and perhaps even something outside the horoscope, as well as encompassing all that is within it. The Sun most contributes to our ego, the person we think we are, the person we identify with. Aspects from other planets to the Sun (and the Sun's sign and house placement) affect the way we identify ourselves and they affect our opinion of ourselves. Do we have a good opinion of ourselves or do we have a poor self-image? Do we have a self-image at all? Aspects to the Sun shed light on these questions. The Sun may not describe exactly *who* we are, that is too elusive and anyway it is a moveable feast, but the Sun has a lot to say about how we want to be seen. It is an image of ourselves that we take pains to keep, as we feel we can be proud of it. Individuals will sometimes glory in their Sun attributes, bask in whatever the message of their Sun is. Hardly surprising, therefore, that, en route to adulthood, teenagers have a need to indulge in hero-worship.

Jung and his followers use the word 'individuate' to describe the process of becoming a distinct entity. Basically, if one is individuated then one is clearly distinguishable from others of the same species. Arguably, the Sun describes the impulse behind the individuation process.

The Sun isn't only about ego and identity. In the same way that the Sun keeps and holds the whole solar system together, the planet seems to have an integrating role in the horoscope, rather like the leader of an orchestra. The glyph looks like a cell with a nucleus in the middle and, similarly, the Sun may contain a clue as to what lies at the centre of our being: what is our nucleus, our core, our essence. Our character as opposed to our personality.

The Sun in a chart describes how and where we want to be recognized and, in being recognized, our identity is reinforced. If recognition is not possible or is not sufficient, then solar psychology is not above plain old attention-seeking. Thus, the Sun says much about how we glean our sense of identity, our sense of 'I'. Indeed, to some extent, whenever we use the word 'I' we are coming, at least partially, from a solar perspective.

Life, Vitality and Will

The Sun is the source of all life energy on Earth and similarly it contributes greatly to the general will and vitality of the person; perhaps to the notion of a Divine Spark. Its strength in the birth chart indicates the basic urge towards life and towards being. Those with a 'sunny' disposition are people who can enjoy life and radiate their presence; their vitality is strong. One can imagine that for some people their Sun radiates like a 150-watt light bulb when they walk in a room, whereas others get by on 40 watts. People usually feel at their most alive when carrying out the message of their Sun. For instance, you may have the Sun in the Third House and feel 'switched on' in classroom situations, or perhaps it is in the Fifth and you find it easy to light up at a party. When in strong aspect to a planet or point in the chart, the Sun gives the other body vigour, power and strength. Just as the Sun in the sky provides light and heat, anything that is touched (a house or another planet, for instance) by the Sun in our charts is at once illuminated and warmed. Whatever the other planet (or point) is, the spotlight is put on it and it is invigorated. Aspects (see Chapter 5) work both ways of course, so conversely planets tapping into the Sun (such as Saturn) can sap its power and strength, rather as sunglasses subdue the intensity of sunlight.

Goals

The Sun will contribute much to the most important events and decisions in life. Essentially, it is concerned with our life purpose and therefore our central aims and goals and where our inner spirit takes us. Basically, it has much to say about our quest. Obviously the whole chart speaks of our purpose, mission and quest but the Sun seems to play a central role here by almost driving the rest of the chart, or so it seems. Driving force or not, the Sun is certainly an area to focus on in the chart.

Purpose, Intent, Direction

Coming from a solar perspective, one might say 'I want' (the Moon is more 'I need'), 'This is my purpose, my intention, my direction'. Or 'Here I want to be myself. Here I want to be special, here I want to be unique and an individual in my own right.' The Sun symbolizes that part of the self that centres on itself. Aspects to the Sun describe the ease or difficulty an individual may have in both accepting themselves and in being self-centred (although other parts of the chart are relevant here, too). Thus, the condition of the Sun has considerable impact on a person's self-confidence and self-esteem, attributes that are of course not stationary: confidence can both grow and wane over time.

The Heroic Quest

A life's purpose can be described as a heroic quest and the Sun in the horoscope contributes to where and by what means we may become a hero, at least in our own small way. Where the Sun is, we are the central character; it is the place in the chart where the main light is shining. Before embarking on the heroic quest, the Sun describes our image of the hero: who or what we look up to and seek to emulate (this may be based on an early image of our father), although this isn't usually as conscious as it might sound. A hero by definition is an upright person whose integrity is unquestionable. The heroic figure is purposeful and self-reliant, a leader rather than a follower. Heroic quests, whatever their complexion, all share certain features:
 • The hero has to have a quest, purpose, task or challenge. Usually the task is something that the hero does both for him- or herself *and*, at the same time, which makes a contribution to the Collective. Successfully carrying out the quest ensures the hero a degree of fame and a tiny slice of eternity.
 • In order to carry out the task, the hero has to leave safety, security and familiarity, as symbolized by the Moon. He or she has to forge out into the unknown.
 • There will be obstacles and triumphs along the way. Basically, the task has to be big enough for there not to be any guarantee of success. Imagine watching a Hollywood movie. There has to be some chance that the hero is not going to make it, otherwise there is no story and no excitement; the audience might as well be watching paint dry. In astronomical terms, the potential for heroic failure is symbolized by the fairly rare possibility of a solar eclipse. Here, to all intents and purposes, the Sun 'goes out'. The sky is momentarily dark, albeit in daylight hours. The word 'eclipse' comes from the Greek and means 'failure, abandonment or disappearance'.
 • There will be helpers and jealous rivals to make the task easier or more difficult (these tend to be shown by the aspects to our Sun). It is easy to see why heroes attract enemies because, when they are in the spotlight, others inevitably are put in the shade. In the same way, in the sky, the Sun is very bright and very hot. All other stars pale into insignificance against it; indeed, we don't see other stars when the Sun is out.
 • There will usually be temptations, offered by the 'baddies', for the hero to slip from grace and take the easy way out. Such temptations are also shown by our solar aspects. If the hero does give way to temptation then, having lost the essential heroic ingredient of integrity, s/he ceases to be a hero but takes on the shape and colouring of a different planetary energy.

Of course, as well as meaning honest and upright, integrity means being complete or undivided. The circle, which is essentially the glyph for the Sun, is an age-old image of wholeness: it is undivided.

The Father

The Sun in the horoscope is always descriptive of the father; both of the biological father and subsequent father figures. At the very least it shows the individual's experience of Dad. Having said that, all charts will have many different significators to describe both parents. Nevertheless, the Sun (and Saturn) usually describe some very basic facts about the father, including, for instance, what he did for a living. The house position of the Sun often says which areas of life the father found most important – maybe even more important than the owner of the horoscope – for this area of life took him away from his child (although those with the Sun in the First House may have felt that they *were* the most important aspect of their father's life). Thus, on some level the child's attention starts to head in the same direction; s/he has learned what *is* important, where to focus, where to put their attention. While the house position will often show where we felt his attention was focused, the sign and aspects usually say something about what happened to him and what he was like. Indeed, the Sun can be viewed as describing the father's heroic quest and how successful – or not – he was at it. Where there are several father figures in the life, the Sun will usually describe an aspect of each of them, however much they seem to differ as individuals. The Tenth/Fourth Houses and their rulers also do this, of course. If the father is completely absent, as is quite commonly the case, his role in the person's psyche and developmental process is often even more important. The individual then weaves a story (based to a greater or lesser extent on the reality of the situation) that explains his absence.

What is Important to Us

Whether describing what we thought father found important or not, the Sun in the chart describes those areas of life we consider to be essential, those areas and qualities to which we attach importance. Its position in the chart describes where we focus our attention. Its house placement will often show where, how and for what reason we first attracted attention – usually in childhood. The area associated with the Sun may describe the area where we are most naturally in the limelight.

Husbands and Men in General

The Sun not only describes the father but also often describes (along with Mars) the male partner or central man or men in a woman's life. Even if she has no men in her life, the solar principle does often describe an inner image of male figures. Ideally, women live out this image for themselves but the advent of feminism, and women leading their own, more independent lives, seems to have made little difference to this oft-noted observation by astrologers.

A Future Orientation

The solar principle is concerned with the future, it describes the direction one is heading towards (hence Apollo being an archer), as opposed to the Moon, whose concern is the past and where we are coming from.

In Mundane and Business Astrology

As the Sun is the boss of our solar system and is associated with success, prominence, power, honour, fame, influence and leadership, perhaps it is not surprising that the Sun represents the monarch, the overall ruler or figurehead of a country or organization.

Metal

Gold. This is the most lustrous and valuable of metals. Its yellow colour is reminiscent of the Sun itself. Like the reputation of the very best hero, it will not tarnish, rust or fade, and these are the qualities which make it so valuable. Gold is usually linked to eternity, and couples exchange eternity rings to suggest enduring love. Diamonds also probably come under the solar umbrella as they are valuable; they glisten and are scarce. Crystals, being a symbol of the self, are also solar.

The Body and Vitality

The major organ is the heart which, from the moment of birth, works non-stop until we die. It is a pumping machine which provides the power needed for life.

The Sun also undoubtedly contributes to our overall vitality. And, more esoterically perhaps, it is probably behind our basic 'life force', that mysterious energy which animates our whole being and thus may contribute to our ability to shrug off disease. What modern medics would call the immune system, perhaps. Significantly, and perhaps supporting this view, is the fact that, to the Greeks, Apollo was the patron of medicine and father of Asclepius, the god of medicine. A god so skilled that he could bring the dead back to life. The circle, as we have seen, is an age-old image of wholeness and therefore health. The words 'health', 'whole' and 'holy' all come from the same Old English root word, *hal*.

How to Interpret the Sun – Recapping the Main Points

By House Position

Firstly, the house position of the Sun will show what is likely to be one of the most, if not *the* most, important area of life to the individual. It is through the activities of this house that the individual may achieve most recognition and feel most alive. As has been noted, it often describes the area of life where the child first gained attention. For instance, the Sun in the Third House often describes a circumstance where the youngster shone at school, perhaps gaining honours or becoming Head Girl or Boy. The Sun in the Sixth House will often describe a child who was noticed because s/he was ill. Little wonder, then, that if one got 'strokes' for the given life area that it would continue to be important throughout life. The house position of the Sun will often indicate what drew the father's attention, too. In the Sixth House perhaps he was perceived as always being at work; in the Eleventh out with his mates or serving the community; in the Twelfth behind the scenes, and so on. The house that the Sun rules (the house that has Leo on the cusp) will add important information concerning the Sun in the horoscope. There is usually a relationship between the activities of the Leo-ruled house and the house in which the Sun is found.

By Sign

The sign of the Sun often works as an adjective. To illustrate this, let us imagine someone with their Sun in Scorpio in the Fifth House. Basically, this person feels that creative self-expression is essential to life, that *playing* (Fifth House) is what is important. Imagine that the individual loves going to the theatre; in Scorpio, the individual will favour melodrama, plays dealing with the major themes of life – birth, sex and death. Opera and tragedies would probably be enjoyed but (overly) light entertainment might not. Or maybe our person with the Sun in the Fifth House feels that children are the most important ingredients in the world; in Scorpio, the individual may have possessive children or be possessive of their own (or other people's) youngsters. And so on. Chapter 3 provides plenty of information which can be used to decipher Sun signs (there are also many books available on the zodiac). The important thing to remember is that the Sun is less a description of how one actually is and more a description of the direction in which one is heading: the person one is striving to become, and the goal and the challenges that have to be faced en route.

By Aspect

The Sun will invigorate and give strength to whichever body it touches in the chart. There is an opportunity for some illumination with respect to what that body signifies. For instance, the Sun shining on Mars (imagine a tight aspect between the two) will increase the individual's physical strength and general hardiness, as well as fortifying the essential qualities of courage and daring, and potentially increasing impulsiveness and recklessness, too.

The Moon ☽

'They fuck you up, your mum and dad,
They may not mean to, but they do.
They fill you with the faults they had
And add some extra, just for you.'

Philip Larkin, *This Be The Verse*

Astronomy

Even though the diameter of the Sun is about 400 times that of our Moon, the Moon looks about the same size as the Sun when viewed from the Earth. The reason for this is that although the Sun is much larger, at 93 million miles/150,000 million kilometres away it is also much more distant. Astrologers often comment that the seemingly similar size of the Moon and Sun reflect the equal importance that the Moon has in the horoscope. Its nearness to us also reflects the idea that it is associated with those things that are of the closest concern. The apparently similar size of the Sun and Moon is what makes total solar eclipses possible, because if the conditions are right, from our viewpoint the entire disk of the Sun is covered by that of the Moon.
  • Mean distance from the Earth: the average distance is a mere 239,000 miles/384,000 kilometres.
  • Diameter: with a diameter of approximately 2160 miles/3476 kilometres, the Moon is about one-quarter the size of the Earth.
  • Period of rotation: the Moon turns on its axis every 27.3 days, which is roughly the same time that it takes to orbit the Earth. Because the durations are so similar, the Moon always shows us the same face. The far side of the Moon was first observed by humans in 1959 when an unmanned Soviet spacecraft photographed it. Ten years later, on 20 July 1969, US astronauts Neil Armstrong and Buzz Aldrin were the first men to walk on the Moon.
  • The Moon's light comes from reflecting just 7% of the Sun's rays. The Sun is about 400,000 times brighter than the Moon, even at Full Moon.
  • Spending just two-and-a-half days in each sign per month, the average daily motion is 13 degrees 12 minutes, or roughly one degree every two hours.

Mythology

There is extensive lunar mythology in all cultures. Goddesses associated with the Moon have usually been concerned with matters of fertility, child-rearing and agriculture. Countless worldwide festivals are also associated with the Moon; for instance, Easter falls on the first Full Moon following the Vernal Equinox in the Northern Hemisphere (this is why Easter Sunday can fall anywhere between 22 March and 25 April).
  In Greek mythology the principal goddesses associated with the Moon are: Artemis, the maiden who is associated with the crescent or waxing Moon; Demeter, the mother or mature woman who is associated with the Full Moon; Hecate, the crone or wise woman associated with the waning Moon.
  Artemis was the Greek version of the Roman goddess, Diana. The daughter of Leto and Zeus, Artemis was the twin sister of Apollo and it is said that she assisted in his

birth (see page 76). Indeed, as well as protecting the very young, she was goddess of childbirth. More especially, she was the virgin goddess of the hunt, and one of only three goddesses who were immune to the enchantments of Aphrodite (the other two being Hestia and Athene). She was friendly with mortals and gods alike, and was a great protector of young women and wild creatures. She is often pictured dancing through the forests and meadows in her silver sandals with a band of nymphs following on her heels. Basically, Artemis's role was to preside over women's transition from girl to woman. She helped young men, too, in their transitions into adulthood. While Demeter corresponds to the mother archetype, Artemis is the maiden, autonomous and complete in herself. She is usually portrayed as determined, courageous and fierce, in the same way that her brother Apollo (and the astrological Sun) may be linked with integrity and heroism. Artemis is often portrayed as an upholder of purity and virtuous behaviour. When Actaeon the hunter spied her naked while bathing, she changed him into a stag, whereupon he was ripped apart by his own dogs. According to Homer, Artemis's mother, Leto, was insulted by Niobe who boasted that she had twelve children while Leto had only two. As punishment, Apollo killed Niobe's six sons and Artemis killed her six daughters. Here one can see the fiercely protective nature of the goddess.

Demeter, the Full Moon goddess of the harvest and of fertility, is representative of the fully mature woman. The Greek word *meter* means 'mother' and Demeter translates into something akin to 'earth mother'. The major story associated with Demeter concerns the time when her daughter Persephone was abducted by Hades. Not knowing what had happened to her daughter, Demeter was driven to despair and either forgot or was too grief-stricken to look after the Earth. All living things started to wither and die (a metaphor for wintertime) until she was reunited with Persephone in the spring. This story serves to illustrate the strength of maternal feeling; it is a force so powerful that it can override all else.

If Artemis is the maiden, and Demeter the mother, then the waning Moon Hecate is the goddess to associate with the older or post-menopausal woman. Often described as the crone or wise woman, she is usually depicted as having three heads (either three dog heads or one head each of a dog, bear and horse) and with these heads she is all-seeing and all-knowing. As the goddess of crossroads she can see in every direction. While the wise woman can offer advice when people are at a crossroads in their lives, old age is scary and thus Hecate was often viewed as a frightening creature and something of a witch. Hecate's wisdom and seemingly supernatural powers are illustrated by the fact that she was the only one who knew about Hades' abduction of Persephone. Indeed, she was made a goddess of the underworld as her reward for helping Demeter to find her daughter. In her role as underworld goddess, Hecate looked after the souls of the dead and ensured they reached the underworld safely. All three Greek lunar goddesses are concerned with transitional states; with Hecate the concern is with the latter years and with the end of life itself.

Mother and Baby

The Moon represents the mother and baby in us all. The Moon by sign, house and aspect will usually describe, and describe very graphically, certain aspects (but not all) of how we experienced our mother. This description fits the woman who gave birth to us, as well as other subsequent caretaking figures in our childhood, and especially those who taught us about women and mothering. Our experience and image of mothering are supremely important. Mother is not only the life-giver but potentially the one who can take life away. A provider of milk, comfort, unconditional love, containment and safety on the one hand, she is also the one who can withhold those things: the devourer, destroyer and baby-eater. She can carry the image of the suffocating mother as perhaps in the image of the witch, spider or octopus. Or she can be a siren or a sexual mother and one who has the capacity to castrate. There is also the image of the all-knowing, all-understanding, non-judging wise woman.

The physical and emotional nourishment provided by early caretakers can help produce secure and contented children and adults. Alternatively, when the process goes wrong, then individuals may feel empty, unfulfilled and insecure, with a range of emotional and even physical difficulties. As astrologers we know that the process is much more complicated than the simple 'childhood causes adulthood' type of equation, for the individual is born with a birth chart before they have a childhood. Nevertheless, the horoscope can provide a means for working through the ways that the past has imprinted the individual with behavioural patterns as adult.

The emphasis on the Moon alone in the chart as describing the mother is often exaggerated because the MC/IC axis and their rulers, plus planets in the Tenth and Fourth Houses, are all descriptive of early caretakers. Even planets – any planets – in Cancer can also provide information. The emphasis that should be placed on the baby/infant half of the partnership tends to be underplayed. The Moon symbolizes that part of us which is vulnerable, needy and dependent. That part of us which is still a needy infant inside.

Behaviour and Habits

Anyone who has been closely involved with a baby will know that babies are responsive beings from the word go. They respond to emotional expressions like a beaming smile within the first few weeks of life. Emotions such as joy, disgust, anger and sadness can be reacted to and expressed within the first three months. Presumably babies are born with these emotional abilities to help them survive by forming strong bonds with their caregivers. Whatever the exact mechanisms occurring in babyhood, the Moon describes the way in which the individual habitually reacts and responds throughout life. As an infant, the individual will have learned which signals would ensure that their needs were met. As an adult, the habits and, to some extent, body language continue. Almost any important activity going on in the horoscope can contribute to behavioural patterns but the Moon is especially concerned with that aspect of behaviour which is to do with *reaction*. Such reactions are not only very immediate, they are automatic and unconscious and are thus almost instinctive.

Needs, Safety and Protection

The Moon has much to say about what we need (as opposed to consciously want) in order to feel safe. To some extent, it is what we may cling to for security; what gives us a feeling of rootedness in the world. The Moon describes our whole attitude to the notion of being protected and of protecting others. How do we protect ourselves, how do we protect others? The Moon describes what we are likely to sense about given situations (for example, whether we think them dangerous) and what we say and do in those situations in order to keep ourselves or others safe.

We all have a tendency to fall back on our Moon whenever we are in situations that feel threatening in any way. Our Moon describes those things we tend to find comforting or at least familiar, so it is little wonder that at times of difficulty we tend to fall back on lunar behaviour. Some examples might help. A Moon in Cancer person might literally go back to mother, while someone with their Moon in Gemini might take a course or read a book. A person with the Moon aspecting their Mars may become touchy or fly off the handle when under stress, even if their behaviour is seemingly controlled the rest of the time. Alternatively, they might roll up their sleeves and get involved in a new project. A Moon-Jupiter person will want to lift themselves out of the situation, perhaps pretend it doesn't exist, and broaden their horizons, whereas Moon-Saturn will tend to draw themselves inwards, batten down the hatches and protect their resources.

Moods and Feelings

How any of us might behave is usually linked to how we are feeling, both about ourselves and about the world in general. If we feel positive, we will usually reflect back an optimistic and cheery mood. If we feel angry or depressed, then we will tend to reflect back those feelings, too. Basically, the Moon describes our moods. Some people exhibit a wide variety of mood states, while others appear temperamentally to be always much the same. Our Moon describes the everyday ebb and flow of our feelings – the moods we may get into and why. How we feel about ourselves and our general mood will influence the vibes we are sending out but, more than that, the kind of signals we give out will, in turn, affect how other people feel about us. In physical terms, the Moon has no light of its own and it reflects the light of the Sun. Similarly, in psychological terms, the Moon is largely about the mirroring and reflecting backwards and forwards that occurs between people. The Moon is the planet of feedback. Our capacity for nurturance is also a reflection of how we feel about ourselves and the world. If we feel good about ourselves we can take care of others, but if we feel dreadful we may not have sufficient resources to get much beyond our own needs.

Our Moon describes what we have an instinctual feeling for. An easy way of getting into interpreting Moon placements, and in particular aspects to our Moon, is to think in terms of the sentence 'sensitive to ...' So a Moon-Mars person may be especially sensitive to danger and discord, while a Moon-Uranus type may be especially sensitive to the plight of the outsider and perhaps personally sensitive to feeling rejected.

The Past and Attachment

Along with the IC and Fourth House, the Moon describes our background, roots and heritage: where we are coming from, in a number of different contexts. Whereas the Sun has a future orientation, the Moon is concerned with the past and memories of the past, whether these are conscious or not. The Moon describes patterns of behaviour which tend to drag us back. Our Moon may describe stories of attachment to people, places, things or ideas. Such feelings and memories may prevent us moving forward but they do provide feelings of safety, belonging and familiarity. In old age, when people sometimes feel that they have little to look forward to, there is often an urge to look back. Thus, lunar psychology tends to be active not only in early life but in old age, too.

The Moon and the Everyday

As people enter their twilight years they tend to become much more involved with small domestic matters. Affairs of state dwindle in importance in comparison to the state of one's garden or the lunchtime menu. This too is lunar, for the Moon is concerned with the daily round. It is about everyday life, unlike the Sun which symbolizes major life decisions. The Moon describes how we strive to maintain an inner sense of emotional and physical well-being, and it is everyday life that facilitates that, whatever our age.

The Principle of Actuation

Rather as the starting pistol going off heralds the beginning of a race, the Moon plays an important role in astrology in that the lunations (New and Full Moons and eclipses and, to a much lesser extent, Quarter Moons) make things happen. The astrologer uses various techniques to assess what is likely to be going on in a person's (or nation's) life at any given time. One such technique is to study the planets in the sky (transits) and see where those planets touch factors in the individual's natal chart. Lunations trigger the 'events in waiting' into actual happenings.

Home

The Moon is descriptive of how good we are at accommodating others and adjusting to a gamut of everyday life situations. It can also literally describe our home. However, the IC, aspects to the IC and the ruler of IC, as well as all planets in the Fourth House, are usually more pertinent in this respect. Nevertheless, the Moon is a significator of home, especially in an emotional and atmospheric sense. Home is a place where we feel safe, it is akin to our adult womb, a container, a place we retreat to, a place that might give us emotional or physical anchorage. Home is also a base from which to go out and do solar things. Thus, our Moon can describe:
* The environment and decor of our home.
* How we live (e.g. tidily, disorderly).
* Where we live (e.g. abroad, in a caravan, by the sea, in a converted church, by a railway, etc.).
* What we may be like to live with (how easily we can accommodate others).

The Feminine Principle

Along with Venus, but even more so, the Moon can be taken to represent women as a whole and, while for everyone it will say something about important caretaking figures, in a heterosexual man's chart it will almost always be descriptive of his female partners or of how he experiences women. The reader needs to bear in mind that projected energy tends to be more dramatic and graphic in its manifestation than when the individual lives it out for themselves. Thus, a woman with the Moon in Leo in her chart may not behave like an attention-seeking drama queen but the female *partner* of a man with the same placement is quite likely to do so.

The General Public and the Masses

The Moon represents the public as a whole and the feelings of the masses. TV personalities, successful politicians and the like often have a prominent Moon (e.g. conjunct the Ascendant or MC) because their skill lies in feeling the pulse of the audience and responding accordingly. In mundane astrology, the Moon is always taken to describe the people.

Food

The Moon is the only significator in the birth chart of food and eating habits, although certain signs (e.g. Taurus and Cancer) are especially food-driven. The Moon in the chart will literally describe:
- Food in a wider context. As we have seen, the Moon describes how we sustain others on a variety of levels, how we feel sustained, what *feeds* us, what *feedback* we need, and what kind of feedback we automatically tend to give to others. It also shows how we interpret feedback, plus the fact that the kind of feedback we elicit from others in turn influences our reaction to them.
- How and when we eat (e.g. quickly, slowly, regularly, huge meals, small meals, when angry) and why. For example, some people eat for comfort, while others find that anxiety ruins their appetite.
- What we eat (e.g. sweet, spicy, vegetarian, salty, meaty).
- Eating disorders (e.g. anorexia, bulimia) and their cause and treatment.

For example, someone with the Moon in Capricorn often likes crunchy food; in Gemini, perhaps a lot of variety on the plate; in Sagittarius, foreign food; in Scorpio, fish. With the Moon touching Mars, there may be a liking for spicy food and a tendency to eat quickly. The Moon in close contact with Venus usually denotes a sweet tooth and a mother who might placate her children by dishing out sweets.

The Body

The Moon governs the tides and, since we consist of 70% water, it is not surprising that the Moon is associated with all hormones and fluids in the body, including the lymphatic system, the menstrual cycle (a woman's own personal tides) and in all matters pertaining to pregnancy and childbirth. The Moon also has rulership over the stomach and breasts, although the zodiacal sign of Cancer is undoubtedly important here, too. The Moon describes how we digest experience and how we digest our food and has a role in most aspects of the digestive system. Alongside the zodiacal sign of Cancer, the Moon is also associated with memory.

Metals

The Moon can be associated with silver – both the colour and the metal. Silver is a rare, expensive and lustrous metal, though considerably less prized than gold. It is easy to work, being very malleable and therefore capable of being hammered thin or drawn into wire. In the same way that the Moon reflects the light of the Sun, silver is the most reflective metal and for this reason has been used since ancient times to make mirrors.

It has also been used for thousands of years to make jewellery and ornaments and, in the previous century, for various photographic processes. Aluminium is almost definitely another lunar metal. Interestingly, some researchers have linked Alzheimer's disease (dementia characterized by memory loss and a return to varying degrees of infancy) to aluminium absorption. The Moon can always be associated with the principle of absorption, as well as babyhood, receptivity and reflection. Aluminium can be used as an alternative to silver in making mirrors and in some photographic techniques. The usual lunar link with food and eating can also be made; food is often covered with aluminium foil and sometimes eaten with silver cutlery. Possibly stainless steel, another metal commonly used to make cutlery, can also be linked to the Moon.

Other Traditional Associations

• Receptacles that hold things: cups, cauldrons (a crescent container in which to brew lunar potions), chalices, containers, cradles, chests, coffins, shells, bowls and boats. Many of these items begin with the letter 'c' in the English language; itself a letter that looks like the crescent Moon and, when turned on its back, becomes a container. One is also reminded of the croissant.

• Mirrors, pearls and water itself are largely signified by the lunar principle, as are all things that reflect, although Neptune can also be the significator here. The menstrual cycle, the sea, the tides – things that fluctuate and, like the Moon, go through phases.

• There are many foods that have been considered lunar but the principal ones are milk, seeds, eggs and foods derived from such ingredients. Matters of domesticity, all activities related to childbirth (obstetrics) and fertilization, as well as catering, are lunar. Both types of nursery – horticultural and child-related – are also strongly linked to the lunar function.

• Animals that have been associated with the Moon are many and various. Certainly, animals that have been used to represent mother either in the nursery or in the sense of Mother Earth have a lunar link. Bears and whales are prime examples. Creatures have been ascribed to the lunar function for a host of reasons. Some are by virtue of being nocturnal or because they are especially fertile (e.g. rabbits), a source of food or simply because they are mammals and milk-producing. Crescent horned animals (e.g. cattle and deer) and those able to change their appearance (e.g. chameleon) have also been traditionally ascribed to the Moon. Cats are often associated with the Moon, not least because they can see in the dark.

The Moon Through The Signs

Moon in Aries - ☽♈

Behaviour

Typically, those with their Moon here respond quickly, strongly and spontaneously and may be in the habit of 'butting in'. Full of fervour, this can be the person who rushes to the defence of others; the one who jumps in to help with lightning speed. There may be an instinct for danger and a need to be at the scene of the accident, trauma or tragedy first. Basically, the person is competitive in matters of caring and territorial about people with whom they are emotionally involved. Not only territorial about loved ones but fiercely protective of them, too. Often, they just have to be the quickest and most involved 'mother' in a given situation. They can go for what they want with drive and passion, and basically want their needs met now. A major characteristic in most situations is of being early.

Skills

Leadership. Speed. The ability to act independently. Can be a powerful advocate for others. Excellent in emergencies.

Needs

This is the person with a strong need for action and to be doing something. Typically they want to be able to act without interference from others and without the imposition of any kind of restraint.

Nurtures Others by ...

Rushing to their defence. For example, the individual may 'argue the toss' for you when you are languishing in hospital and not getting your needs met. Or they may complain on your behalf when you've been given an inadequate meal in a restaurant and are just too timid to sort it out for yourself.

Under Stress

Impatience can be a major behavioural trait under stress. Sometimes there can be an impatience with those who refuse to get better or move on. A tendency to flare up (and cool down) quickly is common, as is the potential to take everything personally and get hurt easily. This person can be touchy. They may too hasty in responding to meet another's needs, often assuming (inappropriately) that the other person's needs are the same as their own – which they might be in emergencies (in which Moon in Aries people excel) but often won't be in more day-to-day situations where we are all different. The strong impulse to mother and to take action can sometimes lead to bossy and domineering behaviour. Often the individual just *has* to lead and certainly to do things in their own way. Co-operation can be difficult, although other chart factors (such as a prominent Venus or a Libran emphasis) can provide the capacity to co-operate.

Parenting

'Quick mothering' might be a key phrase here. This can manifest as having children when young and sometimes before they are really ready to do so. Often there would have been a strong or brave caretaking figure in the childhood. Perhaps this was a parent who was a pioneer for the place, time or circumstance in which they lived. Typically there will have been an experience of no-nonsense, let's-not-cry-over-spilt-milk mothering, with the individual and/or their caretaker believing that they just have to get on with things and roll up their sleeves. An image for the caretaking figure might be of a bird feeding its young in the nest: the bird has to arrive quickly, rapidly distribute food to the nestlings and get back out there to find more. There is no time to hang around. Also, of course, the nestlings compete for the parent bird's attention. Moon in Aries can sometimes indicate competition with the mother or conflict with her, but it can also describe a close relationship where mother is put first. Sometimes it is descriptive of a parent who is good with a needle and always knitting or sewing, a mother who is sharp in a number of different ways.

Home and Food

Typically there will be few frills and a corresponding dislike of fussy furnishings, chintz and sometimes even curtains. Functionality will usually be more important than comfort or looks. As in most things, the individual may go for what is expedient. In house, garden and office, classically there will be a preference for all things that are low-maintenance. Time-saving gadgets may also be favoured. There might be a liking for hot food and for spices, for food that is 'gingered up' a little. Fast food; when hungry, the need to eat *now*. Preparing meals yesterday (i.e. early) so they can be served quickly today. Eating quickly.

Moon in Taurus – ☽ ♉

Behaviour

Typically the type is steady, realistic and calm. They are slow to get upset and not easily ruffled. There can be a huge dislike of change, even when change may be what is required. The principal way of protecting the self is not to rush into things. The usual fluctuating behaviour, moods and feelings to be associated with everyone's Moon don't seem to apply here. The word 'immediacy' is simply not in the dictionary. I remember one student with both the Sun and Moon in Taurus who related how he *had* to walk to work along the exact same route every day. Apparently he had been the same when going to school! The perfect image of this type is of a cow steadily chewing her cud, unmoved by all that is happening around her unless action is really required. The need for material security is usually very marked and the type will often create or attract a reasonable degree of financial security if not actual wealth. Money, food and general comfort are of supreme importance.

Skills

This is a very tactile placement. Any or all of the five senses may be highly developed but skills involving touch and an appreciation of texture are nearly always strong. There can be an instinctive understanding both of their reliance on the material world and a feeling of interconnectedness with the Earth itself. There can be business acumen and skills with investments and most things to do with money, the land and property.

Needs

Material security and physical comfort have to be in place, and the individual *has* to know where their next meal is coming from in order to feel safe. There is often an unsentimental appreciation of nature, animals and the countryside, and an ability to be restored by gardening, working with matter and luxuriating in the body. Sex, massage, shopping for clothes, cooking and especially eating are the kind of activities in which this type revels.

Nurtures Others by ...

Being constant and stable, by hanging on in there. By being practical and not getting ruffled. Perhaps by providing food or massage, etc.

Under Stress

The type can be ponderous and laborious, unable to move or change. Materialism, conservatism and laziness to the point of downright inertia can also be marked. Many an inadequate relationship has survived because a Taurus Moon partner cannot bear either to rock the boat or to give up the nice house or comfortable lifestyle. The desire for a quiet life will lead some with this placement to avoid conversation if they think it might be in any way difficult; as always, the blessing and the curse of this placement can be the inability to move. Sometimes the Moon in Taurus person will simply not understand what the other person is talking about; they can feel secure merely from the physical presence of the other person and be blissfully ignorant of any restlessness or dissatisfaction that might be felt by them.

Parenting

The placement of the classic Earth Mother, a Moon in Taurus's experience of parenting may be of a mother who put practical considerations and the need to make her family feel secure over other issues; a caretaking figure who sought to provide stability and anchorage. One who perhaps wanted to keep things simple, didn't want to make waves and tried to avoid complicated emotional scenes. Sometimes such a parent may feel threatened by the more intellectual concerns of her children or by their need for adventure and exploration.

Home and Food

There is often a leaning towards the conventional and conservative, with a preference for soft colours and natural materials such as wood. There is often an appreciation of simple food. Some will like rich food but usually the person doesn't want it to have been fiddled about with too much. In all things this type has no sympathy with what it might see as fads. There may be a liking for starchy foods and especially potatoes. A slow metabolism with a solid build can be expected, but other chart factors have to agree.

Moon in Gemini - ☽ ♊

Behaviour

Fluctuating moods and feelings are to be expected from those with this restless, adaptable and versatile Moon placement. Always interested in what others think and feel, the type can be very impressionable. The impressions may not be deeply made but they are many and various, and those with this Moon feel all the different tugs made upon them. These are tugs made by others but also all the different pulls from within their own psyche. Bright, light and chirpy behaviour can be expected plus an ability to cope well with shifting goalposts. At home in libraries, bookshops and internet cafés, the typical Moon in Gemini will always be on the go, in their body as well as in their mind.

Skills

The ability to reflect and accommodate a variety of viewpoints will often be strongly developed and may make for a good writer or journalist. Frequently there is an instinctive feeling for language and languages, sometimes mimicry. Verbal dexterity may be matched digitally; these people will often be very good with their hands and strong on hand/eye co-ordination. There is often a marked capacity to do several things at once.

Needs

To be able to alight socially hither and thither as the mood takes them and as opportunity allows. They need conversation, whether the dialogue is with another person or in the pages of a book. Enough dialogue can enable the individual, after considering all the options, to know what is right for them. There is a need for emotional issues to be explained. A dislike of heavy emotional situations often goes with the territory. Although inevitably it will be those who can provide some anchorage who will be attracted to this child of the universe, Moon in Gemini souls respond best to those who keep them interested and keep them guessing. Some with this placement will feel more than usually nourished by light reading, and many will be restored by frequent changes of scene and a variety of activities. They may thrive on trivia, novelty and frivolity as well as more intellectual pursuits.

Nurtures Others by ...

Lightening things up, by being interested, listening and communicating. By being flexible and adaptable and by fitting in with the needs of others.

Under Stress

A scattered, all-over-the place quality can apply to this Moon. Restless, irresolute and unreliable behaviour and difficulties with commitment can result. Decisions made often have to be changed as outside influences and competing aspects of their own psyche jostle for supremacy. There can be a tendency to rationalize feelings as a way of protecting themselves. Sometimes there can be a tendency to avoid real life by over-analysing situations to the point where they aren't actually experienced in reality, only in their head.

Parenting

In childhood the individual will often have received mixed messages and perhaps have absorbed the notion that they must try to please everyone, however contorting that might feel. Often the early message picked up is that they need to accommodate others in order to feel safe and secure. Often the Moon in Gemini person is the family member who is 'elected' to be flexible and fit in. This placement can describe mothering from different sources (e.g. where there are literally two mothers), sometimes an important relationship with an aunt (such as the mother's sister) and sometimes that the mother figure needs someone (her children) to talk to. Not uncommonly, the mother found it difficult to arrive at settled views of her own and instead reflected the views voiced by stronger members of the family. Sometimes this placement is descriptive of a mothering figure who is forever catering for people who all eat something different and maybe come in to eat at different times. Sometimes it describes a chatty, gossipy, caretaking figure. Frequently a childhood is described where news is a major feature, whether this involves newspapers lying around, the radio always being on, the TV being watched or simply neighbours dropping in for a chat. Twins often feature in the family pattern.

Home and Food

A home full of books, magazines and correspondence can be expected with this placement. Depending on the chart overall (and especially the IC and Fourth House), there may be many visitors and a great deal of comings and goings generally. The Moon in Gemini also often indicates having several homes. There can be a curious willingness to try different foods and a yen for experimenting with menus. The ideal meal might consist of a little bit of this and a little bit of that. Snacking (e.g. frequent light meals) and TV dinners may appeal. Reading newspapers and magazines or doing crosswords or jigsaw puzzles while eating is typical of this Moon.

Moon in Cancer – ☽ ♋

Behaviour
The Moon in its own sign will often be descriptive of an individual who is in touch with the Inner Infant: that part of themselves and others which is needy, dependent and vulnerable. There is usually a well-developed capacity to nurture, mother, care for and to generally protect. The need to be at the receiving end of such nurturance and protection is also likely to be very strong.

Skills
At best, here is someone so attuned to how another is feeling that they instinctively know what to do to improve that person's comfort and well-being. The 'other' doesn't have to be human – the vulnerability of a puppy or a kitten will normally also be felt to a greater than usual degree. This Moon can also be associated with a strong imagination which can be useful in artistic and literacy pursuits. A feeling for the past can give rise to particular talents with history and all matters surrounding the nation's heritage. Skills in cooking are common.

Needs
Usually there is a strong need to be mothered and a need for someone or something to care for and protect. To feel emotionally safe, and also safe in their home environment, is usually felt to be essential, as is a feeling of belonging, thus the nesting instinct can be strong.

Nurtures Others by ...
Classic nurturing behaviour, such as attending to others' needs, cooking and home-making. This Moon may nurture others by letting *them* mother; by being a big baby themselves.

Under Stress
There can be timidity and a tendency to hide. The inclination to cling to the familiar, perhaps even running home for safety, can get in the way of moving forward. Those with this placement need to cultivate their instinctive feeling for the past without getting stuck in it. Going back can also imply going back over old wounds and this, coupled with an attentive memory, can make the type prone to brooding. A mood might be traced back to some distant hurt that everyone else has long since forgotten. Touchy, crabby and moody behaviour can go with the territory. Under stress, the Moon in Cancer person may choose not to communicate what is going on but instead to retreat into a mood. Sometimes this placement can contribute to fusspot or 'clucking hen' behaviour and may also contribute to a big baby sub-personality. Some with this placement will stifle independence in others and prevent them going forward. Most will have experienced some degree of this kind of behaviour from their own caretakers.

Parenting

As has been noted, a very symbiotic mother/child tie is common. This does not necessarily mean that the relationship would have been good or happy – the whole chart has to be studied for that kind of information. The placement merely suggests that the relationship would have been more than usually powerful. Often there will have been a very yielding quality to the principal caretaking figure. Not uncommonly the mother may have preferred her children as babies or infants, and thus it is not surprising if some with this placement have learned to keep the infant side of themselves very well developed. The mother's relationship with her own mother may be of interest; indeed, all the womenfolk in the family might be worthy of particular study. Not infrequently, the mother or principal caretaking figure may have been a carer or professional mother (e.g. she may have fostered children or run a nursery). It is hard to get away from the image of a perfect 'mumsy' kind of mother (e.g. always there, warm and understanding) with this placement, but a home life with an emphasis on guilt and emotional blackmail is also often likely, all the more so if Pluto is part of the lunar equation.

Home and Food

The lunar Cancerian home may be a place of retreat and sanctuary or a home to all sorts of waifs and strays (human and otherwise). Many with this placement will live by the water. Living in the house of their parents is a common manifestation. Food is usually seen as very important and as a great source of comfort. Dairy foods are often particularly enjoyed.

Moon in Leo – ☽ ♌

Behaviour

Typically, the Moon in Leo person has a tendency to dramatize their feelings. Usually no stranger to attention and appreciation, those with this placement often also have a strong need for acknowledgement and recognition. This need often translates into a person who responds well to praise. At best, these types respond with warmth, generosity and magnanimity. Moon in Leo people, especially women, often end up in positions of power, perhaps as the head of an organization. Men may hook up with someone in that role even if it does not apply to them themselves. Leader or not, there is often a feeling of nobility about those with this placement. The individuals have a sense of their own importance and won't easily do things they consider to be beneath them.

Skills

This lunar placement is often found in the charts of therapists and others whose job involves the illumination of others in various contexts: perhaps to shine light on another's behaviour or possibly to act in the role of some kind of promoter. The typical Moon in Leo person likes dramatic displays of emotion. There is a liking too for vibrant colours and heroic storylines. Not surprisingly, therefore, the entertainment industry abounds with this Moon placement. Many will like the opera and most will feel at home in the theatre, even if in a spectator role.

Needs

There is a strong need to be best at something. Perhaps to have the best home, to be the most loved child or to have the brightest children. There can be a need for recognition and attention. If circumstances and finances permit, this is a person who enjoys going out and having fun.

Nurtures Others by ...

Giving them lots of attention, by inspiring others and giving them confidence.

Under Stress

The vulnerability of less evolved souls may stem from their mistaken belief in their own publicity or their susceptibility to flattery. One-upmanship and undue competitiveness can also create problems. A more difficulty placed Moon can give rise to drama-queen tendencies, pretentiousness and exhibitionism, although this is less likely when found in an otherwise more self-effacing horoscope. Needing to be centre-stage themselves can prohibit others from receiving their due share of recognition. More dominant personalities may tend to take over their environment.

Parenting

This placement implies either giving and/or receiving parenting that gives the child confidence and permission to shine. People with this placement want their parenting figures to feel proud of them and equally want to feel proud of their own children. The mothering figure at best would have been a warm, strong and creative person, perhaps something of a lioness who gently cuffs her cubs if they misbehave and who wards off danger with a ferocious spirit. Often the mother figure wanted a lot of attention herself (she may have been something of a drama queen, even) and so the Moon in Leo type may have got into the habit of giving attention to others. Sometimes the mother gave lots of attention and the Moon in Leo person continues to expect it. Occasionally there is mothering where the mother wants to show her children off and maybe put them on the stage. The Moon in Leo may play this parenting role themselves or have been at the receiving end of it. As always, aspects to the Moon and the chart overall need to be carefully weighed.

Home and Food

Typically, those with this placement like to have a home they can feel proud of. Some will be impressed by a luxurious and pampered lifestyle. Often there is a flair for interior decoration. The placement may be descriptive of a home with colour, vibrancy and a feeling of creativity about it. Typically, the Moon in Leo likes to be monarch of all they survey and are best suited to wearing the trousers in the home. I have not noticed any special food preferences with this Moon placement.

Moon in Virgo – ☽ ♍

Behaviour

This is not the warmest of Moon placements, nor descriptive of a person given to spontaneous displays of strong emotion or affection (unless other chart factors provide this), but Moon in Virgo types can be very attentive to another's needs and accurate in meeting them. Strong on humility and gentleness, above all this is a helpful, kindly Moon and also one packed with common sense. While instinctively wanting to serve, many feel less comfortable in the role of boss. This can be because of an innate tendency to worry. Easily stressed and nervous, those with this Moon can easily get into the habit of feeling unequal to the task, whatever that task may be.

Skills

There are often skills with precision and detail plus an ability to discriminate and prioritize. The Virgo Moon can be good at organization.

Needs

To be useful. Even if they think they are sick of their job, typically those with this placement feel most comfortable if they are working, or at least being of service in some way. These people are usually industrious and in any event usually derive comfort from keeping busy. Typically, this is the type who cannot *just* watch TV. There is a need to be able to independently get on with the matter in hand. A need for tranquillity is also often marked.

Nurtures Others by ...

Taking care of them and by doing something practical. No task is beneath them and no detail too small to attend to.

Under Stress

If the Moon is receiving difficult aspects then this placement may be prone to fault-finding, carping and nagging. The individual may also don the hairshirt of the martyr, always attending to what others don't want to do. Often the individual will tend to be over-critical in relationships and certainly prone to over-analysing emotional situations. Self-critical and self-questioning, this type may never feel truly satisfied by what they do and will tend to hear criticism from others even when it is not there. Frequently there is dissatisfaction with their life but no confidence to take the steps to improve it. Underestimating their abilities and generally doing themselves down are other common manifestations. Some with the Virgo Moon need to learn to face challenges rather than always setting goals which they know they can easily meet.

Parenting

Often there will have been some kind of illness in the family or early environment. The mother may have been ill herself or may have run around nursing other family members. Many with this placement will have experienced parenting figures as being quite prudish, overly concerned with perfectionism and what the neighbours might say. One woman with this placement reported how, when she was twelve, she came home and told her mother she had been abused in the park. Her mother's first reaction was to get the child into the bath and scrub her clean! An overly critical parent is common and many with this placement will also be critical of their mother or other caretaking figure. The criticism can work both ways.

Home and Food

For women especially, this is often the placement of the person who lives independently. Being rather picky in emotional matters and liking to live in the way they want, many will choose to live on their own. Some will seek a perfect home life and thus will inevitably feel dissatisfied because life just isn't like that. Many will be unhappy or critical about the actual building in which they live. Ideally, this will act as a spur towards achieving an improved home environment but many with this placement are too anxious to make decisions about where to live. There can be a tendency to hold off for too long for something more ideal. If the chart is a mutable one overall, those with this Moon can be prone to missing out through dithering. One might expect Moon in Virgo types to be picky about food, such as being diet-conscious, non-smoking vegetarians who consume large volumes of vitamins. This is rarely true unless Virgo is also on the Sixth House cusp or strongly represented elsewhere in the chart.

Neither are Moon in Virgo homes always immaculate: most with this placement prioritize other areas of life above housekeeping. For others, a clean and tidy home is essential.

Moon in Libra – ☽ ♎

Behaviour
Disliking all that is crass or crude, this placement suggests grace, social polish, charm and refinement. The dislike of any kind of discord or disharmony, whether in the home or in relationships, is usually very marked. Some with this placement will do anything to avoid making a fuss or engaging in any form of confrontation. Usually there will be a tendency to cover up social embarrassments.

Skills
Diplomacy and persuasion. This is a good placement for anyone in a go-between or bridge-building occupation. They might be a lawyer, wholesaler or agent; an individual whose role lies between the customer and producer or between warring factions. There is a capacity to bring people together and thus a habitual tendency to match-make.

Needs
For many, the need for relationship is very marked. This individual simply does not feel comfortable on their own, sometimes even if merely embarking on a trip to the shops. Their dependency stems from the need for companionship and mirroring from another person. The mirroring will work both ways, of course; the individual will tend to reflect the behaviour and needs of whoever they are with.

Nurtures Others by ...
Instinctively knowing the right thing to say and by being able to look at things from your angle. Basically, they will agree with you or at least express disagreement so gently that you are persuaded to change your own point of view.

Under Stress
The vulnerability of this person stems from their need for social approval. As with other placements in Libra, there can be indecision, often about which course of action will please others more. While those with this placement are in the habit of playing peacemaker, curiously they can arouse anger in others. This will often be caused, at least partially, by their inability to be straight and authentic in their dealings. The striving to please everyone can result in their not fully pleasing anyone. Typically, Moon in Libra types can be relied upon to behave appropriately but not necessarily sincerely or authentically. Some with this placement will be downright flattering and ingratiating. At worst, the abhorrence of unpleasant scenes and the need to keep everything nice can mean that the Moon in Libra individual is incapable of dealing with the deepest emotions and feelings, both their own and those of others.

Parenting
At least one caretaking figure will usually be experienced as being yielding and accommodating. At best, they will inculcate in the Moon Libra child the virtues of being kind, helpful, obliging and generally considerate of others. More negatively, the principal caretaker may simply be seen as making the most strenuous efforts to avoid any form of confrontation. Sometimes a high personal (and sometimes family) cost can result from this insistence on keeping the peace. There can be the kind of home life where a not-in-front-of-the-children strategy is employed. The mother figure may not

be very warm, passionate or demonstrative (unless other chart factors provide these qualities) but will exhibit grace and the qualities of being a lady. Rarely one to make waves, she can even be the sort who might be able to overlook her partner's infidelities. Very occasionally she is experienced by her child as being more of a wife than a mother, and of putting both her own relationship needs, and the needs of her partner, well above those of the children.

Home and Food

A harmonious and possibly beautiful home is positively required for those with this arty Moon. Classic styles (at home, in clothes and in the arts) are usually favoured. This also tends to be tidy placement for, as in most areas of life, this person needs order. There is some tendency towards a sweet tooth and those with this placement may be in the habit of standing on the scales; they are frequently over-concerned with their weight.

Moon in Scorpio – ☽ ♏

Behaviour

All else being equal, this person needs to be deeply involved emotionally in whatever they are doing and whoever they are with. The type responds to life with passion and intensity. There will usually be deep feelings about the activities associated with whichever house of the horoscope is occupied by the Moon. Many will be patriotic and possessive of their home, land and country. This placement can be descriptive of the person who either leaves you in no doubt whatsoever about what they are feeling or who feels it safest to hide what's really going on. Both modes of behaviour are possible in different circumstances. When the individual feels safe, or if they have a more extrovert, trusting personality, then the full flood of their intensity, emotionality and passion may be on view. This is the full-on Moon in Scorpio type and also sometimes descriptive of how the introvert may behave when in private and feeling safe. Frequently, though, there is a secretive, proud, intense quality which accompanies a feeling of vulnerability with this placement. Often this individual feels most comfortable when being enigmatic, secrecy being a way of protecting themselves or others. Typically, the type will protect you by keeping your confidences and will expect the same kind of discretion in return. There is often a proud emotional nature here, tinged sometimes with revenge; this can be the individual who wouldn't give you the satisfaction of telling you what is going on. Trust rarely comes easily.

Skills

This is an emotionally sophisticated placement and will often be found in street-wise people who don't flinch from life and who understand the emotional realm. Their emotional strength and perceptive skills can give rise to an ability to bring others through crisis.

Needs

There is usually a strong need for intimate relationship and often for sexual contact. This is the person who wants to be passionately involved with something or someone, but to feel safely involved. The Moon in Scorpio type can be very sensitive to what they consider as acts of betrayal on the part of others. Thus, there can be a strong need for loyalty and privacy.

Nurtures Others by ...

Being close and by encouraging confidences. Not opening up to everyone can be very seductive if you are the person with whom those rare openings occur. A feeling of confederacy can be what precipitates a feeling of closeness for some.

Under Stress

Letting go of difficult feelings can be hard. Some can be overly possessive, jealous and vengeful if they don't feel that their needs are being met. Some thrive on emotional drama to the extent of being crisis-junkies. Such individuals can create storms in seas which were previously calm. Depending on other chart factors, these people tend to love and hate totally. They may take everything too personally and lack objectivity unless this is provided by other chart factors. Shrewd and manipulative, the type can be overly suspicious and self-protective. The cultivation of trust will solve most problems.

Parenting

There is often a history of some early traumas (perhaps deaths) in the family in the early life. Sometimes the mother figure may have been undergoing some kind of crisis when the individual was born or was very young. Frequently the caretaking figure is experienced as being very strong and, depending on the condition of the Moon overall, may have been experienced as domineering or even scary. She will rarely be known for her milk-and-water temperament. A sophisticated understanding of the concept of emotional blackmail will have been learned around the family hearth. Not infrequently there will be jealousy issues surrounding the mother figure; she may be the cause of these in others or may exhibit these characteristics herself. As with those with a Scorpio Ascendant, whatever is going on will have been absorbed by those with this Moon. Sensitive and suspicious, little will have been missed.

Home and Food

Some privacy in the home is usually required and, despite the need for intimacy, many with this placement like to live alone for at least part of the time. They may like to be possessive of their little bit of space. Also, home can be the place where they want to hide. Many like seafood such as prawns, and some like raw food. Therefore an appreciation of Japanese cuisine is not uncommon.

Moon in Sagittarius – ☽ ♐

Behaviour

Warm, buoyant but fairly casual behaviour is to be expected. The type is open and candid, often with a sense of humour and a Tigger-like quality. Tact is not usually a strong point and there can be a generalized clumsiness, both physically and in relating to others. The instinctive feeling of this Moon is that there is more to heaven and earth than the rational intellect might lead one to believe. Innately there is faith in life and in the notion that everything that happens has a meaning and purpose.

Skills

There is an ability to see the larger picture and an ability to imbue others with faith. The inclination to teach and give advice is often well developed; indeed, teaching and preaching may be the habitual attitude.

Needs

Inevitably, there will be a strong need for space and freedom, and a need to explore on both physical and emotional levels. These individuals need the space to be able to search and quest after the big questions in life and to be able to roam as far afield as possible both mentally and emotionally, even if not physically. Those with this easy-come, easy-go Moon will often seek to protect themselves by keeping as free from responsibilities as possible.

Nurtures Others by ...

Encouraging them to be more adventurous and by imbuing them with their own buoyant, philosophical stance. They also encourage others to take their own broad view of a situation. They like to nurture others by taking them on some sort of caper or helping them to spread their wings.

Under Stress

Sometimes this type lays themselves open to charges from more pragmatic types of naïveté, and of looking at the world through rose-coloured glasses. There is often a tendency to believe the best and to overlook the obvious flaws in a given plan, coupled with a habit of overestimating themselves and others. Recklessness, carelessness and a too laissez-faire attitude can be part of the picture. Those with this restless Moon will often have a tendency to believe that the grass is greener elsewhere; this can sometimes lead to a habitual 'moving on' lifestyle. For some there can be difficulty in keeping emotional issues in proportion and some will be prone to living on an emotional roller-coaster, especially if this is borne out by other chart factors. This placement can sometimes be reminiscent of a large, floppy dog in its mannerisms. There can be exaggerated gestures, exaggerated feelings; hysteria even, in the roller-coaster types. Others may exhibit judgemental, moralistic tendencies if other chart factors concur.

Parenting

Often a caretaking figure will have had a tendency to over-react emotionally, and the individual with this placement may do so, too. Usually someone in the family has strong difficulties in keeping things in proportion. Some parents may have been religious or have held strong views on morality or politics. A snobbish, social-climbing aspect to the childhood is also not uncommon. Sometimes there is a parent prone to squandering the family resources; if not actually a gambler then they are overly laid-back with money.

Home and Food

Many with this placement will live abroad for part of their life. Certainly the type feels very comfortable with foreigners and with new people and new situations, as these represent another opportunity to learn and explore. The Moon in Sagittarius person may live in or near a religious building; for example, in a house across the road from a monastery or church, or in a flat in a converted church. Some might live in an educational setting. Most will have a liking for the wide open spaces. There may be a liking for food that is foreign to the culture in which they were raised. Some will get into dietary regimes which are linked with philosophical or religious beliefs. Unless other chart factors indicate a homebody, few with Moon in Sagittarius will be particularly domesticated or tied to a particular hearth, for there is something of the gypsy and nomad in the soul here. In all things, Moon in Sagittarius types don't like to be confined.

Moon in Capricorn – ☽ ♑

Behaviour

The behaviour of those with this unsentimental Moon tends be 'correct', sometimes somewhat austere and given to high standards of conduct. There is a strong need to be respected and taken seriously, and individuals with this placement will seldom behave in a way that might threaten to destroy that respect. For some it is important to be a pillar of society. There is usually some caution and shyness about expressing their feelings, especially on the part of men towards women. There is often a need to be in charge of their feelings, so some degree of emotional self-control is to be expected. Classically, the type behaves in a self-effacing, non-flashy way. The type feels most comfortable when they are in charge but will tend to be realistic about their own talents and may therefore be less pushy than other, equally ambitious, types.

Skills

There is usually an instinctive feeling for organization and structure. These people can put just about anything into some kind of order. Practicality and an ability to master many different materials can feature. Innately this is a carpenter, shipwright, dentist, sculptor and architect. A feeling for the land and tradition can give rise to many rural skills. This placement can also be associated with professions that involve mothering, homemaking and caretaking skills.

Needs

There is a need to achieve, to feel that they are producing something tangible, that they are building something up, contributing to society, in however humble a way. There is a need to be doing something that can be measured and quantified. The type is usually very sensitive to all aspects of the ageing process and typically has a strong need to feel materially secure in old age.

Nurtures Others by ...

Taking responsibility. This can include emotional responsibility where the individual absorbs all the responsibility for something going wrong, even when it wasn't remotely their fault. The Moon in Capricorn person can be quite hard on themselves. Classically, the type nurtures others by rolling up their sleeves and getting on with things, by getting everything organized and in order. Those with the Moon here may nurture you by introducing a degree of realism into situations.

Under Stress

They can be overly dour, pessimistic and negative in attitude. Everything in the day-to-day life can take on an inappropriate weightiness. The type can be in the habit of thinking that life has to be burdensome. Materialism and meanness can also be part of the picture. Undue shyness and caution in emotional matters can cause isolation, as can a life overly dedicated to work. Some may be strict when a more yielding approach is required. Many will have a problem with what they see as childish behaviour in others.

Parenting

Many will have received early caretaking which emphasized achievement in some way. There is frequently some feeling of lack or austerity in childhood. Sometimes this placement simply describes an early life where everyone is working very hard and there isn't a great deal of money. Sometimes the mother will have taken on the role of the father, possibly having had to support the family financially. Often she will have been a professional woman. Indeed, as with Venus in Capricorn, men with this placement are often attracted to women in professional jobs. The Moon in Capricorn conjures up the feeling of a caretaker who was dutiful and responsible but perhaps a little bit rigid. A parent who was afraid of getting it wrong, and therefore carries out the child-rearing following certain rules. Playing it by the book in this way might mean the setting of clearly-defined boundaries of behaviour, such as always sitting down to meals on time. Some kind of clock-watching in the family is often a feature. Being raised in an institutional setting is within the symbolism of this placement but has to be borne out by other chart factors, too. The experience of having parents older than the norm is also a frequent manifestation.

Home and Food

As always, the IC and IC ruler are more pertinent significators for their home, but two classic images emerge from this placement. One is of a spartan existence in a rural setting complete with dry-stone walls. Another image is of somewhere more up-market and classy but nevertheless understated. As with planets in Capricorn generally, there is nothing flashy about this lunar placement. Usually there is a liking for natural materials such as stone. In culinary matters, the individual sometimes likes food with a bit of crunch. The tendency will be to under-eat rather than over-eat, as self-indulgence isn't usually part of the picture unless it is provided by other chart factors.

Moon in Aquarius – ☽ ♒

Behaviour

This is usually a friendly and sociable Moon, despite being somewhat emotionally detached. Cool and rational, this is also a very independent and emotionally self-sufficient placement. Although there is frequently great curiosity about people, there is no need to talk about feelings and often there is a general distrust of them anyway. Often the individual would have been raised to be independent and emotionally self-sufficient. There is a need for an almost scientific approach to life; to search for the truth and to arrive at rational decisions. Often there is an instinctive awareness of the larger picture and a disinclination therefore to get stuck in their own petty emotional problems. At best, the type sympathizes with the needs of all of humanity and has a strong belief in community, reform and in bettering the lives of people everywhere. Perhaps because of their common touch, well-known lunar Aquarians sometimes enjoy great popularity with the general public (e.g. Princess Diana, Marilyn Monroe and George Best). In relationships, the type tends to feel most comfortable with friendship. Men with this placement seem to have a strong need for female companionship. Some are able to establish strong platonic links with women. A good example of a man with the Moon in Aquarius is John Lennon. Some of the sentiments expressed in his songs reflect his lunar placement while his wife Yoko Ono is the living embodiment of it. Curiously, many European men with this Moon are attracted to American women or American culture. It might be noted that the USA has its Moon in Aquarius.

Skills

Sympathy may be extended to the plight of the many. This is potentially a humanitarian, progressive and altruistic Moon. There can also be resourcefulness in finding solutions to problems. Often there is inventiveness and a knack for repairing and designing gadgets. Sometimes a marked, seemingly instinctive, understanding of machines, computers and technology can feature.

Needs

Many a lunar Aquarian will feel nourished by nature and the wilderness. Subjects such as astrology will often sustain them because these people need concepts and ideas. Seeing a pattern at work in the universe will often be especially comforting. There is a strong need for space and freedom, especially in domestic and emotional matters.

Nurtures Others by ...

Being very understanding and interested in you in a detached and impersonal way. They will listen carefully and impartially, and rarely be shocked. This can be a non-judgemental Moon. Some will cultivate others' independence and encourage freedom of thought and action. The Moon in Aquarius type may care for you by telling you the truth as they see it.

Under Stress

Some with this placement may feel more comfortable with machines and gadgets than with people. At worst, the type can be detached, aloof, out of touch with their feelings and emotionally self-contained, to the point of downright coldness. Warmth and the capacity to get more intimately involved with others will, of course, usually be found in other parts of the horoscope. Nevertheless, the shunning of emotional ties can border on the autistic in extreme cases. Opinionated, know-it-all behaviour can also feature.

Parenting

The Moon here may denote a parental figure involved in community affairs, perhaps in some kind of reform. A mother who worked in social housing would be one example. It will also often describe a caretaking figure who was devoted to her friends. A frequent manifestation is that of having an independent, and therefore often a single, mother. It is also a classic placement for those brought up in a kibbutz or in other situations where parenting is given by a larger group. Independence will have been fostered in such situations but sometimes there would have been a lack of emotional feedback. The mothering figure may have been more of a friend to her children, treating them as equals, rather than a traditional mothering type. Few with this placement fully believe that blood is thicker than water. They may well have friendly relationships with their family but the family members may each operate independently, not really as a unit.

Home and Food

Often there is a liking for plenty of light; big windows are ideal, as are top floors in high-rise buildings. The lunar Aquarian may prefer living on their own, but certainly they are likely to believe in everyone living by their own standards and generally doing their own thing. Computers and the latest audio equipment may feature strongly in the homes of those who can afford such things. The home may also be strewn with the individual's own inventions and gadgets. There is often a mix of the old and the new.

Moon in Pisces – ☽ ♓

Behaviour

Any planet in Pisces is particularly prone to being contaminated by other planets plugging into it, so there are endless possibilities for the way in which this particular Moon might manifest. Certainly this is an impressionable Moon but the impressions received may not always reflect the true reality of the situation. It will rarely be conscious, but some with this placement distort things so they appear to be how they would like them to be. Perhaps the distortion is to see oneself or others through rose-tinted spectacles. Part of the reason for the distortion is also that this Moon is exceptionally imaginative. Those with this placement often have a need to believe in magic and miracles, and to believe that anything is possible. Basically, there is a need for the spiritual and the romantic. The type feels nurtured by situations where they can feel emotionally lifted or by situations where there is at least a faint possibility that they might be whisked away. Part of the reason for their strong need for escape can be an acute sensitivity to all the suffering in the world and a marked preference for avoiding that suffering. In practice they rarely do so, for life is simply not like that and often they are too sensitive. The type will often be in the habit of making sacrifices for others and of feeling sorry for people. They feel vulnerable themselves and can sniff out the vulnerability of others. Becoming involved with others' problems can often be a way of avoiding their own dilemmas. Some with the Moon here have a need for others to be in need of rescuing. Moon in Pisces people will often be in the habit of collecting society's waifs and strays. This can be the placement of the lost-soul junkie. Equally it can describe the person who is in the habit of feeling sorry for themselves and is always on the look-out for potential rescuers. As always, the whole chart has to be studied. Often the Moon in Pisces manifests as someone who feels much more comfortable if they can simply relax and let go. Those with this placement rarely feel comfortable when they are confined in any way.

Skills

This can be a super-sensitive placement conferring compassion, empathy and intuitive understanding. The sensitivity can be so marked that it is not uncommon to find psychic abilities. Typically, there is a tremendous capacity for mirroring and reflecting the feelings of others. Some with this placement will make good counsellors and carers, and others will be adept at acting. The type will often be able to mix with people from all backgrounds and are often unusually at home with those on the periphery of society. Many feel quite comfortable with people who have mental disturbances or criminal leanings. There will often be strong artistic skills, with the fine arts, dance, drama and music providing the most likely arenas.

Needs

Some lunar Pisceans may need sympathy and a shoulder to cry on. Alternatively, they may have a need to take on the role of saviour themselves and so are in need of willing victims. Some degree of wonderment, romance and magic in the life can work wonders for their emotional well-being. Some will like to merge with others and with their environment; others feel safest if they can retreat and withdraw. The type tends to protect themselves by swimming in and out of situations and by remaining uncommitted wherever possible. Typically, the individual will be nourished by the arts and spiritual pursuits.

Under Stress

The impressionability of the type can lead to difficulties with focusing and they can be vacillating, vague, disorientated and diffident. Escapist behaviour and sometimes a tendency to seek comfort in alcohol or drugs is common, as are situations of co-dependency, where the individual is sober themselves but their loved one isn't. Indolence, irresolution and a tendency to be too easily led can also feature: the Moon in Pisces person can be very gullible. An avoidance of anything rough, crass, difficult and uncomfortable can make for laziness and dishonesty but only if borne out by other factors. Integrity and strength ideally will be suggested from other parts of the chart. The setting of boundaries and keeping to them can be difficult unless Saturn is also strong.

Parenting

The mother or other caretaking figure in early life will sometimes have been viewed by the individual as something of a victim, hence their own habit of rescuing. They are actually saving their mother. Sometimes the caretaking figure was one who habitually made sacrifices, and the individual has either learned to do that too or has learned to avoid getting themselves into that kind of situation. Typically, the boundaries between mother and child are weak, and emotional boundaries are something that this person may need to develop. Separation can be difficult with this placement.

Home and Food

There is a strong need for the home to be a place of sanctuary and retreat. Many will prefer a home by the water. Some degree of chaos may be tolerated in exchange for a comfortable artistic or bohemian atmosphere. Music will usually feature strongly in the life. I have not noticed any special food preferences but in culinary matters, as elsewhere, the type may be very open to experience.

The Void-of-Course Moon

The Moon is known as 'void-of-course' when it is not going to make a major aspect (the Ptolemaic aspects – the conjunction, opposition, square, trine and sextile) to any planet *before* it leaves the zodiac sign it is occupying. Thus, in terms of aspects, the astrologer is only interested in those that are applying to the Moon, because separating aspects have already happened. Some astrologers go further than the Ptolemaic aspects to include the quincunx and parallel, which appreciably cuts down the amount of time that the Moon is actually void. Leaving this controversy aside, as the Moon changes sign every two-and-a-half days it follows that it will be void for a variable period once every two-and-a-half days. In a horary chart, the void-of-course Moon makes a very strong statement; no matter what the question, the answer is always: *nothing will come of the matter*, but it is a moot point as to the extent to which one should consider the void Moon on a day-to-day level and whether it is worthy of consideration at all in natal charts.

On the day-to-day transiting level, the void Moon is usually associated with false starts and errors. Purchases made at the time of a void Moon are supposed to be little used or not quite right. Similarly, enterprises formed or events that start while the Moon is void may prove costly or go wrong in some way. A famous example of this is the Grand National horse race for 1993 which, following various incidents at the outset, was eventually literally declared void. Some astrologers go further and avoid making decisions or appointments when the Moon is void, believing that any decisions made will be unrealistic and any appointments that are arranged will go awry. The general consensus is that the time of a void Moon is best suited for spiritual and non-material activities, that it is a good time for activities such as meditation, play or sleep; a time for 'being' rather than 'doing'.

I have no doubt that one should avoid having a void-of-course Moon for the start of any major enterprise. Therefore, in electing a chart for an event almost every astrologer would steer clear of having a void Moon. However, I am not convinced that on a day-to-day level one should worry about it too much. I have found that nothing goes wrong with appointment after appointment made during the void Moon unless there are also other factors that predispose to upset plans (e.g. transiting Saturn opposing your Mercury). Undoubtedly, sometimes things do indeed go pear-shaped when the Moon is void but, of course, many more things also go wrong when the Moon is not void! Another point to consider is that, while they may occasionally prove costly in terms of time or money, sometimes upset plans should perhaps be welcomed for the challenges and opportunities they present. Be that as it may, in the natal chart a void-of-course Moon is thought by some traditional astrologers to prevent an individual from having children. Personally, I have not seen any evidence for this but perhaps more research is required. Even if there turns out to be some truth in this idea, it will certainly only be the case if other chart factors also strongly point the same way.

One example of a famous person with a void-of-course Moon was the late Robert 'Bobby' Kennedy,[1] also known as RFK. Robert was the seventh of nine children and the younger brother of President John F. Kennedy (JFK). When he was elected President, JFK made Robert Attorney General and he became his right-hand man. It took years for Robert to get over the grief caused by John's assassination and arguably he lived in his brother's shadow for a number of years. However, in 1964 he became Senator for New York and on 5 June 1968 he was assassinated during his campaign for the Democratic Presidential nomination. He was a strong Presidential hopeful who fought his election very emotionally and on an anti-Vietnam War ticket (he had initially been pro-war but later recanted) and, in keeping with his whole political career, pledged passionately to deal with urban poverty and Civil Rights. Had he lived, it seems extremely likely that he would have become President. RFK's Moon is in almost exact sextile to his Sun but that aspect is separating; therefore, his Moon at 28 degrees 27 minutes Capricorn will not form any further major aspect before it enters Aquarius. His void Moon falling as it does in the Tenth House may be relevant to the fact that although Kennedy seemed to be destined for the White House, to use the usual void-of-course phrase, *nothing came of the matter* because he was shot before he could get there. The void Moon certainly didn't prevent him having children; coming from a good Catholic family, he sired eleven in all!

There are various clues pointing to Robert's early demise. For instance, seven of his planets fall in either the sign associated with death (Scorpio) or in those signs associated with winter in the Northern Hemisphere (Capricorn, Aquarius and Pisces). Even more telling is the fact that Mars is almost exactly setting (several public figures who have been assassinated have had Mars on the Descendant or in the Seventh), as this shows the potential for being attacked – and in Scorpio, it shows that the attack could potentially be fatal. In RFK's case, one might imagine that he could be a man who would easily *feel* attacked by others. One wonders how he would have managed the feelings of guilt and self-condemnation had he become President and survived in that role for a longer period than his brother. Even the seemingly wonderful Jupiter on the MC is debilitated in Capricorn, and it rules the Eighth and is opposed by Pluto. The chart generally lends weight to the theory of planetary dignities (see pages 216-18); for example, perhaps the fact that the Moon is in its detriment in Capricorn is as telling as the fact that it is void.

Curiously, Indira Gandhi who, like Robert Kennedy, was also assassinated, had a void-of-course Moon at 28 degrees Capricorn in a separating sextile from her Sun in

Scorpio. Diana, Princess of Wales and Jimi Hendrix were also born with void-of-course Moons. However, I don't think void Moons can be taken as indicating the likelihood of being cut down in one's prime unless other factors *strongly* point that way. Possibly a void Moon in a natal chart may be indicative of a situation where an individual may seem set on a particular course in life but, for some reason, 'nothing comes of the matter'. Although this may seem fanciful, at times it can feel as if the individual loses out because their choice of path is at odds with the destiny of the cosmos as a whole.

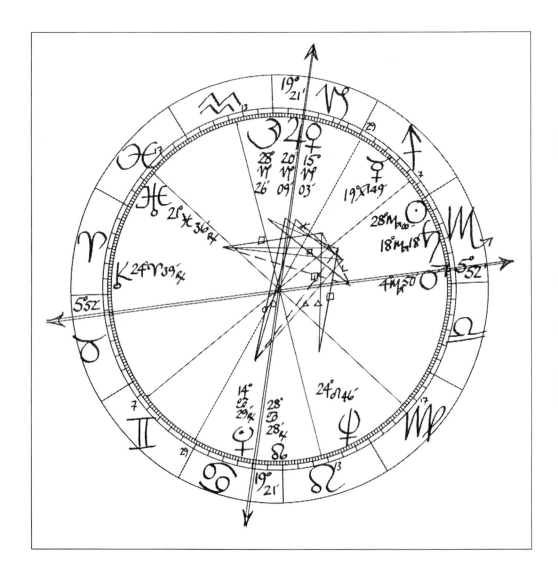

Mercury ☿

*'Better to remain silent and be thought a fool
than to speak out and remove all doubt.'*

Abraham Lincoln

'If ignorance is bliss, this boy is in for a life of undiluted happiness.'
School report quoted in *The Times*

Astronomy

Mercury is the nearest planet to the Sun and can never be more than 28 degrees away from it. This means that in the horoscope it will always be in the same zodiac sign as the Sun or in the sign preceding or following it. Mercury's proximity to the Sun also means that it cannot be seen much after sunset or long before sunrise. The planet has no moons and no atmosphere. Its content is thought to be about 70% metal.

• Mean distance from the Sun: approximately 36 million miles/57.9 million kilometres. The orbit of Mercury is very eccentric so the actual distance ranges from 28 million/45 million kilometres to 43 million miles/69 million kilometres.
• Diameter: approximately 3030 miles/4878 kilometres. After Pluto, it is our solar system's smallest planet.
• Sidereal period (approximate time for planet to orbit the Sun): 88 days.
• Retrograde motion: 20 to 24 days, every four months or so.

Mythology

The Greek version of Mercury was the god Hermes who was the product of an affair (or more likely a one-night-stand) between sexual adventurer Zeus and a nymph called Maia. This fling was one of the many infidelities committed by Zeus that his jealous wife Hera had to suffer, and the arrival of Hermes was living proof of Zeus's duplicity.

On his first day of life Hermes went out to steal oxen that his brother Apollo was looking after. (In some versions of the story, the theft occurred in the first five minutes of life!) One can deduce that Hermes was easily bored and out looking for mischief! To avoid detection, Hermes tied giant sandals backwards on the cattle's hooves, so it looked as though they were being led in the opposite direction to the way they were actually being taken. On his own feet he put enormous sandals made of myrtle twigs and tamarisk.

Hermes stole fifty heifers and, of these, he took two of the fattest and, having ingeniously produced fire by rubbing two sticks together, he cooked them. He divided them into twelve to share with the twelve great gods of Olympus. He hid the rest of the herd.

By sunset he had crawled back into his cradle, apparently all innocence. But Apollo, using divinatory powers, realized the situation and took Hermes to his father Zeus for punishment. Hermes denied all knowledge of the theft but Zeus eventually extracted a confession from him. Hermes then had to talk himself out of the tight corner he had got himself into but did so with such skill that Zeus, far from being angry, was amused by his son's ingenuity. He did chastise him but he also assigned to him various tasks.

The story continues but it already highlights key Mercurial traits: those of duplicity, deceit, ingenuity, trickery, resourcefulness, the capacity for negotiation and for commerce. And surely all those cattle in hiding were the earliest form of kidnapping – the seizing of a valuable asset so one has something with which to negotiate.

The Mercury Complex

More than most of the other planets, Mercury can be described and assessed astrologically either in a light, simple way or in much more complex terms. Viewed simply, Mercury is concerned with communication, travel and thought; with making connections both mentally and physically. For additional information on the traits and life areas associated with the planet, particular attention must also be paid to the whole Mercurial complex: that is to any planets in Gemini (and, to a lesser extent, Virgo), any planets in the Third House (and the ruler of the Third House) and what these planets are doing by sign, house and aspects.

Communication

Mercury in the horoscope will describe:
- What we *think* about. Although simplistic, even the sign placement can be relevant here. For example, the mind of those with Mercury in Taurus might tend to gravitate towards supper and money-making, whereas those with Mercury in Sagittarius may ponder on the meaning of life, or think about their next trip abroad.
- What we *talk* about. This will be related to what we tend to think about, such as money, relationships, food, politics, God, and so on.
- *How* we talk, how we communicate. The entire Mercury complex has to be examined here but especially significant are the aspects to the planet. Mercury will have much to say about our style of communicating. Do we have a low voice, a high voice, a loud voice or do we whisper? Do we stammer, talk quickly or speak slowly? Is our tone angry, sarcastic, polite, bored or something else? Do we answer letters immediately or not at all? Do we write long letters or short ones? Are they factual, flowery, emotional or witty? How are we on the telephone – do we love it or hate it, do we spend all day on it or hide behind an answer-machine, and why?

More on Communicating and Messages

What can make astrological interpretation so difficult is the fact that each planet and symbol in the horoscope has to be assessed in the light of all the others. Arguably, this is particularly the case with Mercury because the planet acts as an 'agent' for all other planets in the chart. Our Mercury will describe how we convey other planetary messages, assuming that we do. It acts as a kind of switchboard in the psyche, delivering messages to different aspects of ourselves and also delivering messages from the various parts of ourselves to the outer world and those within it. Thus, Mercury may not only go some way towards describing messages in terms of their content but will also describe the way messages are conveyed, received, processed and digested.

The Role of Mercury in Relationships

The way messages are conveyed is crucial to the way in which they will be received. This reminds us that Mercury plays a huge, indeed central, role in relationships – all relationships – for most problems in relationships start off as communication difficulties. Either there is an inability to communicate effectively or an inability to listen or understand.

Language, Consciousness and Understanding

Zeus decreed that Hermes was to assist the Fates in the composition of the alphabet and this fits neatly with the Mercurial association with language. Here one can appreciate the role that Mercury plays in matters of self-development for there can be no coming to consciousness without language. When we know what something is called we can dialogue with it and we can dialogue about it. This may be a child recognizing a cat but equally it can be an adult recognizing that the emotion being experienced is shame or jealousy or grief. When we have the name for something, we can start to understand it. When we understand, we can forgive both ourselves and others. Understanding a situation more clearly also provides a way forward. Little wonder that psychotherapy is often dubbed the 'talking cure'. Hermes is able to move freely among mortals and the gods, the upper world and the underworld, thereby clearly showing that it is the Mercurial function that allows us to tap into our unconscious. In fact, any kind of mental probing and questioning requires the input of Mercury.

Mental Functioning

While it is not possible to judge intelligence from the horoscope (intelligence is probably largely a learned and therefore Mercurial process), Mercury nevertheless has much to say about our mental processes. Our Mercury describes how we digest and process information, and we will do this according to our own particular world-view as shown by the rest of the chart. As messenger of the gods, Hermes was the one god who could go anywhere; he could talk to mortals, he could talk to the gods, and he can and did deliver messages between them. Similarly there should be no limits as to where our minds can go. While physically we may not be able to go anywhere, in our heads we should be able to do so.

School and Early Education

The Third House may be a better significator of our school days but Mercury will also be relevant. Perhaps the Third House more accurately describes the actual environment that comprised school, whereas Mercury says more about the early process of learning and making connections.

Siblings

Mercury (together with planets in the Third House, the ruler of the Third House and, to a lesser extent, planets in Gemini) accurately describes our brothers and sisters. We might have none; they might be older, younger, male or female; we may have argued with them, brought them up or been brought up by them. We may have adored them or hated them. There may have been sibling rivalry and jealousies and potentially a whole host of other scenarios. The work, health and all other details about our siblings will be shown.

Hermes was the messenger between the Sun (father) and the Moon (mother) so perhaps it should not be surprising that Mercury is often active at the time of both conception and childbirth. One can also see Mercury as being the messenger between the Sun and the Moon in the fact that siblings often deliver messages to and from their parents to their brothers and sisters. We use our siblings as intermediaries, we get them to deliver difficult messages, such as 'Tell Mum I'm staying out tonight'!

Negotiation, Deals and Trading

Mercury in the horoscope will show how skilled an individual may be at negotiating and making deals. As messenger of the gods, Hermes was entrusted with making treaties. In our own small way, we too are making treaties all the time whenever we are trying to reach an agreement with anyone about anything. A successful treaty or deal has been arrived at when all parties feel happy about what has been agreed. Related to the idea of treaties is Hermes' second job, which was to promote commerce. Interestingly, Hermes was the god of profit (whether lawful or unlawful – the Mercurial function is completely amoral), the god of eloquence and the god of games of chance. Mercury has a major role in any kind of trading, any exchange or indeed anywhere where an agent or middle-man is involved. This obviously includes travel agents, literary agents and all the rest. In the retail trade, the wholesaler is an agent, being the intermediary between the producer and the customer. Similarly, the shopkeeper is the middle person between the manufacturer and the consumer. Buying and selling may involve considerable networking; it certainly involves a lot of discussion. The art of the trader is to overcome the buyer's hesitation by the use of subtle and persuasive words. Little wonder that Hermes was the god of eloquence, the god Logos.

Transport and Short Journeys

It is not possible to have commerce without transport. Goods have to be conveyed from A to B. The word 'conveyed' and the idea of conveyance are perhaps the nub of Mercury. Planets in the Third House are probably more relevant than Mercury in terms of describing transport, school, short journeys and even siblings, but Mercury is also a major significator in these matters. Any planets in Gemini, plus the ruler of the Third House, will provide additional information. As always, if something is true, it will be shown in many different ways in the horoscope. The whole Mercurial complex will describe:

• Short-distance travel and all aspects of getting from A to B. This, of course, applies in the sense of both mind and body. The place where we learn about making connections in the mental sense is, of course, school.
• Where we go and why we go. Do we make short journeys for pleasure, to get to work or for other reasons?
• How do we go? Do we travel by bus, car, train or bicycle? Do we go the long way round or via the shortest route, and which factors influence our choice? Do we take lots of trips or do we tend to stay at home? (Note that Sagittarius and Saturn can be

associated with trains. Mercury itself, or those with a Geminian emphasis, often love bike-riding. Neptune and the water signs can signify travel on water. A lunar or Cancerian influence can suggest caravanning. Mars always favours speed whereas Saturn tends to be slow but sure, and so on.)

Hermes, Travel and Trainers

In terms of conveyancing goods and people, Hermes' third job was to maintain the rights of travellers. His role was largely a protective one. To guide the traveller, heaps of stones (the Greek word for a heap of stones is *herma*) were placed where roads branched off, and also at crossroads marking boundary points and landmarks. When we hit a crossroads in life, we need to be able to call upon the Mercurial traits of detachment, lateral thinking and resourcefulness. Hermes' journeys also extended to conducting the souls of the dead to the underworld. He is known here as Hermes Psychopompos and is sometimes differentiated from the celestial Hermes.

Aided by gold-winged sandals given to him by Zeus, Hermes was the swiftest god; no one could get somewhere faster than he. (Ideally, our brain works at that kind of instantaneous speed also.) In today's mercurial society, it is easy to think of trainers and other similar soft shoes as the contemporary equivalent of Hermes' sandals. The Mercurial person will favour these because they allow a speedy entrance and a speedy get-away. Nor do they make much noise. Mercury will always favour anonymity, because one can get away with things if quiet and anonymous.

Theft and Lying

In some versions, Hermes indulged in theft five minutes after he was born. Thieving and precocious behaviour are often linked to premature weaning and that term is meant not in the sense of milk (though maybe that too) but in terms of good parenting. (Zeus, Maia and Hera were all pretty non-existent as parents.) Antisocial behaviour has often been linked to a feeling of rejection by the parents and especially by the mother figure. But not being too close to parents, especially the maternal figure, also can endow blessings, such as the blessing of having to be resourceful, of going out into the world and experimenting – trying this, trying that – and generally cruising around. A strong, protective maternal bond tends to curb that tendency and thus the gift of experimentation is also curbed.

Hermes had one heifer to play with and he made a *lyre* and a tortoise shell out of it. Here, of course, we have the original liar in the other sense of the word. Our Mercury will say something about the way each of us lies, our reasons for lying and our manner of doing so. Mercury is concerned with the dissemination of information and almost all information conveyed is, at best, only going to be a half-truth. Facts can be misleading, anyway: most facts are actually opinions or stories. Perhaps all ideas are stolen – few if any are wholly original. So while Mercury does indeed describe theft in the usual way that we think of the word, there are also the more obtuse ways of thinking about what constitutes theft.

Mercury Retrograde

Retrograde motion occurs when the Sun seems to be moving faster than another planet so that this other planet seems to be going backwards when viewed from our own terrestrial perspective. Mercury spends a period of roughly three weeks in this apparent state of backward motion once every four months or so. Since time immemorial, astrologers have viewed retrograde Mercury with variable amounts of trepidation because many associate it with times when communications are more likely to go awry. Letters, emails or other messages may fail to arrive or arrangements made will be upset or go wrong in some way, usually due to crossed wires. Ventures started during this period may have to be re-done. It is a time to associate with misunderstandings, transport problems and bungles of all kinds.

The traditional interpretation of Mercury retrograde undoubtedly has some validity but, in my view, it should probably not be taken too seriously except when supported by other chart factors, such as many hard aspects to Mercury or a void-of-course Moon. In practice, one finds many examples where things go exactly according to plan when Mercury is retrograde and, in any case, deviations from the prescribed path need not be viewed negatively. A retrograde Mercury may even be useful in certain situations; it may mark an ideal time for catching up on old correspondence, for instance. And it may be good for any situation where one is going back over what one has said, thought, written or failed to write in the past. It is a good time for double-checking and re-doing. However, when electing a chart to start a venture (such as a business) it is probably advisable to avoid a retrograde Mercury, if at all possible. In forecasting work, the years when Mercury changes direction by progression are usually felt to be significant but I am not convinced that a retrograde Mercury in the natal horoscope has much significance.

Youth

In spite of his playfulness, thieving and pranks, Hermes was popular with the gods. His resourcefulness and ability to talk to anyone and go anywhere meant that he was a most valuable ally. Time after time, he is seen getting the gods out of all kinds of sticky situations in the same way that resourcefulness and clear thinking, indeed lateral thinking, gets us all out of tight corners. The other reason for Hermes' popularity was perhaps because he didn't take himself or life too seriously; he was light, fun, youthful. Similarly we tend to take a benign view of youth and overlook some degree of youthful mischief-making.

Mercury and Urban Life

In her sadly out-of-print book *Mercury*,[2] the astrologer Pam Tyler observes that the Mercurial person is well-disposed to urban living. In the city so much is happening and everything is transient. The individual can be largely anonymous; s/he is free to observe, without necessarily being observed. As Pam points out, the Mercury character is the original voyeur; living life vicariously, on the outskirts and uninvolved. City life and Mercurial life are about keeping things loose, being ever able to move, shift and dodge as the circumstances necessitate. The city is the home of commerce and is also the habitat most favoured by thieves.

Mercury in the 21st Century

Today's society is distinctly Mercurial, as evidenced by people increasingly living in cities and also the increasing problems with youth, transport and education. The advent of the mobile phone could hardly be more Mercurial! It is also hard to escape the feeling that humans are bored; this leads to a faster and faster sound-bite culture, which, in turn, arguably creates even more boredom. Just as in eating, where there is greater flavour to be gained from slow chewing, so it is with living life. Being youthful also seems to be the underlying impulse behind modern man and woman. Homœopaths might interpret all this as society being in a syphilitic (destructive) age of its development. In olden times, the treatment for the disease syphilis was made from the metal Mercury.

Metal

Mercury (also known as quicksilver) is the metal to associate with this planet. Although defined as a metal, it is actually a heavy, silvery, odour-free and highly toxic substance which evaporates quickly when hot but becomes a liquid at room temperature. With an atomic weight heavier than lead, it is so dense that the heaviest of objects can float in it. The term 'mad as a hatter' comes from the time when hat-makers rubbed mercury nitrate into cloth to preserve it. Over time, its inhalation caused personality changes, tremors which became known as 'hatter's shakes', nervousness and sometimes dementia. The glyph for Mercury looks a little like a man wearing a hat. Hermes wore a broad-rimmed traveller's hat called a petasus. Hats, of course, protect us from the heat of the Sun and the two planets can never be far apart in the sky. I have observed that hat-wearers often have the two planets tightly conjunct. If the conjunction is tight and found in Aries, the zodiac sign associated with the head, the individual almost definitely will be a hat-wearer!

The so-called silver fillings in most people's teeth are made up of an amalgam of metals, 50% of which commonly used to be mercury (the rest consisting of silver, tin and other metals). Given that it is probably the most toxic non-radioactive metal currently known, there is concern as to the safety of its use, a concern which has led to its usage being banned in some countries. Various diseases have been linked, rightly or wrongly, to mercury poisoning, including multiple sclerosis, Alzheimer's, Parkinson's and chronic fatigue syndrome. The metal is a neurotoxin which means it affects the nervous system – a bodily network strongly associated with the planet. Some of these diseases share similarities with so-called mad hatter's disease; Parkinson's sufferers have similar tremors, for example.

The Body

Given that it is the role of the nervous system to carry information to and from the brain to the other organs and parts of the body, there can be little doubt that Mercury plays a major part in its functioning. The lungs and the whole apparatus of breathing also belong to the Mercury/Gemini complex. So do the hands but, in as much as our legs help us to get from A to B, Mercury can inform us about all our limbs.

Hermes carried with him a winged staff with two serpents entwined around it – one usually thought to be female and the other male – and this caduceus has become the insignia of various branches of the medical profession. This could have come about because the staff allowed Hermes to impart sleep on whomever he chose, or because Hermes came to be associated with alchemy, which is the forerunner of both medicine and pharmacology. Whatever the history, suffice it to say that one of the snakes can be taken to represent yin energy, and the other is yang energy. The staff around which they are entwined can be interpreted as the spinal cord. The crossing of the serpents occurs seven times and almost definitely symbolizes the seven chakras – the centres of electro-magnetic energy in the body. The caduceus could also be taken to represent the DNA double-helix.

In the World at Large

Along with planets in Gemini and the Third House in a nation's chart or other mundane map, Mercury's area of operation includes everything to do with a nation's language(s) and the whole telecommunications industry, including postal and telephone services. The nation's schools and libraries, and attitude to education generally, will also be part of its remit, as will transport. Being concerned with commerce, Mercury in a nation's horoscope will contribute information about what the nation trades, how it trades and who it trades with.

Mercury Through The Signs

Mercury in Aries – ☿ ♈

Other people are inevitably going to feel rather slow to the Mercury in Aries person, who likes to get to the point – the nub of the matter – quickly and without needless circumnavigation. This is especially the case if the Sun is also placed in Aries. This is a direct, no-going-round-the-houses, quick-thinking, fast-talking and often tactless Mercury. There can be a capacity for instant decision-making and sometimes the quick arriving at solutions to problems. On the down side, negotiating and seeing another's point of view may not be so easy. There can also be a tendency to jump to conclusions prematurely and to speak for or make decisions for others. In classroom and communicative situations generally this individual cannot wait to give an answer. In essence, the individual is competing to say 'I know that'. Frequently this is the person who writes in books (putting their personal stamp on the text) or underlines or highlights the main points.

Mercury in Taurus – ☿ ♉

Clear, step-by-step learning or teaching can be a feature. There can be a talent for expressing things with simplicity, a gift for conveying information to others in a steady, keep-it-simple, building-blocks way. There is often a liking for information to be presented as visually or logically as possible. Perhaps for this reason, this placement can be associated with tarot cards (especially with the Sun in Gemini) for here one touches information. There may be an interest in the arts or a tendency to think about money and material considerations a good deal. There could be many comings and goings to do with property and land. A pleasant voice is the norm, especially if the planet is coupled with Venus. There can be slowness over decision-making and a reluctance to change their mind. Entrenched ideas belong here. This is the kind of placement that accords with the individual who hangs on to computers or other equipment rather than update them, because of a liking for the comfort and familiarity of an old machine. In communicative matters the individual may appear to be unaffected by grief or joy due to Taurus's naturally stoical bent.

Mercury in Gemini – ☿ ♊

Here, in the sign of its rulership, Mercury is strongly placed, implying an agile mind and one open to new ideas and experimentation. What the individual may lack in conviction and staying power may be more than compensated for by verbal and mental dexterity. Opinions will be less swayed by moral bias and more influenced by facts. Curious and easily bored, this individual may have the capacity to process a great deal of stimuli at the same time. Typically, the individual will be a great talker and always on the go, dashing from A to B, thinking on their feet and talking with their hands. This can be the person who will read anything and listen to anybody. There is a need to sample as many ideas as possible. There may be a liking for crosswords and word and card games.

Mercury in Cancer – ☿ ♋

There can be a liking for recording information or a need to do so. Thus, this is an excellent placement for the diarist or curator. This may be the person who records lectures, because there can be a need to be able to play things back, to be able to replay the past, to go back over things. Often there will be an interest in history. Memory and touch may go together, and some people with Mercury here particularly like feeling things with their hands. One famous actor with Mercury rising in Cancer (and therefore very strongly placed) has a notorious reputation for handling women's breasts (Cancer). This is a good placement for the restaurateur because it combines commerce (Mercury) with food and nurturing (Cancer). There can be a need for a mother figure to talk to. Many with Mercury here will take on this role for others. An attentive and sympathetic communicator is implied. However, the receiving and conveying of facts can be skewed by emotion, and personal experience may colour the individual's attitude to interpreting data, without their even being aware of it.

Mercury in Leo – ☿ ♌

Expressing their opinions with confidence, or at least with the appearance of confidence, can go with this placement This person may be good at bluffing. Pride can be the biggest impediment to learning, as it can be so hard for the Mercury in Leo individual to admit to their ignorance in the first place. Learning often requires starting from the bottom and this may not come easily to this potentially know-it-all type. However, these difficulties may not be such an issue if the Sun is placed in Virgo or Cancer. There can be an ability to express information with colour and drama. An audience can bring out the orator and after-dinner speaker, if the rest of the chart inclines that way. The planet of commerce in the sign of banking makes this an excellent placement for those who work in banking or similar industries. Typically, while being rather subjective in their views, this person is also often very loyal – this is not someone who talks ill of their friends.

Mercury in Virgo – ☿ ♍

An analytical and rather sceptical placement, this is someone who, all else being equal, strives to be objective. Classically, the individual is meticulous with information and gifted at classifying and categorizing it. The Mercury in Virgo person knows how to make information useful. Good with details, there can be a marked capacity to deal with any amount of complexity and intricacy in terms of learning, analysing and using information. It is good for any kind of specialist. Often there is an interest in health and an urge to talk or write about such matters. Work is typically the other subject area that dominates both thought and discussion. Frequently there is little tolerance of fools, but the critical faculties can be offset by an appreciation for the little absurdities of life and the sense of humour that can result from that.

Mercury in Libra – ☿ ♎

A capacity for reflecting back the opinions and ideas of others can mean that those with Mercury in Libra may have the gift of ensuring that other people feel understood. These individuals may know what others think even if they are not always so sure of their own opinions. The capacity to reflect back can make this a useful placement for the counsellor if the chart overall agrees. At best, Mercury here lends a gracefulness in self-expression, a high degree of tact and an ability to convey things in the nicest possible way. This can make the Mercury in Libra person very persuasive if not always totally honest. Some with this placement find it possible to agree with both sides of opposing factions! Others, always weighing things up, can find any decision-making process difficult. The placement is useful for those involved with the administrative side of the beauty industry, and useful too for work in public relations and diplomatic fields.

Mercury in Scorpio – ☿ ♏

This can be a very pithy and witty placement for Mercury. Some with Mercury here will be skilled at delivering witty one-liners. This placement is great for conspiracy theorists for there can be a tendency to take a somewhat cynical, dark or unflinchingly honest view of human nature. Often there is an interest in psychological matters – if not academically, then certainly in simply trying to fathom what makes others tick. There is an interest too in sex, death, medicine, the occult and potentially all of life's mysteries. Although this placement can indicate a person of few words – one who doesn't give away more than is necessary – it is also often descriptive of someone who, when they do talk, speaks with great passion and intensity. So much so, that others may be loath to disagree when they are in full melodramatic flood. Mercury here can indicate tremendous mental stamina: the individual who is still awake reading or studying when others are tucked under their duvets. Or it may be the individual who understands and can illustrate the notion of mind over matter. Once the mind is put to something, then anything is possible. Jealousy can be a strong feature in sibling relationships. Strength in the hands and limbs can also feature.

Mercury in Sagittarius – ☿ ♐

A broad-minded, fun-loving Mercury, this placement can be associated with people who travel a great deal – especially if the rest of the chart confirms this. It is an ideal placement for the travel agent, tour guide and long-distance lorry-driver. There can be great skills at spinning a yarn so the telling of tall (fishing!) stories belongs here. While there can be a certain sloppiness with respect to accuracy or the details of a given story, there is often a wonderful capacity for imbuing an anecdote with fun, sparkle or meaning. Individuals with this Mercury can be great at seeing the wider view and getting the gist of the matter in hand. It is an ideal placement for anyone called upon to comment on religious, philosophical or political matters. Sagittarius is a sign often concerned with the morals of a particular situation, so this can be a fairly judgemental Mercury. However, those with this placement can also often be generous in thought, tending always to give others the benefit of the doubt.

Mercury in Capricorn – ☿ ♑

There can be a marked ability to discipline their thoughts, to remove extraneous mental clutter and to really concentrate on the matter in hand with Mercury here. An efficient and organized brain makes this a great placement for any number of administrative tasks and also for any activity that requires mental discipline. Many golf players have Mercury here and it is also ideal for anyone involved in dentistry and osteopathy. Individuals with this Mercury tend to be both careful with information and careful in what they say. They don't like to open their mouths without good reason. Typically, they want to be respected for their ideas and dislike being thought of as stupid. The taking of elocution lessons so that one speaks properly would be within the symbolism. There can be a tendency to be influenced by the ideas and opinions of their father. Certainly, this realistic and down-to-earth placement inclines towards conservative thinking but also to a dry sense of humour.

Mercury in Aquarius – ☿ ♒

People with this sceptical and fairly objective Mercury come to their ideas and opinions independently. They may listen to the views of others but won't swallow these wholesale. In the world at large, they tend to question political spin and advertising jargon. Mercury in Aquarius individuals are interested in the truth as they see it, and when being told something, often the first question they ask of themselves is: 'Is this true?' Many Mercury-Aquarians are interested in human nature and in the natural world. Knowledgeable with wide interests, the placement can also give rise to the infuriatingly opinionated know-it-all. It can describe people with strong convictions who are not frightened of contradicting others, whether or not it is appropriate to do so. The typical Mercury in Aquarius person is not scared to call a brick a brick. Equally, you know that if they tell you, 'You look wonderful', they mean it. Sincerity is a watchword here. There can be open-mindedness but once the mind is made up, it will not be easily changed.

Mercury in Pisces – ☿ ♓

A common manifestation of Mercury here, in its fall, is of an individual having a weak sense of direction. They so easily get lost, even in places they know well. This is not a very critical placement for Mercury and oversensitivity and impressionability can lead to misunderstandings and a distortion of the facts. Nevertheless, there can be a marked capacity for getting into other people's heads and for reflecting their views and ideas. This can be a very empathic placement. Some individuals with Mercury here are able to almost telepathically infiltrate the mind of others. There are sometimes issues to do with a sensitivity to sound and sometimes issues of pronunciation can feature. Some will have perfect pitch or a gift for mimicry (many an impressionist has Mercury here), especially if Gemini is also strong in the chart. There can be also be an appreciation of the value of learning experientially. This is the placement to associate with dance or drama therapy, for instance, and sometimes with communicating through the medium of dance or music.

Venus ♀

'All charming people have something to conceal,
usually their total dependence on the appreciation of others.'

Cyril Connolly

'When you feel bad about yourself you reverse your magnet and repel people.'

S. A. Grafio

Astronomy

Known since prehistoric times and visible to the naked eye (though not more than three hours after sunset or three hours before sunrise), Venus is the brightest object in the sky after the Sun and Moon. Reflecting about 80% of the sunlight hitting it (the Moon reflects a mere 7% of sunlight), Venus would appear much brighter than our Moon were it not for the fact that the Moon is about one hundred times closer to us. Our nearest planetary neighbour, Venus is often thought of as our sister planet, being similar in size, mass and density to the Earth. Its environment is extremely hostile, though, being very hot (hotter even than Mercury) and completely dry. Venus is covered with swirling dense cloud composed of sulphuric acid droplets which not only trap heat but produce acid rain which evaporates long before it reaches ground level. The cloud contributes to the planet's yellowish colour which has been the inspiration for poets for centuries. The majority of its surface is thought to be composed of volcanic material and live volcanoes may still be erupting there. Many of its surface features are named after female figures. Its orbit is the most nearly circular of any planet (round, like the female form) and its rotation rate is the slowest of all planets (reflecting perhaps the lazy quality that is sometimes attributed to Venus). In common with Uranus, but unlike every other planet, Venus rotates from east to west which means that its dawn is in the west, instead of the east. As an inferior planet (its orbit lies between the Sun and the Earth), Venus shows phases when viewed from the Earth through a telescope. As with the Moon, these phases vary from a large, bright crescent when it is nearest the Earth to a small, silvery disk when farthest away. As with the Moon, Venus is associated with the feeling realm and of course feelings, by their very nature, go through phases.

• Mean distance from the Sun: approximately 67 million miles/108 million kilometres.
• Diameter: approximately 7521 miles/12,104 kilometres and therefore only slightly smaller than the Earth.
• Sidereal period (approximate time for planet to orbit the Sun): 225 days. Due perhaps to its very slow rotation of 243 days, Venus has no magnetic field, reflecting the psychological quality of passivity with which it is associated.
• Retrograde motion: no more than 43 days in a year. Some years not at all.

Mythology

Venus to the Romans, Ishtar (literally 'brightest star') to the Babylonians, Freya in Nordic mythology and Aphrodite to the Greeks, mythology surrounding this planet is inevitably feminine. The Fates decreed that Aphrodite had but one divine duty, namely to make love and to encourage others to do so, and therefore she presided over the survival of the species. Once she was caught by Athene working at the loom (Athene's province), apologized profusely and never did any work again. Similarly, Venus in the horoscope can describe areas where we choose to be passive, if not downright lazy. There are various versions of Aphrodite's origins, the Homeric one being that she was the daughter of Zeus and the sea nymph Dione. Another more popular version from Hesiod describes her as having risen as a fully formed goddess from the sea on a scallop or oyster shell, out of the foam in which Kronos had tossed Uranus's genitals. In this version of the story, she was a goddess without parents. *Aphro* means foam but presumably in this instance semen is implied. From the name Aphrodite we get the word 'aphrodisiac' – a food, drink or other substance that arouses or intensifies sexual desire. Aphrodite is supposed to have appeared on a scallop shell, and many seafoods (notably oysters) are credited with having aphrodisiac properties.

Aphrodite's constant companions included doves, sparrows and the three Graces (or Charities) – these were the beautiful, smiling, some say dancing, daughters of Zeus and the Oceanid Eurynome: Aglaia (radiance and splendour), Euphrosyne (joy and merriment) and Thalia (abundant cheerfulness). The Graces were always charming, gentle, polite and graceful. They dressed Aphrodite, soothed her, bathed her, arranged her hair and massaged her with ambrosial oils. Wherever they went, they ensured peace and happiness and instilled in others the joy of living that comes from art, music, dance and love.

A most beautiful goddess, when Aphrodite arrived in Olympus all the gods wanted to marry her, making many of the other goddesses jealous of her. To try to stem possible trouble, Zeus married her off to Hephaestus (the Roman Vulcan), the club-footed craftsman and god of the forge. Thus, this was an arranged marriage between the ugliest god and the most beautiful goddess. Hephaestus was lame, ugly and usually described as bad-tempered but his skill as a craftsman was matchless. Robert Graves tells us: 'Every Bronze Age tool, weapon or utensil had magical properties, and the smith was something of a sorcerer.'[3] Hephaestus's forge was housed inside a volcano, hinting perhaps not only of strength but smouldering passion. Hephaestus used his skills to make lavish jewels and adornments for Aphrodite, his greatest gift being a girdle made of fine gold, in which he wove magic filigree fibres. The magic girdle ensured that gods and men would fall hopelessly in love with its wearer. The already beautiful Aphrodite seldom loaned the girdle to others and hardly ever took it off.

It seems that Aphrodite didn't mind being married to Hephaestus; in some versions of the story, it is said that she liked being married to him because she thought she might enjoy greater freedom to pursue her affairs. Of course he did notice her philandering and he did mind, once setting a trap for her and Ares and causing all the gods to laugh at the pair of lovers when they were caught together naked in a net. One might conjecture that Aphrodite would seem more beautiful when cast against someone so obviously physically flawed as Hephaestus. Or one might say this marriage was a union between outer and inner beauty or between art (Aphrodite) and craft (Hephaestus). Of course she would have valued the adornments he gave her, just as many a woman has stayed married for the economic advantages to be gained from so doing. The marriage might also be viewed as a marriage between opposites, as most partnerships are. Perhaps another reason why Aphrodite stayed with Hephaestus is because he thought she was wonderful. How difficult it is to turn our backs on those who truly love and admire us.

Aphrodite had countless affairs, both with gods and mortals. Her most famous liaison, and one which seemed to last, was with Ares (Mars). Hephaestus was peculiarly Martian too, working as he did in a forge. With Ares there is the quality of Mars in Aries; with Hephaestus, Mars in Scorpio. Aphrodite had three children with Ares (and children also with Adonis, Dionysos and others) but none from her union with Hephaestus.

Aphrodite was frequently the cause of jealousy. Sometimes she experienced it herself, and her rivalry with Athene and Hera set in motion the Trojan War. Since Aphrodite was in charge of continuing the species, it is not surprising that rivalry was so often part of her behavioural package, for it is frequently rivalrous feelings that hurtle people into liaisons, given that potential partners become much more attractive when everyone else fancies them, too. The competition speeds things along, for if people had time for their feelings to cool off, they might think twice about getting involved.

Enjoyment, Pleasure and Happiness

Our capacity to enjoy life and to be happy has surprisingly little to do with our life experiences but is largely decided by our intrinsic nature. The Venus principle says much about our capacity to appreciate beauty, to appreciate the world around us and those within it. Venus shows where and how we get pleasure out of life and, to a large extent, what we enjoy doing. It shows what gives us joy (Jupiter can also have a bearing here) and makes us happy. Aspects to Venus will show how easy we find it to accept what we have been given by others or the cards that life has dealt us. The strength and flavour of our Venus will show how easy or difficult we are to please (though the Moon, with its desire to accommodate others, and Jupiter as indicator of both faith and buoyancy are also relevant). Our Venus placement will also show what steps we take to make others happy. Words like please, pleasing and pleasure all have the same root and all come under the Venusian umbrella. When considering your Venus, ask yourself what gives you pleasure, what makes you excited and aroused, what makes it worth getting out of bed in the morning? Your Venus – its sign, house and aspects – may not be descriptive of all the answers to those questions, but will provide a good starting point.

The symbol for Venus looks like a hand mirror (and Aphrodite is often pictured carrying one) and the planet, alongside the Moon, seems to signify something of the mirroring process. For instance, when people fall in love, they do so at least partially because the other person is falling in love with them. People usually find each other mutually attractive or unattractive. It rarely happens that an individual likes a person who dislikes them; not for long, anyway. Similarly we feel pleased when we please another.

The Feminine Principle

Whereas the Moon describes that aspect of the feminine which might be termed 'maternal', Venus represents women in the role of maiden or femme fatale. In a heterosexual man's chart, it will often be projected outwards and very literally describe his female lovers. A man's Moon will also describe the women in his life and the two images, lunar and Venusian, may harmonize or clash with each other. A classic scenario occurs when a man marries one of his female images but, feeling deprived of the other, has an affair with a woman who embodies the missing characteristics. Gay men are more likely to fall for men who are described by their Sun or Mars than their Venus, and gay women may be drawn to women who embody their Moon, Venus or Mars. With everyone, the Fifth and Seventh houses, and their rulers, also give many clues to relationship choices.

The Principle of Giving

Venus describes a person's desire and capacity to give, whether they are giving their time, their affection, their money or giving way in a dispute. At such times, the needs of the other are given precedence and priority over the needs of the self. Our Venus says much about how easily we yield under pressure. The person who vibrates strongly to this planet tends to cave in easily. While giving usually arises out of a desire to show love (using the word 'love' in its widest sense), it is possible to be giving for more dubious motives; in Venus mode we may submit merely because it is easier to do so and because we want to avoid opposition. We may merely be too passive to fight. Or maybe our need to be popular is too great. We may even be prepared to buy our way into another's good graces. Of course, Venus is as much concerned with sharing as it is with giving. When studying your Venus, ask yourself how easy is it for you to share? What aspects of yourself or your possessions do you share with others and how? What is easy to share and what is more difficult? Venus is about accepting as well as giving, whether it be accepting another's love, help, time or gifts.

In ancient times, in Greece, and the Middle East, the word talent was used to describe a weight or a coin. Our talents and accomplishments, and money itself, all come under the umbrella of Venus, possibly because there is a relationship between how we 'spend' our time, our energy, our money and our affections. Our way of giving of ourselves, our way of loving the world we find ourselves in, is through our talents, whether these are artistic or otherwise. We may have a talent for gardening, so a stranger may walk past our garden and derive pleasure from our flowers, or maybe we are grinding coffee beans or frying bacon, and the smells we create potentially give pleasure to others, however fleetingly. As Bolen[1] tell us, Aphrodite always did what pleased her, similarly, we don't usually grow flowers or grind coffee beans solely to please others, we do it because we want to. Nevertheless, grinding the coffee beans or growing the flowers in our garden are a way of giving to the universe; arguably, a way of giving pleasure and a kind of love back to the planet. Shopping comes into this category, too. When we purchase something, we are in effect saying that whatever we have bought is of value to us. If we buy a loaf of bread we are saying we want bread. Sharing and reciprocity comes in here as we give the money and in turn receive the loaf.

How We Give and Receive Affection

Still basically on the subject of giving, our Venus describes how we feel about being close to another person and how we achieve this. How easy is it for us to give and receive the love and affection of others? For example, the Venus-Jupiter person may pour affection over everyone while fearful Venus-Saturn, perhaps no less loving in the right circumstances, may be more cautious and self-protective. Venus-Neptune may express their love by rescuing you, Venus-Pluto by encouraging deep intimacy very quickly. Of course, such scenarios will inevitably come complete with a much larger psychological pattern as described by the whole complex surrounding the planet.

Venus, Love and Intimacy

There are many different types of love: erotic, fraternal, spiritual (agape) and maternal love. Relationships may be characterized by feelings of strong liking, affection, tenderness, devotion or, especially with the input of Mars, lusty passion and desire. Venus is significator or at least co-significator of all expressions of love, and especially so when it comes to the romantic variety. While romantic love may or may not have a sexual outcome, it always has a sexual aura. Venus represents the passive, attracting, sharing aspect of the sexual act unlike its partner, Mars, whose job is to chase and make conquests. Venus can be associated with flirting and foreplay, Mars with penetration.

More generally, Venus is the significator of love and enjoyment in the widest possible sense. The planet describes our attitude to all social interactions. It describes whether we are a party animal and whether we are sociable, asocial or antisocial.

Venus is similar in size to the Earth and is also a planet that is quite near to us in terms of relative distance, although not as near as our Moon. Both planets are close to us in the way that our feelings are close to us. Little wonder that Venus is a planet to associate with intimacy and not just in the obvious relationship sense. The artist is also being intimate with us by sharing something of their inner self.

The Cosmic Peacemaker

The psychology to be associated with Venus can result in either war or peace. On the one hand, the astrological Venus describes the urge for harmony and peace and our ability (or not) to achieve this. In Venus mode we find points of agreement and similarity; as we have seen, here we are prepared to give in. Here we want to equalize and balance and are willing to yield. There is an urge to reciprocate and co-operate with others. The principle of co-operation is key to the planet and also to the success of all relationships. Moreover, greater potential for peace comes with equality as, arguably, so does happiness.

The Civilizing Effect

The more civilized an individual or a society is, the less likely they are to engage in war or other kinds of dispute. Manners and courtesy are distinctly Venusian attributes and are characteristic of civilized behaviour. The need to be liked and loved civilizes people by knocking off the raw edges in their behaviour. Coarse and discourteous behaviour is decidedly anti-Venusian. Polite, civil behaviour increases good feelings between people, minimizes discord and maximizes the chances for agreements to be made. On the other hand, overly courteous behaviour leads easily to sycophancy and insincerity. Overly sweet, fawning behaviour and the tendency to flatter are also potential behavioural traits that can be laid at the door of this planet.

The Charm Offensive

In Mars mode we might say 'I want what I want', whereas in Venus mode, we say 'I want what you want'. However, the Venusian principle is not necessarily an unselfish one; it can be quite the reverse. We are more likely to get our own way by setting out to please (and certainly not to displease or offend) the other party. When charming, we are more likely to get our own way and Venus is very much the significator of charm. To charm someone is to appeal to them personally, to cause them to be enamoured and entranced by you. In other words, in true Aphrodite style, if we are very charismatic, we catch and captivate, perhaps almost bewitch the other person. The word 'charm' actually means magic spell; the spell used to be given in the form of a chant or verse which was recited in order to make something happen. Perhaps like Aphrodite's girdle, it was used to make someone fall in love. Later a charm came to mean an amulet to ward off evil or bring good luck, and from that came the charm bracelet.

Jealousy, Rivalry and Self-Valuation

In the same way that we can't determine intelligence from a horoscope, we cannot easily measure depth of feelings from the horoscope either. However, what we can determine are motives and outcomes. In any event, the experience of passionate feelings for another represents the very antithesis of feeling safe and secure. When 'in love', feelings of jealousy and insecurity are so easily aroused, and feelings of safety and security fly out of the window. The degree to which we may or may not feel threatened when the object of our desire so much as talks to or even looks at another person is largely based on the extent to which we do or do not feel OK about ourselves. The equation roughly goes: insecurity plus desire equals jealousy. Our Venus (its sign and house placement and, more especially, any tight aspects it might be receiving) has a bearing on our self-valuation, especially in terms of whether we feel attractive, lovable and, possibly, sexy to others. If we feel reasonably attractive and lovable, then we will be less prone to feeling threatened by potential rivals. If we don't feel confident in such matters (perhaps Venus is receiving hard aspects from Saturn or the outer planets) then we will more easily feel threatened, provided also that we have strong feelings for the other person. Thus, Venus attributes are often causative factors behind conflict, in the same way that quite often wherever Aphrodite went, war often ensued. Conflict often occurs in response to jealousy, whether that jealousy is fuelled by love, money or some other valuable commodity. It can occur both on an individual basis and also provide the true motives that propel a country into war.

Money, Self-Worth and Violence

Along with the Second House and its ruler(s), our Venus says much about our values and therefore can also be associated with money. Are we tight with a buck or do we have holes in our pockets? How easy is it for us to earn and spend generally, and what do we spend our money on and why? (But note that the Second House is frequently an even stronger indicator of our earning and spending potential.) What we find beautiful, or for some other reason value highly, we will be willing to pay for. When we are in love we value the other person and, to some extent, find them beautiful. Beauty is indeed in the eye of the beholder. When we are well-paid, we feel valued and we value ourselves more. When depressed, spending money often lifts the spirits, at least temporarily. How much people charge for their services provides a strong clue as to how much they think they are worth. Venus is a planet to associate with equality and inequality, and perceived inequality in terms of our looks, our income and our ability to attract love can, as we have seen, stir up feelings of jealousy and, in turn, conflict. Wearing her magic girdle as she did, rarely lending it to others and hardly ever taking it off, Aphrodite operated from an unequal vantage point.

Richard Wilkinson, a professor of social epidemiology, has shown, using many examples, that however rich a country may be, that country will be more violent, dysfunctional, sick and depressed if the wealth gap between the social classes grows too wide. For instance, according to Wilkinson, people living in Harlem have shorter lives than the people of Bangladesh who live in greater poverty but whose lack of wealth is equally shared among the overwhelming majority of the population.[5]

How We Attract Others

Our Venus describes those attributes that others find attractive or admirable about us, usually without any special effort on our part. Birds sing and other animals make noises to attract a mate (Venus is a co-significator of music); other species use other attributes such as size, colour or pheromones to attract. Our Venus shows our own particular human equivalent of birdsong or plumage. So when considering our Venus, we need to ask what have we got that others want, admire or desire? This can apply to the possessions we own, the people we attract, our looks or our character. Because of its mirroring effect, Venus also describes, to some extent, what we are attracted to. Our attributes can make us more valuable but, as we have seen, can also have the potential for arousing jealousy and envy in others.

Venus and Magnetism

In the same way that Venus shows how we attract others, the planet probably literally has rulership over magnetism in the physical sense. The link with Uranus may provide a clue. We know that Venus concerns itself with the principle of attraction, while Uranus is the planet of repulsion. Uranus was, for instance, revolted by his children. Possibly the two planets symbolize the positive and negative poles of a magnet.

Tastes and Values

Venus has much to do with our capacity for comparison and ability to evaluate and make choices. We are coming from a Venusian position whenever we consider whether we like this or we like that. In other words, who or what do we value most, what is our taste, who do we choose? Our Sun sign seems to be at least partially descriptive here but Venus is a major component, too. Our taste (as shown for instance by our choice of lovers and friends, the clothes we choose, the adornments we wear, the paintings we buy, the music we listen to or play) gives out a message of exactly who we are. Knowing what we value and showing what we value is a way of defining ourselves. The people we knock around with help us to define who we are, too. The person we have on our arm (so to speak) can increase or decrease our value in the eyes of others. When we love someone, that person may not necessarily make us more valuable, but we certainly feel more valuable. Little wonder that the Sun – the body we most associate astrologically with identity – is close to Venus in the sky, for our identity is very much linked to our taste and our values. Self-valuation is intimately linked to the extent to which we are able to live according to our value system. As a rule, we feel bad about ourselves – our self-valuation plummets – when we act contrary to our values. We also don't feel good if we have to dress in something we'd rather not, perhaps to wear a relative's cast-offs if their style of dress is widely different from our own.

Venus by sign and aspect will say a lot about our likes and dislikes; to some extent it describes what we find beautiful. Aphrodite insisted on being valued and admired and inflicted horrid punishments upon those who neglected her. This perhaps gives a clue to the importance of surroundings and appearances. People who live in run-down areas or less than beautiful housing estates sometimes complain about the way that the estate gets vandalized, covered with graffiti, and so on. Arguably, this wouldn't happen if people were living in homes they found aesthetically pleasing.

Venus and Dress

Related to our aesthetic sensibilities is the way we choose to dress. Do we dress to please ourselves or to please others? Either way, our Venus placement and aspects significantly contribute to our dress sense and also may describe what we find pleasing in the way that others dress and present themselves. Venus with Jupiter may over-dress (flounces, bright colours, high fashion or opulence), while Venus-Saturn may choose to under-dress (toned-down colours, natural fibres, old clothes, traditional styles), while Venus with one of the outer planets may seem to follow the fashions and/or go for the avant-garde.

Vanity and Avarice

Aphrodite's mirror and her penchant for getting into contests to decide if she was 'the fairest of them all' all point to the fact that she took excessive pride in her appearance. Conceit and vanity are major Venusian traits and one is reminded that vanity comes from a Latin source meaning 'empty'. Venusian behaviour can also be overly-indulgent (of the self or others) and ingratiating. The individual with Venus run rampant may be given to flattery and is easily flattered themselves. Adolf Hitler had his Sun, Mercury and Venus in Taurus, and Libra on his Ascendant, making Venus one of the most powerful planets in his horoscope; and (speaking very simplistically) surely avarice was a strong motivating factor with him. According to Steven Erlanger in *The New York Times*,[6] Hitler amassed huge wealth, lived on a grand scale and very much enjoyed the luxuries his wealth brought him. Apparently he earned about eight million reichsmarks from *Mein Kampf* alone: 'From the time he became chancellor until his death in 1945, Hitler received some 700 million reichsmarks in corporate payments.' It was money that would have been donated for the growth of Germany as a whole, but money to which he seemingly had unlimited access.

The Arts and Music

Many parts of the horoscope potentially have a creative or artistic side (e.g. the Fifth House, planets in Libra and Pisces, Neptune), but one of the contributions of Venus is that of harmony. Not all artistic, creative or musical forms are harmonious but, where they are, the Venus placement and aspects will be the reason. Music and the arts generally are major vehicles for the giving and receiving of pleasure. Additionally, songs are a frequent way of expressing love.

Physical Characteristics

The Venus principle leans towards the soft, round and sweet. Prominently placed or linked with the Moon, it may describe a sweet tooth, for instance. When linked with Mercury it suggests sweet words. The Venusian principle is accumulative and given to ease, indulgence, luxury and comfort. It dislikes anything rough or harsh and is generally passive in nature.

Metal

The Venusian metal is copper. The Latin word *cuprum* comes from the island of Cyprus where Aphrodite first appeared. The metal is reddish and lustrous and easy to mould and shape, being flexible and very malleable (as we have seen, all things Venusian 'give'). A good conductor of heat and electricity, copper is second only to silver in its ability to conduct electricity. The electrical industry is one of the greatest users of copper – a fact that makes the link between the severed genitals of Uranus tossed into the sea, and the birth of Aphrodite out of that sea, all the more interesting. Another link with Venus and Uranus can be found in the fact that a major homœopathic remedy for epilepsy (surely a major Uranian disorder) is *cuprum*. Copper and money go together as many coins are copper alloys. Apparently, many gunmetals also contain copper and it is widely used as a component in agricultural poisons and water purification. It is also used in chemistry tests for sugar. A policeman's truncheon used to be called a 'copper stick' – at best, the job of the police is to keep the peace.

The Body

Venus is associated with venous blood and female genitalia. Venus will be one of the significators in venereal (sexually transmitted) diseases. Its main contribution to ill health lies in its penchant for over-indulgence (e.g. of food or sex) and inclination to sloth and laziness.

Venus Through The Signs

Venus can never be more than 48 degrees from the Sun in the horoscope, which means that it will always fall in the same sign as the Sun or in any one of the two signs before, or two signs after, it. As with Mercury, it can be difficult to spot the sign of a person's Venus, unless the planet is strongly placed or prominent for some other reason. Not surprisingly, people with Mercury and/or Venus falling in the same sign as their Sun usually resonate more strongly to their Sun sign than those whose Mercury and Venus are in different signs. The following notes must therefore be used very cautiously. As always, aspects to Venus will be much more important than its sign placement. The oft-used word 'relationship' in the following pages can often be used to mean all kinds of relationships – not just romantic ones.

Venus in Aries – ♀ ♈

The myth of a knight on a white charger rescuing a damsel in distress is a likely motif in relationships but there is no way of knowing whether the Venus in Aries person is the knight or the damsel (gender doesn't come into it here). A certain amount of excitement – danger, even – can feature in the love life and competition is often a theme; many with Venus here will get themselves pursued or fought over. Falling in love feet-first is a common manifestation and, as with Venus-Mars contacts, there can be a tendency to love in haste and repent at leisure. Venus and Mars are in detriment when found in each other's signs, as is the case here, and yet the feminine (Venus)/masculine (Aries) mixture seems to lend a certain sparkle to many with this placement. Many are gifted at the charm offensive and this is often a very popular and alluring Venus (Hollywood stars George Clooney, Marilyn Monroe, Doris Day, Audrey Hepburn and many others have it). Those with it can attract by virtue of being very direct and seeming almost innocent. Straight men may be attracted to the full-on type of woman, someone who may prove to be more than they can handle.

This can be a selfish and uncompromising placement, and some with Venus here give off signals that seem to say 'If you love me, you will give me what I want' or 'If you love me you will let me be myself'. Commonly, the Venus in Aries person is showered with gifts and surprises from their partner who is usually trying to prove that, to them, their beloved comes first.

Making rapid emotional and financial decisions is the norm as Venus in Aries individuals usually make strong, instant decisions as to whether they like something or someone. This person spends (emotionally and financially) on impulse.

Some will make strong statements in matters of taste, perhaps by wearing bold colours or dramatic styles. Typically, Venus in Aries types tend to cut their hair or hem-lines. It's a good placement for a hairdresser, if other chart factors concur.

Venus in Taurus – ♀ ♉

Venus is strong and at home here in its own sign, suggesting a marked capacity for enjoying life's many pleasures. Indeed, a love of the good life, certainly the comfortable life (good food, fine wines, art and music), often applies. Equally, many others gain pleasure from the simple things in life: nature, gardening and the countryside. There is often a strong sense and appreciation of touch, texture and form. This is an ideal placement for anyone who works with fabrics and it is also ideal for anyone whose life involves touch – the masseur or healer, for instance. If you want to please a Venus in Taurus person, opt for a tactile approach or produce things that feel nice or smell good. In romantic matters, be prepared to go slowly and steadily as Venus in Taurus doesn't like to be pushed (those with the Sun in Aries may be quicker on the uptake, though). Some with Venus here will attract by virtue of their voice or their touchy-feely, tactile skills or, more simply still, with their body. Many will have a good dress-sense, some will have a beautiful neck or throat.

Constant in most matters, Venus here can be associated with enduring affections and long-term relationships. However, there is a need for intimate relationships to have a strong physical contact, and if this is lacking the individual may 'play away' but, even then, will often choose to come home in the end. This can be due to the aforementioned enduring affections, because of a horror of change or because of a liking for their creature comforts; comforts that may be more readily available at home. Venus is potentially at her most materialistic in Taurus. Those with Venus here undoubtedly appreciate their body and yours but usually also like to know that there is money in your bank and theirs.

Classically, Venus in Taurus types show love through food – food and sex often come together in this sensual, orally-fixated Venus. This is a good placement for accumulating money but then, potentially, so are all personal planets falling in Taurus. Money can sometimes be gained through the construction or food industries or through the ownership of property.

Venus in Gemini – ♀ ♊

Those with Venus here may attract others with their speed or agility of thought, their conversation, or simply by being difficult to pin down. Often there is a gift for language and an appreciation of literature or poetry, and sometimes an attractive speaking or singing voice. This is a placement to associate with 'sweet words' and thus can describe someone who knows how to put others at their ease, and generally how to communicate tactfully, pleasingly and gracefully. The beautiful appearance or graceful use of the hands can also be a feature. Valuing language and education, as they do, few with this placement will be attracted for long to someone whose main attributes are their looks or their money.

A Venus in Gemini individual may be a consummate flirt and some will have little difficulty in juggling several love interests and multifarious social commitments at the same time. However, those with this placement can often also be found to be all talk and no action. In other words they can be elusive lovers, always beckoning and teasing but with no real intention of delivering. Commonly, they don't want to commit themselves because they know how easily bored they can become. Most with this Venus like to play games with lovers and friends and to keep both emotional and social situations 'light'. In fact, emotionality can be a real turn-off for some with this placement. On the other hand, anything novel or quixotic usually will appeal. However, the main thing they may want from relationships is communication. They also, on some level, often seek someone they can learn from.

Venus here implies a socially skilled individual, someone who is curious about and able to mix with all types of people. All else in the chart being equal, the Venus in Gemini person is born to network and to be a social butterfly. Many are curious about the romantic lives of others and, with their wide social circle, may have a penchant for matchmaking. In artistic matters, there can be a gift for any genre that requires a capacity for comparison. While the whole chart has to be taken into account, this placement favours loving relationships with sisters or a longing to achieve something akin to such a happy sibling relationship with the partner.

Venus in Cancer – ♀ ♋

Those with this Venus may attract others by exuding a homely, sympathetic, romantic, soft quality; by either seeming to be a child in need of nurturance and protection or by coming across as maternal, protective and all-accepting themselves. Venus in Cancer can be translated as 'the charming mother', and parental roles can loom large in relationships. There is usually a love of nesting and some will marry in order to have a home and family or for reasons of security. Some will never love anyone half as much as they love their own mother.

Classically, if they are attracted to you, those with this placement may skirt around the issue (or somehow propel you into skirting around the issue) and sidle their way into your affections. Some need to learn that faint heart never won fair anybody. The issue is often that the individual is frightened of getting hurt; taking risks with their affections is not an option. Once involved, there can be a tenacious, clinging propensity in relationships; letting go of lovers is rarely easy. Some with this placement hook up with childhood sweethearts or evermore carry a torch for an early love. Others marry long-standing boy/girlfriends whom they have been dating since the year dot. As well as implying a tendency to linger over past love affairs, this placement can be associated with an appreciation of the past generally. This can translate as a love of history or antiques, or sometimes as a sentimental valuing of objects because of the memories they carry.

In social matters generally, those with Venus in Cancer show they care for you by helping you to feel as if you belong; sometimes this is done through humour, as shared laughter always strengthens bonds between people and increases feelings of safety. Many with Venus in Cancer spend their money on beautifying their home or on buying property and, if other chart factors agree, money can be made through real estate (e.g. Donald Trump has Venus here).

Venus in Leo – ♀ ♌

Classically, those with Venus here like to be courted and pampered and hate to be ignored. At worst they are blatant attention-seekers but at best they understand another's need for acknowledgement too; they know that love and attention boost an individual's self-confidence and self-esteem. Thus, they are often skilled at hooking their preferred lovers as well as attracting people generally, simply by beaming their spotlight, warmth and charm upon them. How many of us can ignore being flattered in this way? Venus in Leo switches on 'high voltage' attention but, in turn, gets a lot of notice back. Many with this Big Cat placement are expert at both giving and receiving 'strokes'. Venus here can be associated with warmth, generosity and passion. Provided that they can seek out and bask in the warmth they need from the world at large, and provided that their partner makes them feel special too, they can be very loyal to that partner and generous towards them. If the rest of the chart accords, this charitable and warm-hearted placement can also be associated with generous gestures in the wider world.

Inevitably, emotional matters will be dramatized and made more colourful, wondrous or tragic than they actually are. Thus, this is a good placement for drama, opera and the entertainment industries generally. When projected outwards, this Venus often describes a person who is attracted to more extrovert, creative or glamorous types who can be shown off. It is the placement of so-called trophy wives and also with the idea of keeping up with the Joneses. Certainly, people with Venus here like partners they can be proud of and possessions they can feel proud of, too. Some are attracted to celebrity figures. There can be a liking for gold and precious (and even non-precious) gems. Some will spend their money on jewellery or make money from it. The placement can also be associated with banking. Many with Venus here have a special love for children.

Venus in Virgo – ♀ ♍

Those with Venus here may attract others by their apparently wholesome, modest and unassuming nature (although less so if the Sun is in Leo). They also may be attracted to people who tend to be overlooked by others; with their own particular eye for detail, no one is overlooked or missed out as a potential object of interest. However, given that Venus in Virgo tends to be discriminating in relationship matters, most objects of interest (human or otherwise) may be dismissed. What Venus in Virgo does appreciate is kindness. They can also be attracted to others who do their job (whatever it is and however humble) with care and precision. Similarly they can attract others by exuding these qualities themselves. The placement can be associated with relationships with people met at or through work.

Virgo is an independent sign and, even when involved, individuals with Venus here ensure that they remain whole unto themselves. Classically, the Venus in Virgo person shows they like you by listening to you and by catering to all your little whims. Potentially an excellent nurse, they know how to take care of you. They may also try to improve you and this can mean a certain degree of criticizing and analysing.

Venus in Virgo can be associated with discerning taste in all matters. The ability to sort out the beautiful or valuable from the non-beautiful or non-valuable can be a useful trait for those employed in the art world. It is also useful in most other industries, in terms of knowing which people to employ and which to avoid. In their taste, Venus in Virgo types tend towards understatement. Not liking things to be too flashy or showy, even if well-off, they may tend to dress down rather than up. Charity shops were just made for Virgo (and Pisces) types. Classically, they go for natural materials and fibres and appreciate products that are well-made and clothes that are tailored and cut beautifully.

Venus here can denote a particular love of animals (Brigitte Bardot has this placement) if other factors concur. Financially, this can be a successful Venus, perhaps because of the tendency to put love and care into their work or because of a tendency to think small with respect to money. Whoever first said 'take care of the pennies and the pounds will take care of themselves' may have had Venus here.

Venus in Libra - ♀ ♎

Venus, a planet much associated with relationships, is strong here in the sign most associated with marriage, civil partnership and one-to-one relationships in general. This gives us a clue about how prominent the theme of relationship is for individuals with this placement. They can be attracted to refined, gracious, cultured, congenial types and, in turn, may attract others by exuding these qualities. Uncouth behaviour is usually a no-no for this Venus. More importantly, the Venus in Libra individual enjoys the companionship of others and doesn't like to be alone. They may love the idea of marriage and be idealistic about the married state; so much so, that some seem almost set up for disappointment. They want union so much and so fervently want things to be agreeable that seeing the other person as he or she really is can prove difficult. The individual can be more in love with the idea of partnership than with the actual partner, so it is little wonder if the person, getting wind of this, strays.

Good at appearances themselves, the Venus in Libra type can easily be taken in by a charming smile and superficial good looks. Libra is an indecisive sign and Venus here can describe someone who lacks firmness when making relationship choices. Trading in their partner for a newer, younger model is rarely the goal but is certainly sometimes the outcome of the Libran penchant for being seduced by someone who is taking an interest in them.

Good at sharing, in relationships the Venus in Libra type can expect everything to be reciprocal. This can mean that they find the giving or taking of individual decisions and actions quite hard. Both Libra and Venus are concerned with peace and this can lead to an ability to compromise and to achieve conflict-free relationships. Given that they value peace, harmony and good relations so highly, these individuals tend to be diplomatic and often have good negotiating skills. Some will have the ability to heal and soothe others by managing to say the right thing and to say it charmingly. However, the reverse can also be true; the tendency to avoid confrontation at all costs can lead to scenarios where nothing is actually dealt with, so that when things come to a head (as they inevitably do), what began as an initial difference of opinion becomes an all-out battle.

Shared involvement in art, law or music often brings couples together and it is not uncommon for these subjects to be strongly shared throughout life. The financial state can be much altered for good or ill through the alliances that are formed with other people. Financial gain may also be made from the arts or sometimes through the law courts.

Venus in Scorpio - ♀ ♏

Venus is in its fall in Scorpio, where we find the planet of love and peace in one of the most uncompromising and passionate of signs. Indeed, it is the sign most associated with resentment, revenge and the deepest, almost congealed feelings. Little wonder therefore that the typical Venus in Scorpio individual doesn't enter into relationships lightly. Nor do they leave them lightly. 'If I love you I will die for you' can be the platform from which many with this very loyal Venus operate. While associated with the most passionate and possessive feelings and actions, some with Venus here may not necessarily be all that possessive themselves but will often arouse such feelings in others. Love and competition tend to go together with this Mars-ruled Venus and rivalrous, tumultuous feelings between siblings, friends and lovers are the norm. As a general rule, those with this Venus don't find it easy to share; they can be frightened that someone is going to steal their lover or their valuables. The reverse is also often true: some with this Venus are excessively generous and can lose out because of that generosity. As always, half-measures don't usually figure with planets in Scorpio.

People with this placement will go for partners who seem deep, complex, mysterious or unfathomable and may, in turn, attract others by exuding a still-waters-run-deep quality themselves. What you see is not usually what you get with Venus in Scorpio and that, or some quality of forbidden fruit, can be part of the attraction. Relationships often have a degree of mess, or at least drama, attached to them with this Venus. Perhaps because of the influence of Pluto, Venus in Scorpio relationships often have an element of the taboo about them. For instance, it is not uncommon for lovers to have to fight to have their relationship accepted because of race, religion, previous romantic entanglements, complicated finances, same-sex issues or some other prejudice. The main difficulty for those with this placement can be that of trust. If Venus is the only planet in Scorpio, the individual may be too trusting of those they are involved with and will get their fingers burnt because of it. Conversely, if Venus is one of several planets to be found in the sign, the individual may smell rats where none exist, so that friends and lovers feel that they are being watched and controlled all the time.

In matters of taste, this placement can be associated with a liking for many art forms and sometimes for strong colours. If the rest of the chart concurs, money may come through the dying process (e.g. caring for the terminally ill or working as an undertaker), through inheritance, insurance or some other aspect of the corporate world.

Venus in Sagittarius – ♀⚺

Many with Venus here will attract others because of their buoyant good humour or carefree, expectant attitude to life. They may also attract others by virtue of being foreign or will be attracted to all things foreign. As a rule, Venus in Sagittarius is attracted to the adventurous, generous and casual, and is repelled by what is small and mean-spirited. Some attract others with their dynamism (e.g. Tina Turner). Relationships with those involved in education, or with people from different cultures and with different beliefs, are the norm because relationships can be a way of exploring the world and of educating ourselves. Relationships where one person converts to the other's religion are not uncommon. For some, shared moral values can be an especially important factor in all their friendships and relationships. Often there is a *c'est la vie* attitude to love affairs and optimism triumphs over experience for many. Typically, when love affairs end, the Venus in Sagittarius person is not going to sit around moping for long. As with life generally, love affairs may be enthusiastically viewed as adventures and certainly not as an end in themselves. More attracted to the future than the past, typically this person likes novelty and fun and may be able to provide it for others. But, being restless, they may not hang around for long if bored. In relationship matters, there is a need for plenty of space and freedom. Some with this placement want to explore many relationships; few will embrace commitment easily. Appreciating fun, humour and an adventurous spirit as they do, many with this placement tend to exit if the atmosphere becomes too intense or heavy. They can be idealistic in love, but the reality of relating to the same person on a 24/7 basis can be hard, so much so that the grass may often seem greener the other side of the fence.

When called upon to teach others, there can be an ability to do so in a positive and upbeat way, thus instilling in the pupil the joy of learning. Typically, the individual themselves just loves to learn. There can also potentially be a love of God and an attraction for many kinds of religious and philosophical experiences.

Generosity with money is implied with this placement, and some will be fortunate in overseas financial affairs if the rest of the chart concurs.

Venus in Capricorn – ♀ ♑

Women especially with this placement may appear self-possessed and can attract by virtue of their dignity, poise and professionalism. Men are attracted to what they see as classy, up-market types. In work, and also in social situations, there can be an attraction for those who seem businesslike and professional; there can be a liking for people who are in control. Or the individual may attract others by displaying these qualities themselves. Venus in Capricorn types take their relationships seriously and have few illusions about love. They are often willing to make strenuous efforts to make their relationships work. Partners are often encountered through professional activities. Venus here can also be associated with love affairs in which there are age differences between the partners. Attracted to security and success, Venus in Capricorn women, especially, often go for older men; they marry their fathers in some way. Age differences or not, some enter into relationships for reasons of status or security. Attracted to appropriate behaviour themselves, most with this placement can usually be relied on to behave properly; even if insatiable in the sack, they are not likely to embarrass you in public. In romantic as well as in social situations, there is a need to appear dignified and to feel respected. Few will indulge in behaviour that might lessen that respect.

When prominently placed (e.g. on the Ascendant), Venus in Capricorn can, on occasion, give rise to exceptional looks; it can signify beautiful bone structure, flawless skin or excellent teeth. Sometimes this placement can be associated with a cool, dry, no-frills quality. In public at least, feelings tend to be kept under control. But it is also often the signature of the *professional charmer*. For instance, there are many professional singers, not only of rock (Capricorn!) or classical music but most other musical genres too, who have this Venus. Perhaps this is not surprising because many songs define what love is. Through song, people talk about the reality and often the pain of love – all of which is in keeping with a Saturnian type of Venus. Examples include Frank Sinatra, Edith Piaf, Elvis Presley, Robbie Williams, Alicia Keys, Justin Timberlake, Bjork, Britney Spears, Placido Domingo and Dolly Parton. Sun Capricorn Annie Lennox has her Venus in Scorpio but it is conjunct Saturn, which gives it a Venus in Capricorn flavour. This placement can also be associated with people who deal in gemstones or work with valuable rocks, such as those who make or sell jewellery.

Venus in Aquarius – ♀ ♒

The beauties of nature and the companionship of friends bring happiness with this placement. There is usually a marked affection for friends, and commonly friends become lovers and lovers turn into friends. There isn't a huge dividing line between the two. Some with Venus in Aquarius attract others with their refreshingly different, possibly quirky, open and friendly demeanour (or are attracted to such qualities), while others attract by virtue of their seeming coolness (e.g. Marlene Dietrich).

While this Venus often indicates a friendly, sociable, even convivial, person in general terms, when it comes to getting involved in a more intimate way there can be a tendency to play it cool. A huge percentage of possible liaisons may be rejected or at least kept at a friendly, but detached, arm's length. Thus, while this is the placement of the individual who adores their friends and generally always needs a pal, there can also be something of the lone wolf about this Venus. Friends and lovers can come from all walks of life; this person mixes with everyone, irrespective of creed, colour, class or income. In fact, the preference is usually for someone who is both different and ordinary: someone outside their own predictable social circle. There is usually something at least slightly unconventional about Venus in Aquarius relationships.

As with all personal planets falling in Aquarius, independence is a keyword and one manifestation of Venus in this sign can be the idea of the independent woman (either being her or being attracted to her). Another is that the choice of partners and friends will always be arrived at independently; these individuals are not affected by the expectations or values of their family, of society or of their other friends. Interested in what makes people tick, those with this Venus tend to be more attracted by the inner person than by outward appearances; sincerity is a character trait that is highly prized. Commonly, they attract others by taking an active interest in them. Some with this placement like to feel that they are helping other people to make progress in their lives, and they are usually attracted to others who are similarly interested in humanity.

Frequently there is an enjoyment of nature; a beautiful landscape (the wilder the better) can really stir the spirit. There can be a liking for gadgets and a willingness to spend money on them. Money may also be made and lost through electronic and technological services as well as through friendships.

Venus in Pisces – ♀ ♓

This is a romantic placement and one that conjures up the feminine images of princess, mermaid, ballerina and movie star. Quite a passive placement, there can be an ability to seduce others without the individual apparently having to say or do anything, except maybe flutter an eyelash or two. Some may themselves be easily seduced and open to almost anything. There can be a tendency to lose themselves in relationships. As with Venus/Neptune contacts, love can involve losing or surrendering the self in some way and often demands that some kind of sacrifice be made. Equally, relationships can be a route to escaping the drudgery of everyday life. Classically, the Venus in Pisces type wants or needs to devote themselves to something or somebody. Venus is exalted in Pisces and one reason for that can be attributed to sexism (the essentially passive and alluring nature of this placement) but another, possibly related reason, is that Venus here finds it so easy to co-operate. On the down side there can be difficulty in standing firm.

Some Venus in Pisces individuals have problems committing themselves emotionally; they don't know if they love you and may just want to bask in your loving them. Commitment can imply the closing of doors to other possibilities. Ever reluctant to lose sight of the initial wistful, romantic quality of a love affair, love is definitely not linked to ownership with Venus in Pisces, and many with this placement get hooked up in scenarios which don't involve binding contracts. Some with this placement may feel more comfortable in a platonic relationship or end up in one. This can be because the person is drawn to a more spiritual and universal idea of love; for some, the sexual act can feel far too crass.

Depending on the chart overall, some with Venus here will attract others by seeming to be insecure and dejected. A possible scenario is that the other person simply feels sorry for, and wishes to rescue, Venus in Pisces. On the other hand, some with this placement are attracted to people who, for whatever reason, are weak and unable to get their lives together. Addictive patterns can feature, so relationships with dependency and non-dependency issues can go with the territory, as, on occasion, can deception in financial matters.

On the plus side, Venus in Pisces types have the potential to heal others by virtue of their accepting nature, a quality that can make them very easy to be with.

This placement can be associated with a love of music and, more especially, an appreciation of dance. As with Piscean placements generally, money can be spent on shoes and there can be a fondness for having their feet massaged!

Mars ♂

'Serious sport is war minus the shooting.'

George Orwell

'Violence is the repartee of the illiterate.'

George Bernard Shaw

Astronomy

- Mean distance from the Sun: approximately 142 million miles/228 million kilometres.
- Diameter: approximately 4222 miles/6794 kilometres.
- Sidereal period (approximate time for planet to orbit the Sun): 687 days
- Retrograde motion: roughly every two years for nearly 80 days.
- Moons: Mars has two moons; Deimos (panic) and Phobos (fear), discovered by Asaph Hall in 1877.

Mythology

To the Romans, Mars was held in high regard as a defender and protector of the community. He was the god of spring, fertility and agriculture as well as war. However, the Greek version of the god (Ares) had a poor reputation and was seen as uncontrolled and too easily provoked. Homer repeatedly described Ares as being bloodthirsty, stupid and not knowing right from wrong. He was represented as wounded, defeated and whining. Loyalty to his men or his children, or to simply wreak revenge (like his mother Hera), was his primary motivation. Perhaps this is not surprising given his parentage: philandering Zeus hurling thunderbolts from Mount Olympus for a father and the jealous, vengeful Hera for a mother. Ares' first tutor was Priapus, who taught him dancing and warfare. As well as being god of gardens and vineyards, Priapus lent his name to priapism, a condition characterized by a painfully erect penis incapable of ejaculation. Ares had no wife and is best-known for his affair with Aphrodite, the goddess of love, who was married to the disabled smith-god Hephaestus. Ares fathered many children including four with Aphrodite. He was the only god who took steps to protect and take action on behalf of his children and others he cared about. As always, the Martian impulse pushes us to get involved, admittedly perhaps to interfere inappropriately, but coming from a Mars perspective the individual is never a bystander.

Companions to Ares on the battlefield were his sister Eris (Discord), and her son Strife, plus his own two sons, Phobos and Deimos (Fear and Panic). In wars, Ares is often depicted as fighting on the so-called wrong side. In the Trojan War, he fought against the Greeks (his own people) and basically was fighting against his own best interests. Similarly, when we are too easily provoked, we are also usually fighting against our own best interests; we are likely to get ourselves into serious trouble and court displeasure from those who may otherwise have supported us. Whenever we decide to stick our neck out and assert ourselves in some way, whenever we say 'I want', we risk disappointment as the other party can refuse us. In other words, we become vulnerable.

The Principle of Doing

Mars represents the principles of passion, drive and doing. It converts whatever it touches in the horoscope into fuel and therefore into action. Mars by sign, and especially by aspect, will often contribute information as to how we set about doing things: what spurs us into action and the kind of action we take.

Daring and Vulnerability

Mars rules Aries, the first sign of the zodiac and, like that sign, the planet can be associated with a drive to be in at the start of things. Whenever we do something for the first time, e.g. initiating a new activity or project, we may get it wrong and make a fool of ourselves. As the Greek god Ares, Mars was god of war but by no means the god of victory; in fact, he often lost. As soon as we dare, we are vulnerable because we might lose or make mistakes. The Mars in our charts may show where we dare to put ourselves on the line and take a risk. In this area, we may dare to deviate from the consensus view and strike out on our own. Risk-taking contributes to the progress of a society; if no one had ever dared, there would have been little progress. Our Mars will show where, when, how and in what way we may dare to show our strength. And when we have dared, our cards are on the table. What we want is clearly expressed and can be denied to us. In Mars mode we say 'I want that' and we then become vulnerable because others can say 'No'. Mars has rulership over the male genitalia and one only has to consider the male sexual organs, which hang outside the body and can easily be axed, to understand how vulnerable the Mars principle is.

Strength and Courage

Our capacity for daring is often an indicator of how much we can take something on the chin, how prepared we are to put ourselves on the line, to make a fool of ourselves, even. Thus, our Mars will say much about the nature of our strength (physically and psychologically), our capacity for courage, our ability to endure, to rough it and survive in less than perfect situations.

The Principle of Assertion

Myths associated with Mars often depict him as fighting on behalf of others. This, arguably, is a positive manifestation of the Martian impulse. However, we often miss the extent to which we are personally involved in the issue, the extent to which we are actually defending our own ego and personal interests. Basically, our Mars is concerned with the way we assert ourselves and which areas of life make us want to assert ourselves. To assert ourselves is to declare our interests, to affirm, to be positive, to maintain our position in the face of pressure not to do so.

How we go about getting what we want is a large part of the survival/assertion aspect of Mars. In Mars mode, we want our own way and are prepared to fight (or at least assert ourselves in some way) in order to get it. People vary hugely in the manner in which they go about getting their needs met: some will turn on the tears, others will pull strings behind the scenes, some will sulk and some will argue the toss. Some are taught that it is wrong to be selfish (perhaps Mars is in hard aspect with Saturn) and then may find it difficult to ask directly for something they want. Others may have been raised in an overly competitive environment and have picked up the cues that the only way to survive is to push themselves forward. Still others (perhaps with a prominent Venus) will have learned the charm offensive. Whatever the methodology for survival, we can become more conscious of the underlying psychology and perhaps learn new strategies by studying our Mars placement and aspects.

Being assertive does not mean riding roughshod over another, although a mishandled Mars can indeed impel us to do just that. This is a common misuse of its energy and explains why Mars has such a poor reputation. Good practice in assertion requires the use of Venus as well as Mars, for a degree of compromise and a healthy respect for the needs of others are often required for successful outcomes to be achieved. However, concentrating only on the Mars end of the spectrum, it is easy to see why we may find it hard to be assertive. Such difficulties may be linked to planets that are in aspect to Mars or more prominent than Mars. Perhaps we find it difficult to be assertive because we want to be popular and fit in (Venus). Perhaps we lack confidence or are fearful (Saturn). Perhaps we feel impotent (Saturn and Pluto). Maybe taking the easy way out seems much more attractive or we want to be viewed as a nice person (Venus), and so on.

Defence, Territory and the Causes of War

The qualities associated with Mars are needed to defend our territory, whether the territory is our body, our children, friends, house or country. Our Mars will describe what we construe as being our territory. It will also describe with whom and in what situations we are most likely to feel threatened. Clearly, Mars has an essential protective role to play and only becomes problematic if the individual (or country) is overly territorial or feels too easily threatened. Iron is the metal to associate with Mars and interestingly, iron deficiency (anaemia) has been shown, in studies with incarcerated young men, to be a direct cause of aggressive behaviour. In other words, it is when we feel weak that we feel more easily threatened. It is precisely at those times that we are more likely to strike out aggressively. Arguably, all disputes between people, and all wars between nations, arise out of a situation where the individual or group feels threatened by another individual or group.

Mars and Crime

Whereas Venus urges us to find points of agreement, the Mars principle urges us to see points of disagreement and dissimilarity. As well as showing the difficulties we may have in defending ourselves, our Mars may also describe a tendency to be too eager to fight, perceiving threats from outside where none were intended. A mismanaged Mars can incline towards aggression and antisocial behaviour. Crime of all kinds, not just violent crime, owes a lot to the Martian impulse. Theft, for example, is a selfish and uncivilized act and it also requires considerable daring. Criminals have no regard for the victims of the crime. Theft also implies that the thief wants something *now*: there is no patient attempt to obtain the object, whatever it is, the hard way, through work or saving for it.

Survival, Competition and Sport

Mars describes our desire and will to survive. Fighting for life implies being attached to living and so perhaps Mars, as well as Venus, can be taken as a barometer of our capacity to enjoy life. Mars helps us live. It is also Mars that we associate with all forms of competition. Sport is a good vehicle for expressing the competitive spirit because we can compete with ourselves as well as with others. Viewed in this light, competition can also be seen to be a major motivator toward excellence. Aspects to our Mars and, to some extent, the planet's sign and house, will indicate what we feel about the whole area of competition in its various guises. It will also describe whether or not an individual is a good loser.

The 'Oomph' Factor

Because the Mars principle is so honestly go-getting, when prominent it can add great spirit and gusto to the personality, although when unrestrained it can also suggest much forcefulness. Nevertheless, Mars contributes to the idea of personality. A weak Mars implies a lack of get up and go, a lack of 'oomph'. While we are all taught not to be selfish, the reality is that no one likes a doormat. And we don't trust someone who toes the party line, and we are rightly suspicious of too much sweet talk, because we like to know where a person genuinely stands. On the whole, people value individuality, they value a person who has guts. Providing it is not uncontrolled, people value the Mars principle because it is honest and it gets things done. A prominent Mars increases the fiery quality of a chart and can help to offset some of the problems associated with a lack of fire.

Sex

In sex and romantic love, Mars is concerned with chase, conquest and penetration. Our Mars by sign and aspect will say much about how we experience our sexuality. It will show what we find sexually exciting as well as what others may find exciting about us. In sexual matters, as elsewhere, how do we get our needs met? With what ease or difficulty do we pursue what we want? In a woman's chart (along with her Sun), Mars will often describe an inner image of men, especially younger men. Such an image may well reflect the kind of men she becomes involved with (romantically or otherwise) or finds attractive. Gay men will often be attracted to either the Mars or solar principles in their charts, too.

Fighting Disease and Depression

When working well, Mars helps us to fight off unwanted pressure from the outside world. It can also give us the 'oomph' to cope with internal psychological pressure. Mars may also have some bearing on the body's ability to fight off ill health and disease. In diseases such as cancer, we hear that people have 'won' or 'lost' their battle. Indeed, a healthy response to cancer, in terms of survival, is to give full rein to the messages associated with the Sun and Mars.

People who have become depressed are usually having problems with the Mars principle. Sometimes this is because what is considered inadmissible anger is being turned inwards on the self. Sometimes it is because we feel crushed and powerless. The act of doing something, and thereby discovering that we are not helpless and impotent, is often a major route out of a depressive phase. And as perhaps any sex therapist will concur, if people can be helped to express their anger, resentment and negative feelings, then their sex lives become more satisfying. In various contexts, unexpressed anger creates feelings of impotence.

Physical Characteristics

The Mars principle is hot, sharp and fast. Mars will tend to quicken the expression of whichever planet it touches in the horoscope and whichever house it is found in. Areas touched by Mars will be speeded up and the individual may be impatient to express what that area signifies. In that particular area, if in no other, the individual may become heated or come on strong.

Metal

Iron, the metal associated with Mars, is used wherever a defence is required: in gates, armour, helmets and tanks, for instance. Basically, iron is used to prevent threats from outside penetrating within. The purpose of the old so-called Iron Curtain between the USA and USSR was a barrier between the two nations. Iron is an abundant metal which has been used since prehistoric times to make tools and weapons. Flexible but nevertheless tough, it is also very reactive and corrodes easily. Objects made from iron will rust and disintegrate quickly if they are not protected. So, despite their strength, objects made from iron are also vulnerable. Mars is a major significator in all occupations and industries that use the metal, such as industries which make or use tools for agriculture, building, warfare, the kitchen or the operating theatre. Mars has been known since the earliest times as the red planet, due to its reddish colour created by the iron oxide on its surface. Individuals with red or rusty-coloured hair inevitably have the planet strongly placed, often in contact with the Ascendant.

The Body

As well as the male genitalia, Mars has rulership over muscle where a lot of heat is made and stored. We talk about 'putting muscle into something' when we are exerting strength. Arterial (oxygenated) blood can be particularly associated with the planet and 65% of the iron to be found in the body is found in the red blood cells. A lack of iron (anaemia) is the most common nutritional deficiency and can have ramifications for our intake of oxygen. Physically, as well as psychologically, when we feel strong we feel as if we can breathe; when feeling weak, we don't.

Mars is a significator in all kinds of surgery, accidents and injuries. Accidents, by their very nature, are caused by misplaced energy and are therefore at least partially Martian. Uranus is also often in the picture as being a significator of the unexpected and shocking. Bites and biting (and love bites) also come under its domain, as do burns, cuts, grazes and stings. Mars rules all inflammatory situations (psychological as well as physical) and thus will always be in the frame in any kind of 'itis' (tonsillitis, colitis, hepatitis, and so on) or ulceration.

In the World at Large

Again, Mars will be a prime mover in any inflammatory situations. In a nation's chart it will say something about how territorial and aggressive the country is. The army and military generally come under its domain. When symbolizing young men, it will have much to say about the youth of the nation and will be one of the significators for criminal activity and internal troubles such as rioting. Mars may be associated with right-wing politics, which tends to favour free enterprise and competition.

Mars Through The Signs
Mars in Aries – ♂ ♈

General Characteristics

Working well, Mars in its own sign adds courage, ardour, strength and daring to the horoscope, plus a capacity for taking quick, decisive action. Not afraid to get involved, Mars in Aries contributes leadership potential to a chart. This placement inclines to independence – an insistence on doing your own thing and in your own way. Indeed, the Mars in Aries person may prefer to do things on their own as everyone else can seem so slow! Not a strategist, the Mars in Aries type tends to be direct, straightforward and self-motivated. It is a great placement for competitive sports, particularly any kind of racing. Anger may be easily aroused but typically will die down quickly, too. There is a swashbuckling quality to this Mars which conjures up images of Robin Hood and the Scarlet Pimpernel.

Under Stress

If borne out by other chart factors, this placement can be associated with feelings of frustration and often rash, brash, pushy and unco-operative behaviour. The person may 'strain at the leash' to start things but not necessarily finish them. The type can lack staying power – a capacity for endurance needs to be found elsewhere in the chart. There can be an overly developed tendency to 'look after Number One'. Mars here can also be accident-prone, with the head and face being particularly prone to scarring.

Sexually

Directness in sexual matters can be expected, plus a liking for the chase, but the individual may not be so interested in the long haul. The ardent feelings felt for someone can fizzle out when that individual has been caught. At best, Mars here can mean that a person is not frightened to take the initiative, at worst it can indicate someone who lacks subtlety. There can be an attraction to daredevil or dynamic types. As Stephen Arroyo has noted,[7] there can sometimes also be an attraction for those in uniform.

Mars in Taurus – ♂ ♉

General Characteristics

For many with this practical and realistic Mars, striving for material security takes top priority. This person may compete with you over ownership. They might compete when shopping, liking to find the bargains before you do, for instance. The desire to accumulate can be strong. Certainly, there can be a need to conquer the material world or at least to feel that they are not going to be crushed by it. For some, tremendous determination can result in business success and it is also an ideal placement for the construction trades and agriculture. There is a need to see concrete results for their efforts. The type may get their own way by refusing to budge; winning the everyday battles of life by simply standing their ground and 'hanging on in there'. Depending on the chart overall, there can be an enormous resistance to change, and asking a Mars in Taurus person to move can be like waving a red rag at a bull. And this may be the main feature that gets others angry – that *they* have to do much of the bending and accommodating in various situations.

Under Stress

A risk to their security, or a call for change, is what is likely to arouse anger. This can be a very angry placement if only because the anger is so often controlled and restrained that, if and when it does blow, it can be explosive. There can be tremendous stubbornness, a tendency to bully and, depending on the chart overall, a 'might makes right' attitude. Neck pain can sometimes result from pent-up anger or unexpressed sexual feelings. Some people inadvertently (or purposefully) express anger and passion with the help of material objects. Mars here can be associated with plates crashing or flying – the proverbial 'bull in a china shop'. In mundane terms, Mars here can be associated with aggression towards or from the police. It can be an anti-peace placement.

Sexually

As with material possessions, those with Mars here can be very possessive of their partners. Arroyo points out that Mars in Taurus men, especially, like to be the big provider in their relationships.[8] It is a kind of 'this-is-what-men-do' (pay for everything) way of operating. This is potentially a very sensual and sexual placement. In romantic matters, as elsewhere, the hallmark of Mars in Taurus is patience and stamina. A person's voice or neck can be the great attractor or detractor.

Mars in Gemini – ♂ ♊

General Characteristics

Tremendous resourcefulness is the hallmark of this placement. These people can often get themselves out of, or talk their way out of, any tight corner. Frequently there is dexterity in activities requiring quick body-eye co-ordination, such as in tennis, football and darts. Competition in communication is implied, perhaps following on from having to compete with too many voices around the breakfast table or something similar. There can be a liking for debate, with the individual being able to argue from opposing points of view. This individual is likely to enjoy newspapers, journals, word games, crosswords and the like. Driving may be enjoyed and there may be mechanical skills. This is a good placement for the journalist competing for stories, the salesperson, taxi-driver or mechanic. A good deal of everyday coming and going and many short journeys are implied with Mars here.

Under Stress

The person be argumentative and prone to point-scoring. Well-delivered barbed comments and sarcasm can be the norm. Conflict, or at least competition with siblings, is highly likely. There can also be a tendency to be accident-prone, such as often cutting or burning their hands. Surgery involving hands and limbs is also possible if other chart factors concur. Some people are prone to respiratory infections. Mars here can also be associated with insect bites and stings.

Sexually

This type is full of curiosity; they want to know about sex. What do other people get up to in bed and why, and what's it like? Aside from the mind, the part of the body that may be of most interest is the hands. There can be an attraction for younger lovers or perhaps it is the person's own apparent youth that others are attracted to. They will tend to be attracted to those with a fine mind or at least a glib tongue, and also to the writer, the teacher or the person who can sell snow to the Eskimos. Good communication, having a dexterity with language, can be the turn-on here. Typically, the Mars in Gemini person won't like relationships to get too heavy or formulaic, but will stay attracted to a partner who can keep things light and fun.

Mars in Cancer – ♂ ♋

General Characteristics

Those with Mars in its fall tend to get what they want in a roundabout kind of way. This placement implies either fighting for family, tradition and heritage or fighting against it, depending on the chart overall. In any event, going into battle when loved ones are felt to be under threat is the norm. This is a fiercely protective Mars but may be prone to interfering inappropriately. Fighting for the home can sometimes occur literally, such as when there is a dispute over the ownership of land, or following marital breakdown. Some experience of domestic discord in early, if not later, life is implied. In some cultures and times, the home may be given over to the State for war purposes. For some, fighting for their home will mean issues of patriotism; perhaps involvement in the Territorial Army, Home Guard or simply arguing with the family over matters of ownership. A lot of energy can be directed into home improvements; this is an excellent placement for do-it-yourself activities.

Under Stress

The sensitivity to threat can make for an overly defensive and touchy attitude, and to easily feeling slighted. Unexpressed anger can also lead to the holding of grudges. Dangers and malign intent from others may be perceived on very scant evidence. The difficulty in being direct can lead to sulks and smouldering moods. There may be some tendency to gastric upsets and stomach ulcers, but only if the rest of the chart concurs. There is often a sensitivity to eggs and sometimes to other dairy products.

Sexually

Potentially, this is a very responsive placement. An ability to create safety and a need to feel safe are often key in sexual relationships. There may be an above-average need for fidelity and a partner who comes home each night. Unresolved anger, or competitive issues with mother figures or even the result of premature weaning, can spill out into other relationships. A sexual fixation on women's breasts is not uncommon and there can be an attraction to men who have developed chests, too.

Mars in Leo – ♂ ♌

General Characteristics

Mars here can be associated with gallantry, chivalry and fighting for their honour. Anger can be aroused by the real or imagined superiority of others. The Mars in Leo person doesn't like to be made to feel small, and feelings of injured pride can be what spurs them into battle. This is a great placement for chess (a game where two royal houses do battle). More active pursuits might include jousting, duelling (honourable warfare) and fencing but more especially boxing, whether as observer, partner of the participant or actual fighter. Pride may be taken in sporting prowess. Fighting for or against king or country may apply with this placement, thus both republicans and royalists can have Mars here.

Under Stress

This 'medal*lion* man' Mars may be prone to bluff and boasting, to giving an appearance of strength while closer inspection reveals nought but bravado and bluster. Some with Mars here may be too proud to express anger. A common manifestation is for the individual to feel insulted and personally attacked far too easily. For instance, the slightly barbed joke or comment is not easily forgotten or shrugged off. The fixed quality of this Mars can ensure that the person holds on to their anger. I am reminded of a friend who still talks and fumes about a time when, sorting through produce to find the best fruit on a market stall, the stall-holder quipped, 'This is not fucking Harrods, dear.'

Sexually

The person may be attracted to creative types and certainly to those who are wholeheartedly committed to something. There may be a need to be proud of, or even to be able to show off, their partner. If trying to impress a Mars in Leo person, buying the best theatre tickets might be an idea. Chase a Mars in Leo person by showing them that they are special. Meanness or small-mindedness will be the ultimate turn-off. Generally speaking, the Mars in Leo person may turned on by fun and also by a bit of drama.

Mars in Virgo – ♂ ♍

General Characteristics

This is an ideal placement for the artisan, the carpenter, the craftsperson and the individual who is some other kind of specialist. Mars in Virgo can be fuelled by the irritation caused by faulty functioning and bad service; ideally, the individual puts energy into improving the situation. There is a tendency to get angry over little things, even to waging war on insects (and other small pests). Adaptability, coupled with an ability to master detail, can lead to technical wizardry of all kinds. Mars in Virgo conjures up the notion of military service, ambulance-driving or involvement with organizations such as the Red Cross. Arguments at work are possible with the individual getting angry if, for whatever reason, they are not allowed to do their job properly or are accused of not having done it well enough.

Under Stress

This can be an irritable, carping, nagging Mars. Not usually prone to dramatic outbursts of anger and passion, unless the rest of the chart suggests it, there can be anger at their own (and others') inadequacies. For some, the difficulty in accepting their own imperfections and those of others can get in the way of accomplishing anything at all, and yet Mars in Virgo is best when actively doing something and being helpful. There can sometimes be a tendency to project their own critical faculty on to others, in which instance the person may erroneously feel that they are being attacked for minor imperfections.

Sexually

Although the cliché of the Mars in Virgo individual repeatedly washing themselves and disliking the messiness of sexual relations is unlikely to be true very often, nevertheless, this placement can be associated with a degree of finesse and fastidiousness in such matters. Women with this placement who project their Mars may be prone to attracting partners who are overly critical. Some may attract others by virtue of their kindness, conscientious or skilfulness in some area, or they may be attracted themselves to people with similar qualities. The Mars in Virgo person may be perceived as being attractive because of being 'small but perfectly formed', or they may find this quality attractive in others. Understatement is likely to be more of a turn-on than the reverse but, as always, the whole chart has to be studied.

Mars in Libra – ♂ ♎

General Characteristics
Mars, in its detriment, can be associated with a tendency to go into battle over perceived injustices. Those with Mars here put energy into adjusting imbalances as they see them. Winston Churchill and Margaret Thatcher both had Mars here. The capacity to fight other people's battles makes this an excellent placement for the law and indeed for any vocation which involves taking sides while at the same time seemingly following a drive for peace, harmony and conciliation. Some with Mars here can charm their way out of a paper bag. Some are extremely gifted at getting what they want, smiling sweetly as every request is granted. There is sometimes a need to do things in partnership with another person, whether this is going to the shops or some larger project. Many with Mars here act or wage some sort of war to gain the approval of others. The deaf percussionist Evelyn Glennie, who could be defined as 'beating out a harmony', has Mars in Libra on her Ascendant and I have seen this placement with other drummers.

Under Stress
The person can be competitive in relationship; either competing for a partner or competing with their partner. They may project aggression onto others, seeing themselves as the reasonable, fair and peaceable one, and others as pushy and hostile. Mars here can be very partisan. Arguments, discord and unrest can be created due to a tendency to fight too strongly from one side or to try to force an unrealistic co-operation between factions. Often feelings have to be acknowledged and aired before peace can be arrived at, and Mars in Libra may not pay enough attention to this.

Sexually
They are civilized – not keen on coarseness or too much rough and tumble. They are attracted to charming, civilized types or they attract others through their own charm and reasonableness. They will actively seek out partners, and can be direct and decisive about such matters. An early marriage or important committed relationship is very typical.

Mars in Scorpio – ♂ ♏

General Characteristics
Mars is strongly placed here in its own sign. Strong on subtlety, those with Mars here may undertake tasks with the gentlest of covert movements. There is a tendency to control their strength. Despite this, those with Mars in Scorpio tend to do nothing by half-measures. Often they will act in secret and this placement can make for a good strategist. There can be tremendous endurance, and once a course of action has been

embarked upon there is an unrelenting ability to see it through. Individuals with this placement tend to get their own way through what might be termed 'psychological warfare' – an ability to penetrate the psyche of the other person. A probing attitude and a tendency to leave no stone unturned inclines to thoroughness in action. Some with Mars in Scorpio are fuelled into battle by matters of loyalty. Betrayals are not easily forgiven.

Under Stress

There can be difficulties in releasing anger. For some with this placement the feelings go so deep, and are so emotional and perhaps irrational, that it is difficult to rant and rage. But problems in expressing difficult feelings can lead to an inability to let go and forgive. This is turn can lead to vengefulness and a cynical outlook.

Sexually

They tend to be drawn to strong, still-waters-run-deep, silent types or at least to those with a degree of emotional depth. They may attract others by displaying these qualities themselves. There will usually be sexual secrets in the lives of those with this placement emphasized, and an ability to penetrate such mysteries in the lives of others. Mars here can be associated with a passionate nature and an intense emotional life. When emotionally involved, the person can be quite jealous, sometimes suspecting infidelity for no good reason.

Mars in Sagittarius – ♂♐

General Characteristics

Those with Mars here have a need to fully believe in why they are involved in the projects that attract them. The placement implies fighting for or against a belief system. Potentially, it can mean war on behalf of or against their own god or other people's gods. Fighting abroad, or getting oneself into various scrapes when overseas, is also within the symbolism. If prominently placed, Mars in Sagittarius can give rise to tremendous zeal with respect to what the individual believes. This may or may not have anything to do with religion, but the potential for arguments over education, politics or religion is high. This is a restless, adventurous position for Mars, ideal for travellers and outdoors types. It is ideal, too, for the Boy Scout and Girl Guide, and also for anyone who enjoys walking. The imposition of limits or responsibilities can feel especially aggravating to those with Mars here.

Under Stress

If prominent and receiving stressful aspects, those with Mars here can become self-righteous and prone to getting on their high horse over the perceived incompetence or moral sloppiness of other people. 'Moral outrage' is a good phrase for this politically clumsy placement. This can also be the placement of the cowboy – the undisciplined person who executes tasks in a sloppy, casual style. Accidents while over-stretching themselves, while they are overseas or while horse-riding, although not the most common manifestations of this placement, are well within the symbolism.

Sexually

There can be an attraction for sporty or outdoor types, or even merely to the leg and hip areas of the body. Some may be attracted to tomboys or be attractive to others because of their own tomboy characteristics. There is a need for sex to be fun; for some, a limitless supply of sexual partners can be a way of exploring and learning about the world. Mars in Sagittarius can be rather rumbustious for more subtle types but, as always, the chart as a whole has to be studied. Sexual relationships with those from other cultures and sexual adventures while abroad may feature.

Mars in Capricorn – ♂ ♑

General Characteristics
Mars is exalted in Capricorn; the Martian energy is harnessed in Saturn's sign, resulting potentially in tremendous self-control, self-reliance and executive ability. If prominent, it adds a responsible, hard-working quality to the horoscope with the capacity to focus and sustain energies. Depending on the chart overall, this is an ideal placement for those who work on the land or with rock or stone. It is ideal, too, for a military career or anywhere that strength can be harnessed. Yoga may be enjoyed, for instance. If ambition is shown elsewhere in the chart, then Mars in Capricorn can give the capacity to fight their way to the top. Fighting for or against authority (and sometimes the personal father) is a common manifestation of Mars in Capricorn. The individual may either be someone who gets angry at the perceived conservative attitudes or pettifogging of those in authority, or who becomes enraged at perceived threats to customs and traditions that have stood the test of time. Any planet in Capricorn can have a strong sense of class and those with Mars placed here can feel threatened by people who come from a different social class to their own.

Under Stress
People with this self-sufficient, stiff-upper-lip Mars may defend themselves by adopting a reserved and dignified outer shell, forever fighting off any evidence of vulnerability. Unresolved feelings of anger towards their father may unconsciously spill out on to other authority figures, such as the boss at work. More specifically, Mars here, especially in contact with Uranus, can suggest either the person themselves or their father having knee-replacement surgery.

Sexually
Sex and status can go together, with individuals significantly increasing their own status or significantly improving the status of others. There can be sexual attraction to older men and father figures, and sometimes to those who work on the land or beneath it (e.g. farming and mining) or who have a spartan lifestyle. Or sometimes there can be attraction for men who are austere, granite-like or harsh. Some with Mars here may attract others by exuding such qualities themselves. Age differences are common in relationships. There can be an attraction for those in authority or for those with an air of authority. In romantic relationships, as elsewhere, the principle of control can be key.

Mars in Aquarius – ♂ ♒

General Characteristics
Potentially the placement of a truly independent spirit, some with Mars here expend a good deal of energy in defending the ways they differ from others. They may dislike being thought of as being the same as everyone else. Indeed, there can be a fighting for or against unconventionality. Some with Mars here feel threatened by others who appear to be uncontrollable and independent; therefore, this may or may not be an

unconventional placement. In terms of anger, a lack of freedom for themselves or others can be what makes this individual see red. This is a good placement for a person who fights battles for the group, whether the group is large or small, local or international. Anger can be aroused by perceived injustices and unfair practices suffered by various members of society. Such injustices can provide the fuel towards action. This individual will often also fight battles for their friends or, at the very least, be happy to roll up their sleeves to support and generally be helpful towards their friends. The sign placement of Mars will often describe the nature of their tools: in Aquarius, computers and other technology are implied. Individuals with Mars here may have skills either in electronics or electrical appliances and, more specifically, in information technology.

Under Stress

They may get angry over matters of intolerance, as they see it. A tendency to get angry with friends, instead of seeing how much they have in common, can frequently occur. Like Mars-Uranus contacts, but less so, this placement is ideal for any kind of freedom-fighter. There can be an insistence on doing things in their own way, and a tendency to feel annoyed when not allowed to do so. Some with this placement believe they should be free to do exactly what they want, when they want, and without restraint. When angry, some with Mars here will behave in a cold, aloof and brusque way.

Sexually

Many with Mars here will have an experimental, broad and open-minded approach towards sexual matters. Alternatively, life may ensure that such a position has to be struggled for. For some, the choice of partner may be an act of rebellion. Sexual relationships and complications with friends often feature in the life, with friends becoming lovers and vice versa. They may attract others by seeming to be different, sincere or honest, or may be attracted to such qualities in others. The quality of detachment is likely to be in evidence. The placement can signify attraction to those involved in technology, electronics and so on.

Mars in Pisces – ♂♓

General Characteristics

Depending on the chart overall, those with Mars here may have a tendency to drift into situations and, once in them, to be swept off-course. A degree of focus and discipline needs to be provided by other parts of the horoscope. Typically, Mars in Pisces types assert themselves by being difficult to get hold of. Escapism and elusiveness are the great survival mechanisms. Like a fish swirling under foliage, with some species even throwing up ink or dust, Mars in Pisces can have a gift for camouflage. This is not an aggressive position for Mars but some with the placement prominent will fight for the underdog. The suffering of others can be what causes anger. This is a good placement for service to others as well as for those who direct their energies into the arts or mystical matters. It is also good for decorators and painters (I have seen Sun conjunct Mars in Pisces several times in the charts of people whose fathers were decorators). In terms of sport, it is an ideal placement for fishing, swimming and all water sports.

Under Stress

Although obviously not applicable to everyone, Mars in Pisces is a common placement in those prone to drink and drug addictions. Mars here can also be associated with alcohol-related violence. Often the individual will, at some point, be on the receiving end of such behaviour. The anger of those with Mars placed here tends to be diffused and free-floating, and might alight on anyone or anything.

Sexually

There can be tremendous sensitivity in sexual matters and here, as elsewhere, the individual can take on the role of rescuer. This is a romantic and idealistic Mars that needs (and may be able to provide) a degree of sensitivity, mystery and fantasy. It is a tremendous placement for dancing and for wooing lovers on the dance floor. This is a common placement in those who have multiple marriages. It can also be found in those who pursue a promiscuous lifestyle. The reason for this is a strong urge to merge with another, a yearning for union, perhaps for the ultimate sexual-cum-mystical experience. In addition, there is often a general openness to others, an ability to seduce and be seduced; this Mars is not a very discriminating one.

Jupiter ♃

'A positive attitude may not solve all your problems,
but it will annoy enough people to make it worth the effort.'

Herm Albright, quoted in *The Boston Globe*

Astronomy

Fifth furthest from the Sun, Jupiter is by far the largest planet in our solar system, being twice as big as all the other planets combined (the Sun, being a star, is not included here) and 318 times larger than the Earth. After the Sun, Moon, and Venus, Jupiter is also usually the brightest object in the sky (occasionally Mars is brighter). It is often mistaken for a star but is actually three times brighter than Sirius, the brightest star. It has a fast rotation period (less than ten hours) with turbulent weather patterns of violent storms and extreme winds. Along with Saturn, Uranus and Neptune, Jupiter is one of the so-called gas planets, being composed principally of hydrogen and helium. Being so much larger than the others, it is physically like a huge balloon, reflecting its psychological quality of buoyancy. The Great Red Spot (larger than the Earth) was discovered on its surface in 1664 and is thought to be a complex storm of rising gas moving in a counter-clockwise direction. Jupiter has a barely visible ring system that was discovered by NASA's Voyager I in 1980.

• Mean distance from Sun: approximately 484 million miles/778 million kilometres.
• Diameter: approximately 88,800 miles/142,800 kilometres at the equator.
• Sidereal period (approximate time for planet to orbit the Sun): 11.86 years. This means that Jupiter spends about one year in each zodiacal sign before moving on to the next.
• Retrograde motion: once a year for about 4 months.
• Moons: more than 60 satellites are known, most of them recently discovered. Many of the recent discoveries are very small indeed and have not yet been named. Gallileo discovered Jupiter's four large moons (Io, Europa, Ganymede and Callisto) in 1610 and they can be seen easily through a telescope. These moons and many others are named after Zeus's mythological lovers.

Mythology

Alerted by his father, Ouranos (Uranus), that his sons would usurp him, Kronos decided to swallow his children as soon as they were born. Zeus's mother, Rhea, secretly gave birth to Zeus in a cave in Crete and deceived Kronos by giving him a stone wrapped in swaddling to swallow, instead of the child. Therefore, right from the beginning Zeus was lucky and protected, being the only one of Kronos's children not to be devoured by him. Rhea put the infant Zeus in the safe-keeping of nymphs. These nymphs (actually the daughters of the King of Crete and called Curetes) beat their bronze shield whenever the baby cried so that Kronos wouldn't hear him. Raised on milk and honey, Zeus had a good upbringing. Similarly, people with Jupiter prominently placed (or in their Fourth House, for example), often do have a childhood of abundance (whether in material, moral or religious terms). Zeus's 'good' upbringing resulted in his feeling confident that he could cope with anything. Zeus was suckled by the goat Amalthea, and in gratitude he gave her a place among the constellations. To the nymphs he gave one of the goat's horns, conferring upon it the ability to refill itself indefinitely with whatever food or drink was requested. This was the horn of plenty, known as cornucopia. Similarly, Jupiter in the horoscope is the place where some kind of abundance – our own particular horn of plenty – may be found.

When Zeus reached adulthood, he took Metis (meaning wisdom and prudence) for his first wife. Metis gave Kronos a drug which caused him to disgorge first the stone he had swallowed and then all of Zeus's brothers and sisters. Metis knew more than all people and gods put together and Zeus was frightened that she might become too powerful and dethrone him, so he swallowed her whole. Jupiterian types have this tendency: larger than life themselves, they can dwarf and overshadow the presence of others.

Zeus and his brothers, Hades and Poseidon, divided the universe between them. Poseidon took the oceans and rivers, Hades the underworld, and Zeus took the heavens and dominion over the gods.

As ruler of the heavens, Zeus was somewhat warlike; from the heights of Mount Olympus he hurled down thunder and lightning (which can be interpreted to mean enlightenment). In horary astrology, Jupiter rules high places – and the top of mountains is an advantageous place for Zeus to be, for here everything that is going on below can be seen (the Jupiterian impulse is always to see the whole picture, the overview). The mountain top also symbolizes the Jupiterian reluctance to 'come down' in emotional terms.

Zeus's mythological love life may yield the most clues to the psychology that is associated with Jupiter. Continuously unfaithful, he romped his way through many romantic adventures. He was a great actor and could pretend to be any creature that it suited him to be. For instance, if Zeus wanted to seduce a swan, he could turn himself into a swan. He could also often bluff his way out of tight corners to prevent his philandering being discovered by his jealous and vengeful second wife, Hera (Juno). Zeus and the jealous spouse are familiar characters in Jupiter-style relationships (e.g. Jupiter tightly linked with Venus or Mars, or in the Seventh House). As god of wind, Jupiter was a super-stud; he spread his seed far and wide and fathered many children. Similarly, Jupiter in the chart may describe where an individual is at their most fruitful.

Buoyancy and Luck

The house where Jupiter is found is often an area where we are lucky, where we can get away with things. Sometimes it just describes areas where we think we can do so but eventually come unstuck by over-reaching ourselves. Nevertheless, our Jupiter placement usually describes an area where we can enjoy a certain measure of protection. Frequently, wherever Jupiter is or with respect to what it is touching, things just fall in our lap, without any special effort. Sometimes it is through being in the right place at the right time; Jupiter is very much a planet to associate with opportunity. Where Jupiter is to be found, we tend to feel confident and optimistic and have faith as to the good eventual outcome of events. The Hundred Million Dollar Question is whether things turn out all right because we expect them to or whether we are more confident because we are used to fortunate outcomes. Even when things do go wrong and Jupiter is the significator, Jupiter confers a certain buoyancy and bounce to the proceedings. Fans of Winnie the Pooh will know that Tigger must have a prominent Jupiter and Eeyore a strong Saturn. While Jupiter has its negative side, it has to be said that a mismanaged Jupiter is more difficult for those involved with the individual than for the individual themselves. One might find it difficult to live with Tigger but Tigger himself is probably totally happy! Note that Saturn in aspect to Jupiter, or even prominently placed elsewhere, tends to restrain the more over-the-top potential of the planet.

Generosity, Wealth and Abundance

With matters to do with planets touched by Jupiter and in the Jupiter house, the individual can, and often is, very generous, benevolent and charitable, though sometimes in these areas we also lord it over others. In the Jupiter area we may have more than we need and therefore have something to give. Although Jupiter has nothing to do with money per se, it can certainly be linked with prosperity in the same way that Saturn can be linked with poverty. Where Jupiter is to be found we are often wealthy in the sense that we abound in something valuable. Jupiter confers plenty, abundance, a profusion of something, bearing in mind that abundance is a relative concept – a cup of rice might be huge if compared to someone else's spoonful.

Confidence, Optimism, Joy and Gambling

Jupiter confers confidence and optimism wherever it is found and can also be associated, at best, with the idea of joy and joviality. The person who vibrates strongly to this planet will be upbeat and good-humoured. Where an individual is optimistic they will be prepared to take a risk. Little wonder, therefore, that Jupiter is the planet to associate with all forms of gambling, both with shrewd acts of judgement and with the over-optimistic, ill-judged and ill-conceived variety often encountered in betting shops and casinos.

Growth and Expansion

Our Jupiter position by sign, house and aspect shows where and how we seek to grow. It also shows where we need room to grow. Growth implies moving forward, going beyond current limits; it implies looking beyond the seeming perimeters of the current situation and glimpsing its meaning and possibilities. As always the planet is concerned with distant horizons, with a world that is both in the future and far away.

Physically, Jupiter is large, light and buoyant, like a balloon. The planet tends to inflate or expand the principles associated with any other planet or point it touches in the horoscope. So, for instance, Venus-Jupiter might expand the social life, incline one to over-spend and have lots of lovers. Mars-Jupiter will expand the competitive and enterprising spirit and expand the urge to fight and romp around having adventures (sexual and otherwise), while Jupiter-Saturn might increase a responsible, dutiful attitude. Many words that start with the prefixes 'over' and 'extra' have Jupiter as part-significator, implying, as these prefixes do, some degree of excess.

Greed, Dissatisfaction and the Urge to Explore

Where Jupiter is placed in the horoscope, we can want more and more and expect more and more. The Jupiterian impulse can be greedy. Greed, in turn, often leads to dissatisfaction and to the feeling that the grass is greener elsewhere. More positively, a key feature of the planet is the urge for exploration – in Jupiter mode, we always seek to explore and go further. In Jupiter mode we want more and sometimes erroneously believe we are entitled to more. Contentment is antithetical to the urge to explore, a desire which inevitably is born out of feelings of dissatisfaction and restlessness. Such feelings can be useful; without them there could be no growth or progress. Dissatisfaction prompts the individual to pastures new and also into taking a gamble. The urge to move on is easier to satisfy where there is lack of responsibility and a lack of ties generally. The nature of an individual's restlessness and urge to explore may manifest as an urge to travel, but exploration can take many other forms, too. The particular manifestation will often be described by the planet(s) in tight aspect (especially hard aspect) to Jupiter. Linked with Venus or Mars, the individual will seek to explore through relationship; if linked to Mercury, the exploration may be more cerebral, and if linked to Neptune, there may be a taste for exploring spiritual matters.

Space and Freedom

Being hampered limits one's capacity to grow and s t r e t c h. Jupiter rules the zodiac sign Sagittarius and, in common with that sign, the Jupiterian impulse prompts a dislike of responsibilities and a dislike of limits of all kinds; in Jupiterian mode we like to be at liberty. The areas of life associated with the house where Jupiter is to be found (or rules), and the planets it touches in a chart, always want to express themselves in a big way and need a lot of space to do so.

Travel and Higher Education

Linked to the notion of exploration is Jupiter's concern with long journeys – both physically and mentally. While travel does indeed broaden the mind, so can the educational process and, in particular, those educational activities which are concerned with meaning or which will take the individual further in terms of social understanding or advancement. As for long journeys, it is a matter of some debate as to what constitutes a long journey. Perhaps a long journey will inevitably mean going abroad but mostly a long journey in this context is one where a degree of exploration and a broadening of one's horizons is implied.

Belief and the Search for Meaning

Our beliefs dictate the extent to which we may be visionaries. The overly Jupiterian individual – the great opportunist, gambler, optimist or promoter – believes that anything is possible. Without either self-belief or belief in some kind of higher power – basically, without the notion of positive thinking – nothing is possible. Our Jupiter, together with planets in the Ninth House (particularly) and, to a lesser extent, planets falling in Sagittarius, will have much to say about our search for meaning. Life becomes much more joyous if we believe that it has some kind of larger significance; without a sense of meaning and purpose, life can feel very bleak indeed. The umbrella embracing our religious beliefs and practices, our philosophy of life and therefore our moral code, our politics and any other beliefs we may be attached to, all belong to Jupiter and the Ninth House. As well as describing where we may find or look for God, Jupiter can also describe areas where we may play God; for example, by being in an advice-giving role.

Jupiter and Wisdom

The word 'wisdom' comes from a source meaning 'to make known, give information of, to show, direct, lead and guide'. Thus, the application of wisdom can embrace many roles from tour-guide to advice-giver to cleric. To be wise, an individual needs to be able to glimpse the wider and deeper implications and meanings beyond the current situation. Wisdom is the capacity to judge correctly and that is only possible when one can judge something in the light of a greater whole. Arguably, the acquisition of wisdom also requires the input of Saturn as well as Jupiter, given that reality and responsibility are part of the territory.

Jupiter and Society

Jupiter with its 12-year cycle, and Saturn with its 29-year cycle, place the individual in the context of a wider society. Indeed, the manifestations of these two planets create society. The word 'religion' comes from the Latin *religio*, meaning 'bind together'. Religion does bind people together; communities of all kinds are often founded upon common belief systems, even if, nowadays, these are not necessarily religious. Arguably, society is defined by its common morality and, at their source, laws are based on ideas of right and wrong. Thus, while Saturn is implicated in the administration of the law, Jupiter is concerned with the moral precepts underpinning those laws.

Getting Away with Murder

It would be a mistake to think that Jupiter is all goodness and luck; Jupiter has its malign and dreadful aspect as potentially does every planetary energy. As Eve Jackson has noted,[9] mass murderers, and criminals generally, often have highly focal Jupiters; the serial killer is, in a sense, playing God and in some cases even believing that they have a God-given right to take the lives of others. It is actually Saturn that keeps humans on the path of the straight and narrow through the exertion of control, discipline and everyday 'oughts' and 'shoulds', whether these are imposed from within or imposed by society.

Hypocrisy, Inflation and Grandiosity

Jupiter can be associated with politicians, the clergy, people in sales and promoters of all kinds. Such occupations trade on faith; the priest doesn't say God may exist, but says that God does exist. The sales person doesn't say this might be the best vacuum cleaner, but says that it is. The shadow side of faith is doubt. Zeus was always skilled at bluff and hypocrisy and, as Jackson also points out, hypocrisy is another potential Jupiterian trait. Hypocrisy literally means feigning, pretending, giving a false appearance of virtue or goodness. Whenever we are being hypocritical and thus are 'faking it', we tend to speak in true Jupiterian style with exaggerated conviction or empty words. In Jupiter mode we may be grandiose: full of large plans and prone to inflation. In other words we are puffed up with vanity, pride, pomposity and inappropriate ideas. Interestingly, the work of Françoise and Michel Gauquelin[10] has shown that Jupiter can be associated both with actors and politicians. Glenda Jackson, Ronald Reagan, Arnold Schwarzenegger and Clint Eastwood are obvious examples of people who have pursued both career paths.

Jupiter and War

Still on the more difficult manifestations of Jupiter, the planet's association with war needs also to be touched upon. Zeus was a warlike god (as well as being the father of Mars, the god of war), and given that wars are inevitably fought over matters of religion or the relative wealth of one cultural group over another, perhaps the Jupiterian influence is not surprising. Also with its propensity for exaggeration, Jupiter has the potential to inflate a merely tense situation to the extent that it becomes an inflammatory one.

The God of High Places

People in high places often have affluence and influence. If Jupiter is found in your Eleventh House of friends, for instance, then perhaps you have friends in high places. Linked with anything social in the horoscope, the influence of Jupiter inclines to social climbing. Also to patronage; the Jupiter type may seek to protect another. If assuming too great an air of superiority, the type can also be patronizing. Taken to an extreme position, patronage can result in condescending behaviour to those of lower social status. In other words, snobbery, arrogance and haughtiness are also traits that can be laid at the door of a Jupiter running rampant.

Extravagance

The more common negative trait to associate with Jupiter revolves around its penchant for extravagance, and we need look no further than a dictionary definition of the word to get a good feeling for the planet:
Extravagance
1. A wandering beyond proper limits; an excursion or sally from the usual way, course, or limit.
2. The state of being extravagant, wild, or prodigal beyond bounds of propriety or duty; want of moderation; excess; especially, undue expenditure of money; vain and superfluous expense; prodigality; profusion; waste; lavishness; unreasonableness; recklessness.
3. Something that is an indulgence rather than a necessity; luxury.
Source: *Webster's Revised Unabridged Dictionary*, 1996.

Aunts and Uncles

Not so many miles away from the concept of patronage may be the fact that Jupiter is traditionally associated with uncles. Possibly Jupiter also embraces aunts, although more work is needed to confirm this notion. Historically, aunts and uncles have often taken a mentoring role in families; at best they have been on hand to guide and possibly provide financial assistance to younger family members. The reason that uncles, as opposed to aunts, may have been ascribed to Jupiter may be because uncles, in days gone by, were usually better financially placed to assist in this way. I am indebted to Jane Struthers for pointing out that the word 'uncle' is slang for a pawnbroker, a trade ruled by Jupiter.

The Body

The liver is the largest gland in the body, weighing 2-4 pounds/1-2 kilos. In keeping with the psychology associated with the planet that has often been called the 'greater benefic', the liver's role is to sort out what is beneficial for the body. The liver has a greater capacity for regenerating itself than any other organ and, of its many functions, one is detoxifying drugs and alcohol. In other words, the liver helps us to get away with abusing our body by protecting us against noxious substances. Another function is to de-saturate fats (fats themselves probably owe much to Jupiter), converting them so they can be used by the body. Health problems where Jupiter is the triggering factor are usually caused by excesses of some kind. With Jupiter there is a tendency towards surfeit and congestion, fullness and over-production. Growths of all kinds – including cancerous growths – owe much to the planet, as does obesity. Whereas someone with Saturn strongly linked to personal planets will incline to leanness, those who have Jupiter links to the Sun, Moon and Ascendant (or its ruler) may incline to corpulence.

Metal

The Jupiterian metal is tin. A malleable substance, tin is added to other metals to make them go further. Tin can make another alloy appear more than it is. Tin is mostly used for its protective properties – for instance, it is used to coat other metals to prevent them being corroded or attacked by chemicals.

Interpreting Jupiter

Perhaps the first thing to say is that, in practice, the aspects to Jupiter and its house position are always going to be far more important than its sign position. The sign position takes on more interest if Jupiter is rising or is prominently placed elsewhere. The interpretations that follow must be treated with caution, therefore – they are more designed to set the reader thinking. To give an example, I have no doubt that the Religious Society of Friends (the Quakers) vibrates most strongly to the zodiacal sign of Aquarius and yet, in practice, if one did a statistical survey of Quakers one would be unlikely to find Jupiter placed more frequently in Aquarius than in any other sign. My next-door neighbour, for instance, is a Quaker but her Jupiter is in Sagittarius. However, the Aquarian element is perhaps added to this by the fact that her Jupiter tightly squares Uranus and falls in her Eleventh House.

Jupiter Through The Signs

Jupiter in Aries – ♃ ♈

If strongly placed (e.g. rising), Jupiter here can describe an individual characterized by their capacity for big trouble and sometimes over-the-top (perhaps attention-seeking) behaviour. Adding enthusiasm and confidence to the chart as it does, it can indicate a crusading and pioneering spirit. Individuals may have a liking for large-scale projects and run the risk of biting off more than they can chew. While less confident souls may be particularly prone to giving in to peer pressure and following trends, more confident types will be the first to set them. This Jupiter placement is an enterprising one, able to seize opportunities. It has leadership, trouble-shooting and trend-setting potential and is also ideal for work in sales. This individual may be able to promote anything, whether it is religion, politics or something more commercially based. Religious or political views may be pursued with zeal and, especially if borne out by other chart factors, there is potential for leadership in these areas.

Jupiter in Taurus – ♃ ♉

This placement is often indicative of someone who is fortunate in financial or material terms, or who at least feels that they are. If the planet is prominent and other chart factors concur, this person may even simply attract wealth. It is an ideal placement for fund-raising activities. If prominent and receiving stressful aspects, it can be indicative of avarice, greed and self-indulgence, but frequently those with Jupiter in Taurus are not overly acquisitive at all. Instead, the philosophy that 'God will provide' may be much in evidence. There can also be an appreciation of nature's bounty and an enjoyment of the good things in life. Not given to wild flights of fancy (unless the rest of the chart provides these), Jupiter here tends towards a stoic, pragmatic philosophy of life.

Jupiter in Gemini – ♃ ♊

This placement suggests a breadth of knowledge, a love of reading and wide interests. Generally, the individual can be optimistic about their ability to learn and communicate. However, Jupiter is in its detriment in Gemini and success can be muted by restlessness, superficial knowledge or a tendency to spread oneself too thinly. Many comings and goings, a deluge of communications and plenty of short-distance travel will often be the norm. Some interest in or capacity for teaching may be indicated; especially for teaching overseas. It can also be good for writing and publishing generally. In religious matters, the typical individual with this placement will believe that all religions are roughly saying the same thing and may be reluctant therefore to commit themselves to any one Church. It is a good placement for the study of comparative religion, literature or politics. It can also be associated with schools, journeys, tour guides and multi-subject degrees.

Jupiter in Cancer – ♃ ♋

Jupiter is exalted in Cancer, possibly because both the planet and the sign share the principle of protection. Often the individual has strong feelings about protecting their family, heritage or country. For some, the placement may mean turning their home into a haven for those who share their beliefs. Wealth may be acquired from real estate or via the family, especially from the mother's side. The person's culture or religion may also be inherited through the mother, as is the case with Judaism. Or there may be involvement with religions which pay particular homage to the mother principle. Often enjoyment may be gained from history. It is a good placement for the cook and homemaker though, if prominently placed (e.g. rising), obesity may prove a problem.

Jupiter in Leo – ♃♌

This is a warm, generous placement, which, if prominently placed in a chart, can add confidence and leadership potential. There can be an appreciation of grandeur with Jupiter here and a liking for show, pageantry and doing things in a big, stylish way. Often there is enjoyment to be gained from film, theatre and socializing. Egotism and a reluctance to play second fiddle to a higher power can limit the capacity for religious faith. More religious types may favour what might be called High Church. Some will feel at home with churches and religious practices that have a certain amount of pomp and ceremony. There may be pride in the person's church, school or university and a keenness to show it off as being, in some way, the 'best'. This is an ideal placement for a school or university governor, church leader or local councillor.

Jupiter in Virgo – ♃♍

This is potentially a conscientious Jupiter with the individual having strong work ethics and believing in the importance of good service. This can mean, of course, that the individual simply does too much but it can also suggest joy in their work and the potential for working overseas. However, the meeting of little (Virgo) and large (Jupiter) can result in the individual getting bogged down by trying to digest too much information. Finding the wood for the trees may not be easy for some who have Jupiter in the sign of its detriment. Worrying over things too small to be worthy of so much concern is also implied. There is likely to be a preference for more modest displays of religious practice and Methodism probably belongs here. A discriminating or even cynical attitude with respect to political or religious matters may be the norm. (Flaubert,[11] who is credited with the phrase 'God is in the detail', had his Jupiter in Aries in his Sixth House, a house linked to Virgo.)

Jupiter in Libra – ♃♎

The opportunity for exploration, and perhaps for growth generally, will tend to come through relationships. This is a person who may have an optimistic 'hope over experience' attitude to marriage and partnership in general, even though there can be a restlessness when within the married state. There can be indecision in arriving at a preferred set of religious, political or philosophical beliefs or convictions. There may also be indecision about entering into serious relationships and sometimes a holding out for a seemingly 'better catch'. Marriage and partnership are likely to be greatly affected by matters of philosophy, religion or politics, and vice versa. Taoism and its appreciation of peace, co-operation and the principles of yin and yang may strike a chord. Most will prefer to travel in the company of another person and may even have been introduced to the joys of travelling through a well-travelled partner.

Jupiter in Scorpio – ♃ ♏

The planet of breadth hits the sign of depth. Thus, in matters of higher education or with respect to political or religious affiliations, there is a requirement for more than superficial teachings or political spin. The individual has to feel emotionally involved in what they believe. Reconciling the experience of the death of a loved one with the notion of a God may be difficult. Integrating their views about sex with those held by church or society may also be problematic. The capacity for faith, will-power and determination is strong and may be applied to any life areas that Jupiter touches in the horoscope. Involvement in, and possible material gain from, investments, insurance, legacies, alimony or taxes is implied but has to be borne out by other chart factors. There may be an interest in the occult and all matters pertaining to death and life after death.

Jupiter in Sagittarius – ♃ ♐

Jupiter placed in its own sign gives the planet a certain amount of strength in any horoscope in which it is found. It is likely to add a degree of buoyancy and fun to the chart, as well as a liking for travel and perhaps an interest in other cultures and their differing religious beliefs and practices. The individual is likely to have strong beliefs concerning the importance of education. If the rest of the chart concurs, this is a good placement for anyone working in a religious educational setting (e.g. a teacher in a church school). There is often a liking for the outdoors, and walking holidays may be favoured. If prominently placed, this Jupiter can give rise to the planet's more notorious traits; for instance, extravagance, carelessness and getting matters out of proportion.

Jupiter in Capricorn – ♃ ♑

There is often a clash between optimism and pessimism, and between extravagance and miserliness, with Jupiter in the sign of its fall, but while individuals with this placement may be overly cautious in matters of risk-taking, they are often big on responsibility, duty and integrity. The type may also be big on making economies, disliking, as they often do, any kind of waste. Wealth will often come (or sometimes be lost) from or through the father. Not uncommonly, poverty in childhood is often replaced by relative comfort in old age. The father can take on an exaggerated significance in the life although, if other factors concur, he can be rather a remote figure. This placement lends a conservative tinge to the horoscope because of a fundamental belief in tradition, hierarchy and the Establishment. Some may be overly respectful towards those in authority. There is often an appreciation of the land with Jupiter here. It is also a good placement for the geologist, jeweller or anyone whose life is touched by large rocks.

Jupiter in Aquarius – ♃ ♒

Future-orientated, progressive in thought and reforming in spirit, if prominently placed, those with this Jupiter can believe in the power of ordinary people to do good. Jupiter here inclines towards a wide social circle and strong beliefs espousing freedom, humanitarianism and democracy. It is an ideal placement for Voluntary Service Overseas. In matters of faith, as elsewhere, there is an inclination towards tolerance and universality, at least in theory. The main problem can be an intolerance of intolerance. The Religious Society of Friends (Quakers), with their view that God is in everyone, belongs here, as may many an organization with the word 'Friends' or 'Brotherhood' in its title. Also Christian Science, which is practised by people of different denominations and faiths. It is an ideal placement for the studying or teaching of scientific or technological subjects and also for aviation.

Jupiter in Pisces – ♃ ♓

Jupiter is strong in its own sign, increasing the imaginative faculties and potential skills in drama, music and the arts generally. Sometimes unworldly and somewhat chaotic with money, this is also potentially a charitable, compassionate and generous Jupiter. However, I have frequently seen this placement occur in those who are hopeful of benefiting from the charitable and generous impulses of others! In matters of belief, the individual will usually be drawn to spiritual matters, mysticism and New Age subjects, or simply to agnosticism. Travel can be the great escape – sea voyages, idyllic island hideaways and spiritual retreats all come within the symbolism, as does travel for artistic, musical or merely hedonistic reasons. Often there is a wish for sanctuary and seclusion with Jupiter here. Any propensity already shown in the chart towards taking on the role of saviour or victim will be increased.

Saturn ♄

*'I guess I just prefer to see the dark side of things. The glass is half-empty.
And cracked. And I just cut my lip on it. And chipped a tooth.'*

Janeane Garofalo

Astronomy

The second largest planet in our solar system, visible to the naked eye and the outermost planet known to ancient peoples, Saturn is considered to be very beautiful because of the effect created by its ice rings. These are only visible from the Earth with the aid of a telescope and were first observed by Galileo in 1610. Made of variably sized chunks of ice and rocks, the rings are wide (about 185,000 miles/300,000 kilometres in diameter), but very thin (about 0.6 miles/1 kilometre thick).

• Mean distance from Sun: approximately 886 million miles/1,427 million kilometres.
• Diameter: approximately 74,900 miles/120,536 kilometres in diameter at the equator (about 10% less at its poles) and therefore about 9.4 times the diameter of the Earth. It is thought that its oblate shape (e.g. it is flatter at the poles) is caused by its fast rotation (10-11 hours) and gaseous composition (hydrogen and helium).
• Sidereal period (approximate time for the planet to orbit the Sun): 29.46 years. This means that Saturn spends about two-and-a-half years in each zodiacal sign and therefore its average movement is 1 degree per month/12 degrees per year.
• Retrograde motion: once a year for about five months.
• Moons: more than 40 are known. Most of the moons are small but some, such as Titan (about 3200 miles/5150 kilometres in diameter), are larger than Mercury or Pluto. Many of Saturn's moons orbit around the edge of the planet's rings. They help to keep the rings in place, and for this reason they are sometimes known as shepherd moons.

Mythology

Having reduced his father to impotence (see Uranus), Kronos headed a new dynasty. Together with his siblings, the Titans, he ruled over the whole universe. He married his sister, the earth goddess Rhea, and they had three daughters – Hestia, Demeter and Hera – and three sons – Hades, Poseidon and Zeus (Pluto, Neptune and Jupiter). Kronos was told by an oracle that his position would be supplanted by his children, so he attempted to avert the threat by swallowing his children as they were born. Zeus managed to escape being swallowed and when he reached manhood his first wife, Metis, gave Kronos a drug which made him vomit up Zeus's other siblings. The story is really about the fact that we will be supplanted by our children. As we get older, if we are not careful, we do tend to suppress the next generation, sometimes by stopping their progress and sometimes by not allowing them to learn by their mistakes. The next generation is supposed to take over from us and they do. This brief outline of the story contains some of the important themes of Saturn. Among them, the reality of the ageing process, the need to take responsibility in life (alone among his siblings, it was Kronos who dealt with his father), feelings of guilt (for castrating his father) and potential low self-esteem (in assuming that his children would usurp him and presumably that they didn't love or respect him sufficiently).

The Saturn Complex

Saturn lends a cold, heavy, slow, dull, dry, immobile quality to whatever it touches in the horoscope. Its principles are those of contraction, control, inhibition, definition and limitation. There is nothing showy or fluffy about the qualities that this planet represents.

Saturn contacts by house, aspect and, to a lesser extent by sign, describe those areas of life where we lack confidence, where we feel we 'ought' and 'should' do better. When we hear an individual frequently apologizing, we are usually listening to the Saturn voice in their chart. Basically, Saturn describes our conscience, what Freudians would term the super-ego. As many an astrology teacher has noted, this is the part of the chart where it seems that there is a inner voice reminiscent of a stern schoolteacher always telling us to do better, be better, try harder. Saturn can deny, delay, restrict, restrain and generally slow down, even cripple at times, the development of whatever it touches. This is because our fears limit us, as do our physical infirmities, and so does the real world sometimes. Perhaps the purpose of Saturnian denial and restriction is to test the validity of what we are doing or the reality of what we think we want.

The Reality Principle

Perhaps, above all else, the Saturnian principle concerns itself with reality. While there are different types of reality, reality here means worldly reality, the so-called bottom line; the often cold, harsh facts of life. The fact that, in worldly terms, we all die, is a major example. A realistic attitude to life includes an appreciation of limitations. An awareness that time, our resources, life itself, is measured out to us and perhaps shouldn't be wasted. When we understand the limitations of a given situation and are aware of our own limitations and the limitations of others, we can save time and save resources, for no longer do we need to waste energy in trying to achieve the impossible. On a less positive level, when an individual is too strongly identified with the Saturnian view, their negative attitude can prevent them from glimpsing possibilities. When we are depressed, for example, what *is* possible can seem impossible. At best the Saturnian principle makes us prudent, at worst it narrows our vision and therefore narrows our scope.

Boundaries, Limits, Rules and Regulations

Saturn in all contexts rules boundaries and the imposing and enforcing of limits, whether these limits are physical or psychological, self-imposed or imposed by the family, employer or the State. Firstly, there are physical boundaries as in walls, hedges and any other kind of barrier. Then there is the notion of self-control and self-discipline, which might be defined as self-imposed boundaries on one's own behaviour. Discipline, whether self-imposed or imposed from without, is enforced to keep the uncivilized and uncontrolled at bay. Adherence to rules (keeping within the boundaries) implies the notion of obedience as well as discipline.

Parents and most people in professional situations set boundaries of behaviour and timing. Parental rules are designed to protect the child and to educate him or her about the limitations, constraints and restraints that living in the material world implies. Parents control us and, ideally, teach us to control ourselves. Rules, regulations and the exercise of control, both in the family and in the larger context of society, are there to provide protection for ourselves and for others. Contracts, which also set out the bounds of behaviour, are designed to protect both parties. Contracts save time and increase clarity; all parties know what their responsibilities are and what the limits of their brief are. The rules are laid out.

The Father

Saturn is one of many potential significators in the horoscope to describe the father. However, in my experience, in Western society at any rate, Saturn is often less descriptive of father as an authority figure but certainly describes areas of life where he had a lot to learn and/or teach us. Saturn can describe something of all the other authority figures in childhood and be descriptive of the mother, too, although she *is* often in the role of disciplinarian. The prominence or otherwise of Saturn in a chart usually gives a clear indication of the 'feel' of a person's childhood in terms of strictness, work, authority figures and sometimes material lack. It shows us how hard (if prominent or making substantial hard aspects to personal planets and angles), or not, the childhood actually was.

Fears and Defences

Too many rules or too tight an enforcement of them generates fear and anxiety. Fear keeps us out of danger but it also potentially inhibits behaviour and crushes spontaneity and creativity. Saturn is the great inhibitor of our actions, both potentially protecting us by curbing our impulsiveness and crushing us by putting a dampener on our resolve, confidence and ability to act. Of course, successfully facing our fears contributes hugely to our feeling more confident and capable.

While Saturn by no means has monopoly over pain and difficulty (all planetary principles can potentially give rise to both pain and pleasure), the activities of Saturn in a horoscope often do describe some of the most painful and fearful areas of people's lives, especially when they are young. Fear is often related to an expectation of some kind of pain. It is fear that makes the rabbit freeze or the antelope run: defensive strategies that protect both species. The purpose of pain is to bring something to the individual's attention and can thus be life-saving. Defences protect us; the Saturnian principle is only difficult when the individual is either over-defended or under-defended. Inadequate defences leave the individual vulnerable and exposed, while too many defences block progress, imprison and curb the capacity to take risks and enjoy life. Generally speaking, when we feel anxious or frightened, we want things to be structured, organized and defined because then we feel we have some control over what is going on.

Time

The greatest restraint on our activities is time or the lack of it. The number of hours in a day, the number of years in a life: Saturn governs it all. While time is the ultimate boundary, it enables us to structure and order our lives. Without it there would be chaos. People who have difficulty with time-keeping inevitably have problems with the Saturnian principle. The Greek word *chronos* means 'time' and from it we get chronic (long-lasting), chronology (a time line of facts), chronicle (an account of events in the order they occurred), chronometer (time-keeper) and many other time-related terms.

Saturn and the Shadow

The qualitative feeling of Saturn is heavy and slow, and whatever Saturn contacts in our horoscope, or wherever it is found, can feel unsophisticated, gauche and hampered. Like any slow and heavy creature, the Saturnian areas of our chart can feel awkward, graceless and clumsy – in early life at least. Usually we don't want others to see this clumsy animal within ourselves, which is why Saturn has been correlated with the Jungian idea of the 'shadow' – that unconscious part of ourselves which we not only attempt to hide from others but often successfully conceal from ourselves as well. However, as with so-called 'missing elements', Saturn can sometimes describe an area of over-compensation in the horoscope.

Saturn and Quality Assurance

Given that Saturn is associated with the fears that we are not good enough or have not carried out a particular task well enough, the psychology associated with the planet leans heavily towards improved standards and also to guilt when such standards have not been reached. Thus, Saturn contributes to the notion of high standards and 'good' behaviour. A strong Saturn keeps us out of prison because it is the inner voice of conscience (and sometimes the threat of punishment) that ensures that we obey society's rules. Breaking the rules results in individuals being locked up behind the highest walls and tightly controlled in all that they do; in other words, transgressing the rules can result in the punishment of being placed in the heavily Saturnian environment of prison. The image of prison is a useful one for the planet, because sometimes, although often self-imposed, the life areas associated with the house where Saturn is to be found can feel a bit like gaol.

Becoming an Authority

Saturn will often show those areas where, over time, we may excel. Our Saturn by sign and house can show where we have become or may become an expert, an authority. Saturn's remit is not really about theory but is concerned with learning by experience. When young, we are often deprived in the areas with which Saturn is concerned in our charts (e.g. Saturn's house position and aspects). It may be no one's fault, but usually we experience some kind of lack here. We have to find and learn about it – whatever 'it' is – for ourselves. We tend to learn Saturnian lessons over time and in the School of Hard Knocks. Wherever our Saturn is, we have much to learn when young but may, when older, also have a great deal to teach. So in the chart area where Saturn rules or is placed, we are offered an opportunity to learn thoroughly. And we become our own best authority in this area because we had to learn the hard way. It is here that we can follow the alchemists by turning lead into gold. The lead is our initial experiences of inadequacy, lack and impoverishment and the gold is what we may transform those inadequacies into.

Vocation and Work

Alongside our MC, Second, Sixth and Tenth House planets and rulers, Saturn can also provide clues to how we earn a living, simply because, as has been noted, our Saturn areas can show where we can become experienced and adept.

The Harvest

Related to the process of maturing and the idea of experience is the notion of the harvest and the idea that we 'reap what we sow', and that unless we have sown our seeds and tended the crop, there will be nothing to harvest. Saturn ensures that what we reap is what we sow – not a grain more, not a grain less. With Saturn we don't get anything for nothing. Putting in the time and effort does reap rewards and so Saturn can be associated with fruition as well as with deprivation. Thus, the qualitative feel of Saturn is not so much mean as exacting.

Skin and Bones and the Ageing Process

The skin provides the first defence, the first physical boundary between us and the outside world and, as such, forms a protective barrier. The skeleton provides the structure in the body. It literally keeps us upright and provides a frame, a coat hanger on which all anatomical parts hang or in which they are encased. Our skeletal framework changes as we get older, as does our skin. In fact, we substantially deduce a person's age by how upright they are and by the amount of wrinkles they have. Bone is the hardest substance in the body and the most enduring – when buried, all flesh disintegrates but the bones remain. Similarly, when in Saturn mode, we want to do things that will last and stand the test of time. Saturn also has rulership over teeth. As we get older our gums recede and more actual tooth is exposed – we become, quite literally, 'long in the tooth'.

Saturn describes all matters concerned with the ageing process. Age imposes the greatest restraint on our activities. If too young, we are unequal to a number of tasks. Likewise, in advancing years, while some things become possible, many things become impossible. The average eighty-year-old cannot leap over fences nor dance the night away. Hearing and disorders of hearing have also traditionally been ascribed to Saturn. Diseases influenced by Saturn will usually be characterized by some state of deficiency, caused for example by malnutrition or poverty. Or diseases associated with other aspects of the ageing process, such as calcification which causes hardening. Depression – the so-called 'common cold' of mental illness – is the great Saturnian malady with transits from Saturn prone to bringing us 'down', and natal conjunctions or hard aspects to Saturn from the Moon, Mars, and Jupiter in particular, resulting in an above-average incidence of depression.

More on Health

Possibly because of its tendency towards psychological denial, the sign placement of Saturn sometimes equates with vulnerable areas of the body. Thus, for example, Saturn in Pisces (to use a comparatively light-hearted example) may, for instance, describe a difficult relationship with footwear (e.g. the wearing of ill-fitting shoes) resulting in hard skin (Saturn) on the feet (Pisces) and bunions and corns. A Sun in Pisces in hard aspect to Saturn, or Saturn in the Twelfth House, may indicate the same tendency. Our Saturn sign placement or aspects often also describe an aspect of our father's health problems and often, in very general terms, the cause or partial cause of his death. Thus, Saturn in Aries might point to a stroke or cerebral haemorrhage, for instance.

The Metal

Saturn's metal is lead. It is the heaviest, dullest and most impenetrable metal, used in places where a high degree of protection is required. It is the least conductible, least malleable and most inflexible of metals. Radiologists use lead aprons for instance when taking X-rays to protect themselves from the radioactivity. Over time, metals which have isotopes heavier than lead eventually turn into lead, thus the age of the various metals can be deduced by the amount of lead present in the ore. Scientists also use lead for measuring time. The earliest industrial disease – lead poisoning – was known as Saturnism and is characterized by fatigue, headaches and depression. Lead used to be added to petrol to slow an engine's combustion.

Saturn Through The Signs

Saturn is in each sign for two-and-a-half years and thus the aspects made to and from the planet and its house placement are likely to be much more telling than its zodiac sign. The sign in which Saturn is placed will have some relevance but the exact manifestations can vary hugely depending on these other factors. Nevertheless, it is hoped that what follows will prompt some useful ideas. The sign position will become more important if Saturn has prominence in the chart for some reason – for instance, if it falls on one of the angles. Given that Saturn is in a sign for so long, it will say something about what is happening at more collective levels. For example, when Saturn is going through Gemini, society at large is likely to be discussing educational standards and methods, and perhaps matters of literacy, language and grammar. Any faults in transport systems would probably come under scrutiny, too.

Saturn in Aries – ♄ ♈

Saturn is in its fall in Aries, perhaps because of the potential clash between the more primitive, childish go-getting qualities of Aries and the civilizing, restraining, adult nature of Saturn. Some kind of stop-go situation is implied, a feeling of frustration as if, like Mars-Saturn combinations generally, one is trying to drive at full speed with one foot on the brake. Saturn here often describes life lessons around the issue of competition and also courage. There can often be an unconscious fear of coming first but equally a fear of not coming first. One woman had Saturn in Aries in her Ninth House opposing her Moon; she applied to go on a very high-powered training course but was refused entry into the course because she didn't have a first-class degree. The fact was that she was competing with her mother, and when she realized this and applied for a more suitable course, she was successful. This course was actually a much more realistic option for her.

Sometimes, there can be a caution about starting things with Saturn in Aries, an anxiety about taking the initiative to do or say something, fearing that perhaps one is being rash, impulsive or pushy. Saturn in Aries types often have an expectation of opposition to their plans. While some will find it hard to push themselves forward, others who are fearful of being crushed may adopt a more authoritarian style. At best, this placement adds grit to a chart and a capacity to rough it. Saturn here can be the signature of the 'battler' and the stunt artist, because some people will become, through facing their fears, expert on the art of daring. Combining as it does the principles of combat and discipline, this is an excellent placement for the soldier and for those engaged in martial arts. Potentially there is an ability to curb, discipline and harness their more aggressive and impulsive impulses.

Saturn in Taurus – ♄ ♉

In mundane terms, it can be a difficult time for farmers, potters and others in so-called Taurean trades when Saturn is transiting this sign. Generally speaking though, on an individual level, this position can be associated with slow and steady economic growth. Nevertheless, there is often a fear of poverty and a tendency to exercise care with their resources although, as always, the whole chart must be studied. While some will have come from a background of economic hardship, the reverse is often the case. The lessons of Saturn in Taurus are often concerned with ownership. Individuals may feel their life choices are limited: that they are in prison, either because of material lack or because of material abundance. A life deliberating over what they do and don't value may be the result. And the need to define exactly what they value, what they are worth in the widest context, may be precisely what is required of those with this placement.

The other fear for some is of not being productive. There is a strong need to accomplish something tangible with Saturn here. Taurus is a ponderous sign and Saturn a heavy planet; the combination of the two furthers stability, patience, tremendous realism and steadiness of purpose. It is excellent for work in construction, architecture and design, for there is a capacity to exercise tight control over their material and to be able to give it structure and form. Some individuals with Saturn here may take responsibility for feeding the nation in some way. Some will take responsibility for the material or economic circumstances of others. This can therefore be the placement of a treasurer or accountant and is a common enough placement in the charts of philanthropists. There can be guilt about ownership and guilt about not using money carefully, so creating a certain tight-fisted quality. In fact those with Saturn in Taurus usually are careful with money, whether they decide to hang on to it or give it away. The father-figure may have been overly concerned with economic matters or sometimes with sensual pleasures.

Saturn in Gemini – ♄ ♊

Individuals with this placement will tend to be serious about matters to do with learning and communication. This can give rise to the individual who is something of an authority on how to write properly or an authority in some area of knowledge. This is an excellent placement for a journalist, editor or educator. Some will grapple with fears around their capacity to express themselves. There can be a reluctance to commit themselves, either verbally or in print, perhaps because of an expectation of being misunderstood. One friend of mine prefers writing with a pencil so that what she has written can be rubbed out. Basically, the type takes the time to avoid misunderstandings, and they can take such pains to do so that misunderstandings are precisely what do occur. The difficulty can be in communicating with spontaneity. Classically, the type knows the dangers of blurting things out and so keeps their own counsel – sometimes when verbal expression is precisely what is required. As with any Saturn placement, there can be a variety of scenarios in childhood but fearing oneself to be a slow learner in contrast to the seemingly superior schoolwork done by a brother or sister or by schoolmates can be one manifestation. Some with this placement will have missed out on early education but many will have been sent to the best schools and may have had parents who were teachers. An extremely articulate, Scrabble-playing, literate family can be the norm. Sibling relationships will almost always be of interest; the individual may be very affected by elder siblings or by their responsibilities towards younger ones. Sometimes aunts and uncles (as parents' siblings) feature in the life more than usual. Fears concerning articulation may find expression in a physical way, as in the individual having difficulties in walking, speaking or hearing, for instance. One woman of my acquaintance has a congenital problem with her arm and so cannot easily 'talk with her hands'. Saturn here can also contribute to the likelihood of such disorders as carpal tunnel syndrome.

Saturn in Cancer – ♄ ♋

During the years that Saturn goes through Cancer, society may be pondering on the question of what the responsibilities of parenthood actually are. Questions about discipline versus a more caring, understanding approach may be in the air. For the individual with this placement, as well as for society as whole, there is the notion of working hard to feel safe. The lessons of Saturn in Cancer are lessons concerning safety and protection. How not to over-protect on the one hand and the dangers inherent in being under-protected on the other. Family responsibilities can be weighty with this placement. The understanding that the family is not only a source of protection against a harsh world, but that it can also serve as a form of imprisonment, goes with the territory. In an otherwise more unconventional horoscope, Saturn in Cancer may describe an individual who takes a dim view of the past or of the family unit. Some individuals will have experienced a strict home life or some early family or domestic austerity with this placement. It can be a hallmark of a disciplinarian parent, a dutiful mother or merely anxieties about the family – fears of losing the family or worries about individual members. Saturn in Cancer implies a strong sense of family responsibility and many with this placement will take care of their parents in old age. Both sign and planet are defensive by nature, and this is a good placement for those who work in the security and defence industries. This includes the armed forces. Whoever first said that 'a man's home is his castle' may have had Saturn in Cancer, because the notion of defending their home and family (and sometimes country) is a strong theme here. For this reason, there may be a liking for castles and other types of fortified homes. Depending on the chart overall, the individual may be cautious about expressing their feelings and generally feel rather vulnerable. Some will deal with these feelings by making their body their defence; making it hard like rock through body-building, for instance. Saturn in Cancer can also be associated with crustaceans, reptiles and amphibians with hard skins, especially when falling in the Sixth House of pets.

Saturn in Leo – ♄ ♌

Individuals with Saturn here often have fears around drawing attention to themselves but equally (and often less consciously) have fears around being unacknowledged, too. There is usually a tendency to underestimate their creative abilities. Additionally, many feel inhibited when centre-stage, and yet many with this placement are skilled at drama and creative writing or some other form of self-expression. Many with Saturn here have a fundamental fear of failure and pride is often their worst enemy. This means that there can be difficulty in taking risks in expressing and exposing themselves generally. It is important that Saturn in Leo individuals find time for creative pursuits and that they give themselves permission to simply experiment and have fun. Contrary to what they may think, other people are not looking at them or laughing at them. The father will often have been a creative man although not necessarily sufficiently appreciated for this. For example, one person's father was an artist in *gold*-leaf work in castles and similar buildings but the uniqueness of his skills went largely unrecognized while he was alive.

Especially when other chart factors concur, Saturn in Leo often describes someone who has a natural air of authority and many with this placement will end up in positions of leadership. The lessons for Saturn in Leo can include those of being in authority themselves but also in accepting the authority of others. It is often not easy for those with this placement to accept and obey the strictures laid down by parents, bosses or others in authority. Even traffic wardens can make these people see red! Some with Saturn here may try to avoid being in authority; they lack the necessary confidence, but perhaps the lesson is to be able to be in charge, to assume the mantle of leadership, willingly but without being autocratic. Basically, they need to trust that others will have confidence in them, even if they don't have it in themselves. Cultivating flexibility is often what is required of those with this placement. Failure to take charge themselves often results in the individual having to deal with autocratic authority-figures, such as the boss who acts as if they are royalty.

Saturn in Virgo – ♄ ♍

In the years when Saturn is transiting through Virgo, society at this time may be asking what constitutes a job well done? Or which responsibilities does the State have for the health of the individual and the health of the nation? On an individual level, this is a good placement for any kind of role which involves time-keeping or 'time and motion' – hence trade union activities. Many with this placement will simply have a job where they have to clock in and clock out. Sometimes there can be employment in hospitals or laboratories. Sometimes in taking responsibility for the health of the public or monitoring such matters. Some with this placement will be frightened that they are not paying enough attention to detail or not executing their job properly, and many will feel that they are 'doing time' in their occupational roles. More positively, this placement can contribute to a psychological profile which takes work seriously; for example, taking care of the tools of their trade, paying attention to detail, being efficient, precise and hard-working. When in hard aspect to personal planets, Saturn in Virgo can contribute to a tendency to worry and, in particular, to worrying about work and health matters. This person can become weighed down with anxiety about trivial matters. And some just expect to be chastised for being sloppy or late and can suffer great anxiety as a result. As a rule, the lessons of Saturn in Virgo are concerned with service; in particular, with how to be of service to others without being servile. Often introducing some kind of ritual into the daily life reduces the feelings of anxiety in those with this Saturn prominently placed. Not uncommonly, the father will have been a craftsman of some kind or have worked in a service industry; possibly he will have been overworked and underpaid. Some parents will have actually been 'in service'. Often the father-figure will have been very work- or task-orientated, possibly at the expense of his family, his health or other areas of life.

Saturn in Libra – ♄ ♎

Saturn is exalted in Libra, for here we have the cosmic rule-maker and rule-implementer in the sign most concerned with fairness and impartiality. This implies the potential for balanced judgements and fair punishments. Thus, this is an ideal placement for all branches of the law and for any work requiring mediation skills. It is also useful for involvement in music (the laws of harmony) and the arts. This is also a good placement for those involved with fair trade, international development and bridge-building between nations and families. Sometimes there is bridge-building in a company between union and management. Whatever the issue, those with Saturn here may be constrained in the decision-making process by the fear that they will judge wrongly. Ideally, the issue of fairness is taken seriously. Taking responsibility for fair play and ensuring that everyone gets a just hearing can be a positive way of using this placement. At best, those with Saturn in Libra realize that co-operation is key to successful living, but at the same time are also realistic about the difficulties inherent in that process. Saturn placed here can yield various manifestations when it comes to the individual's relationships. Some will feel burdened by the prospect or the reality of marriage; others will be fearful of being on their own; many will marry later in life or, if young, marriage to someone older is implied. Frequently, the individual has to learn in their marital-type relationships the difficulties inherent in keeping the peace and also in asserting themselves. One could say that the capacity for and desirability of compromising is likely to be tested. Sometimes, being direct and asserting themselves is precisely what is required. A contract, as opposed to a more casual cohabiting situation, will be insisted upon by some and eschewed at all costs by others. Whatever the actual scenario, it is through partnership that the individual will learn about the realities of give and take; the realities that people have differing points of view and opposing needs. Often the rules of marriage have to be tested, infidelity being the common by-product of marriage that facilitates that process.

Saturn in Scorpio – ♄ ♏

'When authorities warn you of the sinfulness of sex, there is an important lesson to be learned: do not have sex with the authorities.'
Matt Groening, creator of *The Simpsons*

Some with this placement may make it difficult for others to know them on more intimate levels. The feeling is that their privacy has to be defended. There can be a fear of giving their power and autonomy to another, perhaps due in part to an experience of a lack of privacy in childhood or early betrayals. Some with this placement will become an authority in a traditionally Scorpionic subject area – perhaps medicine, psychology or the occult. At best, they will be an authority on emotional issues generally. While often skilled at dealing with other people's crises, many with this placement are terrified of having crises themselves. There may be strong passions swirling around in the Saturn in Scorpio person, but very few would realize it because the individual knows how to control their feelings. However, the releasing and sharing of their inner life can be precisely what is required in order to establish the much longed-for intimacy with others. Nevertheless, the ability to create strong boundaries can be very useful in the practice of most therapies and can be a useful stratagem for survival in the world generally. Childhood scenarios can include an early stifling of sexual curiosity or curiosity about death. For instance, the death of the father can have unusually strong family repercussions. Individuals with this placement often have to find out about sex and sexuality the hard way (through encountering difficult experiences), as the whole subject area is likely to be a 'no go' area in the early home environment. Some with

Saturn here will attract sexual interest from older partners themselves. Saturn in Scorpio must surely be the significator for the 'dirty old man'; not in the individual themselves but when projected on to others (see pages 318-19). Guarding against stormy weather can sometimes manifest as vocational activities in insurance, taking responsibility for joint finances and various occupations involving corporate money. Becoming an authority of either the emotional or practical aspects of death can be another manifestation.

Saturn in Sagittarius – ♄ ♐

This is potentially the placement of the sceptic, as those with Saturn here may be frightened of being too trusting, too optimistic or too ready to believe. Equally, the idea of a life without some kind of higher meaning can be too horrifying to bear but faith doesn't come easily to many with this placement. Sometimes this is because of a strict religious or moral upbringing. Individuals with this placement may operate from anywhere along the sceptical-gullible polarity with respect to their beliefs, whether these be religious, political, moral or simply their beliefs about the outcome of a project or situation. Whatever the religious upbringing, this is commonly a placement of people who adhere to a strict moral and ethical code, and who feel guilty if they transgress it. Sometimes there can be a self-righteous attitude and a tendency to judge others for their perceived moral lapses. If the rest of the chart confirms it, Saturn here can help to produce an academic – the person called upon perhaps to prove they are bright, educated and wise. Indeed, this is a good placement for any kind of teacher. Often there will be an interest in the rules of a particular academic subject or an interest in subjects that have strong rules, such as science or mathematics. The lessons with Saturn here are often those concerning trust. How to be able to take risks in life and to go out into the world and explore, yet to have a realistic awareness of the dangers inherent in risk-taking. Some with this Saturn will become expert on the whole notion of taking risk. This is an ideal placement for people who travel – perhaps in connection with their work – especially to places that are largely uncharted and unexplored. Some will have experienced the down side of living life on the edge, or living life while trusting to luck, through a parent. This placement is synonymous with the gambling or wayfaring father, for instance, although this is just one of many possibilities. Saturn in Sagittarius can provide a gift for long-term planning and, where humour is also suggested elsewhere in the chart, a talent for comic timing.

Saturn in Capricorn – ♄ ♑

Saturn falling in its own sign suggests that discipline, duty, obedience and a sense of responsibility will feature strongly in the life, or that the person thinks it should. Commonly, the individual will have shouldered considerable responsibility at an early age or watched a parent do so. Often there is a particular closeness to the father or an identification with him. He may have been older than the norm. His life may have been dominated by work or duty. Tradition often plays a major role in the life; some will feel that there is a tradition that they have to live up to or sometimes defend themselves against. Sometimes the situation is one where the family, village or town in which they were raised was rather old-fashioned – and this can be either appreciated by the individual or disliked by them. Usually the liking for tradition increases with age. Typically there is a marked need to achieve something tangible, measurable and durable in the life and a marked need to feel in control. This person wants to be respected and taken seriously and may be overly sensitive with respect to their reputation. The fear of failure or censure can be very marked with this placement. It is not surprising, therefore, if this individual is one to keep to the rules; one to try to avoid putting a foot wrong. Some will want to achieve at all costs and will judge themselves severely if their results fall far short of their expectations. There can be a tendency to expect far too much of themselves and sometimes of others. Success may come late for some but ideally it will come eventually. Those in more subservient roles may become rather dour over time and youngsters will inevitably attract authority figures (such as employers) who are hard taskmasters. On the plus side, this Saturn increases a feeling of perseverance in a chart and an ability to conquer adversity. Depending on the chart overall, there can also be tremendous organizational skills here, plus patience, dedication, efficiency and a liking for order coupled with a strong sense of duty. There is often an abhorrence of the thought of being materially dependent, and frugality may result. Saturn in its own sign can be associated with strong defences, including walls. The Berlin Wall was built when Saturn was conjunct Jupiter (a large wall!) in Capricorn and came down during its next Saturn return when Saturn in Capricorn was conjunct Neptune (a dissolving wall!).[12]

Saturn in Aquarius – ♄ ♒

The lessons for society at times when Saturn is transiting Aquarius, and also for individuals with this placement, are usually concerned with tolerating people who are different in some way and accepting those who pursue alternative lifestyles. Some may have early experiences of feeling punished for being in some way 'different'. It is not unusual for individuals with this placement to have an underlying fear of not fitting in, a fear of being an alien. And yet, at the same time, there can be an abhorrence of the idea of being ordinary and a drive towards expressing themselves with originality. How to be unique and recognized as such, coupled with still being an ordinary member of Joe Public, can be the mission here. The lessons for this placement are often found in the realm of friendship. Some with Saturn here distrust others who appear to be too friendly, and yet there can be this fear of not fitting in and maybe a reserve about breaking through the reserve of others. Learning to trust in that which is new and progressive can also be a theme. Ensuring that change is implemented responsibly, and taking positive steps to deal with the social barriers that separate people, can be a positive way of using this placement. Some with this Saturn may work with people who are traditionally marginalized by society, while others may become authority figures in the world of technology. Saturn in Aquarius can suggest a strong sense of social responsibility and, while there can be a distrust of groups, taking responsibility for the developmental progress of a group of people, whether it be small or large, formal or informal, can provide a positive use of this Saturn. Saturn here can suggest the formation of friendships with older people and also the desire to feel on friendly terms with authority figures (such as their employer). On occasion, the placement describes a father who was perceived as always being out with his mates rather than being at home; hence the potential distrust of group situations.

Saturn in Pisces – ♄ ♓

This is a gentle Saturn placement with not very many boundaries. This individual will stretch any rules or limits placed on their behaviour. Not always strong on self-discipline and maybe wanting to escape rules and regulations, those with Saturn in Pisces may be prone to poor time-keeping. There may not be much appetite for areas in life which demand a high standard of boundary-keeping or -setting. Having said that, the combination of Saturn and Pisces can make for great artistic and often spiritual discipline in those whose charts suggest an interest in such matters. Basically there can be an openness to spiritual matters and yet, often, a fear of being too open, a fear of being sucked into something outside their control. Nevertheless, Saturn here can describe the individual who sets aside time to meditate and then actually does it. It is also a useful placement for those involved in the music industry and many exceptional actors also have it. This is perhaps because the more flexible boundaries lend themselves more easily to entering into the psyche of another character. On occasion, the weak boundaries can make the individual particularly prone to being led or manipulated into situations against their will or against their own best interests. They are also prone to easily feeling guilty about matters which may or may not be their responsibility. The lessons with Saturn here often involve sacrifice and acceptance, and demand humility in some way. This placement can also sometimes indicate someone who takes responsibility for clearing up the mess in various contexts and situations. There can be a fear of chaos and/or a dislike of situations where they are out of control. Frequently there will have been a parent who was a victim (possibly of alcohol) or unable to cope for whatever reason. The individual may end up taking responsibility for them. If other factors concur, perhaps the father was weak or absent. This placement sometimes indicates that the individual may be more than usually badly affected by alcohol.

The Outer Planets

Visible to the naked eye, the previous seven planets (including the Sun and Moon) have always been known and until recent times have provided sufficient symbolism to reflect the human experience.

However, things have changed radically over the last century. The 20th century witnessed the advent of the telephone, space travel and huge technological advances. The discovery of electricity alone, and with it the production of countless time-saving electrical appliances, has transformed everyday life. The social and medical changes have also been huge – the contraceptive pill alone created a revolution in sexual behaviour. In the so-called developed world, at least, life is much more stimulating, difficult and complicated than it ever was. It is also moving at an alarming and increasing speed. Astrologers such as William Lilly in the 1600s could make precise predictions because there were fewer possibilities and many more moral certainties – there were only so many things that were likely to happen and people's views of the world wouldn't differ so much. In Lilly's day, clients were not encouraged to think in terms of personal autonomy and free will. The astrologer's job was to tell the client their fate. Nowadays an astrologer looking at the chart of a child cannot even imagine the occupational possibilities (for instance) that might exist for him or her, even a mere twenty years down the line. The philosophical stance of astrology has shifted, too, with many an astrologer now taking the view that one's fate is something to be negotiated and worked with. The major sweeping and revolutionary changes in the world in the last 200 years have been mirrored by the discovery of the outer planets – Uranus, Neptune and Pluto (discovered in 1781, 1846 and 1930 respectively) – and the attributes associated with them. The far-reaching effects of global warming, and economic expansion in the East, will no doubt be best described by these planets too, and perhaps also by other bodies that have been discovered since and others that have yet to be discovered.

Uranus ♅

'Technology is the knack of so arranging the world that we don't have to experience it.'

Max Frisch

Discovery[13]

Uranus was accidentally discovered by musician and keen amateur astronomer William Herschel[14] on 13 March 1781 in Bath between ten and eleven at night using a 7-foot/2-metre telescope. Its position in longitude was about 24 degrees of Gemini at the time. The planet had been observed many times before (it is borderline visible to the naked eye), even as far back as the 1600s, but had previously been categorized as a star. Uranus has a number of large but very thin rings which were not discovered until the late 1970s.

Astronomically, the planet has always been full of surprises. Astrologically, Uranus is concerned with various ways of being different, so perhaps it is not surprising that physically the planet is also unique. It spins on an axis that is tilted so much that the planet looks like a spinning top turned on its side. Because of this tilt, the Sun shines directly over the North Pole and directly over the South Pole alternately every 42 Earth years. Uranus is a gas planet, composed mainly of hydrogen and helium gases. It is not thought to have an internal heat source but does have a very powerful magnetic field. Methane in its atmosphere, interacting with sunlight, is the cause of its blue-green colour, a colour reminiscent of the zodiac sign of Aquarius, of which Uranus is co-ruler. Also in line with Uranian symbolism is the *Voyager 2* observation that Uranus radiates an ultraviolet light which has been dubbed 'electroglow'.

Astronomy

- Mean distance from the Sun: 1.78 billion miles/2.87 billion kilometres.
- Diameter: 32,300 miles/52,000 kilometres. Over 14 times larger than the Earth.
- Sidereal period (approximate time for the planet to orbit the Sun): Uranus has an orbit of 84 years and thus spends seven years in each sign.
- Retrograde motion: retrograde each year for about five months.
- Moons: Uranus has at least 27 satellites, most of them named after characters in Shakespeare's plays, although Ariel and Umbriel are from Alexander Pope. The five main moons – Titania, Miranda, Oberon, Ariel and Umbriel – are much larger than the others. Titania and Oberon were discovered by Herschel in 1787, Ariel and Umbriel in 1851 by William Lassell, and Miranda in 1948 by Gerard Kuiper. The spacecraft *Voyager 2* found ten moons hidden within Uranus's rings in 1986. More moons or 'moonlets' (they can be very small) are being discovered all the time.

Mythology

According to Hesiod, in the beginning there was only Chaos, an empty void. This void gave birth to Gaia (the Earth). Gaia bore many children but first she bore the sky: Ouranos or Uranus. Gaia then gave birth to the mountains and the sea. Note that the sky is very far away and Uranus concerns itself with the psychological principle of distance. Uranus became her mate and her equal as he 'covered' her on all sides. As a couple, they became the parents and grandparents of the Olympians, and Uranus may indeed be a significator of grandfathers. Their children included the Cyclopes – Brontes (thunder), Steropes (lightning) and Arges (thunderbolts) – who resembled other gods but had only one eye in the middle of their foreheads, the twelve Titans, and the Hundred-handed Ones (the Centimanes) who had fifty heads and a hundred arms each. Uranus is always involved in all situations involving mutations and deviations from the norm. In the myth, presumably the mutations occurred because of in-breeding and incest (Uranus had bedded Gaia, his mother); boundaries have been crossed which aren't supposed to be crossed, from the point of view of civilized Greek society, anyway. The Uranian impulse always does impel the crossing of boundaries. In modern day terms, one example of boundary-crossing includes tinkering with nature through genetic modification, cloning, etc. Mary Shelley's *Frankenstein* is perhaps *the* Uranian story of all time and can be interpreted as a warning of the implications of such practices.

In any event, Uranus in the horoscope describes where we are different – psychologically, physically or in our life choices. Continuing with the story, Uranus found his children very ugly and banished them to Tartarus, a place so far beneath the Earth that it takes a falling anvil nine days to get there. Some interpretations of the story describe Tartarus as being Gaia's womb, others as her bowels, and therefore that Uranus pushed the children back inside her. Whatever the story, Gaia wasn't happy to lose her children. First she mourned them and then she got angry and planned her revenge. She created flint and made a huge sickle, and then gathered together Kronos and his brothers to ask them for help. Only Kronos (Saturn), the youngest Titan, was willing to assist, so Gaia gave him the sickle and, when Uranus came to lie with Gaia, Kronos castrated him and threw his testicles into the sea. From the blood that fell on to the Earth sprang the three Furies (the Erinyes) – the goddesses of revenge. And from the foaming sea and Uranus's discarded testicles, Aphrodite was born.

General Characteristics

Collectively, Uranus is concerned with new ideas breaking into society. Such ideas may be breathtaking in their scale and in the revolutionary changes they bring. Uranus embraces most inventions, many discoveries and, in particular, technological advancements. Such advancements lead to progress and the saving of time and often freedom from some kind of drudgery or enslavement, at least for some people. Difficulties inevitably occur because the Uranian impulse pays no heed to the ethical or emotional repercussions of such technological forging ahead. The action of the planet operates in a completely undemocratic and often stubborn and wilful manner. Uranian energy is the most unco-operative of all the planets. It is the planet of the dictator because, if prominent, it can give rise to a perverse, autocratic and fanatical bent. In today's world, issues such as cloning and genetic engineering are at the forefront of the Uranian urge. People are initially shocked by developments brought about by the action of Uranus (the contraceptive pill, the computer, the World Wide Web), which at a stroke not only revolutionizes society but leaves many of its members out in the cold. After all, two-thirds of the world don't even have a telephone, let alone a computer terminal.

Uranus Turns into Saturn

In the English language, the two planets are almost an anagram of each other. Curiously, most things Uranian eventually become Saturnian: whatever shocks society today usually becomes accepted, institutionalized and taken for granted tomorrow. The rebellious teenager becomes rather conventional, ten or twenty years down the line. As Nick Kollerstrom has pointed out,[13] the age of uranium ore (the metal associated with Uranus) is measured by the presence of lead. Since isotopes heavier than lead (as uranium is) eventually turn into lead, which is Saturn's metal, the older the mine, the more lead and less uranium it will contain.

Rebellion

Both in collective and personal terms, Uranus challenges all that has become stuck, sterile or predictable. Its message is fiercely anti-Establishment and unconventional. Uranus will always force the breaking of rules and the crossing of boundaries. The concern of Uranus is to challenge the status quo and to break with the past and with tradition because, from the Uranian point of view, clinging to the past can only hinder progress. When an individual is touched by the Uranian impulse, there may well be a need to turn their back on family, State or some other voice of authority. All the outer planets challenge the constructs of Saturn, albeit in different ways. In the case of Uranus, the challenge is to authority, tradition, the status quo and to time itself. Uranus is concerned with liberation and freedom while Saturn is concerned with control and safety; two concepts that do not sit comfortably side by side.

Revolt, Revolting, Revolution

The word 'revolution' literally means to turn over. It often implies returning to a former recurring position (as with a music record that moves at so many RPMs – revolutions per minute), although is usually interpreted as civil disobedience. Indeed, the word 'revolt' means to cast off allegiance, to fall away to a rival power, basically to disobey whoever is in authority. Some of society is inevitably revolted by some of the sweeping changes ushered in by the action of Uranus. Conversely, finding something repellent, repulsive, disgusting – basically, revolting (which is how Uranus saw his children because of their deformities) – is usually the motive behind a revolution; something is perceived as being so disgusting that it has to be changed drastically.

Contempt, Castration and Rejection Themes

As with the myth, Uranus is *the* planet to be associated with castration of all kinds and here one can include any situation where something has been cut out or cut off. This includes surgical procedures where something is removed. For example, the chart of a woman with Moon in Taurus (throat) in opposition to Uranus told the story of her mother (Moon) who had had her thyroid gland removed. Mars – the planet to associate with surgery – was also plugging into the equation by square aspect.

An individual 'cutting out' and becoming emotionally detached from their feelings is another example of Uranus at work. Feeling estranged from family or society are common Uranian experiences. In some cases, the individual loses touch with the fact that they themselves have rejected society or the 'other' by turning their back on them. Rather like Ouranos with his children, the Uranian impulse is often to reject. Rightly or wrongly, the individual feels they have been left out in the cold and so they go off in a huff. Rejection, alienation, estrangement and feelings of isolation are major emotional experiences to be associated with this planet, especially when it is in aspect to personal planets and angles in the horoscope.

Contempt, Revulsion and Magnetism

The novelist Iris Murdoch, in her novel *A Fairly Honourable Defeat*, suggests that the opposite emotion to love is not so much hate as contempt, and surely this is a key Uranian emotion. It also provides a clue to the complementary and antagonistic relationship that exists between Venus and Uranus. To hold someone in contempt is to despise them, to consider them so inferior that it is beneath our dignity to have anything to do with them. Contempt is a common enough feeling among adolescents, who of necessity are struggling to assert their independence. It is often their elders' values and tastes (Venus) that are considered particularly abhorrent and from which they take great pains to distance themselves. Although one might interpret the myth as being about the fostering of their independence, in banishing his children, Ouranos provided an early example of contemptuous behaviour. The word 'contempt' is also used in legal circles, such as when an individual fails to respect the authority of a court of law or legislative body and, by flouting the rules, can be charged with contempt of court.

Venus and Uranus appear to be the significators behind the principles of magnetism, both in emotional terms but also quite literally in physical terms. Venus governs the principle of attraction, as when a positive pole meets a negative pole, and Uranus governs the principle of repulsion, as when like poles meet each other. Little wonder, therefore, that Uranus is the planet associated with electricity and all matters of an electrical and electronic nature.

Split Ups and Breaks

In all contexts, like the metal uranium and the idea of nuclear fission, Uranus is the planet to associate with splitting; with separating one portion of something from its other part. This can be seen in the case of relationship splits: if there is a clear and stark severance of relations between people, Uranus will usually be involved. In these days of complicated family structures, Uranus is also often a significator of step-relatives: for example, Uranus falling in the Fourth House and sometimes the Tenth can imply a step-parent; in the Fifth it can indicate step-children; in the Third it can point to step-siblings.

Whereas Saturn can be associated with brakes Uranus rules all kinds of breaks. Anything from broken crockery to broken families. In health matters, we might include broken bones if Saturn were also involved. In ordinary parlance, an individual may say 'Give us a break'; in other words, 'Let me off the hook for breaking the rules'.

Societal Rejection, Deportation and Exile

The discovery of Uranus heralded a period of immense social and political change in many parts of the world. France was reeling from revolution and America had just gained her independence. In Britain, the Industrial Revolution had driven thousands of poverty-stricken people from the country to the cities. A new underclass dependent on crime emerged, the prisons overflowed and the idea of deportation took root.

Uranus and Australia

Situations where individuals en masse are literally ostracized from society are very Uranian, as are situations where individuals voluntarily decide to emigrate. An example of mass ostracism occurred in the late 18th century in the UK, not long after Uranus was discovered. Britain and Ireland sent about 165,000 of its citizens to the then unknown land (to Europeans) that we now call Australia. From a UK perspective, being shipped off to Australia at that time would indeed have been like being sent to Tartarus; it might have taken a falling anvil the symbolic equivalent of nine days to reach Tartarus, but the sea journey took nearly nine months. In my view, Australia resonates strongly to Uranian vibes, not only because its early white settlers had been rejected by the land of their birth (as they in turn rejected the Aborigines), but because one is aware of there being so much sky and the population tends to live on the perimeters of the continent. The interior (the *out*back) is only sparsely populated. The land mass itself pretty much stands apart from the other great continents. It also has possibly the largest reserves of uranium on the planet. In my experience, Europeans when visiting Australia tend to do so when under the influence of major Uranian transits or directions.

The Urge for Independence

Allied to the notion of rejection is the insistence upon independence. To be independent means not depending upon (and usually not respecting) the authority of another, not being dependent on anything or anyone for one's existence. Standing alone in this way is in itself rejecting to others. It also implies a certain superior attitude, a standing apart, and therefore an aloof stance. At its most extreme, an insistence on independence is not only anti-family but anti-society and even anti-life, given that the planet is one giant ecosystem made up of many smaller ecosystems.

Differentness and Deviation

Uranus forges an independent path in the way that it always prompts contrary action; it inclines movement in the opposite or reverse direction to whatever has gone before. More traditional types view the insistence of following one's own path as a form of deviance, and in a way it is. To deviate literally means to take an *alternative* path and it is curious therefore that the word 'deviant' has such negative connotations. Certainly, all forms of deviation and deviancy are essentially Uranian. Whenever there is 'differentness', the influence of the planet can be felt.

The Prefix 'Un-'

The prefix 'un-' in English reverses the meaning of a word – usual becomes unusual, for instance. A great deal of words that do start with 'un-' accord well with the Uranian position, such as unusual, unconventional, unexpected, unpredictable, unco-operative, to name but a few. The same can be said for words with the prefix 'anti-' and, though less consistently the case, the same can be said of the prefix 'ir-' as in irregular or irreverent.

Physical Characteristics

Uranus operates at lightning speed. The physical qualities associated with its action are fast, freezing cold and taut. There is an extreme sudden and unexpected quality, which in turn is usually experienced as shocking. From the aesthetic point of view, Uranus can be associated with sky- and turquoise-blues and with blue-green colours. Certainly irregular and broken lines and streaks are Uranian. All kinds of explosions, lightning and flashes also apply, and any situation where there is some kind of break in rhythm. Particularly noticeable in mundane astrology, it should be noted that the action of Uranus usually tends towards extremism. The planet rarely delivers in half-measures.

The Body

Physically, all kinds of mutations and deformities (where an individual may deviate from the norm) are Uranian. Also instances where one part of the body is in rebellion (e.g. as in the case of the cancerous tumour) against the body in its entirety. As has been noted, Uranus governs all surgical procedures where a part of the body is rejected to the extent that the surgeon and/or patient decides to remove it.

Any kind of rupture or break is Uranian, as for example when a bone is broken or a blood vessel is ruptured. Spasms and cramps are also Uranian (here there is a sudden break in a bodily rhythm), as are convulsions. Accidents inevitably have Uranus, as well as Mars, 'in the frame', as accidents by their very nature are always unexpected. They also come as a shock.

Metal

Uranium[16] was discovered in 1789 by Martin Klaproth[17] and named after the planet Uranus. It is as common as tin and can be found in most rocks, animals and also in seawater. Although widespread in most places, uranium isn't always found in sufficiently concentrated amounts to make it economically viable to mine. Huge reserves can be found in Australia and Canada, and these countries are major suppliers of the metal. Uranium is very dense and heavy, and is silvery-white when refined. It is weakly radioactive and, like all radioactive isotopes, over time it decays; it is thought that this provides the main source of the heat inside the Earth. Its atomic number is 92, which may or may not be a number to associate with Uranus in symbolic terms. One of the isotopes that make up uranium can be split and it is this splitting (so-called nuclear fission) which produces the energy associated with nuclear power stations.

Interpreting Uranus

The aspects of Uranus and its house placement and rulership should be weighted much more heavily than Uranus by sign. This is, of course, because Uranus spends seven years in each zodiacal sign and impinges therefore more on the collective than on the individual in terms of sign placement. Nevertheless, the sign of Uranus can confirm information already suggested by other chart factors. Thus, for example, Uranus in Libra can be interpreted as a significator for divorce, but only if other factors in the chart also point the same way.

Uranus Through The Signs

Uranus in Aries – ♅ ♈

Most recent transit: 1927/8 to 1934/5. Next transit: May 2010 to 2018/19.
This seems to mark fast-moving periods of radical change with people seeking new sources of excitement. Stories involving speed, recklessness, independence, originality and possible extremism and civil disobedience are to be expected. Uranus in Aries brought the so-called Roaring Twenties and the motor car. The first transatlantic flight, cars and electrical appliances brought the promise of excitement and a new independence. In the West, for the first time, women smoked, drank, cut their hair, voted and went on dates unchaperoned.

Uranus in Taurus – ♅ ♉

Most recent transit: 1934/35 to 1941/2.
This is a very determined, stubborn and practically innovative combination. Uranus in Taurus periods may be characterized by considerable economic changes and shifts in people's values. During the last transit, the world recovered from the Depression but then was plunged into the Second World War. People could not rely on keeping any material security they may have built up, as many were cut off from their land and possessions. One possession that all people have is their body and the safety of that could not be relied upon either. But in the struggle to maintain life, people had an opportunity to free themselves from their more materialistic shackles. In terms of wealth and land, whether by accident or design, the move may be towards a more level playing field with Uranus here. The onset of rationing meant that people in many Western countries became more independent in terms of growing their own food.

Uranus in Gemini – ♅ ♊

Most recent transit: 1941/2 to 1948/9.
This placement may signify new methods of education and a generation of free thinkers; those likely to skip school or rebel at university when of an age to do so. Also a university education for those not expected to have one. The last transit saw the school-leaving age increase in the UK. This combination can be associated with radical, revolutionary, perhaps reforming ideas and with new technology that speeds up communication. Gemini is the sign to associate with dualism. During the last transit, as part of rationing, the British government asked women to shorten their skirts to save cloth – all over the place things were cut into two. Many countries were partitioned as well, often causing separations and a break in communication between friends and families. This was sometimes due to the war (e.g. Germany was divided into East and West Germany) but there were other instances: Korea was split into the North and South; India was partitioned into India and Pakistan; Southern Ireland became Eire and officially separated from Northern Ireland. Various countries also became independent (Burma, India, Sri Lanka) and split from their host country. This transit can be associated with civil war as in fraternal splits, with brother fighting against brother. Both the American War of Independence and the Civil War took place when Uranus was in Gemini.

Uranus in Cancer – ♅ ♋

Most recent transit: 1948/9 to 1955/6.

The last transit spawned the Women's Liberation movement and also a generation of people who wanted to get as far away from home as soon as possible. Women started to question their role as mothers and housewives, and the general movement was towards personal liberty and away from family responsibility. Family life started to change and family breakdown became the norm for a generation willing to turn its back on family values. Freedom from domestic chores became a reality as washing machines and other household appliances gained ground. Some European countries talked of becoming a trading family and out of that was born the Common Market.

Uranus in Leo – ♅ ♌

Most recent transit: 1955/6 to 1961/2.

This particularly stubborn combination can be associated with revolutions in the art world and in how people spend their recreation time. Changes in the world of banking might also be expected. It is a time when that which is bright, dramatic, glorious and bold may take centre stage. Innovation in matters to do with lighting may feature. During the last transit, the world was introduced to the rave (a loud party!), to lasers and, more significantly, a huge percentage of the industrialized world embraced television. The world was also introduced to the bold colours and strong imagery that comprised Pop Art. Possibly people want to do their own thing, rather than follow their leader, with Uranus in Leo. Leaders may also find their span of leadership unexpectedly and dramatically cut short when Uranus is here. During the last transit, the 14th Dalai Lama went into exile and there were many assassinations as well as unexpected natural deaths of leaders. And new and often young heroes unexpectedly emerge when Uranus is in Leo. The last transit marked the first major era of space travel – humankind felt anything was possible and, in a variety of ways, wanted to glory in its achievements. Young people looking for glory signed up to go to war in Vietnam or other places.

Uranus in Virgo – ♅ ♍

Most recent transit: 1961/2 to 1968/9.

This combination can be associated with breakthroughs in medicine, trade union activity and changes in working practices. New and usually small electrical, electronic and technological devices may come on the market. This can herald generations keen to embrace alternative medicine or to clean up the planet. The last transit saw Pluto join Uranus in Virgo (see pages 213-14). It saw farming practices change and also a backlash against pesticides and insecticides. Insects proved to be a surprise feature of this transit (e.g. the Beatles and Buddy Holly's backing group, the Crickets) and insecticide was used in the Vietnam War. Rachel Carson's deeply influential book, *Silent Spring*, appeared. Having discovered that pesticides were residing in all creatures living on Earth, she spoke of the dangers of misusing pesticides and called for a change in how humans viewed and treated the natural world. A new awareness of the health risks of smoking meant that smoking started to be seen an act of rebellion, rather than something that was cool.

Uranus in Libra – ♅ ♎

Most recent transit: 1968/9 to 1974/5.

One might associate this combination with changes in contract law and in the legal system generally. It can arouse a new awareness of inherent injustices in society and can potentially lead to strikes and other civil unrest arising from perceived unfair practice. In the UK alone, the last transit saw the Equal Pay Act, the Race Relations Act, the Sexual Discrimination Act and the abolition of the death penalty. Changes can be expected too in the ways that people conduct their relationships and perhaps a rise in marriage or divorce rates. During the last transit, the Divorce Reform Act was passed in the UK, making it easier for couples to divorce.

Uranus in Scorpio – ♅ ♏

Most recent transit: 1974/5 to 1981.

This combination mixes the Uranian idea of shock and the Martian capacity for violence with the Scorpio predilection for melodrama. Extremist behaviour and explosions of anger are to be expected! In line with this, the last transit saw an unprecedented number of bombings, sieges and murders (including the Yorkshire Ripper murders) in the UK, where there were also race riots and freak weather: snow in June (1975), and the worst drought for 500 years and the hottest summer for over 200 years (1976). Concerned with the truth, as Uranus always is, this combination can be associated with exposés concerning death, sex and corporate finance. The phrase 'date rape' was first recorded in 1975 and punk music began in earnest in 1976. The transit also saw the beginning of 'alternative' comedy.

Uranus in Sagittarius – ♅ ♐

Most recent transit: 1981 to 1988.

This freedom-loving combination conjures up the notion of exciting journeys to offbeat places. It favours progress and innovation (but conversely, possibly strikes and disruptions) with respect to most forms of transport. The last transit saw an increase in air traffic to meet expanding holiday travel. Travel can also be in the mind, and the last transit also saw the beginning of the Internet, the Microsoft Windows operating system, mobile phones and video games, although these did not become commonplace for some years, possibly until Uranus reached Aquarius. The British public were also introduced to the far-flung Falkland Islands as the UK went to war with Argentina. Uranus is always concerned with change and resistance to change, and this combination of a liberty-loving planet falling in a libertarian sign suggests that the main battleground will revolve around people's beliefs and their having the freedom to pursue those beliefs, whether they be political, religious or philosophical. When Uranus was last in Sagittarius, Mikhail Gorbachev introduced *glasnost* (openness) into Soviet policy which heralded many changes in the country, including freedom of speech.

Uranus in Capricorn – ♅ ♑

Most recent transit: 1988 to 1995/6. See also Neptune in Capricorn,
as these planets were conjunct in the early 1990s (exact in 1993).

This can be a cold, hard, anti-inflationary combination and one which might favour right-wing politics and the demands of management over those of the workforce. However, as always with Uranus transits, the reverse can also be true. Uranus can herald periods of reform for governments and monarchies. During the last transit, anything that might be described as 'Establishment' was under threat. Institutions which were solid and, having stood the test of time, one felt could always be relied upon, started to go through radical changes. Some of the safest, seemingly rocklike companies and organizations acted as if they were shaky and could fall down. The early 1990s brought a period of recession. However, unexpected companies and entrepreneurs also emerged, and in South Africa Nelson Mandela was freed from gaol and later elected President. Many established companies went in for downsizing and, from now on, people could no longer have any expectation of working in the same job for the duration of their lives. The last transit saw the end of the Cold War, the Soviet Union and the Berlin Wall, all of which had previously felt immutable.

Uranus in Aquarius – ♅ ♒

Most recent transits: 1912 to 1919, and 1995/6 to 2003.

This combination may herald tremendous growth in terms of technological and scientific advancement but also can give rise to events which require such progress to be made. For example, in May 1997 the first human case of the current spate of bird flu was recorded. Seemingly the strain of this flu virus is similar, if not the same, to that which killed up to 50 million people (one-fifth of the world's population) in 1918, when Uranus was also in Aquarius. Events often conspire to teach humanity that we are powerless in the face of nature when Uranus is here. In differing ways, the boundaries between different peoples are likely to be broken down. Although the World Wide Web had been around for a while, the recent transit through Aquarius saw it reach even greater numbers of people throughout the world. Various members of society may find the strength that enables them to insist upon their freedom during Uranus in Aquarius transits. The most recent transit saw the introduction of cyberpets (!) and Dolly, the first cloned sheep.

Uranus in Pisces – ♅ ♓

Last transit: 1919/20 to 1927. Current transit: 2003 to 2010/11.

There is a sparkly, glitzy, celebratory feeling about this combination which is an ideal one for ice skating and ice dancing as well as many other creative arts. One might expect significant changes to be made in the world of shipping, fishing and the marine world generally. Changes and surprises can also be expected in the film industry as well as on the drugs and alcohol front, and sometimes there can be wars and civil unrest arising from drink or drugs. The 1919 transit of Uranus in Pisces coincided with the prohibition of alcohol in the USA, which actually increased the consumption of alcohol. The current transit has also 'coincided' with an increasing awareness of the prevalence of binge-drinking in the UK and conversely with an increase in pub opening hours. Uranus in Pisces in the 1920s brought talking movies while more radical, offbeat films have surprised some by winning the top awards during the current transit. The current transit sees Uranus in mutual reception with Neptune as that planet falls in Aquarius; both ingresses are ideal for technological advancement with respect to film, video and photography. Doubtless, digital photography and everything else that is digital owes much to it.

Neptune Ψ

'As Arthur C. Clarke has observed: "How inappropriate to call this planet Earth, when clearly it is ocean." Nearly three-quarters of the Earth's surface is sea ...'

James Lovelock

'When we let Romance go, we change the sky for the ceiling.'

George Meredith

Discovery

Appropriately, the discovery of Neptune in 1846 is somewhat confused. It began with mistakes (including the fact that Neptune was mistaken for Uranus at one point), a disappearance and a huge scandal played out in the newspapers. Galileo spotted the planet in 1612 but dismissed it as one of Jupiter's moons. Over two hundred years later, the presence of a planet beyond Uranus was suspected to account for the fact that something was interfering with the gravitational pull of Uranus and pulling it off course. Neptune's position was predicted quite independently by John Couch Adams[18] of Cambridge University and, a year later, by Urbain Le Verrier in France, both using mathematical calculations. Neither knew the other was working on the same problem and both shared the predicament of needing a telescope and an astronomer to actually look for the body in the predicted place. Couch sent his observations to George Airy, the Astronomer Royal, who, perhaps not taking Adams seriously, did nothing to investigate the matter further. According to Caroline Herschel,[19] Le Verrier's superiors in France didn't take much notice of him either but Le Verrier did persuade Johann Gottfried Galle of the Berlin Observatory to look and, with the assistance of Heinrich d'Arrest, Galle found Neptune very close to its predicted position. Neptune was found on 23 September 1846 at 26 degrees Aquarius conjunct Saturn in the same degree. The success of the mathematical predictions was ground-breaking and gave testimony to Newton's Law of Gravity. Newspapers in France accused the British of stealing credit for the discovery and English newspapers, similarly scandalized, accused the French of doing much the same thing. In the end, and after much controversy, Le Verrier and Adams shared the credit for Neptune's discovery. As with Uranus, the planet went through various names before its mythological nomenclature stuck.

Astronomy

Neptune is the fourth-largest planet in our solar system but the smallest of the four gas planets. It is usually the eighth planet out from the Sun except every 248 years, when the orbit-crosser Pluto moves inside the orbit of Neptune for about a twenty-year period (this last happened between 1979 and 1999); at such times Neptune becomes the outermost planet. Neptune has five rings (discovered by *Voyager 2* in 1989), three of which are named Galle, Le Verrier and Adams after Neptune's discoverers. Some rings are narrow while others are broad and diffuse. Adams, the outermost ring, has three arcs which have been named Liberty, Equality and Fraternity. Neptune is a very windy and stormy place and enjoys seasons and temperature changes. Its clouds are thought to be composed of frozen methane and this is believed to be the reason for the planet's blue colour. Various features (e.g. a Great Dark Spot the size of the Earth) on the planet have been known to disappear or shapeshift.

- Mean distance from Sun: approximately 2,793 million miles/4,496 million kilometres.
- Diameter: approximately 30,775 miles/49,526 kilometres; about four times the size of Earth.
- Sidereal period (approximate time for the planet to orbit the Sun): 164.8 years. This means that Neptune spends about 14 years in each zodiacal sign.
- Retrograde motion: once a year for about five months.
- Moons: thirteen are known. The largest moon, Triton, was discovered in 1846 by William Lassell. About two-thirds the size of the Earth's Moon, Triton is known to be geologically active; for example, it has ice-spewing geysers. It is also thought to have a watery environment, which might even support life. The moon is unique for many reasons, one being that it moves in a backwards direction. The other moons (all named after sea deities) are much smaller and consist of Nereid (discovered by Gerard Kuiper in 1949), Galatea, Despina, Naiad, Larissa, Proteus and Thalassa (discovered by the *Voyager 2* spacecraft in 1989), plus five more very small moons, as yet unnamed, which were discovered in 2002 and 2003.

Mythology

After deposing their father Kronos, the brothers Zeus, Hades and Poseidon drew lots for who was to have lordship over the heavens, the sea and the underworld. Poseidon won the seas. Poseidon had these as his main domain but he ruled over lakes and rivers, too. Despite the immense size of territory, he often competed with other gods for various cities and areas of land. In the same way that the sea doesn't usually penetrate inland for very long, he was very often defeated. Similarly, Neptune in the horoscope can describe a place where we are thirsty, never satisfied and always longing for more. Like the sea and our emotions, Poseidon was uncontrollable in his rages; when he didn't get his own way, he became vindictive, causing either floods or drought. This can be likened to the watery disasters we sometimes see when Neptune is making aspect to various planets in the sky; for instance, Hurricane Katrina occurred in 2005 when Neptune was square Mars (although obviously there were other indicators at work too). Poseidon is usually portrayed with his trident, a three-pronged staff usually used for catching fish, which he used to calm waters, to create storms, to command sea creatures, to produce springs of water or to create earthquakes (he was god of earthquakes). The trident has been associated with various religions; for instance, it has been linked with the Trinity in Christianity.

At one point Zeus and Poseidon both wanted to marry the beautiful sea goddess Thetis, but they learned from Prometheus that her son would become greater than his father, which prompted both suitors to abandon her fast. Poseidon turned his attention to another sea goddess, Amphitrite, whom he had seen dancing with her sisters, but she viewed him with distaste and ran away. Like the sea overwhelming the land, Poseidon followed and raped her. Poseidon did eventually marry Amphitrite but not without the intercession of Delphinus (Dolphin) who pleaded Poseidon's case for him. Amphitrite shared Poseidon's kingdom, and in pictures she is often shown by his side; perhaps her responsibility was over sea creatures. Poseidon had nearly as many affairs as Zeus and fathered many children (many of them monsters) – as always, water is the great fertile element. With Amphitrite he fathered Triton who was half-fish; with Demeter he fathered the horse Orion; and with Medusa he fathered Pegasus the flying horse.

Jupiter and Neptune share joint rulership of Pisces and, like the brothers in myth, they have much in common. Both can be associated with various aspects of man's search for meaning, with excesses of all kinds and also with horses, which Poseidon is supposed to have created.

Neptune and the Sea

The mythology surrounding Poseidon, above all else, symbolizes the sea. In many ways, the sea is an appropriate symbol for the planet, being boundless, unfathomable, and its danger and vastness usually being under-estimated.

Erosion of Boundaries

Both Uranus and Neptune challenge the boundaried world-view of Saturn. Although powerful, water has no form, no shape and no edges. In keeping with this, Neptune works by undermining and dissolving what it touches, taking away any sense of definition. Imagine drawing a line on a piece of paper with a soft pencil or charcoal (the line is representative of Saturn); the effect of Neptune is like that of a soggy finger rubbing over the line, it will become indistinct and hazy.

The Ego-less Planet

Because of this erosion of boundaries, in the world of Neptune one feels a part of everything. There is no longer any separation between self and not-self. All becomes One and One is all. While this feeling of oneness is key to the mystical experience as one has to lose oneself in order to merge with the Divine, at the individual level it can be very difficult because, unless one is a truly enlightened soul, inevitably one feels lost and anxious in a universe characterized by nothingness. For when definition disappears, 'nothing' is all that remains except feelings and sensations. For good and ill, being part of the One dispenses with the notion of ego and individuality. As is the case when travelling through thick fog, we quickly lose our way if thrown into the ocean. However, creatures who live in the sea don't appear to have a problem with being lost; they navigate their world with the aid of different senses.

Compassion and Sensitivity

In a world where there is no separation between self and not-self, one is naturally a compassionate being for there are no boundaries to prevent us from empathizing with the suffering of others. We don't have to put ourselves in another's shoes for we are already wearing them. The house where Neptune is found in a chart and the house it rules (the one with Pisces on the cusp) may show areas of particular compassion that are either given or received. It is through our Neptune placement and aspects that we identify with the victim, and through doing so we either become a victim ourselves or are propelled into pursuing the role of saviour. Here we feel sorry for others, here we feel pity. We may think we are merely being sensitive and compassionate but, in truth, our pity is as much for ourselves as for the object of concern. If Neptune is linked to our Fifth House, for example, we might be alive to the suffering of children and want to rescue them, or perhaps we feel compassion for the struggling artist. In the Tenth, our compassion may be for a parent or even our boss or, equally, they may feel sorry for us.

Planets and parts of the chart which hook into Neptune often take on an over-sensitive quality. Here, the individual may be too refined to cope with the roughness, pain and crudity that is part of everyday life. Little wonder, therefore, that some individuals who resonate strongly to Neptune want to escape from the 'real world' altogether. Planets plugging into Neptune often describe the means of escape: for the Venus-Neptune person it might be through romantic fantasy, whereas the Mercury-Neptune type may be addicted to reading or uplifting conversation. Some Sun-Neptune individuals avoid being themselves by fantasizing about being someone else, and so on.

Transcendence and Escape

At best, Neptune urges us not so much to escape but to transcend ordinary reality, to lift ourselves up and touch something more wondrous. The true mystic lives in the world and of the world and isn't simply trying to avoid the bits they don't like. A person of a truly mystical bent isn't trying to escape from discomfort but, perhaps having cultivated a more sensitive perception, is able to see beyond what is immediate and material, is able to glimpse a Divine hand at work, or sense the bigger picture. The person is able, as William Blake expressed it, 'to see the world in a grain of sand'. The problem can be in deciding whether someone does have that greater sensitivity or whether they have merely deluded themselves into thinking that this is the case. As always, Neptune is the planet to associate with *delusions* of all kinds.

One way to get a feeling for Neptune is to remember what it feels like to be under the influence of alcohol. We drink alcohol for a variety of reasons but one of the effects of drinking is that after a drink or two (or five or seven), nothing much matters any more, the work-related stress of the morning disappears in the alcoholic haze of the evening.

Favourite Neptunian vehicles for escaping from reality and anaesthetizing the stresses of daily life include alcohol, drugs, the cinema, and TV. Drugs are routinely used to numb pain, to anaesthetize and to propel people from one state of consciousness into another. Drugs, like alcohol but even more so, distort the individual's perception of time and space so that they are no longer limited by those confines. Rules don't apply any more, either. Without space, time, rules and regulations, anything becomes possible, as indeed it is in the Neptunian world of fantasy, sleep and dreams. Paradoxically, though, in the 'real' world, nothing becomes possible without the structures provided by Saturn – a sense of time, space and boundaries generally.

Film, Music and the Arts

All the outer planets are concerned with collective issues and with fashion of one sort or another. With Neptune, the fashion is in the arts, and in particular, in film, dance and music. Neptune isn't a planet to be associated with feelings in a personal sense but collectively it does describe society's longings and goes some way to creating them in the first place. This is where the artist is involved, for the artist gives form to the dreams, fantasies and yearnings of all of society, however vague those longings might be. And in giving form to them, they become less inchoate and more rooted in a reality. As it slowly moves through the signs, Neptune defines what and who a culture is going to find glamorous: who and what is going to enchant and captivate us.

Watching TV and going to the movies are ways to escape from the harshness of the world or to actually experience that world, but in an anaesthetized form: we can view the world's atrocities from the comfort of our armchair. They are also tools we use to become inspired or, if an artist ourselves, ways in which we inspire others. An audience can lose themselves in what they are watching or feel uplifted by the music they are listening to. Indeed, almost any feeling can be aroused by music, a fact that has been utilized by makers of films and TV programmes the world over. One only has to think of Bernard Hermann's film scores (e.g. to Alfred Hitchcock's movies) for evidence of this.

Most art forms can also be used for propaganda purposes so that an audience can be seduced into believing whatever message the political party (or advertiser or newspaper) wants to send them. In the same way, arguably, newspapers don't so much report the news as make it by deciding which stories Joe Bloggs will be exposed to and the treatment that those stories will receive. Basically, newspapers spend their time creating scandals and in so doing they influence the morality of a nation by telling that nation what constitutes scandalous behaviour. As in newspaper stories and modern-day soap operas, Neptune is a planet to associate with fairy tales. Far from being mere creative fibs, fairy stories distort the germ of the story so that its essential truths cannot possibly be missed. The moral of the story – and there usually is one – is delivered in a palatable form, at once grotesque and benign. In touching upon such stories we are allowed to discover what would happen to us if we followed various courses of action when faced with similar circumstances. As with our dreams, fictional stories allow us to rehearse real life.

As always, Neptune works in an insidious, invidious way. The planet doesn't operate directly; instead it seduces, distorts and envelops. Wherever Neptune is involved, the tendency is to soak everything up; indeed, we become unable to filter anything out. It is like being by the water's edge at a time of flood; there is nothing we can do to stop the waters rising.

The Media and Advertising

The world of newspapers and publishing utilizes other planetary energies as well as those of Neptune: Jupiter we can associate with all aspects of publishing and broadcasting; Mercury with writing; TV and film nowadays need the technological know-how that is associated with Uranus; and Venus is a prime mover in all the creative arts. Nevertheless, Neptune is a major significator in all branches of the media and is particularly central to the world of advertising. The advertiser makes a particular product seem more wondrous than it is, the rough edges are knocked off and the product is presented in the best possible light. Advertising can almost be viewed as a form of propaganda, except that it is not a political viewpoint that we are being sold. Advertisements tells us that if we use a certain face cream our wrinkles will disappear, a certain soap powder and our white clothes will dazzle us with their brilliancy. A guy can turn into Adonis if he uses the right razor. The truth is being distorted and cloaked out of recognition for, of course, white clothes eventually do turn greyish, wrinkles are a reality of getting older, and few men have Hollywood looks and we might not like them if they did. The interesting thing is that the advertising industry (and the movies and media generally) distorts reality in the first place so that people are seduced into believing that it is desirable to be without wrinkles or to look like a movie star. Jeff Mayo[20] lists Neptune's primary function as being that of *refinement* and it is easy to see why this is such an appropriate root principle. When a substance is refined, it is taken away from its original source; its rough edges are removed. The finished product may be more pleasing than the original but it will also usually be more synthetic. Things are usually refined in order to make them appear to be more ideal or perfect.

Another keyword for Neptune has to be palliation, for example where the physician, unable to cure a patient's disease, prescribes drugs to relieve the symptoms. The word 'palliate' literally means to cloak. When palliated, a problem or offence is rendered less serious, the more difficult aspects of the problem are glossed over, whitewashed away. Humans need a degree of palliation in their lives because we need the attendant horrors of living with reality to be made more palatable. We listen to music, go to the movies or enjoy a glass of wine in order to cope with a hard day in the same way that the terminal patient takes morphine to numb their pain and often to avoid dwelling on the reality that they are dying.

The Reality of Neptune

If we view the world from a Saturnian point of view, then Neptune is undoubtedly a planet to associate with lies. Without the boundaries of time and space, there are no clear dividing lines and everything becomes relative. It is through the influence of Neptune that we learn that so-called truth and non-truth, right and wrong, are very elusive terms and that very few things are quite what they seem to be. As always Neptune is at home everywhere except in the measurable and physical world, everywhere except where things are cut and dried. In Neptune's realm two plus two do not simply add up to four. In Saturn mode we recognize that a piece of furniture is a table. In Neptune mode, the table may become invisible. However, we might be able to sense the table's aura!

Loss, Longing and Sacrifice

As we have seen, Neptune is a planet to describe collective longings. It can also describe individual longings, often because we have lost something before we have fully appreciated having it. For instance, someone with Neptune on their IC may leave the country of their birth but then come to long for the place from which they have escaped. Many a Sun-Neptune person longs for a father-figure, often because their personal father was in some way missing or unavailable. Similarly, the Saturn-Neptune person may long for a father and also for structures and a stronger sense of what they 'should' and 'shouldn't' do.

If Jeff Mayo lists Neptune's primary function as being that of refinement, a root principle for Liz Greene is *redemption*.[21] The word 'redeem' literally means to buy out. Today the term can be associated with recovering ownership of an item temporarily pawned by paying a specified sum. In various ways, it usually means settling a debt or making up for something. We might do a job badly but be told we can redeem ourselves by doing something else right. It implies having our honour and reputation restored to us. Like the seashore overwhelmed by waves, when Neptune is involved we often feel overwhelmed by what is presented to us, so much so that we want to put it right, we want to redeem the situation in some way. We long for it to be restored to how it was before. Often we are willing to make any kind of sacrifice to take us away from this feeling of drowning. However, rarely are many of these feelings very conscious. Often the feelings are collective ones: the sign that Neptune is transiting often points to groups of people which society feels guilty about and to which it is keen to make reparation.

As Pluto is generally regarded as belonging to the Kuiper Belt and not of our solar system, Neptune is the planet furthest out from the Sun. Similarly, as we get older, we get farther and farther away from those solar adolescent days of hero-worship; we can no longer imagine we are as-good-as-gold, so aware are we of being tarnished. Making mistakes, what some might call sinning, is the price we pay for maturity, experience and becoming a whole person. So, as we get older and become more and more poisoned and less and less wholesome, we may indeed want to be washed clean and given a clean slate. To be redeemed is to be forgiven, blessed, made holy and reconciled. In various ways, people seek redemption as their life draws to its inevitable close. And some see the act of death itself as a means towards redemption. According to the Christian world view, committing a sin breaks our relationship with God, and of course the story goes that Jesus brought about atonement (at-one-ment) with God by dying on the cross and saving us from our sins. If we are redeemed, then our prior condition was one of slavery and it seems that the term 'redeem' originally referred to the purchase of a slave's freedom. Indeed, the planet is undoubtedly a significator for all matters pertaining to the release of slaves and the Neptunian house, the Twelfth, is also traditionally the house of slaves. The planet is also sometimes important with respect to people from cultures where their ancestors were slaves. Thus, as with Pluto, Neptune can be a planet to associate with some black cultures as well as white cultures where slavery has featured strongly. Thus, perhaps it is no coincidence that a large percentage of those worst affected by the floods following Hurricane Katrina in August 2005 were the largely black Americans of New Orleans and the surrounding area.

Neptune and Resignation

The whole subject of forecasting demands its own book and so the effects of Neptune by transit have largely to be excluded here. Nonetheless, it is worth noting what happens to people under Neptune transits. As well as the usual effects of idealization, loss and confusion, people let go in various ways. If past the first flush of youth, they become less enamoured with hanging on to life. Ambitions and ego needs count for less (which can be difficult if the individual happens to be young). Things don't matter so much any more; in other words, each subsequent Neptunian transit (or progression or direction) makes the individual slightly more resigned to their death and more inclined to consider how they might atone for perceived previous wrongdoings. A keyword is resignation – people become resigned to their lot and, frequently, they literally resign from their jobs or other areas of responsibility. This can be because Neptune undermines our strength and thus we have to capitulate or because circumstances dictate that we feel we are swimming against the tide. Whatever actually happens, Neptune pulls us away from the material and towards the more spiritual or at least unworldly.

Physical Characteristics

Neptune lends a nebulous, amorphous quality to whatever it touches. It subtly sensitizes, refines and potentially confuses whatever it comes into contact with. It is the planet of the unreal and the surreal. It has rulership over things that shape and colour our sense of reality and which may have the capacity to alter it entirely.

Elemental Neptune

The Moon and the watery signs of Cancer, Scorpio and Pisces often share rulership over the sea with Neptune. It is the significator of fog and many, if not all, gases. Neptune seems to have rulership over many artificial and synthetic products – plastic, for instance. The radioactive element neptunium was created in 1940 by bombarding uranium with slow-moving neutrons. Thought at the time to be a wholly artificial element, it has since been found to exist naturally in uranium mines, albeit in very small quantities.[22]

The Body

Neptune can be associated with all types of poisons and also with parasitic diseases. Neptune can also be linked with wasting diseases: insidious conditions where there is no obvious sudden onset of illness but a gradual fading away.

Interpreting Neptune

The aspects of Neptune and its house placement and rulership should be weighted much more heavily than the sign in which it is found. This is of course because the planet spends fourteen years in each zodiacal sign and impinges therefore more on the collective than on the individual where the signs are concerned. Nevertheless, as with all the outer planets, the sign of Neptune can confirm information already suggested by other chart factors. Thus, for example, Agatha Christie had Neptune in Gemini, neatly describing the fact that she had imaginary brothers and sisters as a child. However, this wouldn't apply to everyone born over the fourteen-year period; it works with Christie because Neptune was also making a tight aspect (a quincunx) to a Third House planet (Venus) and conjunct Pluto, the ruler of her Third House. Note that the transits of Uranus and Neptune straddled each other for many years in the 1980/1990s and, in any case, when considering the ingress of any outer planet, it is always worth checking what the others were up to at the time.

Neptune Through The Signs
Neptune in Leo – ♆♂♌

Most recent transit: 1914/6 to 1928/9.

This is potentially a wonderful time for dance, drama and for the arts and creativity generally. And for good and ill, a time of celebrating the self and, with the First World War, for dreaming of heroic glory. Going to the cinema became all the rage during the last transit and, with it, a tendency for people to model themselves on the glamorous movie stars that they idolized. Film studios became big business with, for example, Samuel Goldwyn creating Goldwyn Studios which, after mergers, became MGM, the studio with the famous lion logo. In the UK, the BBC received its Royal Charter. Neptune combined with Leo has a fizzy, glitzy quality of boom and bust about it. Potentially it's a time of serious self-deception, as people can believe that what is possible in the movies is also possible in real life. During the last transit people over-reached themselves and came unstuck. Leo is the sign of banking and the stock market crash (Black Thursday, 24 October 1929) and the resulting Great Depression (during the years of Neptune in Virgo) is an example of the inflationary, speculative and unreal feeling that can be associated with this combination. Compassion for children can be expected and the quantity of children sent out to work was significantly reduced in many countries (including the US) during the last transit. The last transit also saw more than a few 'rags to riches' stories (and vice versa), such as the meteoric rise of Coco Chanel from the humblest beginnings, and the poor farmer from Georgia who started Coca Cola (fizz!) in 1888 and sold it for 25 million dollars in 1919.

Neptune in Virgo – ♆♍

Most recent transit: 1928/9 to 1942/3.

This is the major significator to describe the Depression as it so clearly describes the fact that millions lost (Neptune) their jobs (Virgo) with the result that people longed to be in work. In India, Gandhi was teaching the spiritual benefits of hard work and humble lifestyles. The resultant poverty of the Depression and the idealization of purity that is described by Neptune in the sign of its detriment, led directly to the rise of the Nazi Party and the Second World War. Also to racist policies in other parts of the world (e.g. South Africa). This is a common enough occurrence but smaller nations (Virgo) seem particularly to have been victimized during this time, their boundaries no longer able to keep their more powerful neighbours out; for instance, Poland was invaded by Germany, and Finland by the Soviet Union. Neptune rules chemicals and drugs and Virgo is concerned with maintenance of the body, thus this combination can be associated with the discovery of new drugs. The last transit produced LSD and penicillin. In the USA, Prohibition came to an end, resulting in something of a clean-up in society. Arguably, it was a time of progress in all things small; for instance, this period saw the splitting of the atom. The establishment of the minimum wage in the USA in the late 1930s might also have been good for the 'little guy', the one without economic power. Some of the film titles also mirrored the themes of smallness: *Snow White and the Seven Dwarves*, *Little Women*, *The Thin Man*, *Of Mice and Men*, for instance, and there was the hugely detailed *Gone with the Wind*. The transit favours craft and detailed artistic expression and technique.

Neptune in Libra – $\Psi \underline{\Omega}$

Most recent transit: 1942/3 to 1955/7.

This combination can be associated with a yearning for peace and the dream of a more equal society. This feeling certainly characterized the last transit, falling as it did in the latter part of the Second World War and the years that followed it. In the UK, the post-war Labour government led by Clement Atlee created the National Health Service, the welfare state and also nationalized many industries, the idea being to create a fairer society for all. In the USA, the Democrat President Harry Truman devised a plan for full employment, public housing and a number of other measures which came to be known as the Fair Deal. On the world stage, the general feeling of the last transit was perhaps of an uneasy, illusory peace. The dream of harmonious living also brought about a romanticizing of relationships and, conversely, their dissolution when the dream proved impossible. The ideal of fairness and equality was perhaps most evident in people's marriages. Women had run the country during the war and perhaps were less inclined to play second fiddle when the men returned. Divorce started to become less stigmatized. The generation born with Neptune in Libra would be the first to think that the ideal relationship didn't necessarily require the contract of marriage. The period saw many romantic movies and perhaps a more than usual amount of on-screen relationships mirroring off-screen ones; e.g. Humphrey Bogart and Lauren Bacall, Katharine Hepburn and Spencer Tracy.

Neptune in Scorpio – $\Psi \, \text{♏}$

Most recent transit: 1955/7 to 1970.

Both the planet and the sign love mystery, so this combination should always mark a fantastic period for occult and mystical subjects. The last transit heralded a period of sexual scandals, spy stories and conspiracy theories. In the cinema, spy movies were all the rage, especially with spies and sex coming together in the shape of James Bond. In the UK in the 1960s, Harold Wilson, the then Prime Minister, was accused of being a KGB agent and there was an abundance of real and imagined MI5 plots. In the USA, the assassinations of John F. Kennedy, Martin Luther King and the death of Marilyn Monroe attracted much speculation and many conspiracy theories with young people, especially, accusing their Government of hidden agendas and of telling lies with respect to the Vietnam War. Drugs and sex come together with this combination; the last transit saw the launch of the Pill (1960 in the USA and 1961 in the UK), and with it, society becoming much more open about sex. Indeed the period embraced everything one might associate with the 'sex, drugs and rock 'n' roll' movement. Also within the symbolism of this combination is the fact that the UK saw the end of the death penalty and a relaxing of rules concerning homosexuality. The possibility of a nuclear war was opened up with the Cuban missile crisis and nuclear submarines were created. With its Plutonian rulership, planets falling in Scorpio tend to be good for black culture. During the last transit, the Civil Rights Movement got underway in the USA, with Rosa Parks refusing to give up her seat to a white person on a bus; in the UK, Harold Wilson resisted the demands of white minority leaders in South Africa and what was then Rhodesia.

Neptune in Sagittarius – ♆♐

Most recent transit: 1970 to 1984
(note that Uranus also entered Sagittarius in 1981).

Segments of society may yearn to go far, far away when Neptune is here. The last transit saw films that reflected such dreams of exploration; for instance, *E.T.*, *Star Wars* and *Close Encounters of the Third Kind*. Outer space was very much in the real news, too, with numerous space probes and visits to the Moon. Long-distance travel became the dream of many; people started travelling and exploring the world in greater numbers. With Neptune here, things that are fast, over-the-top, novel, quixotic and exotic are likely to be in fashion (the outrageous Sex Pistols, The Clash and the punk movement all appeared during this period). And in a number of different ways, being foreign may be something to be celebrated. Neptune in Sagittarius can be associated with a longing for a freer, more casual and carefree society with an accompanying dislike of authority, rules and restrictive practices. During the last transit Mikhail Gorbachev started reforming the Soviet Union which led to a much more liberal time politically, economically and in society in general. A longing for life to have some greater meaning and purpose, and a greater openness to people being religious (and non-religious) in their own way, can be associated with this transit. The 1970s brought a rise in the popularity of various religious cults and sects. The musicals *Godspell* and *Jesus Christ Superstar* were all the rage. Cultural shifts in further education are something else to expect from this transit. The last transit saw the birth of the Open University in the UK, an educational institution open to all, regardless of previous education and current life circumstances.

Neptune in Capricorn – ♆♑

Most recent transit: 1984 to 1998
(Uranus was also in Capricorn from 1988 and the two planets were conjunct in 1993).

This pro-Establishment transit can be associated with an idealization of age, of father-figures and of tradition. The last transit saw the disintegration of many institutions and, to a marked extent, the end of Communism. This was symbolized particularly by the dissolution of the Berlin Wall. Old-fashioned authority and authoritarian regimes underwent dissolution and many of the organizations, companies and rules in society that hitherto had appeared as unchanging, and as safe as the Rock of Gibraltar, faltered. The offshoot of this was that people started to idealize and yearn for all things that felt solid, traditional and had stood the test of time. For example, astrology started to embrace traditional ideas and, to an extent, moved away from being psychological. People started to value old buildings and expressed their dislike of modern architecture. Ronald Reagan – a Republican and aged sixty-nine when he came to office – was in the White House for much of the period, and the UK had a Conservative government during almost all of the transit. Films reflected themes already mentioned, e.g. *In the Name of the Father*, *On Golden Pond*, and some movies seemed to idealize grim reality as in *Schindler's List*, *Les Miserables* and *Saving Private Ryan*. Governments may seek to control drugs or the use of alcohol when Neptune is in Capricorn; the last transit saw the 'Just Say No' campaign.

Neptune in Aquarius – ♆ ≈

Last transit: 1834 to 1847/8. Current transit: 1998 to 2011/12.

Neptune is in Aquarius as I write (mirrored by a mutual reception from Uranus falling in Pisces). The combination of Uranian and Neptunian energies is bringing a revolution in the fields of photography, film-making and mixed media. It is a great time for independent film-makers and for those at the cutting edge of the use of special effects. En masse, people are enjoying digital TV and radio and an explosion of gizmos involving phones, MP3 players, cameras and computer technology. The scope of digital photography alone has allowed Joe Public to create an illusion of expertise in picture-taking. Interestingly, photography was born during the last transit with the word 'photography' first being used in 1839 by William Herschel.[23] Opportunities abound in society for people not only to appear expert in areas they know very little about, but also to acquire celebrity status. When asked what they want to do with their lives, youngsters repeatedly report hankering after fame; they don't espouse any particular ambition to do anything exceptional but almost feel it is their right to be viewed as special, simply by virtue of breathing. The spate of reality TV shows reveals that there are no barriers to winning a talent contest, for example; the competitor with the best voice/dance/other talent is actually least likely to be chosen by the public at large, as the opinion of so-called expert judges is eroded and no longer decides the participants' fate. The idealization of ordinariness, with its glorying in the unexceptional, is mirrored in the rise of genetically modified (GM) crops; as in a GM field, every plant belongs precisely to the same species. Individuality, independence and diversity have no place in a GM field. Similarly, political correctness ensures that differences between people are erased. Conversely, this transit can be associated with the introduction of more liberal laws in various areas of life, suggesting an opportunity for greater openness to different lifestyles and freedom to live life as one chooses; for example, the current transit has seen marijuana given a lower drugs classification in the UK, more liberal drinking laws and the introduction of civil partnerships for gay couples. It might also be associated with breakthroughs in the discovery and creation of new drugs; anaesthetics, for example, were discovered during the 1840s. Nowadays the discoveries are likely to be found through the use of genetic engineering and other manifestations of technological know-how. Potentially the transit may give rise to a more truthful examination of ESP, hypnotism, alternative medical practices and various altered states of consciousness.

Neptune in Pisces – ♆ ♓

Last transit: 1847/8 to 1861/2. Next transit: 2011/12 to 2025/26.

Spiritualism was 'born' during the last transit and spread like wildfire. Certainly one might expect Neptune in Pisces to be an ideal transit for all matters to do with psychic phenomena. A general growth of understanding concerning spiritual matters, and greater awareness of subtle energies and vibrational types of healing (such as homœopathy), may be expected during the next transit, plus perhaps greater compassion towards the less fortunate in society. Perhaps more difficult for worldly and financial affairs, it should prove an excellent time for dance, music, watercolours and all free-flowing forms of art. Surely it is an ideal transit for the artist and, no doubt, ideal too for the con-artist.

Pluto ♀

'It takes two to corrupt – the corrupter and the corrupted.'

Marshal Mobutu Sese Seko

Discovery

As early as 1905, Percival Lowell thought there was a planet ('Planet X') beyond the orbit of Neptune and he continued searching for it until his death in 1916. Pluto was eventually discovered on 18 February 1930 at 4 p.m. in the Lowell Observatory in Flagstaff, Arizona, by laboratory assistant Claude Tombaugh (born 4 February 1906). Its position measured in longitude was 18 degrees Cancer, a degree ever more to be linked with Plutonian issues. Some astronomers question whether Pluto is in fact Lowell's Planet X, as it would seem to be too small to be the body he was searching for. In any event, the discovery of Pluto was announced to the world on 13 March 1930. Curiously, 13 March is both the late Lowell's birthday and also the date on which Uranus was discovered.

The story of its discovery is very Plutonian in its style. There is the fact that, although its presence was suspected, its appearance took years to surface; the fact that Lowell had to die before it was discovered; his obsession concerning its existence; and the mystery surrounding it generally. The discovery 'coincided' with the rise of interest in depth-psychology, the rise of Fascism and Nazism in Europe, Prohibition and gangsters in the USA, the splitting of the atom and the subsequent production of the atom bomb. Humans have always had the capacity to kill each other and war has always been a fact of life, but since the discovery of Pluto humanity has had the capacity to wipe out the entire planet.

The name, which was one of thousands of suggestions, was put forward by an eleven-year-old schoolgirl from Oxford called Venetia Burney.[24] (Her grandfather had been the person to suggest the names Deimos and Phobos for Mars's moons.) Perhaps the staff at the Lowell Observatory chose it because of its mythological connections; given that Pluto is so far away and receives so little light, it is ideally suited to being named after the ruler of the underworld. Or maybe they liked the fact that the first two letters are the initials of Percival Lowell.

Astronomy

Whereas the physical image of Jupiter (big and full of gas) can be likened to a balloon, Pluto (small and dense) feels more like a golf ball. Its orbit is highly eccentric. Even though by far the most distant body, on average forty times further away from the Sun than is the Earth, Pluto is closer to the Sun than Neptune for twenty years out of its 248-year orbit. The last time this happened was between 21 January 1979 and 11 February 1999. Its eccentricity includes the fact that Pluto rotates in the opposite direction from most of the other planets and its orbit is tilted further from the ecliptic (17.2 degrees). The orbit is also very elongated, which is why sometimes Pluto is so much nearer than at others. These unusual features led some astronomers and astrologers to propose that Pluto may, in fact, be a huge asteroid rather than a planet, but then there is no precise definition of what a

204 • The Contemporary Astrologer's Handbook

planet actually is. Quite possibly, Pluto is a large Kuiper Belt object (a TNO or Trans-Neptunian Object) and not a member of our solar system at all.

On 24 August 2006, Pluto lost its designation as a planet and joined a newly-formed category, that of 'dwarf planet'. Given that Pluto is associated with *down-sizing*, its demotion seems entirely appropriate. Meeting in Prague, the International Astronomical Union (IAU) upgraded Ceres from being the largest asteroid to a dwarf planet. This new, equal footing between Ceres and Pluto seems fitting given the shared storyline of Demeter (Ceres) and Hades (Pluto) in the Greek myth (see below). The body previously known as UB313 (popularly known as Xena and discovered on 5 January 2005) was also added to the list of dwarf planets. On 13 September 2006, it was officially named Eris (sister of the Greek Ares and a goddess of discord). In the myth, Eris had a lawless daughter called Dysmonia and the body's moon was given this name. Doubtless many new bodies will be added to the dwarf planet list. Readers wising to keep up with the latest developments can do so at www.iau.org

• Mean distance from the Sun: on average Pluto is about 3.67 billion miles/5.9 billion kilometres from the Sun, but due to its wildly elliptical orbit Pluto's distance from the Sun varies enormously. It ranges from about 4.6 billion miles/7.5 billion kilometres down to 2.7 billion miles/4.4 billion kilometres.

• Diameter: Pluto is smaller than the Earth's Moon with a diameter of 1,430 miles/2,300 kilometres. Being so small, and 1,200 times farther away than our Moon, it can only been seen through the most powerful of telescopes.

• Sidereal period (approximate time for a body to orbit the Sun): one orbit lasts 247.7 years but the orbit of Pluto is eccentric. It may spend anything between ten and thirty years in a zodiacal sign.

• Retrograde motion: five months of each year.

• Moons: Pluto's only moon, Charon, was discovered on 22 June 1978 by James W. Christy. Named after the boatman who ferried the souls of the dead across the rivers Acheron and the Styx into the underworld, Charon has a diameter about half that of Pluto – approximately 727 miles/1172 kilometres.

Mythology

After the overthrow of their father Kronos, his three sons Zeus, Poseidon and Hades divided up the universe between them. Zeus ruled the heavens, Poseidon had the sea and Hades the underworld, which he ruled with his bride, Persephone. Hades was god not only of death but of fertility and abundance, too. He was known as Pluto (or Plutus) to the Romans, which means 'rich one', and Hades to the Greeks. He was rich by virtue of all the precious minerals, metals and organic matter buried within the Earth. He was also rich in dead souls. However, his name in this context was often translated into *Dis*, which is the Latin word for rich. The psychology of Pluto can often be associated with words that start with the prefix 'dis-'. *Dis*charge or *dis*miss are good examples, meaning to rid oneself, remove or release. Even the word *dis*tance means the intervening space between objects. When an object is at a distance it is far more remote, as is Pluto itself. Things that are more remote are more inaccessible and often therefore more highly prized.

To return to the myth, the underworld was a subterranean kingdom where the souls of the dead waited for judgement. Heroes went to the Elysian Fields and evil-doers to Tartarus. They were prevented from leaving the underworld by the three-headed guard dog Cerberus, the so-called hellhound. Wearing a helmet of invisibility, given to him by the Cyclopes, Hades spent his whole life totally invisible in the underworld, coming above ground on very few occasions. As he represented the actual finality of death, he would of course be seen only rarely. Basically he was always in the *shade* and, curiously, Hades is an anagram of that word in English. Psychologically, Pluto is associated with the personal and collective *shadow*, aspects of the individual or society which are buried in the unconscious. Hades's invisibility extended to the fact that he was not even talked about; people were afraid that mentioning his name might attract his attention.

The famous occasion when Hades did venture above ground was when he abducted his niece, Persephone. Hades had wanted to marry Persephone (Zeus and Demeter's daughter) but Demeter had rejected Hades as a suitor for her child. So when Persephone was out picking flowers, Hades arranged for a beautiful new flower – a narcissus – to rise up in front of the young maiden. When she stooped to pick it, the earth opened and Hades appeared in his chariot and took her away. In the same way that in all the gangster movies (as in real life) the gangsters are successful only because there is someone corrupt in government (a Jupiter/Zeus figure) who is helping them, Zeus was complicit in the abduction of his daughter.

When in the underworld Persephone ate a pomegranate – a symbol of fertility and possibly of winter (it is full of seeds but they are hidden from view) – and by so doing she made the tie with Hades insoluble. It was agreed that she should spend two-thirds of the year above ground with Demeter and one-third with Hades in the underworld. Roughly translated, this symbolizes the fact that winter takes up about one-third of the year and spring and summer the other two-thirds. There are no children from the union of Persephone and Hades, and this mirrors the fact that fruit doesn't grow in the wintertime.

Survival and Sophistication

While Hades doesn't come out of the story smelling of roses, the myth is really about the need for Persephone to grow up and lose her innocence, an innocence that embraces not only the notion of blameless behaviour but ignorance of the very existence of sin. Hades survives because he is streetwise and knows how to manipulate a situation to his own ends. In order to be able to survive in the real world, innocence is the dubious virtue that has always to be sacrificed wherever Pluto is concerned. Pluto's domain lies in the realm of experience, sophistication and forbidden fruit. To be Plutonic is to be aware of temptation and to have a shrewd knowledge of all that takes place beneath the façade of civilized society. Whereas the innocent person is vulnerable and powerless, the streetwise person is empowered and cannot easily be exploited or duped. They can see what is really going on. Little wonder, therefore, that Pluto is associated with depth-psychology and occult subjects: disciplines intent on penetrating beneath the surface. People who resonate strongly to Pluto will usually have few illusions about human nature. While too great an exposure to the seamier side of life can lead to paranoia (always expecting the worst) and to ruthlessness (the urge to survive at all costs), at best the Pluto gift of being streetwise makes us shrewd and helps us to survive.

The Collective Shadow

All the outer bodies, moving slowly as they do, describe the various trends and fashions in society over time. Such waves of what is 'in' or 'out' through the decades give rise to the generation gap. Pluto will usually describe those elements of society that a particular period of history will get obsessed about and often want to eliminate. Such obsessions will usually be the legacy of what society hasn't dealt with or been sufficiently conscious of in the past. Transiting Pluto reveals material that the collective had previously swept under the carpet. Whereas Saturn contributes to the individual 'shadow' (the personal unconscious), Pluto is representative of the collective shadow (suppressed material from whole generations). As Pluto slowly makes its way through the signs it describes which members of the human race are likely to be persecuted or merely exposed, for whatever reason, at any given time. An individual's Pluto – its prominence or otherwise, and its general condition – will describe the extent to which he or she may get caught up in the maelstrom of a collective fate.

Pluto and Nature

The role of Pluto seems to be to remind us of nature's laws; in particular, the laws of birth, death, decay and renewal. Pluto reminds us that civilized behaviour is only a thin veneer and that lurking underneath is a planet full of animals, plants and minerals in varying stages of a birth and death cycle. Humans are animals and share many of the same basic instincts. Pluto's orientation is pro-survival but not necessarily pro-civilization; often it is quite the reverse. From the Pluto perspective, an overly civilized society takes humans away from their true animal state. The reality is that we are all animals and subject to nature's laws. For example, we die, we decay and we have to relieve ourselves continuously of waste products. Humans share a wild creature's instinct for survival. If food, shelter, employment and other essentials to our ongoing survival become scarce, our behaviour tends to become more obviously animal-like and uncivilized.

Survival, Suppression and Elimination

Sometimes described as a 'higher octave' of Mars, Pluto, like Mars, is primarily concerned with survival. But of course one species (or an individual's) survival is often at the expense of another's. Whereas Mars, a personal planet, is concerned with individual survival, with Pluto the concern is for the species as a whole, even if this is at the expense of the individual or the minority. Whereas Mars fights to survive, the style of Pluto is simply to *suppress* or *eliminate*. At best the qualities associated with Pluto have a strongly *cleansing* and *purging* quality to them. For Pluto forces the exposure of all that is discordant, poisonous and harmful to society or to the individual. Such material, whether physical or psychological, will usually have been suppressed (invisible) and lying dormant for some time. As individuals, we suppress things seemingly for the sake of survival (for instance, the child may cut off from remembering traumatic events in childhood) because we cannot cope (or feel we can't) with such 'taboo' material, often because it is thought to be too embarrassing or shameful. But there usually comes a time when the suppressed material just has to be exorcised. It has to see the light of day for reasons of survival and personal growth and development.

Pluto's elimination process is a slow one with things gradually coming to some kind of crescendo. Pluto is a major significator wherever there is a release of extreme tension, as in a volcano erupting, as in orgasm, as in the baby being expelled from its mother's womb, as in faeces leaving the body. Survival in some way is dependent on something being expelled. Pluto brings things to their inevitable crisis or end point. It has a hand in all kinds of eruptions and purging. Although a boil on the skin, a volcanic explosion or the exposure of a family secret may not be pleasant, it will always be cathartic, cleansing and releasing. Before any kind of renewal can take place, such eruptions are necessary for there has to be a clear-out of what is poisonous and destructive first.

Pluto and Justice

Justice is not usually a word that comes in the same sentence as Pluto, which often brings atrocities too horrendous to contemplate. Nevertheless, Pluto's role does seem to be concerned with dealing with the sins of our forebears, whether these forebears are merely a generation away or many generations down the line. Society doesn't recognize Pluto events as being anything to do with justice because the generation concerned has not been responsible for, and is often completely ignorant of, the sins of their ancestors. Therefore, the particular 'sin' is often merely one of ignorance. Many examples of wars and terrorist attacks might be cited here but I have chosen the example of the thalidomide drug. Thalidomide was first introduced in the late 1950s as a sedative and, because it was deemed to be so safe, was prescribed for nausea and insomnia in pregnant women. Subsequently, it was found to be the cause of severe birth defects in children whose mothers had taken the drug in the first three months of pregnancy. It is estimated that perhaps somewhere between 10,000 and 20,000 babies worldwide were born with severe disabilities as a consequence; many without arms or legs. Here, as elsewhere, Pluto's justice feels more like retribution. As with the thalidomide example, Pluto ensures that something shocking is brought out into the light of day, but the exposure, making a generation streetwise, can prevent further damage occurring. Pluto ensures that society cleans up its act.

Taboos and Prohibition

Perhaps the most appropriate keyword for Pluto was initially posed by the astrologer Richard Ideman; that of taboo. Indeed, the word can be taken as a summation of everything that Pluto is concerned with:
Definition of 'taboo':
1. Forbidden or disapproved of; placed under a social prohibition or ban.
2. Marked off as simultaneously sacred and forbidden (in Polynesia and other South Pacific Islands).
3. Any prohibition resulting from social or other conventions.
4. Ritual restriction or prohibition, especially of something that is considered holy or unclean.
Etymology: 18th-century from Tongan word *tapu*.
Source: *Webster's Revised Unabridged Dictionary*, 1996.

The prohibition of something, and thus its suppression, is what usually gives rise to some of the more difficult aspects of Plutonian activity. For instance, when alcohol was prohibited in the USA, people didn't stop drinking; the sale and consumption of alcohol was merely tossed into the underworld. It is estimated that there were at least 100,000 speakeasies (illegal bars) in New York alone, at one point. Because of Prohibition, organized crime (itself a very Plutonian activity) increased tremendously with gangsters getting richer and more violent as they fought over control of the sale of alcohol and other illegal activities such as prostitution and gambling. Bootlegging and corruption among the police also grew on a unprecedented scale. All this came as a consequence of alcohol being prohibited, a consequence of suppression.

Abuse, Shame and Embarrassment

What is viewed by a society as taboo will vary across generations and cultures. In the individual's chart, as well as showing links to the collective, the placement of Pluto will often signify which so-called taboo activities occurred in their own family and which stories were brushed under the carpet. For some, Pluto in tight, hard aspect to personal planets may describe abuse or mental illness regarding the self or family members. Pluto is usually implicated as a major significator in instances of abuse, mental illness, certain kinds of death and certain kinds of sexual expression. And, as always, victims of abuse feel ashamed even though they may be innocent. Above all, Pluto is concerned with shame and embarrassment. Abuse of all kinds usually results from the suppression of an earlier abuse. The negative side of Pluto arises from the suppression of energies, whereas the positive side of Pluto arises from the reverse of this, the bringing of things to the surface.

On a lighter note, when we accidentally reveal something we shouldn't or make some kind of faux pas, we are embarrassed. A favourite expression of people at such times is 'I could have died!' or 'I wish the ground had opened and swallowed me up.' This latter phrase sounds just like Persephone being abducted and the feeling exactly conjures up Pluto. The feeling of exquisite exposure is very Plutonian.

Hades stood accused of rape or certainly abduction. Pluto is the significator of rape but one shouldn't think of the word purely in a sexual sense. The word 'rape' means to take by force. There is no consultation, no negotiation in situations involving rape. The position of Pluto in an individual's chart sometimes describes situations where this being-taken-by-force kind of violation (not necessarily anyone's so-called fault) may occur. For instance, Pluto in the Fourth House often equates to a childhood history where the person was plucked from the culture of their birth and re-planted somewhere completely different.

Pluto and Death

Both Saturn and Pluto are concerned with death but, whereas Saturn's message concerns the inevitability of the ageing process and our inevitable demise, deaths signified by Pluto in the natal chart often have a taboo aspect to them. Murder, suicide and abortion are the typical exit patterns signified by this body. Pluto can also be associated with what might be termed 'civic death', when, for instance, a person loses their vote or is prohibited from doing certain things in their community.

Pluto and Sex

The final release of tension at the point of orgasm is usually thought to be Plutonian in nature, but Pluto's role in sex goes further and again revolves around what may be considered taboo in a specific culture and time. Abuse is indeed included, for sexual abuse is mostly about the misuse of power. The perpetrator, perhaps like Hades, feels impotent and chooses a victim who is powerless. But as well as abuse, Pluto's reign also incorporates sexual practices which liberated people might construe as acceptable, provided that they occur between consenting adults. These are sexual activities which may be perfectly in line with the natural world or with honest feelings, but which go against the grain of a particular society and time. Thus, prostitution and same-gender sex may apply here. Basically, they are any sexual practices which are outside what society sanctions and which don't have a procreative outcome.

Pluto and the Irrevocable

Hades was known as a god without pity because if a mortal entered his underworld they had no hope whatsoever of leaving. He was deaf to all appeals for a reprieve. Similarly, Pluto seems to be most concerned with situations that cannot be undone or repealed. They are beyond recovery, irreversible and unalterable. Plutonium itself is rather like this, with some isotopes taking more than 24,000 years to decay. Similarly, the slate cannot be wiped clean with respect to society's most terrible atrocities, such as Hiroshima.

Medical Suppression

Pluto is responsible for the burying of material, for storing it, and for the process of bringing it to light. In medical matters, the most powerful drugs have been created since the discovery of this body. Homœopaths and some other alternative practitioners might argue that these powerful drugs don't cure symptoms but suppress them. A disease seemingly crushed or eliminated in one generation raises its head, in a slightly different and usually more dangerous form, in a generation or two later. Even in the same individual, vanquishing a disease in childhood may simply be an illusion. The problem is dormant, not dead.

Pluto and Mental Illness

Pluto is inevitably the main significator of mental illness. In psychotic states, the individual almost seems to be possessed by the elements we associate with Pluto. Paranoia and the experience of being persecuted (both peculiarly Plutonian feelings) often go with the territory. There will be other factors at work too, of course. For instance, Saturn – the planet that provides the barrier between the conscious and unconscious – is inevitably weak in such cases.

Pluto and Disability

Pluto, and possibly Chiron (see pages 306-10), are *the* bodies to associate with most instances of disability in the horoscope, although less so with disabilities such as blindness or deafness. It is probably the case that Pluto is not so much concerned with disability per se as with events and groups of people in society which are rendered largely invisible and possibly powerless. People who are disabled often talk about how invisible they feel to the rest of society and, in olden times at least, people were ashamed of their disabilities. Parents have been known to hide their disabled child. Commonly, Pluto will be found to be in tight, hard aspect to personal planets or points in the chart in people born with a disability, although less so in cases of acquired disability in later life. Or Pluto may be found in the Third House, for instance, when a sibling has learning difficulties. Sometimes the disability may have been caused by some kind of tinkering with nature before the individual was born, or possibly even conceived, and before the damaging effects of such tinkering were known.

Black Culture and Our Historical Roots

White people who have black lovers often have Venus and especially Mars in aspect to their Pluto. In less enlightened times such intermingling was considered to be taboo. However, black people with white lovers do not, on the whole, have the same aspects. This leads me to believe that Pluto has much to do with black culture itself. There is much evidence to support this view. For a start, there is no doubt that, right across the globe, black cultures have been suppressed by white cultures. Also, on the whole, black people fared much better and gained greater political power when Pluto was in its own sign – see Pluto in Scorpio below. As an aside and just playing with correspondences, I note that the English actress Honor *Blackman*[25] has Pluto tightly semi-square her Sun and Ascendant (both the Sun and Ascendant can be associated with one's name). The Sun is always a significator of 'man' and here both the Sun and Ascendant are in the sign of Leo, which is *the* sign to associate with the notion of *honour*!

Pluto can be associated with pre-history, and people who pursue archaeology, genealogy or merely collect fossils will inevitably have the body prominently placed in their charts. Having traced the genetic history of the human race, some scientists have suggested that the most common ancestor for all of us was a woman who lived in Africa some 200,000 years ago. They named her the Mitochondrial Eve. In other words, white or black, the DNA common to all of humanity spirals backwards in time to our earliest origins in Africa.[26]

Pluto seems to be concerned with the absolute nub or essence of something after all the periphery has been stripped off. It is not therefore fanciful to speculate that the body is concerned with the genetic code itself, possibly in tandem with Mercury (see pages 109-20). When everything else has been stripped away, our DNA remains. It is beyond the scope of this book to explore this in any detail but another curious fact is that people who were involved in a homœopathic proving of Plutonium repeatedly had dreams of being in a time thousands of years ago. Some provers also dreamt of being African, Aboriginal or Maori. Frequently they had a dog by their side.[27]

Pluto and Dogs

During the year in which Pluto was discovered (1930), Walt Disney's Mickey Mouse character acquired a pet dog. He was given the name Pluto a year later and appeared in 48 films. Unlike previous Disney dogs, he never spoke as a human – only as a dog! However, my assertion that Pluto is a major significator of dogs has been arrived at through observation – noting the charts of people who work with or keep dogs, and also the transits for the times of dog stories. It is also relevant that Cerberus the hellhound features in the Hades story. People who dislike dogs often complain particularly about dog excrement. As with dogs, Pluto probably has a strong connection with smell and with instincts generally. Most instincts are basically concerned with ensuring the survival of a species.

Bankruptcy and Redundancy

In collective terms, Pluto can be associated with extreme wealth (see below). However, with ordinary mortals, I believe it can also be a significator of bankruptcy, which for centuries was another one of the great taboos. Etymologically, the word 'bankrupt' is thought to be made up of the Latin words *bancus*, meaning table, and *ruptus*, meaning broken, because in Roman times the creditor would break the debtor's work bench as a punishment and a warning to other potentially insolvent tradesmen. In olden times it was considered to be a disgrace to become bankrupt. More important, perhaps, is the fact that the bankrupt person was deprived of their civil rights. As always, Pluto concerns itself with enforced civil death as well as the more literal kind of demise. For similar reasons, Pluto can be associated with the experience of redundancy (the likelihood of an experience of redundancy is strong if Pluto is to be found either in, or ruling, the Sixth or Tenth Houses). When someone loses their job in this way, they have no choice in the matter and thus often feel powerless and impotent, and even ashamed, despite the fact that it is their job that has been made redundant and the loss of employment is no reflection on the individual themselves. Their employer has down-sized. As always, Pluto is concerned with trimming down, humbling, stripping, getting down to the barest bones of something. Down-sizing is one example of this.

Pluto and Comedy

Pluto is often very prominent in the charts of comedians (it might be conjunct an angle, for instance). Laughter is a great release mechanism and commonly one of the things that makes people laugh is seeing others (particularly those in power) being brought down to size. Much of the content of jokes is of a taboo nature. The comedian speaks the unspeakable.

Metals and Minerals

Pluto rules plutonium, which was discovered in secret in 1940 (but publicly reported in 1946) by Glenn Seaborg and others at Berkeley, California. Plutonium is found in trace quantities in naturally occurring uranium ores. One kilogram is equivalent to about 22 million kilowatt hours of heat energy. Pluto also rules oil and coal (valuable fossil fuels which are formed from organic matter), material that was alive on Earth millions of years ago and then forced down by heavy layers of rock. Over time, the increased pressures and heat resulting from the overlying rock transformed the decomposed matter into coal or oil.

In the World at Large

Pluto seems to have rulership over organizations, individuals and industries which wield the real power in society: multinational corporations, media moguls and pharmaceutical companies. Real wealth and power, as in plutocracy, is unseen. People in the criminal underworld also wield power in a silent, unseen way as is the case with gangsters, and they too come under the umbrella of Pluto. Anything subterranean is also embraced by Pluto – abysses, sewers, drains and most aspects of plumbing. Also tunnels and underground railways.

Pluto Through The Signs

Pluto in Cancer – ♇ ♋

Most recent transit: 1913/14 to 1937/9.
Previous periods with Pluto in Cancer: 1423/5 to 1447/8 and 1668/70 to 1692/4.

With so many wars, this period was characterized by the 'power of the shell'. (Cancer is surely the sign of sea shells and all other types of shell.) Pluto in Cancer witnessed the Russian Revolution, the First World War, the Spanish Civil War, and part of the Second World War. Women – in particular mothers – became more powerful because so many men died at war. It was women too who now worked on the land and kept industry going. In many countries, women got the vote for the first time. Family, home and country had to be fought for, it could no longer be taken for granted. The period also saw worldwide economic depression and a flu epidemic which killed up to 40 million people worldwide. For one reason or another, the period saw the beginning of the death of family life.

Pluto in Leo – ♇ ♌

Most recent transit: 1937/9 to 1956/8.
Previous periods with Pluto in Leo: 1447/8 to 1464/6 and 1692/4 to 1710/12.

Often termed the 'me' generation, it is hardly surprising if there emerged a subliminal feeling of 'I have survived' in those who overcame the events of Pluto in Cancer. The concern of Pluto in Leo seems to have been with the impotence of the self against the power of the family or nation. This period saw the emergence of the atomic bomb and horrendous atrocities (e.g. concentration camps, Hiroshima and Nagasaki). In the shadow of such terrors, the individual self had very little power and yet often very powerful individuals seemed to be pulling the strings that made these things happen. After all, this period saw some extremely powerful leaders and dictators emerge, including Hitler, Mussolini and Stalin. The other revolution occurring at this time was in the emergence of TV and with it a transformation in the way people pursued recreation (Leo). TV has also been largely responsible for the cult of fame, personality and celebrity.

Pluto in Virgo – ♇ ♍

Most recent transit: 1956/8 to 1971/2.
Previous periods with Pluto in Virgo: 1464/6 to 1478/9 and 1710/12 to 1724/5.

Pluto was conjunct Uranus for a large part of the time during its most recent transit through Virgo. This period was characterized by revolutions wrought by very small things. This was the time of the *mini* skirt, the *Mini* car and small creatures (insects) in the form of the Beatles! The tiny contraceptive pill gave a new licence to the way that people could conduct their sexual lives. Suddenly there was freedom in such matters. Similarly, the silicone chip (also very small) and computers started to create a whole new world. Many farming traditions were destroyed. The sign that Pluto is travelling through seems to describe who or what is fated to be annihilated at any given time.

Pluto in Virgo saw the destruction of the small and seemingly insignificant – pests and weeds – with the introduction of an array of synthetic pesticides in the 1950s. Rachel Carson's book, *Silent Spring*, published in 1962, was instrumental in bringing the risks to the natural world to the public's attention. The environmental movement emerged from the resultant outcry. Similarly, the period saw the rise of powerful detergents. Adverts on TV showed housewives bleaching the germs away in bathrooms and kitchens. There was an *obsession with cleanliness* and a war on germs (very small things!); all part of the seemingly endless destruction of the natural world.

Pluto in Libra – ♀ ♎

Most recent transit: 1971/2 to 1983/4.
Previous periods with Pluto in Libra: 1478/9 to 1490/1 and 1724/5 to 1736/7.

Libra is the sign to associate with equality, balance and also with marriage. The Pluto in Libra period was caught up in *balance of power* issues. There was an uneasy balance of power and an avoidance of hostility between the USSR and the USA. The exposure of the inequalities between men and women gave rise to the Women's Movement in the West and in moves towards a more equal balance of power between the sexes. This, together with the Pluto in Virgo introduction of the Pill, meant that marriage ceased to be an essential social construct. Couples now could choose to marry or not. The early 1970s saw the start of a decline in people choosing to get married and an increase in the divorce rate. The difficulties that people experience in marriage could no longer be suppressed and now became unacceptable to many. The inequalities facing people with disabilities also started to be noticed, precipitated in the USA perhaps by so many injured men returning from Vietnam.

Pluto in Scorpio – ♀ ♏

Most recent transit: 1983/4 to 1995.
Previous periods with Pluto in Scorpio: 1490/1 to 1502/3 and 1736/7 to 1748/9.

The Aids epidemic started to be recognized around the world and, for the sake of survival, educated society everywhere learned about sex. The subject was taken out of the closet and openly discussed. In the UK, the equivalent to Aids in the countryside occurred with the advent of Dutch elm disease, which almost wiped out the elm tree. But perhaps it was in Africa that Pluto in Scorpio was most powerfully felt. This is also the continent that has borne the brunt of the Aids epidemic. Civil war broke out in Rwanda in 1990, leading to massive genocide in 1994. The last white president of South Africa, F. W. de Klerk, lifted the ban on the African National Congress (ANC), Nelson Mandela was released from prison, and all remaining apartheid legislation abolished. A majority black government followed after the elections in 1994.

Pluto in Sagittarius – ♀ ♐

Most recent transit: 1995 to 2008.
Previous periods with Pluto in Sagittarius: 1502/3 to 1515/16 and 1748/9 to 1762.

This transit can be associated with moral crusades, faith-based political agendas, as well as religious and ethnic divisions and tensions. Pluto entering Sagittarius ushered in a new wave of gambling in the UK with the introduction of the National Lottery and changes in betting laws generally. The transit has brought something approaching a terror of risk-taking in a wider sense. For example, in the UK, many schools which are unable to afford the potential cost of litigation are no longer scheduling school trips in case of accidents befalling pupils. Some local councils report that one-third of their road-building budgets is spent on settling claims to people who have tripped on uneven pavements. Everywhere people are frightened of being sued and thus horizons have been dimmed and exploration curtailed. The sign that Pluto is travelling through usually describes which members of society are being persecuted or at least given a hard time. With Pluto in Sagittarius, it is the Church, followers of Islam, educational institutions and travellers who are having a hard time. September 11 and the Iraqi war have revealed a paranoia about foreigners and those who pursue 'non-white' religions. The transit has seen the persecution of the migrant, the gypsy and those seeking asylum. Potentially this is a placement to associate with ethnic cleansing. The exposure of seeming hypocrisy within the Church and within educational fields has provided prominent news stories. Potentially there could be sweeping transformative changes in the religious world with the 'death' of some churches (and prominent church leaders) and the birth of others. Politicians have been 'outed' for not coming clean about a host of moral principles, such as their sexual preferences, dishonesty around money, travel expenses, and so on. It seems that there is a demolition process at work concerning people's faith in government, politicians and the Church, with suspicion having replaced naïve, innocent, blind trust. In philosophical and religious matters there is perhaps the requirement that the superficial wrappings have to go. People have to discover what is the essence of their belief system and what cannot be destroyed after the periphery has gone. Finally, Sagittarius is a sign to associate with exaggeration; with Pluto possibly signifying terror, we have seen (in my view) an exaggeration of the risk of terrorism.

Pluto in Capricorn – ♀ ♑

Next transit: 2008 to 2023/4.
Previous periods with Pluto in Capricorn: 1515/16 to 1532 and 1762 to 1777/8.

Who knows what the next ingress of Pluto into Capricorn could mean but it might herald the overthrow of governments and companies that have become institutions or the bedrock of a particular society. The impact of global warming might herald natural disasters. Big business and company directors may look vulnerable at this time and, with Uranus squaring Pluto for part of the period, individuals challenging multinationals in larger numbers seems likely. Pluto here is bound to expose the weaknesses of institutions, and is not likely to be supportive of tradition. The role of the father in many a society may be re-evaluated and diseases affecting the older male, or preventing men becoming older, could be on the agenda.

Planetary Dignities

Until the discovery of Uranus in 1781, only seven planets (including the Sun and Moon) were known and these seven planets between them were said to have rulership over all the twelve signs. With the exception of the Sun and Moon, each planet ruled two signs each. More traditionally-orientated astrologers keep to these original ascriptions while those of a more contemporary, psychological bent view Uranus, Neptune and Pluto as rulers or co-rulers of Aquarius, Pisces and Scorpio respectively. Down the ages, most astrologers have suggested that planets operate better, or at least have more strength (some would even say are more 'lucky'), in some signs more than others. Most of the ideas concerning the strength or weakness of planets – the extent to which a planet is 'dignified' or 'debilitated' – have sprung from planetary compatibility. For example, the Sun and Mars are of a similar nature and so it should come as no surprise that the Sun is said to be exalted (dignified) in Mars's sign, Aries. On the other hand, Mars is said to be in detriment (debilitated) in Venus-ruled signs, in the same way that Venus is in its detriment in Mars-ruled signs.

Planet	Sign Ruled	Exaltation	Detriment	Fall
Sun	Leo	Aries	Aquarius	Libra
Moon	Cancer	Taurus	Capricorn	Scorpio
Mercury	Gemini, Virgo	Virgo	Sagittarius, Pisces	Pisces
Venus	Taurus, Libra	Pisces	Scorpio, Aries	Virgo
Mars	Aries (Scorpio)	Capricorn	Libra (Taurus)	Cancer
Jupiter	Sagittarius (Pisces)	Cancer	Gemini (Virgo)	Capricorn
Saturn	Capricorn (Aquarius)	Libra	Cancer (Leo)	Aries
Uranus	Aquarius	Scorpio	Leo	Taurus
Neptune	Pisces	Cancer	Virgo	Capricorn
Pluto	Scorpio	Aries	Taurus	Libra

Rulership

Planets have a particular affinity for the zodiac sign which they rule; the particular planet and sign have much in common and, more telling, the planet can be said to be at home. Everyone feels stronger and safer in their own home and such is the case here; planets in their own sign don't necessarily operate better but they do tend to rule the roost. When in aspect, planets in the sign of their rulership will usually dominate whichever other energies they are touching. According to Charles Carter, there is a traditional idea that says that rulership works better in positive (fire and air) signs than in negative ones (earth and water). Commenting on this idea, he takes the view that Mars in Scorpio, Jupiter in Pisces and Saturn in Capricorn tend to be accident-prone.

Exaltation

The word 'exalt' literally means to 'lift up' and the sign of its exaltation is usually thought to bring out the best in a planet. Often used in religious and biblical contexts, exaltation implies going higher in the heavens and therefore being closer to God. Perhaps, therefore, the planet will operate in less purely personal and selfish ways and instead in ways that incline to the greater good. More prosaically, perhaps, a planet is said to operate in its most characteristic form in the sign of its exaltation. William Lilly talked about the exalted planet being like an honoured guest in the home; such a guest gets a lot of attention and is given the best the host has to offer.

Detriment

A planet is said to be in its detriment when it is in the opposite sign to the one it rules. There is nothing 'good' or 'bad' about this but such a planet often manifests in a way which runs counter to the purpose of the planet. For example, the Sun, which is concerned with the heroic quest, can be seen to be disadvantaged in Aquarius, the sign that has least truck with heroes but instead champions the cause of Tom, Dick and Harry. A planet in detriment may operate against that planet's own best interests and thus, from the point of view of its traditional role, is to some extent weakened. It's similar to a football match: the home team, in its own domain (similar to rulership) is generally thought to be advantaged and the away team is disadvantaged because it has to play in the opponent's home (detriment), in territory which will be unfamiliar.

Fall

When a planet is to be found in the opposite sign to the one of its exaltation it is also weakened and, according to tradition, rather more so than when found in detriment. A planet found in its fall can sometimes describe literal falls or a falling from grace. If exaltation implies closeness to heaven then fall implies somewhere baser, the farthest away from heaven. If we continue with the analogy of a planet being at home (rulership) or not at home (detriment) then, in its fall, a planet is not only away from home but in a place far removed from it. When we are far from home, in an alien culture perhaps, we become primarily concerned with survival. We don't have sufficient resources to be able to think of others; we have to concentrate on Number One. Thus, *if* a planet is disadvantaged in its fall, I think that it is because whatever the planet represents suffers from a feeling of insecurity and therefore a tendency to behave more selfishly.

A Word of Caution

Consideration of essential dignities may be useful, essential even, in horary astrology (where it is a much more complex subject than that presented here), but their relevance is less certain when it comes to working with natal charts. There are several reasons for this and most stem from the times in which these ideas hail. In earlier times, individuals had much less power to rise above their circumstances or to live the kind of life they might be most suited to. Nowadays a man doesn't have to be a warrior or huntsman; nor do women have to be destined for marriage, children and domesticity. If the circumstances of one's society did still decree that a woman had to be a contented domestic wife and mother, then certainly it would be advantageous if she had her Moon in Cancer or Taurus as then she might be well suited for such a role. And it would be advantageous for a man, too, as he would attract such a mate. Having said that, planets that are dignified do usually pack a powerful punch in any horoscope; but for me the issue really is that simply because a planet is stronger or more dominant, it doesn't mean that it is *better*.

Mutual Reception

The circumstance where two planets fall in each other's sign – an example would be a chart that has the Moon in Capricorn and Saturn in Cancer – is known as mutual reception. Where this happens, the planets are said to be dignified and can feel like a conjunction between the two bodies. From my point of view, a double whammy, in this case of a Moon-Saturn nature, has been created.

Chapter 5

Aspects and Planetary Combinations

Part One: The Aspects

The word 'aspect' literally means 'the way a thing may be looked at'. In astrology we use the word to describe the angular relationship between planets and other points in the chart. Each planet and angle (Ascendant, Descendant, MC and IC) is at a distance (measured in longitude) from every other planet and angle; if the distance that separates them is a numerical fraction of the whole circle, the two points are said to be 'in aspect' to each other. The aspects describe how the planets and angles interact; whether they ignite, obstruct, suppress or support each other, for instance.

Between six and ten aspects are commonly employed by astrologers:

Name (Glyph)	Degrees apart	Orb	Type of Aspect	Division of the circle by
Conjunction (♂)	0°	8°	Major – Neutral	0
Opposition (♂°)	180°	8°	Major – Hard/Active	2
Square (□)	90°	8°	Major – Hard/Active	4
Trine (△)	120°	6°	Major – Soft/Passive	3
Sextile (✶)	60°	4°	Major – Soft/Coaxing	6
Semi-square (∠)	45°	2°	Minor – Hard/Active	8
Sesquiquadrate (⊡)	135°	2°	Minor – Hard/Active	3/8
Semi-sextile (⩝)	30°	2°	Minor – Irritating	12
Quincunx (⚻)	150°	2°	Minor – Irritating	5/12
Quintile (Q)	72°	2°	Minor – Creative	5
Septile (✶)	51.5°	2°	Minor – Creative	7

These aspects can be divided either into so-called 'major' or 'minor' aspects or into five basic categories:

i) The 'neutral' aspect, the **conjunction**, where two bodies occupy the same place (or nearly the same place) in longitude. They are lined up next to each other when viewed from the Earth. This is the easiest planetary relationship to spot, though not necessarily the easiest to interpret.

ii) The 'hard' aspects which are sometimes described as 'challenging' or 'dynamic' aspects. They are derived from dividing the circle by an even number such as two (resulting in the **opposition**), four (producing the **square**) or eight (creating **semi-squares**, which are one-eighth of a circle apart, and **sesquiquadrates**, which are three-eighths of a circle away from each other). The hard aspects are very energizing and, because they inevitably indicate struggles, offer enormous potential for personal growth and for making something of our lives.

iii) The 'soft' aspects, which are sometimes described as easy or flowing and are derived by dividing the circle by three (resulting in the **trine**) or six (yielding the **sextile**).

iv) Creative or more rarefied aspects which result from dividing the circle by five (**quintile**), seven (**septile**) or nine (**novile** ⚹) or multiples of 5, 7 or 9. It is possible that division of the circle by higher numbers (e.g. eleven or thirteen) may yield very specific information (such as genetic abnormalities) but more research is needed here. Roughly speaking, the higher the number used to divide the circle to derive the particular aspect, the more specific and often unusual will be the traits and circumstances that are described.

v) The final category applies to aspects that don't neatly fit into the numerological idea of dividing the circle by a whole number; the main one is the **quincunx** (also known as the **inconjunct** in the USA). This is a 150-degree aspect (or five signs apart). The little-used **semi-sextile**, which is a 30-degree aspect (or one sign apart), also belongs in this category.

What about Orbs?
An orb is the distance by which an aspect can deviate from being exact and yet still be felt. Allowable orbs are a matter of some debate. The orbs listed above are those commonly used by astrologers, although I tend to use tighter orbs. The reality is that there is never going to be a sudden point when an aspect will be felt and not felt. What is certain is that the influence of an aspect wanes as it becomes looser. Tight aspects, those that are very close, are always going to be felt very strongly. Imagine an orchestra playing. Planets in tight aspect to each other can be likened to the brass section dominating the piece that is being played. An aspect with a wide orb might be rather like someone striking the triangle at the back of the orchestra. If a great deal else is going on, the triangle will not be heard. And in the same way that we might hear the triangle if we are consciously listening out for it, we might also become aware of something less important in the chart by actively concentrating upon it. After all, whatever the nature of a search, we are more likely to find something if we are actively looking for it. The material described by tight aspects – especially the conjunction, square and opposition aspects – manifests so strongly that it could not be missed by a blind person on a galloping horse. Aspects involving the all-important Sun, Moon or Ascendant are traditionally accorded slightly wider orbs than aspects involving other planets.

What Constitutes a Wide or Tight Orb?
This rather depends on the aspect and possibly on the planets involved. As a rule, though, quincunxes, quintiles, semi-squares and sesquiquadrates are usually allowed an orb of no more than two degrees. A two-degree orb with these aspects might be considered quite wide, whereas a two- or three-degree orb would be considered tight with respect to the conjunction, opposition or square aspects.

All Aspects Aren't Equal
Most charts will yield quite a few aspects and it can be difficult for the beginner to decide which aspects are important and which are not. The answer to this question rather depends on the nature of the specific aspect and how tight in orb that aspect is. Suffice it to say that the beginner student should more or less confine their attention to the conjunction and hard aspects, as these describe the main character traits and basic life story. Trines and sextiles can be added to this simple recipe if they are tight (within about two degrees), as can quincunxes within one degree. Quintiles and septiles can

also be ignored by the beginner unless they are more or less exact.

It is not that all aspects may not be saying something; frequently 'lesser' aspects will underscore a theme already described elsewhere. In summary, you are advised to give a great deal of weight and emphasis to:

- Conjunctions.
- The tightest aspects (whatever aspects these are).
- Hard aspects (especially if they are close in orb).

The Conjunction

Number of signs apart: 0
Degrees of separation: 0
Suggested orb: 8 degrees maximum, except sometimes where the Sun, Moon or Ascendant is involved.

A conjunction always provides a strong focus to a chart, and a certain amount of 'oomph' and motivation. One might say that several eggs have been laid in the one basket. This is an area to hone in on. The ease or difficulty with which an individual may experience planets conjunct will largely depend on the nature of the planets themselves. Do they share a similar nature, for instance? For example, the Moon and Venus share a soft, feminine quality and to some extent therefore may feel comfortable together, whereas the Moon and Saturn bring together two very different energies.

The Opposition

Number of signs apart: 6
Degrees of separation: 180
Suggested orb: 8 degrees maximum, except sometimes where the Sun, Moon or Ascendant is involved.

The role of the opposition in the horoscope can best be understood by considering the role of the opposition party in government. For example, left-wing and right-wing political parties serve to check the extremism of each other, although in practice each will sometimes push the other side towards greater extremism. Oppositions tend to manifest themselves mostly through relationships – the self in relation to another person, the self in relation to a group of people and even the self in relation to society itself. We tend to project one-half of our oppositions and experience that in other people. Where the square aspect manifests as projection, it will be projection on to matter, money or the physical world. The usefulness of the opposition lies in its capacity to foster awareness. An awareness of there being two (at least) sides to a story and sometimes an awareness of the paradox intrinsic in most situations. Oppositions can increase the potential for conflict and extremism but also will often increase the potential for indecision as they can be associated with a lack of equilibrium, and a tendency to see-saw from one side to the other.

Exact oppositions occur across opposing signs and therefore between compatible elements: fire opposes air, and earth opposes water. However, exact oppositions occur between the same mode (for instance, cardinal signs oppose cardinal signs) and this is where the stress comes in. Planets (or other points) are, at least to some extent, in conflict with each other in the opposition.

The Square

Number of signs apart: 3
Degrees of separation: 90
Suggested orb: 8 degrees maximum, except sometimes where the Sun, Moon or Ascendant is involved.

Exact squares occur between incompatible elements but within the same mode, e.g. Aries (cardinal and fire) squares both Cancer (cardinal and water) and Capricorn (cardinal and earth). Thus, squares describe the difficulties and challenges of life. Although these difficulties can manifest in and through relationships, the areas of projection are usually more physical in nature and thus these aspects tend to manifest more in health matters, money, work or in some kind of material reality.

When two planets are in square there is usually some kind of uncertainty about the possibility of bringing the two (or more) energies together. This uncertainty can give rise to fear, nervousness and awkwardness, although this may not be fully conscious. Planets in square tend to be resistant to each other; they get in each other's way and create tension. There is often an uncertainty about the rightness of bringing the particular energies together and thus they can give rise to self-consciousness and guilt. The experience of struggle and feelings of uncertainty that accompany these aspects usually push us into proving ourselves, and in doing so we are offered an opportunity to reach our potential. Squares may block, hinder or impede us if we allow them to and they can describe the areas in life where we feel as though we are knocking our heads against a brick wall. Nevertheless, they also describe areas where we are stretched. Little wonder, therefore, that these are known as the great growth and self-development aspects.

They cannot be ignored in chart interpretation because squares describe where we meet the world and make an impact upon it and where the outer world makes an impact upon us. Although squares do give rise to feelings of anxiety, often people go overboard in manifesting the message described by the planets involved, proving that they can do 'it', whatever 'it' is. All, obviously, depends on the planets involved in the aspect. Squares can also describe where we can get stuck and reach a stalemate (especially with squares between planets in fixed signs), and when this happens something from 'outside' usually forces movement. Squares are energizing aspects, they provide 'oomph' and, rather like an itch that must be scratched, they always demand our attention.

The Semi-Square and Sesquiquadrate

Degrees of separation: 45 (semi-square) and 135 (sesquiquadrate).
Division of the circle by: 8 and 3/8. The semi-square is one-eighth of a circle whereas the sesquiquadrate is three-eighths of a circle. The aspects were introduced by Johannes Kepler and are sometimes scarcely employed by more traditional astrologers who concentrate on the Ptolemaic aspects (conjunction, opposition, square, trine and sextile) and the quincunx, seeing the semi-squares and sesquiquadrates as 'minor' aspects.
Suggested orb: 2 degrees.

Known in the USA as the octile (semi-square) and tri-octile (sesquiquadrate), these aspects are not, in my view, minor in terms of significance, although they are certainly weaker than squares. Like squares, they describe difficulties and challenges presented to us by the material world. They tend to manifest strongly but in a narrower, more specific area of life than the more major hard aspects. On their own, they can perhaps be ignored in individual charts (though not in mundane maps); they become more noticeable, often violently so, when multiple or linked to squares and oppositions. The fact that they are more difficult to spot when looking at a horoscope may reflect the fact that the material they represent is often more unconscious, more deeply buried in the psyche. They are less psychologically obvious but may be more precipitous of dramatic events. When we are less conscious of there being a problem, that problem is, for a time, suppressed and so it is more likely to manifest the relevant energies in a dramatic and explosive way. In other words, periodically, some kind of release is forced.

The Trine

Number of signs apart: 4
Degrees of separation: 120
Suggested orb: this is debatable. Many astrologers will allow up to 8 degrees but I consider 6 degrees to be the absolute maximum and in practice I ignore trines when there is more than a 3-degree orb.

Planets in trinal aspect seem to hold hands; they are allowed to express themselves without hindrance or obstruction from each other. Indeed, each body seems to facilitate, support and reinforce the expression of the other. Trines are not growth aspects because growth inevitably is the fruit of struggle while softness and ease, regrettably, are not. Despite being viewed as so-called major aspects, in my experience trines can usually be ignored in chart interpretation unless the orb is tight. That is because these contacts are so passive, have no 'oomph' and, unlike squares, don't manifest themselves in concrete, material, terms.

Trinal aspects give rise to contentment and pleasure because we feel able to express the energies concerned without guilt or self-questioning. Trines take some of the hard work out of living. Nevertheless it should not be assumed that they are wholly 'good' aspects, any more than hard aspects should necessarily be viewed as 'bad'. It is just that as individuals we don't usually view our trines as problem areas. In fact, we can become complacent with respect to these contacts and such complacency is often not so 'good' when measured in collective or relationship terms – in other words, when measured and experienced by other people. Trines can provide lines of least resistance in the chart in that we tend to fall back on them. They describe areas where the person seems to be lucky and is left unchallenged by others. Here the individual is protected and can get away with things, and may take it for granted that they can do so. They reveal the easier areas of life and, given that most people do opt for the easier life, they can provide clues as to what motivates an individual.

The Sextile

Number of signs apart: 2
Degrees of separation: 60
Suggested orb: this is a matter of some debate. Many astrologers will allow up to 5 degrees whereas 3 degrees might be a more realistic maximum orb.

Sextile aspects are less passive than trines, the other so-called soft aspect, but may actually be more useful simply because they are less passive. Sextiles occur between different but compatible elements; for instance water sextiles earth, and fire sextiles air. Water and earth need each other, as do fire and air. Bil Tierney[1] has used the word 'coax' as a major keyword for the sextile aspect and this feels entirely appropriate. Each body can coax the other into action. There is perhaps some aptitude but that aptitude has to be taken advantage of. Unlike the trine, it is not so much a matter of luck but more a case of opportunity with this aspect. The bodies concerned can work efficiently together; the ability is there but some effort is needed.

The Quincunx

Number of signs apart: 5
Degrees of separation: 150
Suggested orb: 2 degrees

Signs in quincunx have nothing in common in terms of element or mode although they may share sign rulership (Taurus and Libra share Venus as their ruler, and Aries and Scorpio share their Mars rulership) and perhaps that is the issue: the relevant energies don't really see each other. The quincunx is an aspect to associate with stress, strain and friction, without the 'oomph' and possibly without the growth potential of the much more powerful opposition and square series of aspects. Less well understood than those hard aspects and certainly much less powerful, the quincunx does not lead to make-or-break situations. What seems to happen is that planet A interferes with the easy expression of planet B, but not to the extent that it actually prevents or challenges B's operation. Imagine that you live near a hospital, have had an accident and are running to the hospital to have a gaping wound stitched up. The quincunx operates on a somewhat similar way to finding, as you are running, that you have a stone in your shoe. Very irritating. Our quincunxes may make us feel uncomfortable, and annoyed even, but often they are not so stressful that we do anything about them.

The aspect has long been associated with health problems and Charles Carter also linked it with death,[2] possibly because the cusps of the Sixth House and Eighth House are naturally both quincunx the Ascendant (First House) cusp. And possibly it is the underlying stresses and strains in life, which we tend to ignore and which tend to be fairly unconscious, which undermine our health over the long haul. Curiously, quincunx aspects occur frequently between couples, perhaps because signs in quincunx provide the qualities that each could benefit from. For instance, Cancer could do with Aquarian detachment and Aquarius could do with some Cancerian appreciation of all that is familial, and so on.

Note that the semi-sextile (a 30-degree or one-sign separation) comes within the same aspect series as the quincunx but its effects, if any, are negligible. Like signs in quincunx, adjacent signs have nothing in common in terms of mode or element and therein lies the similarity between the two aspects.

Tips on Interpreting the Quincunx: The notes on planetary combinations in the latter part of this chapter do not apply to this aspect because the tension of the quincunx seems to result more from the stress between the signs than between the planets. The best course is to start with the planets in their respective signs and consider what *adjustment* each would need in order to feel comfortable with the other and what *discomfort* will ensue when such an adjustment doesn't take place. For instance, the stress between Leo and Pisces arises because Leo's more egocentric needs (the need to be seen, recognized and be important) are at variance with the Piscean urge towards selflessness. A way around this conundrum might be to embark on selfless acts that would precipitate personal recognition and greater self-esteem. The two signs are also the ones to be associated with drama; acting could be a perfect vehicle because the actor completely loses themselves in the part they are playing and yet attracts applause and recognition. Many signs in quincunx are concerned with freedom versus closeness struggles, the self versus the partner, or the self versus wider world issues. Quincunxes usually underscore themes already written in the chart. On their own, they don't describe major life issues and can be largely ignored, at least at the outset of trying to get to grips with a chart.

The Quintile

Degrees of separation: 72
Division of the circle by: 5 (360 divided by 72 = 5). Note that the 5 series includes the bi-quintiles (144 degrees) and can include the decile (36 degrees), the vigintile (18 degrees) and even the tredecile (108 degrees), as these aspects are all derived by dividing the circle by a multiple of 5.
Suggested orb: 2 degrees for the quintile and bi-quintile; no more than 1 degree for all others in the series.

This is an aspect of creativity. It describes the kind of art form we are drawn to (using the word 'art' in the widest sense) and with which we may become skilled. It is often an area we become obsessed and fixated about and we impose that fixation upon the world at large. For example, I have a bi-quintile between Jupiter and Saturn and it could be said that, as an astrologer, I am obsessed with a philosophy (Jupiter) concerning time (Saturn). It is beyond the scope of this book to discuss the quintile aspect further but suffice it to say that researchers into harmonic theory have noted that quintiles describe the style and technical quality of an individual's work and even the style of their behaviour.[3]

The Septile

Degrees of separation: 51.43
Division of the circle by: 7 (360 divided by 51.43 = 7). Note that the 7 series includes the bi-septile (102.86 degrees) and the tri-septile (154.29 degrees).
Suggested orb: 2 degrees maximum for the septile, perhaps half a degree for all others in the series.

Another aspect of creativity but, unlike the quintile, the septile has a romantic, emotional and feeling quality to it. Septiles have much to say about our fantasy life and about which aspects of life provide inspiration as well as how we may inspire others. Our fantasies about ourselves or about the world may have little basis in reality, of course and, as with all horoscopic factors, septiles can have a dangerous side to them. Septile aspects abound at moments of discovery[4] and also in the charts of discoverers. It is easy to see the link with inspiration at this point, for of course we often feel inspired at moments of discovery.

Dissociate Aspects

Dissociate aspects can only occur when a planet (or angle or other body) is found at the beginning or end of a sign. Basically, the general elemental and modal rules are broken and the aspect is 'out of sign'. One example is a planet falling in Taurus but opposing a planet in Sagittarius. Usually, Taurus opposes Scorpio and Gemini opposes Sagittarius but if a body is at 29 Taurus and the other body is at 2 Gemini, they would actually be in fairly tight opposition. Some astrologers dismiss disassociate aspects but the student can be assured that it is the numerical separation that is important, not the sign relationship. Generally speaking, disassociate trines may be more useful than same-element trines as they are likely to be slightly less passive, and disassociate hard aspects may be slightly softer in their manifestation than same-mode hard aspects.

Applying and Separating Aspects

In an applying aspect, the faster-moving planet is approaching the slower-moving one – in other words, the aspect is about to become exact. In a separating aspect, the aspect has already happened – the faster-moving planet is separating from the aspect that it formed to the slower-moving one. In horary astrology, knowing the distinction between the two is essential because separating aspects refer to events that have already happened. In natal astrology, there still may be some mileage to be gained from thinking that separating aspects indicate events having happened before the individual was born and applying ones refer to events due to happen in the future, but in practice this idea can be misleading. The most important point is that applying aspects are probably stronger than separating ones, but this is an area that requires much more research.

Charts without Aspects

Looking at a chart is an exercise in observation; the astrologer, like the artist, has to learn to see. The astrologer needs to see what makes the horoscope under inspection different from most other horoscopes. On occasion, one difference that can be noted is a predominance or lack of a type of aspect, and this can sometimes provide an entry into understanding the chart. It is also worth noting the planet receiving the most aspects and any planets that receive none (unaspected planets).

• **Charts without conjunctions** This is a common occurrence and it is debatable whether their absence is worthy of any special attention. But given that conjunctions add a degree of self-motivation and focus to a chart, horoscopes without them may incline to a less driven, less goal-orientated and more flexible approach to life.

• **Charts without oppositions** Individuals will tend to be very subjective, often finding it difficult to look outside themselves for other people's opinions, approval, disapproval or feedback generally. There can be a resulting lack of awareness with regards to their own nature and the nature of others.

• **Charts without squares** A lack of drive and 'oomph' is a possibility here, and a lack of squares can be descriptive of someone who is confined to taking the easier path through life, although the strong presence of other chart factors can mitigate against this. Frequently, the childhood was very stable and the person's impulse will usually be to uphold the status quo, rather than to buck against their roots.

• **Charts without trines** If there are a lot of squares particularly, a chart without trines will often describe someone who is at odds with the world and maybe at odds with themselves. It can be descriptive of people who overdo it: people with a lot of energy who like to overturn apple-carts. The person can be in the habit of always thinking that everything is going to be difficult and, for them, it sometimes is.

Most Aspected Planet

It is often worth noting, and thus weighting, the most aspected planet(s) in the chart, as such a body then becomes more prominent in the chart. When it receives numerous aspects, this suggests that the planet is well-integrated into the psyche and life of the individual, and it also suggests that there are many avenues through which the planetary energy might be expressed.

Unaspected Planets

If one includes all so-called minor aspects, there is probably actually no such thing as an unaspected planet. If the astrologer concentrates only on the major aspects (those descriptive of the life and character in a general way), then in some charts some planets will be unaspected. In fact, the tighter the orb the astrologer uses, the more likely it is that one or more planets will be unaspected. Sometimes two or three planets aspect each other but nothing else in the chart, thereby creating an unaspected duo (a 'duet') or trio. Geoffrey Dean and his colleagues in Western Australia in the 1970s did some research into this area and found that planets operating on their own or in duets or trios yield significant information. For instance, they found that people with unaspected Mars were the ones who could be described as 'always busy'. Many prolific writers have an unaspected Mercury, including Agatha Christie whose chart is analysed later in this book. Planets on their own (or in pairs) seem to operate independently, perhaps like sub-personalities; their nature isn't integrated into the rest of the personality. This isn't necessarily a 'bad' or a 'good' thing. Very often the relevant planet(s) has an urgent need to express itself; it seems that the rest of the planetary energies, or other parts of the personality, do nothing to get in the way of this process.

Part Two: Aspect Patterns

Planets in multiple aspect form pictures or patterns in the horoscope and astrologers over the ages have accorded names and meanings to some of these pictures. Astrology students can get very excited when they spot some of these patterns but, in practice, it doesn't matter which aspect patterns are formed. When interpreting any configuration, all the planets, signs and houses involved must be interpreted separately and then built up into an overall picture. The most important aspect patterns are stelliums, T-squares and Grand Crosses because these always describe both the weightiest problems and the greatest achievements in the person's life. Next in line of importance are Grand Trines and Yods.

The Stellium

Very obvious to spot, a stellium occurs when four or more bodies conjunct each other, creating a concentrated 'hot spot' for the astrologer to zoom in on. With such a concentration of energy in the same place, there will be a strong focus upon the affairs ruled by relevant house(s), and the characteristics associated with the relevant sign will also be very strong. An individual's whole *raison d'être* can be shown by a stellium, especially when one realizes that the planets involved are likely, between them, to rule most of the houses in the horoscope. With so many eggs in one basket, a stellium is always going to provide motivation, focus and purpose. Provided that each planet is within 8 degrees of the next, the configuration can be defined as a stellium even if, technically speaking, the planets on either end of it don't actually conjunct each other. However, the strongest example occurs when the planets involved all fall within the same 8 or so degrees, so they are all conjunct each other. Single-mindedness can be the blessing and the curse here: a blessing because there are often a few clear goals; occasionally a curse because the individual's life and viewpoints can become narrowed and lopsided.

The T-Square

This configuration occurs when two planets oppose each other and each is squared by a third planet. The planet receiving the two squares is known as the apex or focal planet and it often acts an engine, driving the other planets towards increased awareness and to resolving the dilemmas posed by the configuration. The point in the horoscope exactly opposite the apex planet (sometimes known as the 'empty leg') often acts as a discharge point, providing an area of the life where the tension can be drained off. Either this, or the apex planet, usually provides the avenue for unlocking the potential of the aspect pattern. Over one-third of people have T-squares in their charts and, where they occur, this energizing configuration can dominate the life and the chart. A T-square usually describes the most pressing problems in the life; by dealing with them, an individual stretches themselves and often makes noteworthy contributions to the world. So while indicative of obstacles and lessons to be learned, a T-square offers huge potential for personal growth.

How to interpret a T-square:

i) Consider each individual planet within the T-square by sign, house, houses ruled, etc.

ii) Look for 'double whammies' within the planets, signs and houses in which the configuration falls, as these provide an entry point for understanding what the major issues of the T-square might be. For instance, if Mercury were square to any planet in the Mercurial signs of Gemini or Virgo, there would be a doubly Mercurial feeling to the triad.

iii) Imagine the planets as people as well as types of energy, and imagine how the three individuals would act if locked in a room together. What kind of stories can be conjured up by the three planetary principles?

Except when there are disassociate aspects, T-squares usually occur with the planets falling in the same mode. As a means of understanding the T-square, some general statements can be made by considering the quadruplicity/mode involved:

• **Cardinal T-squares** Goal-orientated and full of drive and vitality, these types are always on the go. While great at getting things done and pushing things through, impatience and an insistence on action can lead to ill-conceived and hasty decision-making and head-on confrontations with others. Juggling the demands of the self, home, partner and career is the norm.

• **Fixed T-squares** Enduring, purposeful and determined, the fixed type doesn't buckle under pressure. However, stubbornness, inflexibility, the tendency to stagnate and to stick in ruts are the inevitable downsides, impeding both progress and movement. Energies can become bottled up and will periodically explode.

• **Mutable T-squares** The mutable signs are concerned with thought, understanding and communication, and a T-square (or Grand Cross) involving them is good for work in health, communication and educational areas. Versatility and flexibility usually feature but this can sometimes translate into over-adaptability, inconsistency, a lack of resolve and a tendency to avoid problems. Restlessness is the norm and establishing or keeping to goals can be difficult.

Examples of T-square interpretations can be found in Chapter 9.

The Grand Cross

Sometimes known as the Cosmic Cross, the Grand Cross occurs when the planets across two oppositions all square each other. According to *Recent Advances in Natal Astrology*,[5] only 5% of charts have this aspect pattern; certainly it is not common. As with the T-square, the first thing to consider is the mode in which the configuration falls and then to look at each planet individually in terms of its sign, houses and the houses being ruled. A way into interpretation, as always, is to look for double whammies within the planets, signs and houses in which the configuration falls. Many of the comments concerning T-squares also apply to the Grand Cross, only more so. The main difference is that the Grand Cross is more complex and offers more possibilities. While the T-square tends to provide a focus, with the Grand Cross the individual tends to feel pulled in four directions at once. This really is a make-or-break pattern and, while potentially productive of great talent and great things, it has a distinctly Saturnian edge to it. Obstacles that present themselves along an individual's path ensure that, while the achievements and rewards may be great, they are usually hard-won. The reader is directed to the relevant section on the modes on pages 26-9 but here are some brief points:

• **The Cardinal Cross** Ambitious and competitive, a state of overdrive and a high degree of pushiness can be the problem here. An unco-operative insistence on doing their own thing in their own way, coupled sometimes with extreme impatience, inevitably lead to feelings of frustration and sometimes to an accident-prone quality. The establishment of a clear, well-planned goal can help to prevent the individual making poor decisions and zooming off in all directions at once. Cultivating a degree of calmness, poise and patience is key here.

• **The Fixed Cross** Wilful and unyielding, the individual can be incredibly strong, determined and persistent, and great to have on your side in a crisis. However, strong desires and an inflexible attitude can lead to painful emotional situations. Feelings of jealousy, anger and possessiveness need to be acknowledged and discharged rather than retained. Some degree of flexibility needs to be cultivated, as does an awareness that letting go is not a sign of weakness but merely sometimes the right thing to do.

• **The Mutable Cross** There can be a feeling of being blown all over the place by the multifarious pulls upon the person's time and interests. A strong worrying tendency can accompany restlessness, vacillation, lack of resolve, a tendency to duck and dive and a disinclination to commit themselves to anything or anyone. While the individual may feel safest living in a state of flux, they need to cultivate some degree of staying power in themselves, and anchorage in their life, in order to make progress.

The Grand Trine

The Grand Trine occurs when two planets are in trine aspect to each other and both are trined by a third planet. Except in the case of disassociate aspects, all three bodies fall in the same element. Individuals with Grand Trines tend to be cushioned, protected and 'lucky' with respect to the element and houses involved in the configuration, or they expect to be. Sometimes the lack of challenge and general feeling of passivity can give rise to immaturity with respect to the element concerned because the individual doesn't really learn about those life areas.

• **Grand Trine in the fire signs** They often live life in the fast lane and, frequently unaware of any risks involved, seem to be protected in dangerous situations.
• **Grand Trine in the earth signs** They are usually materially lucky: either they inherit or marry money, or for some other reason are buffered against poverty.
• **Grand Trine in the air signs** They usually have wide interests and are rarely short of social opportunities. However, the inclination towards passive learning can result in superficial understanding.
• **Grand Trine in the water signs** They may exhibit all the usual watery dependency needs but they will easily have those needs met and, in so doing, may not acknowledge or overcome the neediness in their nature.

Grand Trines provide stability, yet too much stability easily leads to inertia: the person simply has no inclination to rock the boat. Inertia doesn't stimulate ambition or the impulse to grow. So while Grand Trines can show areas of enjoyment and potential talents, they do not provide the necessary discipline to get off our butts and do something useful with those talents. Such 'oomph' has to be shown elsewhere. As always, the whole chart must be studied.

The Yod
The Yod, also known as the Finger of God or the Finger of Fate, occurs when there are two planets in sextile aspect to each other, and each of them is forming a quincunx to a third planet. This third (or focal) planet is always worthy of attention. Rather as the nib of a pen is the action point of the pen overall, the focal planet is usually a place of especial activity in the horoscope. Sometimes it describes something that the individual seems fated to do; very often there are skills to be developed or goals to be pursued.

The Kite and Mystic Rectangle
The Kite occurs when a planet falls opposite one of the three planets of a Grand Trine, so the fourth planet is connected to the Grand Trine by the opposition and also by two sextiles. The Mystic Rectangle consists of two oppositions where each planet also is making a sextile or trine to another. Not commonly seen in practice, the overall meaning of these configurations is open to speculation. With both aspect patterns the emphasis is on the opposition and soft aspects; these are not patterns that are descriptive of action or especial manifestation in the world. For that reason, undue weight should probably not be afforded to them. What probably can be said is that, unlike the Grand Trine, the individual is likely to be much more aware of their many talents and opportunities and so has a better chance of doing something useful with them. All the more so if one or more of the planets configured is also linked to a square aspect. In both patterns all the planets will either fall in fire/air signs or water/earth ones. This may provide a useful starting point towards interpretation as the chart is therefore either going to have a strong, outgoing, masculine, yang energy or a receptive, feminine, yin feeling to it. Both Kites and Mystic Rectangles may add a feeling of stability and cohesion to the chart and incline individuals towards upholding the status quo.

Part Three: Planetary Combinations

How to Use the Following Section

These notes are brief and designed to prompt the astrologer's thought processes. They will tend to be more accurate when the aspect is a tight one *and* the aspect formed is either a conjunction or a hard aspect. The effects of wide, soft aspects are usually negligible. Where a tight, soft aspect occurs, the interpreter can use these aspect notes together with their understanding of the trine or sextile aspect to arrive at a softer and more appropriate interpretation. Although what is written is geared towards the interpretation of the horoscopes of humans, it should be an easy enough process to gear one's interpretation to the study of other types of charts and also to forecasting work. These notes on aspects will only be useful when applied to the major aspects; they will not work with quincunxes, quintiles and septiles, all of which have to be studied individually. For more detailed help interpreting planetary combinations, see my book *Aspects in Astrology* (Element, 1989, Rider, 2001).

Sun-Moon (☉☽)

All tight aspects suggest some kind of creativity as described by the signs involved. Soft aspects add a degree of stability to the character and the life. Hard aspects may be suggestive of schisms between the parents and also between a person's own wants and needs. Often the demands of the past or of the family challenge the ability to move forward. The conjunction between these bodies places great emphasis on the sign and house in which it falls. New Moon children often have parents who are very similar, and often one parent is literally playing both roles, as might be the case where they are raised in an institution or by a single parent.

Sun-Mercury (☉☿)

The two planets can never be more than 28 degrees apart and so the only possible aspect between them is a conjunction. The subjectivity to which all humans are prone may not be recognized by the individual as pertaining to themselves. There can be potential difficulty in separating from their opinions, ideas and views. Disagreement from others may be taken personally and the views of others may be difficult to comprehend. Depending on other aspects the conjunction is receiving, and perhaps on the sign in which the conjunction is placed, this conjunction can give strength to the mental processes and there can be a recognition of the importance of education and confidence in verbal self-expression.

Sun-Venus (☉♀)

As Venus can never be more than 48 degrees from the Sun, only the conjunction and semi-square aspects are possible. The combination inclines towards an affectionate, popular and soft nature although laziness, self-indulgence and extravagance can also feature. The desire to please and be popular and loved can be over-developed, resulting in a tendency to 'cave in' and compromise too easily. Strength needs to be shown elsewhere in the chart. Relationships are likely to be of primary importance. Venus may decrease the general vitality and vigour of the Sun. Often indicates a love of the father. May indicate a soft and loving father figure, possibly with a 'peace at any price' disposition.

Sun-Mars (☉♂)

Tight contacts between these planets will add vigour, strength and courage to any chart. A goal-orientated individual who is not frightened to dare to do something. There is likely to be a strong need for a cause: something or someone to fight for. Hard aspects incline toward undue competitiveness, a tendency to strain at the leash, living life in the fast lane and wanting to do things now! Impetuosity, impatience and self-interest are part of this package which can describe the trouble-shooter or the trouble-maker. An ideal combination for the forces or for any occupation which requires decisiveness and strength. They will often be at war with the father and/or other authority figures and unwittingly with themselves.

Sun-Jupiter (☉♃)

Optimism, faith, enthusiasm and generosity are to be expected, plus an eagerness to experience as much of the world as possible. A questing, visionary, explorative attitude to life goes hand-in-hand with the desire to grow. A sense of humour, philosophical attitude and carefree disposition can be expected, although the hard aspects especially can also give rise to over-confidence, arrogance and to too high expectations of the self and others. There can be a tendency to gloss over problems and mistakes, and take on too much. The father figure can be experienced as some kind of god, or as being too far away to reach and become intimate with. Sometimes he appears as a success story and feels like too hard an act to follow.

Sun-Saturn (☉♄)

Those with these contacts tend to cultivate a realistic (or overly bleak) view of the world. They take themselves and life seriously, do not trust easily and may set up strong defences. A lack of confidence in early life may incline to the setting of goals that can easily be met and/or a fear of failure. This combination often indicates a strict upbringing and a lifetime spent shaking off the belief that they aren't good enough. Greater confidence and considerable self-reliance can come in later years with the realization that they are their own best authority and, sometimes, an authority figure to others. Self-denial, self-defence and self-discipline can lead to lasting achievements. Unless other factors point to the contrary, this combination often indicates a weak father figure; commonly, there is strictness in the early life, but it usually comes from the mother or from elsewhere.

Sun-Uranus (☉♅)

There is often an identification with the alien or outsider – this individual may feel separate either from the family or from society itself. This combination is usually indicative of a strongly independent spirit and sometimes a wilful, rebellious nature, although a greater mellowness usually comes with advancing years, when the individual has worked through their earlier feelings of rejection and recognizes that it is within their own gift to reject or accept. There is usually an insistence on personal freedom and liberty; this individual will not take kindly to interference from others or to being told what to do. There can be a strong urge to discover the truth or to embark on a mission to share it. An excellent combination for all subjects pertaining to technology and sci-fi. The father figure may be experienced as cold and remote, and a law unto himself.

Sun-Neptune (☉Ψ)

This often describes a yearning for the ideal life and a desire to escape from the harsher aspects of reality. Charles Carter described it as a 'delicacy or remoteness from what is ordinary, tangible and concrete.'[6] If tight, both hard and soft contacts can be associated with compassion, kindliness, sensitivity and an appreciation of subtlety. A weak sense of identity and an urge to glamorize the self can at worst lead to self-deception, missed opportunities and a lack of realism. The refinement and sensitivity of the combination make it excellent for involvement in the arts or in charitable works. An identification with the victim can propel this person into the role of victim themselves or that of saviour. Often there is an idealization of the father figure, although frequently he is weak or missing. The individual, or men in their life, may have to grapple with alcohol- or drug-related problems.

Sun-Pluto (☉♇)

This aspect is usually descriptive of a very driven, single-minded, purposeful and even ruthless nature. For many, self-improvement and self-development become the obsession and huge personal transformations can be associated with this combination. Occasionally there are stories of a criminal-turned-saint or a rags-to-riches experience. There is often a decision at some point in the life to live or die, and en route to that decision, many will undergo despair and self-destructive episodes and have to deal with their (usually) markedly poor self-image. Before this happens, there can be a tendency to sabotage their life, and sometimes to throw themselves into the most difficult situations. There is often a very strong tie with the father figure, although there will often have been something remote about him. The death of the father is usually a particularly painful, but ultimately a hugely transformative and revealing, time.

Moon-Mercury (☽☿)

This is a good combination for talking about everyday matters, and potentially for understanding and discussing feelings. Excellent for keeping a journal; maybe everyone with tight contacts between these bodies would benefit from keeping a diary. It can also be associated with imaginative writing, soap operas and kitchen-sink dramas. Also with gossip on the one hand, and with sympathetic communication on the other. It is to be associated with common sense or the reverse. Hard aspects can suggest a head-versus-heart clash and sometimes memory problems. Moon-Mercury can indicate a mother figure who is talkative and sometimes overly rational or irrational, and may describe important relationships with aunts (especially) and uncles (as the siblings of the mother).

Moon-Venus (☽♀)

The combination provides a strong feminine feeling to the chart but the hard aspects especially suggest a clash between the two feminine principles. It is suggestive of loving feelings, of care and consideration given, received or craved for, depending on the aspect and chart overall. Squares especially are sometimes descriptive of the spoilt child, forever showered with gifts or sweets – although sometimes struggling to find more tangible proof of love. Perhaps Mum wants to be out enjoying herself and is assuaging her guilt at neglecting maternal or domestic matters, whether she imagines that this is the case or whether she really does it. Usually there is a strong wish to be cushioned from physical and material hardship and, ever wanting to keep things nice, some with this combination can be over-accommodating, habitually caving in under the slightest pressure. This is sometimes a duo to connect with great consumerism and materialism, and no one enjoys giving and receiving gifts so much as a strongly Moon-Venus type.

Moon-Mars (☽♂)

Direct and authentic in behaviour, to feel is to act for most Moon-Mars people. Rarely content to stay on the periphery of whatever is going on, these individuals have an urge to get involved. Many will have experienced acute domestic discord when young; or the threat can come without it – either the feeling or reality of being raised on a bombsite can sometimes feature. Sensitive to threat, fiercely protective and easily aroused, this can be a very brave but also touchy and sometimes volatile combination, especially where the hard aspects are concerned. Mum will often have been sexually precocious, young and inexperienced in maternal matters. The individual may grow to be angry with her or strongly protective of her. Non-involvement with the maternal figure is not often an option. This combination can also be associated with all aspects of 'fast food' (including snatched meals, eating on impulse or when angry) as well as with home decorating and do-it-yourself activities.

Moon-Jupiter (☽♃)

Strongly protective of themselves and others, this combination can be associated with a generous, caring nature. Frequently, warmth and hospitality go with the territory but so do over-eating, over-cooking and greed and wastefulness generally. Hard aspects describe exaggerated feelings and a tendency to get emotional issues, and the day-to-day ups and downs of life, out of proportion. Something of the quality of a big baby (emotionally) can continue into adulthood. Eating patterns can be attached to the person's religion or other beliefs. Most with these contacts will feel at home among other cultures and may even live abroad. Mother-issues tend to be exaggerated and she may be experienced variously as social-climbing, hysterical or irrational. In mundane charts, this duo is a signature of mass hysteria or at least huge emotional outpourings.

Moon-Saturn (☽♄)

Hard aspects often describe a lack of warmth and emotional softness in early life. Poverty and a feeling of 'bleak house' is common, so that material survival, and therefore the need for one or both parents to work all hours, takes precedence over other aspects of family life. Usually there is a strong need to feel secure both emotionally and financially and a disinclination to take risks in these areas. Indicative of a frugal temperament, it is excellent for all situations requiring the management of time or money. Men are often shy with women and sometimes frightened of them. Both sexes can be fearful of being emotionally or domestically responsible for others, although some will become an authority in such matters. This is a contact commonly found in professional mothering situations, catering and the construction trades.

Moon-Uranus (☽♅)

This aspect can indicate wilful behaviour and lightning changes of mood. Frequently it denotes unpredictable happenings in childhood and inconsistency in the parenting that was received. It can indicate touchy behaviour due to an over-sensitivity to rejection and perceived slights. Sometimes the need to be independent emotionally (and in life generally) leads to behaviour that is uncompromising and rejecting of others' help and care. Thus, feelings of alienation and separation sometimes feature. There is often a need to change their home life frequently and drastically; this can manifest as changes of partner, home, country or merely a penchant for redecorating. Many for whom this combination is strong feel more comfortable living on their own (living independently). Squares between these planets are often a hallmark of the single parent, especially in women's charts.

Moon-Neptune (☽Ψ)

This denotes sensitivity, impressionability, an accommodating nature and often a longing for unconditional love, nurturance, succour and security. It is often descriptive of a yearning for the ideal (and often unobtainable) domestic and emotional experience. Physically, this can mean the yearning for (or attainment of) the ideal home but it is also frequently descriptive of domestic chaos, maybe because some with this placement want to escape the drudgery of domestic chores. Early experiences of abandonment often feature; the mother figure may be experienced as weak, unstable or a victim in some way. It can sometimes be associated with addictions or with relationships with co-dependency issues. It is an excellent combination both for the arts and for work in charitable and voluntary sectors.

Moon-Pluto (☽♇)

Those with this contact may feel more comfortable when relating with others for intense but short bursts. Some feel more comfortable living on their own. The feeling of being invaded and intruded upon by mother (sometimes), and by people generally (often), can feed a strong need for privacy. There is usually great sensitivity to treachery and betrayal in and out of the home. Individuals rarely live lightly and the aspect often describes a familiarity with and/or an ability to process crises, sometimes due to early brushes with tragedy, death or mental illness in the family. Not afraid to confront and demolish, Moon-Pluto skills can include the empowering of others, the transforming of family situations and the regeneration of homes and gardens.

Mercury-Venus (☿♀)

With this aspect, communication is an art form, resulting potentially in beautiful handwriting as in calligraphy or in words being beautifully expressed. Or there can be the ownership of, or attraction to, a beautiful singing or speaking voice. The ability to say nice things, or to say things nicely, can lead to diplomatic skills. A need to talk about love, coupled with an interest in, or downright curiosity about, the relationships of others, makes this an ideal combination for match-making, networking, love letters and love songs. The aspect frequently indicates an interest or skill in music (the ultimate melodious communication), poetry, literary appreciation or involvement in the arts generally. The two planets can never be more than 72 degrees apart and thus squares, oppositions and trines between the two are impossible.

Mercury-Mars (☿♂)

Decisive, sharp, fast and direct in thinking and communicating, there is usually little subterfuge and no 'going round the houses' in individuals with these contacts. Not afraid to speak the unspeakable, these people can also be verbally combative and competitive in learning environments. There is frequently a history of sibling rivalry or of being brought up in an argumentative household. Easily bored with theoretical discussion, there can be an impatience to learn and an impatience to speak. Sarcasm, wit and a liking for or skill with crosswords, word games and quizzes are all common manifestations. The aspect can also be associated with theft and plagiarism, sexual curiosity, sexual relationships between parties of differing ages (toy boys), fast driving and potential road traffic accidents.

Mercury-Jupiter (☿♃)

Believing the best and speaking in upbeat terms, there can be an ability to imbue confidence in others and/or skills at selling and promoting. Not believing that facts should get in the way of a good story, individuals may be noted for their sense of humour or for telling 'tall' stories. Making sweeping statements and a tendency to bluff can go with the territory, as can misunderstandings, woolliness and a lack of judgement. There are usually wide-ranging interests, especially in matters connected with other cultures, philosophy, politics, ethics or religion. Frequently, this combination indicates a life characterized by a great deal of travelling or, at least, an abundance of everyday comings and goings. This is an ideal combination for work in sales, travel or humorous reading or writing.

Mercury-Saturn (☿♄)

There can be an expectation of being criticized (especially with the opposition aspect) and a tendency to control what they say through fear of being wrong or of saying the wrong thing. This is *the* combination to associate with mental control and discipline. The inclination to learn the rules of a particular subject, coupled with a capacity to avoid mental clutter and frivolity, can lead to mastering an area of knowledge or expertise. While some will reject education and opt for a practical life, others will become expert at grammar, editing and maths. Potentially, the individual can become an authority on writing, learning or communicating, or in areas requiring precise hand/eye co-ordination. The aspect can sometimes be associated with strict schooling, older siblings, responsibilities for siblings and sometimes the death of siblings. It is often descriptive of a lack of education or a lack of books and conversation in early life, or sometimes of the reverse, as in being sent to a school with very high academic standards. Either way, there is often a need to prove their intelligence by gaining qualifications or awards.

Mercury-Uranus (☿♅)

At best, an independently-minded, innovative and original thinker; someone who is not afraid to think for themselves and to express their views honestly. At worst, an individual who sticks pig-headedly to flawed viewpoints. Contrariness, and the tendency to contradict others, can be very marked. Some with this combination just have to think differently to everyone else, and even differently to how they themselves thought only a short time before! Reaching agreements can be hard, due to lightning changes of mind, difficulties in compromising and problems in understanding other people's viewpoints. Some for whom this combination is marked will always get the wrong end of the stick. Tact can also be missing as this combination can be associated with blurting out the truth, which in turn can offend and retard all attempts in any negotiating process. The combination can be associated also with sudden changes of schooling and local environments, school rebellions, expulsion from school, step-siblings, and the experience of being ostracized from a sibling through distance or choice.

Mercury-Neptune (☿Ψ)

This can describe the idealizing of facts or, conversely, the distorting or romanticizing of information. Thus, it is *the* combination of the poet or songwriter but also of the journalist and scientist. An ability to infiltrate the minds of others, coupled with the ability to present information in a positive light (or in whichever light is required), makes this an ideal combination also for the propagandist or advertising executive. It is *the* aspect to associate with the ultimate distortion of information: telling lies (although Mercury-Saturn, desirous of giving the 'right' answer, may be no slouch in such matters). On the one hand, this aspect can give rise to confused thinking, dyslexia, forgetfulness and to getting lost when navigating, and to intuitive, subtle understandings on the other.

Mercury-Pluto (☿♇)

An excellent combination for any kind of research, this combination can be descriptive of the detective type of mind: always analysing, probing and ferreting out information. Knowledge can feel like the means to survival for Mercury-Pluto types who always have a compulsive need to know, take nothing at face value and tend to be suspicious by nature. Many with these contacts will end up in situations where they have to 'bury information', by having to keep the secrets of others. It can be associated with sending or receiving poisonous pen letters or similar slanderous events. Often there is an interest in psychological or occult matters. This aspect can sometimes describe mental illness or disability with respect to siblings, and sometimes it can indicate the early death of siblings (if borne out by other chart factors).

Venus-Mars (♀♂)

Here, the urge to compete conflicts with the urge to please. Learning when to give in and when to stand firm can be the struggle inherent in this peace versus war, loving versus fighting, combination. It is a combination of love coupled with competition, and can be tremendously romantic and sensual. However, there can be a tendency to confuse love with lust and a high degree of impulsiveness about getting involved. This 'marrying in haste and repenting at leisure' combination is also associated with classic battles of the sexes and with romantic affairs and emotional triangles. After all, we can only compete for love, or be valued as the most attractive consort, if our charms are pitted against the attractions of another. The issue of love and competition usually starts in childhood, when siblings or, more usually, one or both parents form part of the triangle. This is also a tremendously creative combination; skills in the fields of drama, needlecraft, hairdressing, dress design and exceptional dress sense (sometimes androgynous dress sense) are common manifestations. Impulsive spending can go with the territory for some.

Venus-Jupiter (♀♃)

A large social circle and often an extensive social life is implied by this fun-loving combination. A generous and over-accommodating placement – there can be a strong desire to please, plus a tendency to gloss over difficulties and to keep on a social 'high'. The urge for social advancement can be a strong motivating factor. Over-indulgence, extravagance and wastefulness are the norm and there is a danger of accruing large debts. Hope triumphs over experience in romantic matters, with individuals tending to be optimistic about getting involved. For some, the grass is always greener somewhere else and the idea of 'putting oneself about' can manifest on a number of levels.

Venus-Saturn (♀♄)

Feeling the pain of love keenly, some with this combination will build defences that not only protect the self, but prevent others getting too close. Awareness of commitments and responsibilities can also get in the way of the individual wholeheartedly immersing themselves in pleasure. This person may feel responsible for other people's happiness. For a host of potential reasons, it may not be easy to abandon themselves to bodily, or other, pleasures, without guilt. But, over time, some will become an authority on love and sexual matters. Women with this aspect often lack confidence with respect to their femininity, often partly due to loneliness in childhood and a lack of physical affection from their father. Dressing themselves either substantially 'down' or 'up' can result. This combination can also be variously associated with prostitution, widowhood, poverty, working with money or taking responsibility for financial matters.

Venus-Uranus (♀♅)

This person has to integrate the need for space and freedom with the need for love. This, coupled with a desire for social and sexual excitement, can lead to on-off relating patterns, and sometimes changing their partners frequently. Onlookers simply don't know who the Venus-Uranus person is going to come home with, or dump, next. Relationships can prosper if space is allocated for personal independence and for some excitement and unpredictability. Valuing honesty in relationships and a disinclination for game-playing can feature; conversely, so can rejecting others before they reject the Venus-Uranus person. There can be great sensitivity to rejection with this aspect, hidden sometimes under a 'couldn't care less' bluff. The combination suggests the choosing of an unconventional mate; the choice of partner can even be an act of rebellion. The person may attract others by being exciting and by virtue of their originality, honesty and apparent independence, but they can also alienate others by a seemingly unco-operative attitude. This aspect is good for work where money is exchanged (e.g. bureau de change). Sudden changes of fortune can occur if the possibility is repeated elsewhere.

Venus-Neptune (♀♆)

Through relationship the individual may seek to fuse with the other and touch the Divine. This is the combination to associate with romantic idealism and fairy-tale romances, and with the capacity to seduce and be seduced. A longing for the unobtainable, and an ability to believe the best about the other person, can lead to gullibility and difficulty in facing the reality of the beloved or the reality of the relationship itself. Some will miss the opportunity to make a relationship ideal by being so busy concentrating on the beloved's imperfections. The combination can be associated with imaginary relationships and also with platonic ones – the meeting of souls (literally or in their imagination) but not necessarily the meeting of bodies. Intimate relations often involve sacrifice and longing in various guises. Some will attract others by virtue of their vulnerability or elusiveness, or be attracted to the weak or vulnerable themselves: someone they can feel sorry for. Individuals may take on the role of victim or rescuer in relationships. A longing for beauty, harmony and peace can feed an urge to escape from the mundane and the sordid. This is an excellent combination for appreciation of, or skills in, the arts and can be particularly associated with dance, especially ballet.

Venus-Pluto (♀♇)

This type may be attracted to the deep, dark and unfathomable or may attract others by exuding these qualities. They can be great charmers, skilled at knowing precisely how to please others. It is often indicative of intense, highly-charged 'fated' relationships or of the perpetual singleton (if frightened of the pain, rejection and trauma of close personal relationships). Often describes a life characterized by short bursts of emotional intensity. Emotional insatiability, avarice, jealousy and the arousing of jealous feelings in others can be part of the picture, as can tortuous, messy, triangular relationships. At best, individuals with this combination may be able to create an honest and deep rapport with another person. Some enter into relationships which have a taboo edge to them, such as same-sex or mixed-race relationships. A strong awareness that beauty is power and a capacity to transform the appearance of themselves and others can lead to interest in or skill in the beauty industries, cosmetic surgery, etc. The combination can also be associated with the regeneration of 'dead' clothes, perhaps by transforming clothes bought in jumble sales. This is a money-and-power combination and on occasion can be associated with such areas as stock market trading, banking and blackmail.

Mars-Jupiter (♂♃)

Ideal for involvement in sales, sport or politics, this is an enterprising, opportunistic and enthusiastic combination, one with a risk-taking propensity and often a liking for trouble. It has an inflammatory feeling about it and there can be a liking for big fights of one sort or another – this can mean anything from watching sumo wrestling on TV to political debate to involvement in actual violence. It can indicate fighting abroad; in various ways, either fighting for or against people who are considered foreigners. It's the combination of the crusader; the person who defends their beliefs, fighting for or against religious, philosophical or political views. It is also descriptive of sexual exploration and adventuring; indulging in horseplay and romping their way through a variety of lovers. In mundane terms, Mars-Jupiter can sometimes be associated with huge protests, such as where the people take to the streets in political marches.

Mars-Saturn (♂♄)

These can describe a life characterized by tests of strength and courage; life situations that demand stamina and endurance, whether physical or emotional. It is an ideal combination for rock climbing, mining, welding, the military or anything else where the person's strength will be tested. Perhaps some kind of hard labour or work with heavy metals, situations which require the control of force or the control of sexual energy, such as in martial arts, yoga, etc. Frequently it is descriptive of a father figure in the army or involved in sport or a trade requiring strength, endurance or the use of specialist tools. For women especially, it may describe relationships with rough, abrasive and even violent men. This can be a contact of the bully and the bullied. There is often an early thwarting of sexual curiosity or a sexual atmosphere in the household, making the sexual experience potentially scary. Feeling powerless can lead to depressive feelings but facing fears with courage can reverse such feelings.

Mars-Uranus (♂♅)

A dislike of any kind of restraint is usually marked and this is potentially the combination of the freedom-fighter, mercenary or revolutionary. More commonly, it describes someone who pushes for reform and progress but it can be indicative of the most impatient, daredevil, hyperactive and extremist behaviour. Sudden outbreaks of violence (especially gunfire) are also possible. This is *the* combination to associate with gun-shot wounds. There is usually a liking for speed and the person can thrive on excitement and danger generally. Sexual experimentation, sex changes and sexual liberation can all be manifestations; the individual will be progressive in their attitudes in such matters or simply keen for excitement and maybe to shock others. It can also be associated with electrical fires, accidents involving machinery, arsonists, firefighters, fireworks and also with modelling (the flashing of their sexuality).

Mars-Neptune (♂♆)

Potentially this is someone who courageously pursues their ideals; at worst, self-doubt can undermine their resolve and the achievement of goals. There can be idealization of the masculine principle and, for men, an anxiety that they are not masculine enough. The illusion and idealization of the notion of courage and strength can lead to body-building activities for some, and attraction to the seemingly macho for others. This is a useful combination for all kinds of sports, especially swimming, fishing and all water sports. Women may get involved with men their granny wouldn't approve of – those into drink, drugs and prison; men who appear to be strong but turn out to be in need of rescuing. There may be weak sexual boundaries, with the individual being unclear about what they want or which signals they are giving out. This is a combination to associate with the seducer and the seduced. Often a gentle pairing, but, as with most Mars aspects, this *can* be a violent combination, due in this case to feelings of impotence or the fact that the person's anger gets diffused and can alight on anyone and anything.

Mars-Pluto (♂♇)

Frequently descriptive of individuals who will not be conquered or vanquished by anyone or anything; potentially there is an unflinching attitude and indomitable spirit that refuses to be crushed. Even in more benign situations, the compulsion to survive, compete and win can be very marked. Frequently there is an early experience of violence, whether sexual or non-sexual; the resulting rage from such experiences can provide a useful fuel towards action, or lead to feelings of impotence. While this combination can be associated with extraordinary acts of courage, it is also consistent with fears of confrontation ('If I lose my temper I will kill someone or they will kill me' can be an inner statement) and a terror about being violent or being on the receiving end of violence. Some will adopt, or have been raised with, a 'might makes right' attitude. Individuals often have to grapple with society's sexual taboos in some way. Gay and mixed-race relationships are frequent life choices.

Slower Moving Cycles

While the approximate length of each cycle is given here, cycles involving Pluto will vary enormously because its orbit is particularly erratic. For example, Pluto may spend twelve years in one zodiac sign and maybe thirty in another.

Jupiter-Saturn (♃♄)

These two planets have a 20-year cycle with the conjunctions staying in the same element for roughly a century at a time, moving from earth to air (currently) and then on to water and fire. They are linked in mundane terms with economic peaks and troughs and with major legislative changes. Both planets can be associated with government and also with the deaths of prominent politicians. Perhaps that is the reason for this combination's linkage with the American 'Presidential death cycle'. Since 1840 the American President in office has died (through natural causes or assassination) every time the two planets have been conjunct (in earth signs) at around the time of the inauguration. To date, the only exception to the rule was Ronald Reagan, who was inaugurated when the conjunction occurred in the air sign of Libra. He was shot but recovered.

In the individual's chart, aspects between these planets often describe steady economic growth. There may be swings between optimism and pessimism, confidence and a lack of it. Individuals can struggle to find faith in life and, when devoid of faith, can become depressed. They usually attract life situations which force their faith in life, God or themselves to be tested. This is *the* combination to associate with scenarios involving moral codes, religious schooling or religious discipline. Not uncommonly, individuals experience the structure and discipline of religion (or other beliefs) but struggle to find its meaning. A strong sense of right and wrong can also lead to guilt whenever the person is unable to live up to their own high standards. There is potential to become an authority on such matters.

Jupiter-Uranus (♃♅)

Both planets are associated with freedom, so it is little wonder that, in mundane terms, this 14-year cycle can be linked with capitalism and the concept of the free market economy generally. It favours change and progress, explorations, innovations and discoveries (the Moon Landing on 21 July 1969 occurred during an exact conjunction). There is a possibility of new religions or cults emerging into society and unexpected happenings in the established Church.

On a personal level, it implies a breaking away from the religion/faith or politics in which the individual was raised. Basically, there is a need to integrate the search for meaning with a need to find the truth for oneself. It can be associated with an insistence on freedom if linked to more personal points in the chart. Mutant growths (and therefore cancers) can also be part of the picture.

Jupiter-Neptune (♃♆)

In mundane terms, hard and even soft aspects often indicate the uncovering of fraud and stories regarding fraudsters. This 13-year cycle can also be associated with stories (and sometimes scandals) involving gambling, horse-racing, media and pharmaceutical takeovers and mergers. The cycle can also be associated with various types of rescue packages and with charitable and humanitarian concerns. Losses in the travel (especially luxury travel) and music industries also occur, as do stories involving shipping.

Individuals with the combination prominent may also have an interest in the sea, sailing, and some of the other areas already listed. Often of a charitable disposition, the person with this combination can also have a religious or spiritual life or, at least, an inclination to pursue God and meaning in various guises. It's an ideal aspect for the pursuit of all kinds of meditative practices.

Jupiter-Pluto (♃♇)

This 12-year cycle is associated with huge power – for good or ill and also with huge money (Microsoft's Bill Gates has the two planets conjunct). In short, it's the combination of plutocracy. It also can signify compulsive gambling and changes in gaming laws and taxation. (In the UK, the establishment of Premium Bonds and the National Lottery both occurred under the conjunction.) Stories involving ruthless leaders, power struggles, mining, recycling and various underground groups can all feature at these times.

In an individual's chart, especially when linked with personal planets and points, it can indicate an enormous drive to achieve something superhuman. Indicative of strong beliefs, it can produce the ability to make the impossible possible, through the strength of the person's own inner certainty. For some, it describes deep religious or political convictions.

Cycles of Saturn with the Outer Planets

These slow-moving cycles are indicative of both political and economic changes, usually with conservative ideology struggling against transformative and revolutionary ideas. Thus, in various guises, the tension between the urge to keep the genie firmly in the bottle versus the impulse to let it out is a common story with these cycles.

Saturn-Uranus (♄♅)

This 45-year cycle is often characterized by news stories involving science, astrology and other 'old' subjects resurfacing in a new form. It might describe scientific/technological visions actually taking root and becoming a reality. Science is pushing back the boundaries, and scientific breakthroughs are cutting time in some way. Often there are deaths of prominent scientists, too. This cycle has been connected with right-wing politics and also with the Middle East.[7] It will often describe times characterized by a breaking away from tradition and a sweeping away of an old order. Charles Carter has described the combination as being 'democratic in spirit but autocratic in method'.[8] Those in authority may impose reform upon the populace and meet with considerable resistance. The cycle can be associated with the control of dissidents in society and also with strikes.

Individuals with hard aspects between the planets often feel a pull between tradition and convention on the one hand and the urge to follow a more radical and unconventional direction or lifestyle on the other.

Saturn-Neptune (♄♆)

A 36-year cycle which André Barbault has linked to socialism and communism, while the late Charles Harvey also linked this combination with the British monarchy (with its themes of duty and sacrifice). Health scares and food poisoning stories may feature in the news and there are usually important deaths at this time involving individuals who are prominent in the arts, especially film and music. As with most cycles involving the outer planets, Saturn-Neptune can herald civil unrest. With this combination, those in authority may be perceived as weak father figures and their authority therefore may be easily undermined.

In the charts of individuals, this is an ideal aspect for those who become an authority on drugs (e.g. the pharmacist, physician or homœopath), alcohol, film, music and spiritual matters. Distorting the nature of responsibility, some seek to escape from it, some dodge society's rules altogether, while others feel guilty for not living up to their own ideals of exemplary behaviour.

Saturn-Pluto (♄♇)

This 33-year cycle can mark a time of paranoia and harshness in society, also with shrinking, hardening and demolition. Generally it is a time of cutting back, pruning and 'getting down to the bare bones'. Some members of the populace are usually impelled to discover the minimum that is required in order to survive. Often, times when this cycle is active herald a period of having to start again, following the aftermath of some kind of tragedy or destruction in society. Thus, the cycle can be associated with the lessons of survival, and with the annihilation of defences and the building up of new ones. The cycle can also be associated with railways and also with India, Pakistan and Israel, who all became independent in 1948 during the conjunction of these planets.

The combination can manifest in various ways in the charts of individuals but a feeling of powerlessness is common, as is a drive to create impenetrable defenses.

Outer Planet Cycles

Cycles involving the outer planets are very slow, last for years and thus will affect millions of people born over a long period. They signify huge cultural shifts, the meaning of which may not become clear until long after they have passed. In individual charts these aspects gain significance either if they are very tight or if they are linked to personal points in the horoscope. Otherwise, they describe something of the times in which the individual was born.

Uranus-Neptune (♅♆)

This 172-year cycle seems to focus on the tension or interplay between the arts and the sciences. The Renaissance (in some countries) and the Enlightenment owe much to this cycle. Nowadays one expects innovations in the music industry and in the arts generally. Electronic music and any areas where technology and music (or the arts) come together can be included here. The rise of digital photography owes much to the recent ingress of Uranus into Pisces, the sign ruled by Neptune. This combination can also be associated with awakenings and setbacks in spiritual and New Age matters. Stories surrounding 'frozen water', such as icebergs, glaciers, snow storms and ice cream, may also feature.

Uranus-Pluto (♅♇)

This 127-year cycle is associated with revolutions in medicine, technology and science. The mid-1960s conjunction of these planets in Virgo was characterized by revolutions wrought about by small (Virgo) things, e.g. the contraceptive pill and the silicone chip from which came computers and a technological revolution. For good and ill, it is a combination to link with nuclear power; for instance, the Chernobyl nuclear disaster (26 April 1986) occurred when Uranus and Pluto were semi-square to each other and forming opposition/sesquiquadrate aspects respectively to the Sun. This combination of planets is potentially the most violent, transformative and far-reaching in the entire astrological lexicon, implying as it does, sudden (and often unnatural) deaths. Adolf

Hitler had the planets in tight sesquiquadrate aspect and these were rendered personal as they fell almost exactly at his Sun/Moon midpoint. Saturn was also involved in the equation.

Neptune-Pluto (♆♇)

Associated with the vision of the period in question and with shifts in the ideals of a culture, this 492-year cycle is concerned with the deepest cultural and spiritual transformations, perhaps with the death of some collective dreams and fantasies and the birth of new ones. Stories involving multi-national corporations, and especially the giant pharmaceuticals, are often in the air. Both these planets like mystery (e.g. the presence or otherwise of the Loch Ness monster) and not surprisingly several writers of detective fiction were born in the 1890s when these two planets were conjunct in Gemini.

Aspects Involving the Angles

Aspects, especially conjunctions and hard aspects, involving the four angles (see Chapter 6) are *very* important but, in my view, don't warrant a cookbook section, as the reader should be able to work these out for themselves. For instance, when assessing the meaning of conjunctions to the Ascendant, Descendant, Midheaven and IC, students can consider the placement of the relevant planet in the First, Seventh, Tenth and Fourth Houses respectively and amplify such information accordingly. However, given the speed with which the angles move, the birth time must be accurate for the interpreter to be sure that aspects to the angles do exist. More information can be found in my book *Aspects in Astrology*.

Chapter 6

The Houses

While the zodiac signs are fixed divisions of the ecliptic (the apparent path of the Sun) and are a division of an *annual* cycle beginning with the Spring (or Vernal) Equinox (in the Northern Hemisphere), the houses are divisions of a *daily* cycle resulting from the Earth's daily rotation on its own axis. Thus, all the planets pass through all twelve houses in a day.

The Thorny Issue of House Systems

There are several different ways that the diurnal (daily) cycle can be divided into twelve and, as there are no lines in the sky (!), it is a matter of some debate among astrologers as to which is the 'right' one to use. Currently there are about a dozen house systems that astrologers commonly use, all derived from dividing up the sky by time or space or an amalgam of the two. It may be that different methods of house division are best suited to different astrological tasks. My own view is that it is not necessary to worry too much about the whys and wherefores of the different house systems. When attempting to interpret a chart, the astrologer should be looking for themes that repeat several times in a chart – this is the only way that accuracy and deep understanding can be guaranteed. When experimenting with different house systems, what the astrologer will discover is that the same themes will emerge irrespective of which house system is adopted. It is simply that these themes and stories may be arrived at in slightly different ways.

The Equal house system is reputed to be the oldest house system as well as being the simplest one to calculate. Perhaps it is because of its simplicity that it is favoured by most of the major astrological schools in the UK. With this system, all houses are of equal size and use the Ascendant as their numerical starting point, so that if the First House cusp is 4 degrees of Taurus, then the Second House cusp will be 4 degrees of Gemini, and the Third House cusp 4 degrees of Cancer, and so on, right around the circle. Simple it may be, but in my experience the Equal house system works well enough and is in no way inferior to more complex house systems. The so-called problem for many astrologers is that, unlike most other systems, the MC/IC axis does not coincide with the Tenth/Fourth House cusps. Near the Equator the MC *will* be near the Tenth House cusp, but at increasing latitudes the gap between the two widens. In extreme latitudes (even in the north of Scotland) the sizes of the houses can become very distorted with time/space house systems; some houses become huge while others can be miniscule. In the most extreme latitudes the time systems break down altogether. Obviously none of this happens with the Equal house system and that is one reason to commend its use. Nevertheless, individuals born in extreme latitudes don't especially favour the Equal house system; they still use time/space house systems to a marked degree.

Using Equal houses, one seemingly has two areas (the Tenth and the MC) to describe Tenth House matters and similarly two areas (the Fourth and the IC) to describe Fourth House matters. This can create anxiety, but it needn't. Firstly, students will find that their Equal Tenth and Fourth Houses and their rulers will describe their career, home and parents very accurately; this system does work. However, one does also need to use the MC and IC in addition, as the angles are always very important. The houses in which the MC and IC fall in the Equal house system can provide extra or confirmatory information. If, for example, the MC falls in the Ninth House it can be taken to indicate that the individual (and their parents) may be more impressed by people who have travelled/are foreign/educated/philosophical than by captains of industry (Tenth), for instance. It may be indicative of a career in a Ninth House subject area. If the MC falls in the Eleventh House then perhaps it is one's friends/the Rotary Club/a charity, etc. that the person seeks to impress or is impressed by. Perhaps the individual aspires to co-ordinate a team or to do things that will benefit the community in some way (as shown by the sign and the whole MC complex). The astrologer can work out the various other permutations of where the MC and IC might fall.

The Placidus house system is probably the most commonly used of all. It is named after the Italian Benedictine monk and mathematician, Placidus de Tito (1603-1688), although astrologers long before him, including Ptolemy (c.100-178 AD) seem to have used a similar if not identical system of house division. The Placidean system is a time-based one and, given that time and timing are so much what astrology is about, its popularity is perhaps not so surprising. Certainly, in my experience, Placidean house cusps are very sensitive. They are useful in forecasting work; the effect of transiting planets movingover the cusps is hard to deny.

Readers wanting to know more about the different systems of house division and their usage and history would do well to visit Deborah Houlding's excellent website: www.skyscript.co.uk

Interpretation and the Houses

While it is possible to dispense with houses and signs altogether, and rely purely on the relationships between planets, for most astrologers the houses are one of the major building blocks of horoscopic interpretation. They have the added advantage of being easy and fun to work with.

The **planets** can be taken to represent the actors in a play and the **signs** to describe the costumes and the characters of the actors. For instance, the Sun describes an image of the hero but what kind of hero – an Eva Peron, a Nelson Mandela or a Robin Hood? The sign and, to a lesser extent, the house where the Sun falls will answer this question. Continuing with the analogy, we can say that the **houses** describe *where* the action of the play takes place. If we were discussing a play in the literal sense, we might say that the drama takes place in the kitchen, boardroom or forest. In the horoscope, the houses are areas of projection. We can be at the receiving end or at the giving end of planetary energies. We can be Robin Hood or Robin Hood can come into our lives. Planets in houses will show where or with whom the energies tend to manifest at their strongest. Continuing with the analogy of a play, the **aspects** describe the dialogue and the action and interrelationships between the actors. Aspects (planetary relationships) also have a significant bearing on character.

Before looking at the twelve houses individually, it is worth considering the circle divided into two hemispheres and also into four quadrants (which are formed by the four angles in most house systems except Equal house).

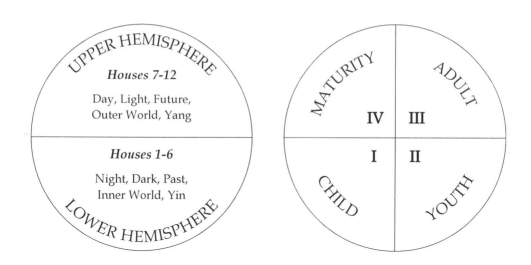

I: First quadrant (First, Second, Third Houses) Here we are born, discover we have a body, learn to walk and learn to communicate and go to school.

II: Second quadrant (Fourth, Fifth, Sixth Houses) Here we become more rooted in the world, we learn about what gives us pleasure, what our talents are and we learn that our body has to be taken care of. We discover romance and the need to work.

III: Third quadrant (Seventh, Eighth, Ninth Houses) Here we learn about co-operating with others and about relationships. Also about death, sex and exploring the world on a deeper level. We come to the big questions in life such as 'Why am I here?', 'Who is God?' and 'What is life about?'

IV: Fourth quadrant (Tenth, Eleventh, Twelfth Houses) We carve out a place for ourselves in the world and contribute to society. We prepare for dissolution.

Although the houses 1-12 follow an anti-clockwise direction, the Sun, Moon and planets appear (from our viewpoint) to move in a clockwise direction.

The Sun's position in any horoscope will give you an immediate idea as to the time of day a person was born. The Sun rises from the First Quadrant and crosses the Ascendant, moving above the horizon (sunrise) into the Fourth Quadrant (morning). It passes across the MC and into the Third Quadrant after midday (afternoon), and then heads down towards the horizon. After crossing the horizon (around sunset – Sun on the Descendant), it travels down into the Second Quadrant (evening). By midnight (Sun on the IC) it is ready to move from the Second to the First Quadrant (where it travels from the lowest part of the horoscope up towards the horizon and a new sunrise).

So, if the Sun is located in the upper hemisphere (containing the Third and Fourth Quadrants), this was most certainly a daytime birth, some time between sunrise and sunset (the Sun was out, there was light). If the Sun is positioned in the lower hemisphere (below the Ascendant-Descendant axis, i.e. the First and Second Quadrant), the birth *must* have taken place when it was dark, after sunset but before sunrise.

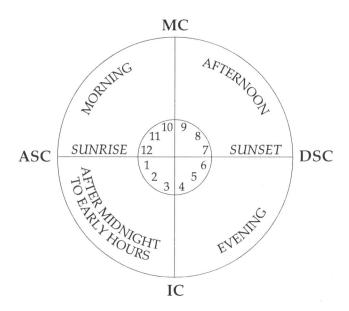

This can also be divided into four segments of time:

• Born between sunrise and midday: the Sun is in the Fourth Quadrant (moving up through the Twelfth, Eleventh and Tenth Houses).

• Born between midday and sunset: the Sun is in the Third Quadrant (through the Ninth, Eighth and then Seventh Houses).

• Born between sunset and midnight: the Sun is in the Second Quadrant (below the horizon, after sunset, through the Sixth, Fifth and Fourth Houses).

• Born between midnight and sunrise: the Sun is in the First Quadrant (moving from the Third House to the Second and finally the First House, just before sunrise).

Keep in mind that sunrise and sunset can vary considerably throughout the year. In Britain, the Sun rises at about 8 a.m. in winter and sets in the mid-afternoon, while in the middle of summer the Sun rises as early as 3.45 a.m. (4.45 a.m. British Summer Time) and sets late in the evening. You might also need to make an adjustment for summer time. For instance, if you were born in the summer months and the clocks had been moved an hour forward, deduct an hour before testing this out for yourself. Finally, keep in mind that the MC and Tenth House (and IC and Fourth House) will rarely coincide in the Equal house method.

It's also a useful way of checking whether the horoscope has been calculated correctly. For instance, if you were born mid-morning, say 10 a.m., the Sun *has* to be located in the Fourth Quadrant (where the Tenth, Eleventh and Twelfth Houses are).

How to Use the Following Cookbook Sections

The 'cookbook' interpretations of the various planets falling in each house must be treated with caution. They are of necessity very brief and superficial, and are only meant to give the general idea and to prompt the reader. Each chart factor has to be analysed in the light of every other chart factor (and in the context of age and culture), and so the most appropriate interpretation of any planet will vary hugely from horoscope to horoscope. This applies to the house positions of the outer planets especially, as these can be particularly complex and far-reaching in their implications. As always, the sign placement and, more especially, the aspects to a particular planet, can drastically alter the ways in which it may manifest.

Planets Bordering on House Cusps

Many astrologers, including me, feel that a planet near to a house cusp also influences the adjoining house, so that if a chart has, for instance, Neptune falling in the Fifth House but very close to the Sixth, the planet can be interpreted as falling in the Fifth *and* Sixth Houses.

What to Do with Empty Houses

As there are twelve houses and ten planets, it can be seen that, for all of us, some houses will be unoccupied by a planet. In other words, the houses are untenanted. A so-called empty house does not mean that the house is less important or that the particular area of life sounds a dumb note. For example, just because you have nothing in your Second House doesn't mean that you'll never earn or spend any money! One simply has to look to the planet that rules the sign on the empty house cusp to find out information about the activities pertaining to that house. Even when there are planets in a house, the house ruler (by sign, house and aspect) will be of interest, but where the house is untenanted it is crucial to pay attention to the ruler. The zodiac sign on the house cusp will also give valuable information about the workings of that house.

The First House and the Ascendant

As with all other factors in the horoscope, interpreting the Ascendant and First House involves seeing the area as a 'complex'. In fact, any time the word 'Ascendant' is used it can be taken to mean the whole complex. This complex is made up of:
- Any planet conjunct the Ascendant and, to a lesser extent, any planet falling within the First House.
- The sign on the Ascendant.
- The ruler of the Ascendant – the sign and house in which it falls and the aspects it makes.
- The Ascendant (or 'rising') sign will often make a general statement, while its ruler will qualify and make that statement more specific. For example, you may have Cancer rising, implying that you go out into the world wanting to care for and protect someone or something. If the Moon (the ruler of Cancer) falls in the Tenth House, the urge to protect will tend to manifest strongly in a professional (Tenth House) role.
- Any aspects to the Ascendant axis, especially if the birth-time is accurate and the aspect is a tight one.

The Ascendant and First House describe **how we approach life**, how we greet our immediate world. It is our personal 'look-out', the lens through which we view the world and through which the world views us. An analogy might help. Imagine you are wearing spectacles with blue-tinted glass, so as you look out on to the world everything will appear to have a blue tint. People looking at you will see you with a blue tint, too. Although you may not be aware of it, other people will be viewing the same world but they will see things differently because they are viewing it through differently coloured glass.

Ascendant and First House material tends to be reinforced by important figures in childhood; we receive (or at least extract) positive messages for expressing ourselves in the manner of this house from those around us. The First House, and in particular the Ascendant angle itself, will often describe the **circumstances surrounding the actual birth**, including who was there and what was said. It will also, to some extent, describe other major **early experiences of childhood**, both in terms of happenings and feelings. Those early experiences colour our attitude to meeting the immediate environment and those within it for evermore; it is as if we always expect it to be that way.

It can sometimes be difficult to understand the link between early experiences and the way we greet the world but there usually is a clear link. Imagine that you were born in the pouring rain (early experience), then you are more likely to go out into the world carrying an umbrella (how you greet the world)!

The Ascendant and First House are sometimes described as the **persona**, which literally means 'actor's mask'. This implies that the First House describes a false self and this is not exactly the case. The reality is that the First House describes an aspect of ourselves that we more readily reveal. It is the part of our character that we show. It is **what we put out in front**, rather as a warrior stands behind his shield. You can think of the First House as describing your badge, your label, as it says much about **the impression we make on others**. In terms of the word 'badge', often the First House can even be associated with our name – especially our first name, nickname or generally the name by which we are known.[1]

Imagine that your whole horoscope is a house, with the usual bedrooms, living rooms, kitchen, bathroom and so on. As a house has many rooms, so too are there many facets to you. There is the you at play, the you at work, and so on, as described by the various planets and houses. Using this metaphor, the First House describes the front door, the façade of your house which may or may not give a true indication of what it is like inside. The front door is the route we must take in order to get out into the world. It is also the way we come into ourselves and by which we let others in. It has always to be remembered that the First House, as well as that important relationship house, the Seventh, has much to say about our relating style. Following on from the idea of the front door being the way into the world, then we can see why the First House is often thought of as describing our journey in life (although of course the whole chart describes our journey) or ourselves as a vehicle. If the analogy of a vehicle is a good one for the Ascendant and First House, then the Sun in our chart depicts us in the role of driver, whereas our Moon casts us in the role of passenger or maybe even as the baggage!

The First House sets the scene for the whole chart and is based on a precise birth time. The birth time is the moment a human being, animal, or even a project, becomes embodied or launched in the world in its own right. Thus, the First House also contributes to the robustness or otherwise of **the physical body** (the body is also often described as our 'vessel') and therefore has ramifications for our health. This is particularly the case with the Ascendant angle itself.

The Sun, Moon and Ascendant: Quick Pointers to their Differences

Imagine life as a journey:

SUN	MOON	ASCENDANT
The driver	The passenger or baggage	The vehicle/the journey
Where I need to go	Where I am coming from	The way I am going
Future	Past	Present/past interface
What I want	What I need	What I am expecting
Character/sense/core	Personality/behaviour Innate behaviour How I automatically behave	Persona/personality and what I show Learned behaviour How I approach life/my entry point
Qualities I am trying to embody/what I am striving to become	Qualities I instinctively use	What I am told I am or should be
What I want to know	What I know already	My window on the world
Recognition/heroism/glory	Comfort/safety	

Sun in the First House

The Sun here may increase self-assurance and leadership qualities but this very much depends on the Sun sign and the aspects to it. If the Ascendant and Sun are in the same zodiac sign this very much strengthens the sign in the chart – the person will strongly resonate to it. In any event, this a self-conscious and self-aware placement. Early experiences of feeling watched or of being given extra attention when young (which the individual may or may not have enjoyed, depending on the sign and aspects to the Sun) will form part of the story of the early years. Thereafter, and not necessarily consciously, the person approaches the world as if the spotlight is on them. The individual watches themselves and may have problems acting in a spontaneous manner. This is not the person to be caught wearing their curlers. One person of my acquaintance has the Sun rising in Pisces. She was the first baby to be born on a particular leap year day and thus attracted the attention of the Press. Curiously, she always disliked being in the limelight after that.

Moon in the First House

This placement suggests someone with a strong imagination who goes out into the world with great sensitivity. Sensitivity to their surroundings and sensitivity to the people around them. Coupled with this is often a marked capacity to adjust to and accommodate others, whatever their needs. Responsiveness is the keyword here. Often this would have come about because of an above-average sensitivity to the mother's needs. Perhaps she was moody, so the youngster would have learnt how to read her moods; how to accommodate her; perhaps even how to mother her, for whatever reason. Often the individual will greatly resemble their mother physically. Some will gravitate towards the role of carer in all they say and do. Others will behave in a way that elicits a mothering response from others.

Mercury in the First House

This person approaches the world with great curiosity. A restless, communicative nature and occasionally a chatterbox (depending on the sign placement and the chart overall). This can be the person who always seems to be going somewhere. I have known several people who deliver the post with this placement! More usually, an inquisitive, enquiring mind will be one of the first factors to notice about this individual. There is a need to analyse themselves and the world at large, and there is a need for feedback from others in order to do so; hence the many questions that individuals with this placement often ask. Mercury here can impart a youthful attitude of mind and a youthful appearance.

Venus in the First House

Keen to create a harmonious environment both in the physical and emotional sense, this individual goes out into world wanting to please. This placement can describe the peace-maker and people-pleaser. There is usually the cultivation of a 'nice' persona; as a child, the person was encouraged to be courteous, pleasant and nice. Often there would have been a lot of messages about appearance. The child may have been told how beautiful they were, and certainly good looks and/or a very attractive demeanour are among the cards this person has been dealt. Venus in some signs certainly confers beauty; in Capricorn, for instance, there is often beautiful bone structure and teeth. Whatever the natural attributes, Venus here often describes someone who puts great effort into being well turned out. Often there is a liking for jewellery or other adornments, too. This is a good placement for a front-of-house person, or someone who works in a receptionist role, as the ability to put others at their ease and create a good first impression can be very marked.

Mars in the First House

An impatience to start the project in hand and an eagerness for action generally characterize this 'hurry up' placement. These people just want to get things done. The perceived slowness of others, and the limitations of being in the mundane world and limited physical body may feel frustrating. Direct, authentic, honest and assertive, the individual may appear more robust than they are, depending on the chart overall and the sign involved. They may feel and have received early messages that they have to be strong; to be some kind of warrior, to take their own life into their own hands. Thus, there can be difficulties in asking for help and generally exposing their vulnerability. There can be an accident-prone and reckless quality, depending on the chart overall, and often there is a scar on the face following an incident in childhood.

Jupiter in the First House

Naturally of a philosophical turn of mind, this individual goes out of their front door with eager enthusiasm, keen to embrace as much of the world into their personal orbit as possible. Thus, there is often a marked yen to travel and explore. In childhood, the person may have taken on board the message that they are lucky and that anything is possible. Certainly this placement adds buoyancy and optimism, and the feeling that life is a journey. Many with this placement tend to live in the future, always looking forward to something. Some will like to be at the forefront of the latest fashions and trends, while others spend time planning their next big trip. There can be a tendency to over-extend themselves; to be overly extravagant and careless with their plans, promises or money. As always the whole chart and the relevant planet has to be studied in its entirety. Sometimes aunts or uncles may play a prominent role in the individual's early life. Self-indulgence may incline to weight problems.

Saturn in the First House

The individual usually approaches life, the immediate environment and those within it, with a strong sense of responsibility. A tendency to take life seriously and often a certain amount of caution and anxiety is present. There is a feeling of a 'slow start'. Frequently hardship or grief early on precipitates a feeling that they mustn't put a foot wrong and that they must leave nothing to chance. There can be a tendency therefore to want to control things and certainly to want to control themselves. A controlled outer image with strong defenses is classic, as is the taking of responsibility at a young age. The individual will often take on the role of the father following his death, illness or defection in childhood. Many with this placement have a lean build and often there is a noticeable bone structure.

Uranus in the First House

Those with Uranus here often look different or in some way are very different from other family members. They may merely be tall; the 'differentness' can manifest in a number of ways. Even if there is nothing obviously different, often they picked up the message that they are outsiders or odd and therefore adopt an aloof and rejected manner. Many go out into the world wearing a badge that says 'I am a card-carrying individualist'. Some approach the world as if they don't want to join the club but instead want to make their way in the world standing alone and independently. As always, a prominent Uranus is uncompromising. Many with Uranus in the First House will be trailblazers for the generation they find themselves in, but as mid-life approaches the rebellious message of youth will probably have become fairly mainstream. And even in youth, those with Uranus in the First may appear to be much more rebellious than they actually are.

Neptune in the First House

Refined, imaginative, frequently artistic or musical, some with Neptune here approach the world and those within it as if they are a camera lens or mirror reflecting who or whatever is in front. Keywords here are sensitivity, impressionability and suscep-tibility. There is often not a strong self-image or tremendous resolve, and the individual can present to the world in a gamut of different ways and embark on one thing and then happily drift into something else. Sometimes the individual in childhood picked up the message that they are fragile, weak, inadequate or unable to cope for some reason. Sometimes ill health explains the reason for this; the physical body may be felt to be delicate. Sometimes the person felt undermined by the environment they were in; for some, instead of toughening them up, early life weakened their feeling of strength and resolve. More frequently they are given the role of prince or princess and the delicacy arises from that. The sensitivity with this placement can border on the psychic, especially if placed in a water sign and conjunct the Ascendant.

Pluto in the First House

Those with Pluto here may approach the world wearing camouflage in some way, although the planet positioned here can sometimes be almost invisible to the observer. For some who have this placement, the world is not seen as a safe place; not safe to expose their true self, anyway. They have to proceed with caution to increase the chances of survival. Often there is a need to keep tight control over themselves. The individual usually undergoes at least one major personal transformative experience in the life. For instance, I know of one woman who changed her occupation from nun to that of psychotherapist; her whole persona, including her personal appearance (and *black* habit), changed radically. Pluto here occasionally equates to the near death of the individual at birth or the near death of the mother. Or there is something thought to be embarrassing in the early life (such as mental illness or being the result of rape or some other assault) which unconsciously makes the person want to hide. Some will be taking pains to hide the fact that they are gay. In any event, this placement often equates with someone who has a strong 'false self'; perhaps someone who 'lives in the closet' about something they almost definitely shouldn't feel ashamed of, but do.

The Second House

The Second House describes **our money, our attitude to money, how we earn it, how we spend it** and **what we spend it on**. Above all else, it is concerned with **our values**. It is the house of possessions, what is traditionally termed **'movable property'** – that is, possessions we can move about fairly easily. The Second House does not describe our actual house, for instance, because that is immovable property and covered by the Fourth. The Second House embraces those 'things' with which we identify. Those 'things' over which we extend our ego. Possessions may augment or detract from the real person. Money and possessions are often the way we choose to bolster ourselves up. Our possessions and our attitude to money, what we do with **our resources** and how we spend our money can all be taken as direct indicators of what we most value in life.

Our attitude to resources will also say something about our **self-valuation**. If we are well-paid for doing a job, we feel valued; if underpaid, we feel undervalued. The Second House says a lot about **what we think we are worth**. It describes **our assets**, not only in terms of material possessions but our personal assets. Planets in the Second House describe those traits that others come to rely on about us, what is dependable about us, what others can count on. What others value about us and what we may value about ourselves. Going back to the issue of self-worth, the word 'worth' is quite a good one for the Second House. 'Is it worth it?' is a question we may ask when faced with a particular task or option. Do we value the issue, whatever it is, enough?

A human's first experience of ownership is the baby discovering its own body. Having a body gives us some feeling of being rooted in the world. Similarly, our possessions contribute to what makes us feel rooted and secure in the material world, what gives us a feeling of stability.

Sun in the Second House
The individual's self-esteem and confidence are often linked to their earning capacity with this placement. This individual can believe that they are what they have. Possessions therefore can be seen to be a way of bolstering the ego. Often the father would have been involved with money; either literally (as in banking) or more than usually concerned with the earning of it. The sign placement of the Sun will often show how the individual earns their money and what they spend it on. Feeling materially secure will often be essential to the person's feeling of well-being.

Moon in the Second House
A secure material and financial life is necessary for an inner sense of security. Earnings may come through catering, real estate or some kind of professional mothering or nurturing. Or the individual may earn their living by looking after the resources of others. Extra resources may be spent on the home, homemaking and family. Frequently, the individual becomes especially emotionally attached to their home and to 'things'. The financial circumstances may fluctuate but the individual will usually be adept at accommodating such changes, despite a need to feel materially secure. In a man's chart, the Moon here can suggest financial gains and losses through women.

Mercury in the Second House
The valuing of education and knowledge will often manifest as the spending of money on books or courses and the short journeys involved in commuting to those courses. If the rest of the chart agrees, and depending on the sign in which Mercury is placed, this

individual might be good in sales, having what is often termed the 'gift of the gab'. More usually, earning a living will involve reading, writing, talking on the phone and so on. The gift of language and verbal self-expression might be one of this individual's greatest and most reliable assets; as may their curiosity. They might value any opportunity where they can talk to people, may value their siblings a good deal and may even benefit financially from their siblings. An excellent placement for the world of commerce; depending on the chart overall, this individual could be curious about the workings of the business world. There can be financial loss through theft.

Venus in the Second House

This placement will usually describe the spending of money on clothes, finery, beauty products and pleasure. The individual will often earn their income in these areas, too. A high income may be valued as being important for the luxuries it can bring. There will usually be a valuing of beauty and art, and the individual is willing to pay to have a beautiful lifestyle. This can be a generous placement (depending on the sign and aspects involved); this person may love buying presents for loved ones. The individual's personal assets can include their personal attractiveness but also the gifts of diplomacy and refinement.

Mars in the Second House

This is a classic placement for impulsive spending but also for the person who can be decisive about investments and able to clinch a deal speedily. It favours the individual who gets paid frequently and quickly; waiting for their money to arrive may not rest easily with this person, especially if Mars is receiving many stressful aspects. This is the person who wants their desires met now. The ability to save is not likely to be much in evidence here! Earnings may come through work with tools, cars, metals and heat. Others may earn their income through more potentially courageous or violent means (e.g. the police or the army) but more frequently the placement merely describes the individual as being willing to fight for what they value. And some of what is valued will be shown by the sign placement of Mars.

Jupiter in the Second House

This person tends to be philosophical about, and therefore generous with, their resources. Innately they tend to believe that God or the cosmos will provide. The personal assets can include optimism, joy, generosity and a philosophical outlook, but profligacy and extravagance can be the pattern for some while others may just feel wealthy and be contented even with very little. Nevertheless, the individual can be greedy as well as generous about resources. A wasteful, easy-come, easy-go attitude is possible if borne out by other chart factors. More usually, the person is simply generous and the extravagance manifests as a tendency to spend today against future expectations of money. Post-dated cheques may be the norm here! The individual with this placement usually values travel and education highly and will spend money on these things. Some will earn their income through matters connected with travel, publishing or education.

Saturn in the Second House

This positions suggests a fear of poverty but not necessarily an experience of poverty. Often the individual feels guilty if they have resources and thus feels the responsibility to look after things. People with Saturn in the Second House are often the ones who proudly tell you how long they have had that dress. The taking of responsibility for money and assets is a common manifestation; sometimes this involves substantial assets, such as when the individual manages a company or large property. Generally the individual feels safest if in control of the purse strings. The prudence with resources can make for great financial security in old age. Personal assets may include a strong sense of responsibility and a respect for age, tradition, etc. The father may have lost rather than earned money or the family may have suffered materially through his death. Ownership carries the burden of responsibility and implies the narrowing and restricting of the individual's freedom. Thus, freedom with this placement can be curtailed either through material lack or through material abundance.

Uranus in the Second House

Sudden reversals of fortune at least once in the life (rags to riches or vice versa) are common with this placement. The income is often earned through, and/or spent on, technology or gadgetry. This individual tends to value progress and freedom, and wants to spend money on things that help them leap ahead and save time. Perhaps for everyone with this placement, money is viewed as important for the freedom it can provide. Some will eschew the treadmill of ownership, viewing it as burdensome and antithetical to freedom, while others will wish to amass wealth in order to buy freedom of choice for themselves and often for others. Personal assets are likely to include originality, independence and a regard for truth. Some will earn their resources through their originality or through possessing some kind of genius.

Neptune in the Second House

The placement can show huge idealism with resources but also sometimes impracticality and even gullibility around money; there is potential for financial losses and scandals with Neptune here, depending on the chart overall. This person may have few boundaries about sharing their assets or, very occasionally, sharing yours! This is the person who can believe 'what is mine is yours and equally what is yours is mine'. This attitude can include the world at large, not merely the person's nearest and dearest. The earning and spending of money on music, art, mystical matters, the interpretation of dreams, hypnosis, alcohol, and so on, is implied with this placement. Personal assets may include an awareness of suffering, compassion and sensitivity. The individual will usually value less worldly attitudes and less worldly people. Some will do well financially because of an almost psychic attunement to the workings of the world around them.

Pluto in the Second House

The house placement of Pluto can often describe where we project the devil, and when found in the Second House the individual can project the devil on to money. Some with this placement will be fiercely anti-materialistic and many will be extremely skilled at managing on a shoestring. Money is associated with power in those with Pluto here and often with their very survival; in other words, it is the means to grant life or death. It is a good placement for welfare rights work, ensuring that others have at least a minimum income and can therefore survive. For most with this placement, there will be a need to periodically have a purge, to throw everything out and start all over again. Pluto in the Second can denote a compulsion to spend (unconsciously throwing their resources away) or a compulsion to save. Bankruptcy can be a manifestation of this placement. Most will have a major transformation (in either direction) at least once in their life regarding their attitude to resources. One man who had been a rich businessman threw it all up to live a more simple life – he became a baker and swapped his Rolls-Royce for a bicycle. The personal assets can include a ruthless, terrier-like determination. Work may involve life and death (e.g. in hospitals or an undertaker's), refuse, gardening, mining, and power and control (e.g. the corporate world).

The Third House

This house is traditionally associated with all manner of **communication** – **speech and writing**, and the general reporting of information. In addition it governs **short journeys**, siblings, **neighbours** and others in the immediate environment, cousins and nephews and nieces, **school and elementary education**. The Third House can be summed up by the idea of **getting from A to B**, whether this is physical or psychological. Physically, the Third House embraces transport and short journeys. Everyday and, usually but not always, brief journeys. Journeys that don't involve much in the way of exploration or adventure – **everyday comings and goings**. It is also concerned with brief communication – **letters**, **emails** and **telephone calls** as well as **books**, **magazines** and the like. Planets in the Third (or, if untenanted, the ruler(s) thereof) will literally describe what interests a person and therefore what kind of books they will read (and write), which magazines they will subscribe to, and what they will talk about. Be aware that the sign and house position of Mercury (and that planet's aspects) will also describe such matters.

The Third House is also associated with **blood relatives**, except for parents who are shown by the Fourth and Tenth Houses. This category can include all sorts of different brethren but the most central relationships defined here are those with **siblings**. Planets in the Third will literally describe our siblings, how they are in every possible sense and our relationship with them. Thus, Uranus in the Third might describe step-brothers and -sisters or siblings from whom we are cut off for a while, while Mars can indicate sibling rivalry or brothers in the army. The Moon here can suggest that we mother our brothers or sisters or were mothered by them.

Our schooldays are also embraced by the Third, the house that is most concerned with accumulating information and disseminating it. School is the place where we learn to connect people, places and things. **Making connections** is central to this house and what today might be termed **networking**. Even in adulthood, the Third House contributes to all facets of knowledge-gathering. The Third House (and, to a lesser extent, our Mercury and any planets in Gemini) is implicated whenever we are learning something and whenever we have to process information or language.

Sun in the Third House

This often indicates someone who shone at school, perhaps becoming Head Girl or Head Boy. Whatever the age, this individual is likely to come alive when in a learning environment. A lot of coming and going in the local environment is suggested – especially if the Sun falls in a mutable sign – plus an eagerness to communicate. This individual might forever be writing letters and emails. The father was probably also interested in learning; not necessarily an intellectual unless the rest of the chart indicates that, but a man who liked to follow the news perhaps or who was always travelling short distances from A to B. His work may even have involved transport. Some with this placement achieve some kind of honours for writing or communication. Honours may also be accorded to relatives for such matters.

Moon in the Third House

Classically the person feels at home in classroom situations. Writing skills are common and the imagination is likely to be well developed. Some will have skills in public-speaking. Many will feel comforted by reading and learning. Just having a book to read can make all manner of situations much more bearable. Often the individual will feel at home in administrative roles. This is the person who can nurture over the telephone and (depending on the sign and aspects) generally hold everything and everyone together in a hectic office environment. There can be the mothering of siblings or an experience of being mothered by them. The placement often denotes attendance at boarding school. Occasionally the Moon here indicates the mental instability of a principal caretaking figure.

Mercury in the Third House

Mercury situated in its own house predisposes to wide interests, a questioning outlook and lots of comings and goings in the local environment. A major emphasis on communication and learning, whether this is writing, talking or reading, will inevitably manifest throughout every area of life. Many with this placement will be fluent, witty and articulate. Others will merely be unable to get off the phone. For most with Mercury here, there will be a lot of contacts; this can be a great placement for those who need to do networking. Skills with languages are also common. A love of cycling is also a frequent manifestation. Lots of activity with regard to siblings can be expected.

Venus in the Third House

Usually indicates a love of knowledge and learning and, in particular, an interest in art, music or singing. An appreciation of or involvement with pictures and art galleries is common. This is the person who attracts others with their curiosity, knowledge or conversation. There may be an ability to communicate tactfully and gracefully. Love affairs conducted by mail, email or on the phone are common. This is perhaps the placement to associate with love letters. Some will fall in love with their next-door neighbour, while others will meet partners in the schoolroom or evening class. A strong bond with a sister is often shown, though sibling rivalry and sometimes incest can also be indicated with Venus here, but this has to be supported by other factors. There is often an enjoyment of and pleasure to be gained through short journeys and weekends away.

Mars in the Third House

This can be a mentally combative and competitive placement but it usually shows an enthusiasm for learning and a capacity to speak their mind. A sharp, decisive mind with wit and speed of thought goes with the territory. Impatience in the classroom and in all learning environments is to be expected; this individual gets angry with themselves (and sometimes with the teacher) if they don't feel they understand. There can be impatience also with transport. Road rage and fast driving are possibilities here but this is also a good placement for the rally driver! A liking for thrillers or adventure stories is common. There can be sibling rivalry and sometimes the misfortune to be bullied at school. Often the schooldays are felt to be rather rough. An accident-prone brother or a brother in the forces is sometimes indicated, if other factors concur. Sibling incest is possible if other chart factors support this. Disputes with neighbours are also possible.

Jupiter in the Third House

In the UK, this will often describe a comprehensive education, or sometimes attendance at a church school. Unless the Jupiter is receiving very stressful aspects, schooldays and all learning environments are often experienced as being enjoyable. For most with this placement, there is an eagerness to acquire and impart knowledge and information, and a curious hunger to learn. This can be a signature of someone who talks a lot and reads everything. However, there can be a proneness to mere surface understanding and other parts of the chart need to provide depth. Those with Jupiter here should maybe strive for the overview of a subject area; there can be a tendency to get bogged down by too much information and too many details. Depending on the strength of Jupiter overall, there can also sometimes be a misplaced arrogance as to the person's mental abilities. More commonly, Jupiter here describes an interest in religion, politics or philosophical matters. It is a good placement for those involved in education, publishing or travel. Certainly, a lot of travel to nearby countries is indicated. There may also be travel to visit siblings living overseas. Others will have learned a great deal from their sibling relationships.

Saturn in the Third House

School may have seemed restrictive or punitive and often there is an early fear to overcome around communicating spontaneously. There may, for instance, be an expectation of being chastised for opening their mouth. There is sometimes a fear of being thought stupid with Saturn here, and knowing the right answer can become the way of defending oneself. Stammering and other speech impediments are common in early life. The experience of feeling ridiculed for how the individual speaks (possibly because of their dialect) is not uncommon. Language barriers generally (e.g. from living in a country with a different first language) are suggested. Some will be overly pedantic in how they communicate, arising out of a fear of being misunderstood. Frequently the individual will have experienced interruptions in their early education. But this is the placement of the eternal student and, in later life, many will become an authority in some area of knowledge. Saturn here also implies burdensome siblings, older siblings or, quite frequently, a lack of siblings. The individual may be late in learning to drive and sometimes can be rather unco-ordinated generally.

Uranus in the Third House

This placement can contribute towards the individual having an original turn of mind and an ability to arrive at opinions and ideas independently. This person doesn't follow the herd. Interested in the truth, as they see it, they won't be frightened to court disapproval by expressing it. Some will forget that the truth is relative and may be prone to extremist views. A liking for shocking others can make individuals with this placement quite out of step with the consensus. So some with this placement may be ostracized by their neighbours (and by neighbours in a more global sense) for being viewed as being far too different in their views. Being cut off from siblings or other relatives (such as cousins) for whatever reason, for a period of time, can also be a manifestation of this placement. Frequently the individual will have step-brothers and -sisters, some of whom they may have been unaware of for many years. A dramatic change of school environment is also often indicated (for example, as the result of a move from the town to the country).

Neptune in the Third House

This placement often indicates an interest in the arts; particularly music, photography or film. Sometimes there may be an interest in mystical subjects. There can also be facility with poetry. Basically, the individual has a need to read and hear things that will lift their spirits and enable them to escape from the rough and tumble of life. There can also be tremendous sensitivity – almost psychic attunement – to what others are thinking and feeling. This can make arriving at and expressing their own views more elusive. Often children with this placement have imaginary companions. Adoptive or foster brothers and sisters are also common. School must be an imaginative and creative environment in order to be an enjoyable experience.

Pluto in the Third House

This placement can give tremendous depth of thought and can be the hallmark of the person who takes nothing at face value. It is therefore an excellent placement for anyone engaged in research or any other kind of investigative work. This can be an individual who has a compulsion to learn and who will leave no stone unturned when trying to get to the bottom of something. There is often an interest in psychological or occult subjects. Sometimes this placement can describe the individual's experience of school as being punishing. It may be paranoia but there is often the feeling of being persecuted by teachers, fellow pupils, siblings or neighbours. Such experiences can also create a paranoid tendency. Sometimes individuals with this placement have early learning difficulties or, more commonly, a sibling with learning difficulties or a decidedly different way of communicating. Some with this placement will have skills in working with those with disabilities, whether the disability is physical or psychological.

The Fourth House and the IC

The angle known as the Imum Coeli (literally 'lowest heaven' in Latin), or more commonly the IC, marks the beginning of the Fourth House in most house systems other than the Equal house system.

Traditionally associated with our **roots, ancestry, home** and **non-movable property**, in a number of different contexts the Fourth House is concerned with the **past**. In common with the Moon, this part of the chart shows **where we are coming from**. The whole complex (planets in the Fourth House, ruler of the Fourth and IC by sign, house and aspect) will literally describe our **ancestry** and our racial and **ethnic origins**. If your family hails from a long line of farmers, this is where that fact will be shown. Our personal history is never-ending; if we could go back far enough we could trace our roots to cave-dwellers and even before that. This leads me to the view that it is the Fourth House and, more especially, the IC angle which encompass what Jung termed the 'collective unconscious'.

The theme of 'where we are coming from' also applies to the family in which we were raised. This area of the chart will have much to say about the **emotional and family atmosphere** in which we grew up. In tandem with other relevant chart factors, it will offer information about one and usually both of our parents, or at least our experience of them. If we are adopted or fostered then this house will contribute information about *all* our families – biological and physical – albeit in different ways. The Fourth describes our **base**, our **platform**, our **foundations**. As the lowest point of the circle, it is the most private house whereas the opposite point (the MC or Midheaven) is the most public part of the chart. The Fourth will describe our **home**, both in an emotional and physical sense (but look also to the Moon here). At home we are **at our most private** and most hidden from the world. At home we walk around with holes in our socks and wearing our oldest clothes. Our home is **our place of retreat**, our **sanctuary**.

The analogy of a tree is a useful one for the MC/IC axis. The Tenth House or MC corresponds to the top of the tree with its branches reaching up to the sky but the IC/Fourth House corresponds to the **roots**. The roots of a tree can go very deep. A tree without strong roots (Fourth) cannot produce much in terms of fruit and foliage (Tenth), in the same way that it would be more or less impossible for a homeless person to have a career or any real status in the world. The Fourth is traditionally associated with **the end of life** and with endings in general. The fruit and foliage of the tree fall to the ground and once again nourish its roots. In the same way, on a daily basis, the individual may go out into the world and pursue their career (Tenth) during the day but at night will return to their home and their private life (Fourth). On a lifetime basis, we will have some kind of role in society (Tenth). Often this is a career, but towards the latter stages of life we retire (Fourth). Retirement can be a very busy time, but in terms of outer-world activity some degree of rest or relief from toil or exertion is implied.

More simply, we can just think that the Fourth House describes something of our home life. It literally depicts our home – where we may live – in a house, caravan or boat, for instance. Do we live by the sea, across from the gas works or next to the pub? Are we in the land of our birth or do we live abroad? Even the name of the road can be shown by this house. For example, I have the Moon in Sagittarius in the Fourth and, at the time of writing, I live in a road called Church Lane! An earlier home was close to a convent. With Scorpio on my IC, the local cinema is called the Phoenix and there are two cemeteries and several undertakers within less than a five-minute walk! This region of the horoscope may indicate who we live with and, along with the Moon, what we are like to live with. It can show the kind of emotional atmosphere we generate in the home. More trivial aspects of our home life – such as decor – will also be described, at least partially.

Sun in the Fourth House

It is important for those with this placement to have a home of which they can be proud. Some will create a showplace. There is a need to be lord (or lady) of all they survey and so this individual needs to be in charge of the house. An awareness and appreciation of the land and their heritage is likely. The family and background are what give the individual a sense of confidence and identity. Many will be proud of and want to show off their origins, perhaps being able to trace their roots back through many centuries.

Moon in the Fourth House

A strong bond with nature, the land and their heritage is to be expected and there may be a strong patriotic streak. People can get emotionally stirred by the countryside with this placement. Home is viewed as a refuge, and the type of refuge and style of home life will be described by the Moon sign and aspects. Although planets here may describe either parent, the Moon in the Fourth is usually more descriptive of a strong emotional bond with the father. There may be many changes of residence in the early life (especially if the Moon is found in a mutable sign) but a more settled domestic scene in later years.

Mercury in the Fourth House

Some with this placement are educated at home, while others are sent to boarding school. Many will come from an environment where there was discussion at the dinner table, and sometimes it is indicative of an intellectual background. Whatever the situation, there tends to be a lot of coming and going in the home environment and a lot of communication also – perhaps phones, radios, newspapers, magazines and TVs in every room. The individual may come from this kind of background or may create it for themselves. Involvement in matters of real estate is possible. Depending on the sign placement and the chart overall, Mercury here can add a nomadic, restless streak to the nature. This is ideal for the person who lives in a trailer or other type of mobile home. Some will have had parents who were involved in education or communication. Siblings can take on the role of parent.

Venus in the Fourth House

It is usually important for those with this placement to have a harmonious home which reflects good taste and is an environment free from discord. Often the roots from which the individual has come are artistic in some way. Many with this placement will have a strong love for one or both of the parents. A parent may have been involved with the arts, the diplomatic corps or the beauty industry. Often there is money in the family and, even where there isn't, at least one of the parents will usually have had a self-indulgent streak. The retirement years can be soft and easy if other chart factors concur. The inclination to entertain at home can be well developed and spare resources are often spent on facilitating this process and generally beautifying the home.

Mars in the Fourth House

Sometimes this placement implies a background where the parents argued. Often it describes a parent as having sexual adventures. Or it might describe a parent who was in uniform. Not infrequently, the individual competes with a parent in various respects and may feel considerable anger towards that person. Sometimes those with this Mars placement come from a war-torn land or have ancestors who fought for their country. Occasionally there is the use of the home for military purposes. Or the home may resemble a bombsite in its untidiness because of all the activity that takes place there! There may be some tendency towards fires in the home or at least burnt saucepans. This is an excellent placement for gardening and farming, and often the parents or other ancestors worked on the land. Many with this placement will enjoy a very active old age.

Jupiter in the Fourth House

This implies a rich ancestry in either moral or financial terms. The person will usually come from a 'good' family, often originally from overseas. Many will be able to trace the family tree back for generations. Some with this placement will have a large home but perhaps all will need a feeling of space in their home environment. A home adjacent to (or in) a church, religious building or stables is not infrequent. Hospitality is often marked. The individual may live abroad for part of their life. Not only in terms of genealogy but sometimes from the perspective of past lives, many with this placement are interested in where they come from in the very widest sense.

Saturn in the Fourth House

Conscious or unconscious fears of homelessness may be described by Saturn here and thus there is often a strong desire for home-ownership. Alternatively, the individual may feel imprisoned by the thought of having a mortgage or a fixed location. Sometimes there are ancestors who worked hard and suffered by virtue of their poverty. Some may have lost their home and it can be this fact that underpins the person's vague fears in this area. The family will often come from a farming or mining community. One parent – frequently the father – may have been a burden or ill in some way, and people with this placement don't usually take the idea of a joyous and easy family life for granted. Taking responsibility for the family, and not uncommonly looking after the parents in their old age, can also sometimes be associated with this Saturn placement.

Uranus in the Fourth House

The individual is often cut off from their roots (e.g. the identity of a parent may be unknown or one or both parents may have migrated from the land of their birth) but may enjoy the sense of freedom that liberation from the family can bring. Sometimes there will have been an experience of a sudden uprooting or unexpected changes of residence in early life. It frequently signifies a step-parent, usually the father. Hence the individual will feel that it is useless to opt for permanence in their home life. Frequently, the individual's home will be full of the latest gadgetry and technology. Often brought up to be independent, there can be a preference for living alone.

Neptune in the Fourth House

This placement will often describe a longing and yearning for their roots. Yearning for their roots implies that the individual has been separated from those roots; perhaps by living far away from their birthplace or possibly because of adoption or something similar. This is the person who dreams of an ideal home whether that ideal home is imagined in a physical sense (such as a cottage by the stream with roses round the door) or in a more emotional sense (an open house that provides sanctuary and spiritual succour to all who need it). At least one parent will have embodied the quality of Neptune, perhaps being a gentle, compassionate creature, or by being a victim or saviour. They might have been missing altogether or just subtly difficult to get hold of. This placement can imply a deeply spiritual parent, one prone to alcoholism or one who works at sea. The possibilities are endless and only by studying the whole chart will the true picture emerge. Spending time creating an ideal home with a quality of sanctuary about it (often by water) is a good way to use this placement.

Pluto in the Fourth House

There is often a very strong tie with the earth, the land and with nature; a feeling for pre-history, the primal roots from which we all spring. Frequently, the person has an experience of being plucked from an early environment (especially the generation born in the mid 1960s who have the Uranus/Pluto conjunction here) and placed somewhere very different and possibly terrifying for a young child. Sometimes, from the perspective of the culture and time into which the person is born, something is considered taboo about their roots or parentage. Pluto here sometimes merely describes having mixed-race ancestry. Or there may have been mental illness or crime in the family. Those with this placement do well if they can find out about all the baggage that precedes them and thus avoid unconsciously repeating dramas of which they are unaware. This is a good placement for genealogy, archaeology and psychology; this individual can gain a lot by digging at their roots.

The Fifth House

Traditionally associated with children, romance, speculation, playing, hobbies and gambling, the Fifth House is concerned with **creativity** and **recreation**. The astrologer Robert Hand, in *Horoscope Symbols*, says the Fifth House is about **doing things for their own sake** – not for the sake of love, money, impressing one's parents, prestige or any of the 101 other motives that spur us into action. Basically, when we are in the Fifth House, we are **at play**. What represents play for one person is not the same for another, but the Fifth describes what we specifically mean by the idea of play. And not only the source of play but how easy it is to play.

The word 'create' means to bring forth, produce or cause to grow. The word 're-create' can be defined as meaning to restore to a good or wholesome condition; to refresh ourselves through some kind of pleasant occupation. Thus, the Fifth is **where we refresh ourselves** through playing and doing things we enjoy. As the house of children, it is the place **where we re-create the child within**. The Fifth is also literally the house of children, as for many people children represent the route through which they re-create themselves. Not only in the act of reproducing but what follows after the child is born – all the play that is involved. Re-creating ourselves through having children, or producing some kind of creative work, is also a means whereby we can achieve some kind of immortality.

As the house of **romance**, the Fifth differs from other relationship houses in that again the emphasis is on enjoyment, having fun and playing. This is the stage of 'going out together' which in some cultures will very much involve sex and in others might not. Play for the child is the means by which he or she learns about socializing. For both adult and child, play is a means of rehearsing life. Rehearsing the real thing. We try things out for the fun of it in the Fifth, just to find out, take a risk, put our toes in the water. When we have a new boyfriend or girlfriend we are doing just that: we are trying them out and we are also learning about relating. The Fifth is the house of **theatre** – the place we go to see a play. Drama is one of the ways that society, in all cultures and since time began, has been able to learn about life in general and about relationship in particular. In watching the actors portray characters and tell stories, we learn the likely outcome of our actions. It is a kind of vicarious rehearsal.

The Fifth can embrace any kind of creativity, but imagine that you are a potter. While you may want your pots to sell, inevitably you have to make them on your own and in your own way. Your pot will be unique to you. The Fifth House is where we express ourselves, it is where we say 'This is me', 'This is how *I* do it'. It has been said that, whatever the topic, the novelist is always writing a barely concealed autobiography. Or, if we know how to, we can look at a painting and tell a lot about the artist. The Fifth is where we reveal ourselves and, in doing so, it is also where we put ourselves on the line – where we take a risk. Indeed the Fifth House embraces all manner of **speculation** and **gambling**.

As always, a story can be made out of the houses unfolding into each other. With respect to the Fifth coming from the Fourth, we can say that we have got our home in order (Fourth) and can now go out and enjoy ourselves, we can now play (Fifth). In the Fourth we got a roof over our head, now in the Fifth we can have children. If we have a secure base (Fourth), we can go out, take a risk or two, and we can speculate a little with life.

Sun in the Fifth House

As with the Sun in Leo, there can be a very strong need for attention and a dislike of being ignored. In romantic situations, the individual chooses partners on the basis of how much they feel loved, and less because they are drawn to the other person. This is also potentially a very creative position for the Sun (the nature of the creativity will be described by the sign involved) and certainly descriptive of someone with a strong appreciation of drama. A love of children (though not necessarily parenthood) is often marked and the individual may feel at their most alive when in the company of young people.

Moon in the Fifth House

There is a need to be creative with this placement; the nature of that creativity will be shown by the sign in which the Moon is found. For instance, in Virgo, the individual may be drawn to some kind of craft; in Gemini they are skilled at writing; in Taurus gifted with clay or massage, and so on. Often the mother will have been creative and imaginative, and an artistic environment may have been the norm of childhood. Some will look after the creative output of others, and this is an ideal placement for the conserver of fine art or an art gallery employee or employer. The individual may have a big family (especially if the Moon is in a water sign) and will feel at home in the company of children and young people. This person knows how to play in a variety of contexts. Taking on the role of parent or child in love affairs is common.

Mercury in the Fifth House

Potentially, this describes the artist as a writer. This position suggests an enjoyment of reading and other literary pursuits, and possibly oratorical skills. This position is perfect for writing for children or communicating about romance or sport. Any sports or games involving hand/eye co-ordination is also ideal and there may be skill at, and enjoyment derived from, playing cards, crosswords and word games. An interest in romantic games is also likely. This is a good placement for all kinds of social networking, including the art of matchmaking. This is the person who will be curious about who is going out with whom. Their own romantic adventures might fill a book, depending on the chart overall. Love affairs in which there are age disparities are common. Lovers will tend to be talkative and always on the go.

Venus in the Fifth House

This is indicative of a love of pleasure and romance. This can be the individual who is in love with love. As well as describing the ability to generally have a good time, an appreciation of the arts is shown. This is the person who loves going to art galleries and concerts. Many will be artistic themselves; as always, the sign placement and aspects are crucial to reaching an understanding of the situation more fully. Spending money on luxuries and beauty products (and skills in the beauty industry) are likely. Good relationships with children are suggested and, typically, there will be more female children than male.

Mars in the Fifth House

Perhaps *the* placement for sporting activities; there is likely to be an enjoyment of speed, action and danger. Depending on Mars's sign, being on the back of a motorcycle may provide the ultimate good time. Sometimes reckless and usually passionate about living life to the full, in romantic matters, this can be the person who lives for the chase and to achieve sexual pleasure. Competition in affairs of the heart is likely and therefore romantic triangles may also be indicated. Romantic enthusiasm and impulsiveness can also make for early pregnancies with this placement. Typically there will be more male children than female, and miscarriages are possible (but other factors in the horoscope must concur).

Jupiter in the Fifth House

This placement implies a love of life and a love of pleasure, and is descriptive of someone who is a gambler at heart. It could suggest literally a gambler, as in putting money on horses, cards or the stock market, and more subtle gambling as in pursuing adventures in romance, creativity and travel to the limit. Huge romantic adventuring may be indicated. Less speculative hobbies involving horses are also possible. This is an ideal placement for someone who is a patron of the arts and generosity is often extended towards children and children's charities. This is a perfect placement for the aunt, uncle or godparent, and some with this placement will have many children. It is a good position for the adult who is described by others as being a big kid themselves.

Saturn in the Fifth House

This placement can be descriptive of someone who is diffident and cautious in romantic matters. More frequently, it describes a person who is frightened of missing out romantically. Saturn here can describe the person who burns the candle at both ends because of this. It usually describes someone who takes all forms of play very seriously and, if creative, will tend to downplay and be lacking in confidence with respect to their artistic endeavours. This is the person who has to learn to be spontaneous. Children can be a source of anchorage for some but many will feel keenly that the responsibilities of parenthood seriously limit the time available for fun. Children will also teach valuable lessons about the nature of playing. Enjoyment of, and skills with, construction, sculpture and tasks involving planning and organization are indicated.

Uranus in the Fifth House

This will often describe creative skills with computers, web design and other technology. Originality is added to whichever creative gifts might be shown elsewhere. This is not a person to follow traditional teachings in artistic education. The placement has an allegiance with rebellious youth and sometimes those with this placement have a particular rapport with youngsters that others find difficult. Step-parenthood is common, as are situations where the person is cut off or separated from their children. Many with this placement may be forced to choose between their need for space and freedom and having children. For some, romantic liaisons, which will usually be unconventional, may be formed and broken off quite suddenly.

Neptune in the Fifth House

Neptune here denotes at best an artistic and/or romantic temperament, at worst someone addicted to escapist pleasures (e.g. drink and drugs) and having an overly developed fantasy life. It favours those who work with children because there is often an ability to enter into the world of make believe. Artistically the placement favours music, drama, dance and film. This can be the person who absolutely loves going to the cinema, for instance. Tremendous romanticism is also often shown and the romantic life will inevitably involve some degree of illusion and sacrifice. Sometimes Neptune in the Fifth indicates the fostering or adoption of children. The person tends to feel sorry for children, seeing them as the victims of society.

Pluto in the Fifth House

A good placement for someone who can become obsessive about some form of creativity. Often it describes someone who wants to leave no stone unturned when it comes to experimenting with life. This can be the person who wants to experience all the pleasures that life has to offer, even if on occasion such pleasures may not turn out to be all that pleasurable! For some, nothing is taboo. There can be a compulsion to push at the boundaries of every sexual taboo. A deep desire to have children can be indicated with this placement, which can also sometimes be indicative of miscarriages and abortions if other factors in the chart concur. Occasionally it equates with putting up a child for adoption (having an 'invisible' child). Romantic encounters in early life make the person street-wise in affairs of the heart.

The Sixth House

Traditionally associated with work, health, servants, employees, clothing and small animals, fundamentally the Sixth House deals with our concern for **maintaining life**, being able to pay the rent and to feed and clothe ourselves. If we don't maintain our daily lives properly we become prey to *dis*-ease.

A major concern of the Sixth House is **work**. This is not the same as our career, our 'calling', though it may well dovetail with that. The concern of the Sixth is about the **daily ritual of life** and it encompasses the notion of work as describing what we actually do all day and our attitude to it. The Sixth has much to say about how we do the job in hand and what we are like to work with. The Sixth implies that there is a relationship between **routine, ritual and health**. Anyone living a religious life would not argue with this, and routine is regarded as essential when raising young children. Work is a major provider of routine and ritual and, for many, sets the structure of their lives. Work provides the means by which we can maintain our life, the way we help to maintain the lives of others, the way we 'pay rent' for being on the planet.

The Sixth describes the way we contribute to the upkeep of the planet and Sixth House energies will say much about our attitude to the notion of **serving others**. And from this it should be clear that it doesn't have to be paid work and we don't have to be an employee. The Sixth has much to say about our working relationships, and frequently our **unequal working relationships**. Thus, not only relationships with co-workers (which may be equal) but our attitude to being, and our experience of being, an employee. The Sixth will also describe our attitudes to employees, if we are an employer. Work is the place where we essentially live out the will of others. Our employees, and in olden times especially our servants and domesticated animals, implemented our will. They served us. And even if we don't seem to employ servants, in a sense we do so all the time. The waiting staff in the restaurant we frequent, the dry cleaners, the youngster who delivers the pizza, the shop assistants – everyone who serves us comes under the umbrella of this house. Thus, our Sixth House describes our attitude to service, both to giving it and receiving it.

Ideally, the work we do each day is the way we bring our psychological attributes and issues together with the physical world. If we don't successfully do this, we become ill as, arguably, *dis*-ease is a circumstance where our inner and outer lives are out of kilter. Thus, the Sixth House concerns itself with the **mind/body relationship**.

In the context of this house being concerned with **maintenance** – maintenance of the planet and those within it, and maintenance of ourselves — then the Sixth also has a bearing on such topics as **diet**, **hygiene** and **clothing**. In practice, our eating habits are more likely to be shown by the Moon, but the Sixth does describe our relationship to routine and ritual and, as such, may contribute information about our eating habits, as food is one method whereby we maintain our bodies. Traditionally, the house is supposed to describe the **cause of physical infirmities** (e.g. working too hard, over-indulgence, etc.) and this works much better than ascribing all matters of health to the Sixth, as some astrologers are wont to do. In practice, the whole chart will offer information about health and disease. This area of astrology is very much a specialist subject and outside the scope of this book.

The Sixth House also has rulership over **pets** and **small animals**. Research has shown that maintaining the lives of animals – having the routine and responsibility of looking after them, as well as the stroking and grooming that is involved in that process – actually prolongs our lives. Even today, pets are still in some sense our servants in that they keep us healthy.

Sun in the Sixth House

This placement suggests that the individual discovers and builds their identity through their job. They can gain confidence and recognition from others through their work. Thus, there can be a need to feel indispensable and to shine at work. There is also a strong 'belief in the importance of good service. For this person, the hero is someone who puts their heart into what they are doing and does the task, whatever it is, well. Often the father inculcated (not necessarily consciously) in the individual the importance of taking pride in their work. Dad may himself have always been at work or have been perceived as being so. The individual may have received attention in early life because of their delicate health. Not surprisingly, therefore, this placement often indicates an interest, job or some other involvement in health matters.

Moon in the Sixth House

A need to work is the key here; the individual feels better if they are being of use. Many will take on the role of mother with their fellow employees and provide the shoulder that others can cry on. Or maybe they nurture others by keeping titbits to nibble in their office drawer. Those less emotionally developed will play 'baby' and be needy at work. Many will have a job that has a lunar aspect to it; for instance, working in a caring profession, in catering, domestic work, real estate or security. This is also a common placement for those whose home is provided by their employer. They literally 'live on the job'. Others will make their work environment look like home. Often the working life of the mother was important to her or the fact that she worked had strong ramifications in the life of the family. People with this placement may be prone to digestive troubles, especially when upset, and care may need to be taken with the diet.

Mercury in the Sixth House

Work that involves writing or communication is the norm here. Jobs that either involve transport (e.g. driving for a living) or travel are equally possible, depending on the chart overall. Chatting with co-workers or customers is likely to be a feature of the working life. In various ways, this is the person who talks for a living. Commonly there is a tendency to worry about health. Nervous strain and worry may be the factors that undermine the person's health. Often found in the charts of agents (and those who run agencies, such as literary agents, travel agents, import-export agents), this is a good position for any kind of 'middle person' role. This can include those who work in almost all areas of commerce and sales. Even the humble shop assistant is the middle person between manufacturer and customer.

Venus in the Sixth House

With this placement, it is important that the individual really values their work, not only that they like the work itself but that they are happy with their co-workers. Congenial working relationships are considered to be crucial. The work itself may call for skills of diplomacy or sociability and is unlikely to be heavy or rough unless other chart indications strongly point that way. Work could be in the art or beauty industries. Jobs involving the exchange of money are also likely. The working environment may also provide the major venue for meeting potential lovers. A love of pets is often indicated and the preference would be for peace-loving and gentle animals. Perhaps a liking for doves, even; the traditional symbol of peace. Health problems might stem from an over-indulgent attitude to maintaining life – perhaps a certain laziness or too pronounced a sweet tooth.

Mars in the Sixth House

Work with metals, cars, heat, knives, machinery or tools may be indicated. This could be the placement of the welder, butcher or surgeon, depending on other factors. A competitive working environment is the norm. There is a need for action and few with this placement will be happy tied to an office environment. If they do find themselves in that situation, they can feel very frustrated. If receiving stressful aspects, Mars here can indicate arguments at work. It is a good placement for anyone whose job involves fighting in some way; perhaps for the rights of co-workers, as in the shop steward of a trade union. Women with this placement often find themselves working in a traditionally male environment. Lovers will often be found at work. Health can be undermined by stress and over-doing things. In extreme cases, frustration at work can lead to misplaced energy and accidents at work. Inflammatory conditions and sexually transmitted disorders can also sometimes be a feature of Mars in this house.

Jupiter in the Sixth House

Jupiter in the Sixth implies work that is concerned with the future in some way; often occupations are in publishing, education, the law or travel. Any occupation which has luck as a feature is also possible, such as stock market activities or being a bookmaker. Whatever the actual job, people with this placement are usually lucky finding work. Colleagues will often come from different cultures and backgrounds and therefore do much to educate the individual in the ways of the world. Health tends to be undermined by over-indulgence in food or drink and a resultant strain on the liver. Disorders of growth and the formation of growths (e.g. cancer) can also be indicated, but the outcome of treatment is usually very positive. Often there is a love of horses.

Saturn in the Sixth House

At its most extreme, this can be the placement of the hypochondriac. Anxieties about the possibility of the body breaking down can result in someone who takes responsibility for their health and isn't frightened to put in the hard work necessary to keep healthy. This placement can be the hallmark of the work-out fanatic: someone who makes their body a defence, even to making it hard like stone. Possibly the father's working life was strongly affected by ill health. Saturn in the Sixth is also potentially the position of the workaholic. Certainly this describes someone who is not afraid to take responsibility and who is willing to put in the time for it. Frequently there are strong organizational skills. Work may involve planning, structure, efficiency, organization or simply keeping to timetables: anything from train-driver to architect. Sometimes the individual works in a job where they can only get so far, possibly because of a fear of the responsibility that promotion might bring. Depending on other chart factors, Saturn here can denote a responsible job, a fear of responsibility or the unavailability of jobs (e.g. in areas of high unemployment). The keeping of crustaceans, reptiles or amphibians as pets (or other creatures with a tough skin) can be shown by Saturn placed here.

Uranus in the Sixth House

The individual is not likely to be suited to a nine-to-five role because too fixed a daily routine would be abhorrent. The ideal boss is one who allows the individual 'to get on with it'; those with this placement will not take kindly to interference or too many rules. This person does best if they can be allowed to do things independently. This is not the office team-player. Frequent and unexpected changes in the working life are suggested; in extreme cases the person may be quick to chuck jobs or is frequently asked to quit. Some will resent the intrusion that the working life makes on their personal freedom. Work with electricity, electronics and technology would be ideal, especially in a freelance or self-employed capacity, as would any working role that allows for originality in style and freedom of movement. The individual will usually be drawn to alternative medicine.

Neptune in the Sixth House

This will often describe a job in industries that thrive on people's need to escape or opt out. These include all areas of the media and the arts, advertising, work in catering, alcohol, pharmacy and anaesthetics, to name but a few. Rescuing, saving and caring for others, and utilizing the skills of compassion, can indicate yet another kind of working life. The job will often demand some kind of sacrifice; for some this is lack of remuneration, for others it is insufficient recognition. Usually very sensitive to drugs and anaesthetics, those with Neptune receiving particularly stressful aspects may also be prone to poisoning and parasites. This needn't only be physical; many with this placement are so open to suffering from co-workers or from the public that they can become a psychic sponge, soaking up other people's negativity. Hopefully, strong boundaries will be provided by other areas of the chart. Work involving subtle energies is a better way of using this placement. Health can also often be enhanced by the use of various healing techniques.

Pluto in the Sixth House

With this placement, work may involve investigation or research. Whatever the trade, it will be pursued with dedication, intensity and passion. The individual positively needs something they can get obsessed about. Some will be drawn to a taboo area, as in the sex industry or undertaking, for instance. Others will work in refuse or sewage. It is also a good placement for those involved with disability. Commonly, the person feels most comfortable in a more hidden role in an organization or employed in more lowly work, where they can hide. It is also an ideal placement for those who work for the police, especially in undercover roles. Perceptive about undercurrents at work, those with this placement need to avoid becoming paranoid when things become tense. Whatever the occupation, most with this placement have to learn about power at work. There can be an above-average risk of redundancy for some with Pluto here. Often there is a love of or involvement with dogs.

The Seventh House and the Descendant

The Seventh House describes one-to-one **partnerships**, both personal and professional. It says much about **how we approach relationships**, what we are looking for and are attracted to. Basically, what 'hooks' us about another person and, quite often, what it is about us that 'hooks' them. We can associate the Seventh with not only **marriage partners** and **significant others** but also with **business partnerships**. Indeed, all partnerships where there is a contract (whether in writing or implied) and also all relationships where a degree of mirroring takes place. This includes, for instance, therapist/client and lawyer/client relationships. In terms of more personal relationships, the Seventh describes both how the partner is and how we are with them. This two-way process occurs because the way we tend to see the other determines how we react to and treat them – hence the term 'mirroring'. As the house of the 'not-self', the Seventh potentially describes what we project on to absolutely anyone else. Thus, someone with Saturn in the Seventh House, for example, will tend to accuse any other person (and not only their partner) of being *controlling* or they may habitually tend to be *frightened* of the other, expecting to be *chastised* – whoever the 'other' actually is (I've put the Saturn words in italics).

Basically, the Seventh describes **what we give to others**, either consciously or unconsciously. Unconsciously we ascribe traits to others through the mechanism of projection (in other words, the traits are ours but we are unconscious of them and 'throw' them on to others); experiencing the 'other' as a literal embodiment of whatever sign or planets are involved. We literally marry the person described in the Seventh. The Seventh will also show how we act when we're with others, especially one other person, so again we are giving away the particular planet or zodiacal energy. Sometimes we give the energy away through our work, as well. For example, an old hairdresser of mine had Venus here and it could be said that he was giving the 'not-self' beauty and value. An actress I knew, who was very attractive but was always cast in frumpy roles, told me that 'other people' were always cast as the beautiful ones. She was disowning her Venus; for her, other people were described by it. Basically, the Seventh is the house of 'out there', 'over there' and 'not me', until we finally discover and own the specific attributes. Thus, the Seventh describes **what we find in ourselves after finding it in someone else first**.

Traditionally, the Seventh is also associated with **open enemies**, as opposed to the Twelfth House, which depicts hidden enemies. It is interesting that the marriage house is also the house of our enemies, but this is not so surprising when we consider the mechanism of projection. The notion of open or public enemies embraces our **adversaries, feuds** and contests of all kinds. It includes the duels of the past and today's **legal confrontations**, lawsuits and litigation. Dealing with both partners and adversaries necessitates **the balancing of our own needs with the needs of others**. Above all else, the Seventh is where we are offered the opportunity to become more conscious and, more especially, where we can learn the art of co-operation through one-to-one encounters.

As well as describing our own relationships, sometimes the Seventh describes our parents' relationship, this often being the first partnership we ever knew and therefore very likely to influence our own relating patterns. The astrologer Manilius also called this cusp 'the portal of death'. In practice, I have indeed found some association with death here. Transits from planets to this angle also sometimes 'coincide' with illnesses associated with the particular planet and sign. This need not be surprising when we consider that the Seventh opposes the Ascendant, which describes the physical body. As an axis, aspects to one side of it automatically give rise to aspects to the other side. Sadly, people also see illness as having little to do with them personally, seeing ill health as coming from 'out there'.

Still remembering that the Ascendant/Descendant is an axis, this Seventh House cusp also often describes circumstances at birth which involve another person – the person in the next bed, the midwife, the obstetrician, etc.

Sun in the Seventh House

The individual gleans their identity through close interaction with another. Sometimes this is the hallmark of the therapist who enables others to discover their identities through a one-to-one encounter with them. There may be an urge to shed light on others or on relationship itself. Many with this placement will, consciously or unconsciously, be looking for or playing the part of father in relationships. Relationships are viewed as being of supreme importance. More introverted souls with this placement will tend to attract egocentric and possibly arrogant partners to whom they may give too much power.

Moon in the Seventh House

People with this placement will usually create relationships which involve strong parenting or caring roles. The individual can play the part of mother or child. Unconsciously, the person is often psychologically married to their own mother, at least in the earlier years of adulthood. Mother's input may even be important when it comes to the choice of marriage partner. Many will want a traditional marital arrangement (but close scrutiny needs to be paid to the sign placement and aspects) in order to have a home and family. The whole family package is usually important.

Mercury in the Seventh House

This person may get someone else to do their thinking. They may see them as being more intelligent and articulate than they are themselves. They see communication as being essential to relationships and may attract a thinking, articulate partner. Or merely attract someone who is a chatterbox! Others will attract partners who work as drivers or in transport more generally. Sometimes the individual is a twin and is looking for a twin soul with whom to share their life. Some with this placement will speak for, or on behalf of, others in a variety of roles and thus this is an excellent placement for those engaged in drawing up contracts between parties and for those involved in mediation and arbitration. Marriage partners are sometimes found though the services of a dating agency.

Venus in the Seventh House

The individual will often regard the other person as beautiful or valuable. This can be the placement of the beautician, hairdresser or artist, or it can describe a partner in such trades. Financial changes (usually gains) through marriage and other partnerships are possible. This placement can describe the likelihood of attracting a loving and affectionate partner, although that person may be rendered weak because of their overly accommodating nature. The individual with this placement may also have all the problems inherent in being a people-pleaser themselves or they may need a partner to teach them the skills of sharing and putting the other person first. For both sexes, this placement can sometimes indicate a female partner. Relationships can have a lazy, self-indulgent quality.

Mars in the Seventh House

This can describe someone who is in a hurry to find a mate, as if there is fierce competition to do so. So an early marriage might be indicated. Relationships will be with people who embody Mars in some way. This could mean a volatile partner and/or a volatile relationship. Equally, Mars could be embodied through the working life of the partner. Thus, hooking up with someone in the armed forces, the police, a worker in the metal or sports industries or a competitive trade (such as sales) would all be examples. It is through relationship that the individual with this placement learns how to assert themselves, how to win and how to compete. To work well, the individual needs to find an outlet for their anger – shared sporting activities are ideal. As with most people, difficulties in the bedroom can give rise to arguments about almost anything; dealing with anger issues can keep such difficulties to a minimum. For both sexes, this placement can sometimes indicate a male partner. For some, Mars here can suggest being attacked or expecting to be attacked; it is easy to project aggressive feelings when Mars is placed here.

Jupiter in the Seventh House

The individual will often put the partner on a pedestal, seeing him or her as little short of a god. The other person will often be large in a number of different contexts and may well become wealthier and fatter after hooking up with the individual with this placement. The partner may be a philosopher, educationalist or come from abroad. Often this indicates a good marriage from the perspective of material gain and social advantage. Some with Jupiter here have a really buoyant and optimistic view of relationship; this can be the placement of the person who enjoys serial marriages and for whom the grass is always greener somewhere else. But it is also potentially the placement of those who are philosophical about the ups and downs of marriage and are quite happy and content remaining with the same person.

Saturn in the Seventh House

This is the hallmark of the individual who takes relationship very seriously. Usually they will want a contract and so will tend to get married, as opposed to co-habiting. Frequently there are fears of both not getting married and fears of doing so. Often the person projects on to marriage the notion that it is an imprisoning situation, which is maybe how the individual thinks one or both of their parents experienced it. Although this placement can delay and even deny marriage, many who have it will marry young because of the fear of missing out. Many of these more youthful liaisons (which are arguably formed in childhood) will founder in the late twenties with the advent of the maturity symbolized by the Saturn Return. Some with this placement will choose an older person, perhaps a father-figure, in order for that partner to take responsibility. But as they mature themselves and feel able to take responsibility, they may then find that their partner is overly controlling. Alternatively, in later life especially, the individual may opt for someone younger so that they themselves can be the one in control. In both personal and professional relationships the individual is offered an opportunity to work through their father issues with this placement. For some, Saturn here is a signature of the arranged marriage, or in any event a feeling that the choice of marriage partner is limited and perhaps circumscribed by parental or other demands.

Uranus in the Seventh House

Uranus in the Seventh can describe the sudden making and breaking of partnerships; for example, deciding to get married almost instantly and deciding to get divorced with equal speed. The partner will often feel like an outsider or will be an outsider in some way; perhaps coming from a culture alien to the one in which they live now. Some with this placement will choose to avoid permanent committed relationships, viewing their independence as being far too important to sacrifice. But even then, suddenly and without warning, they may get hitched in mid-life. The individual may be best suited to some kind of 'open' arrangement in their relationships. Partners who are full of surprises are ideal. Truthfulness and friendship will be central requirements in all one-to-one encounters.

Neptune in the Seventh House

Many with this placement may choose partners that they can rescue in some way; this is a person who tends to be attracted to people they can feel sorry for. At best, the person creates relationships full of sensitivity, romance and compassionate understanding. Some will be attracted to the professional rescuer or the artist/musician. At worst, the individual is just plain gullible when it comes to their choice of partner, projecting God on to the prospective partner and viewing them through rose-tinted spectacles. The overall situation of Neptune (its sign, aspects and rulership), and indeed the chart overall, will describe which way things are more likely to go. In a conscious individual, this placement need not be overly problematic, but for others the role of co-dependent (when married to an alcoholic, for instance) can be the norm. Business relationships should be entered into with great caution as there is potential for loss, disillusionment and personal sacrifice.

Pluto in the Seventh House

Permanent one-to-one relationships can hold a certain amount of terror for many with this placement and some will avoid close relationship altogether. Others may get involved but will have an unconscious compulsion to destroy a relationship once it is formed. A few will find themselves in the situation of helping a partner through depression, trauma, mental illness and even death. Whatever the situation, there is usually a very fated feeling about the relationships the individual gets embroiled in, as if there is a compulsion to get involved with a particular partner and no choice but to do so. Basically, this placement implies intense relationships rather than those of the more milk-and-water variety. Some will embody Pluto by getting involved with someone whose occupation is Plutonian: perhaps the partner will be in the police service, work with refuse or sewage, or perhaps is an undertaker or pathologist.

The Eighth House

While essentially concerned with birth, sex and death, the Eighth House has variously been dubbed the house of legacies or the house of karma. The Eighth does concern itself with the resources of others, the possessions of others, the values of the other person. The resources and possessions of not only our partner, but the possessions of everybody else. Thus, there is the association with **insurance**, **tax** and **legacies** and, if we win money, as through a lottery for instance, then this house is implicated because when we win or gain money in this way, it is other people's money that we are benefiting from. So the Eighth House will very literally describe gains and losses through others, including litigation over tax, **alimony**, dealings with insurance companies and legacies where someone else leaves us their possessions. Its scope also covers **stock market** activities and **investments** generally. Whenever we put our money in any kind of savings we are investing in what is out there and investing in what is not ours. The Eighth embraces any kind of investments that involve other people, whether these are emotional or financial: all **shared resources** and all money belonging to others. **Mortgages** and **bank loans** belong in this house. In his book *The Grip of Death* by Michael Rowbotham (published by Jon Carpenter, 2000), the writer tells us that the title *The Grip of Death* is a literal translation of 'mortgage', when the owner of a house pledges his or her house to another with a handshake ... 'until death'.

Much more importantly, though, the Eighth House concerns itself with the **fundamental** issues of life: **birth**, **death** and **sex**. It is the house of those things that are irreversible and irrevocable; the house whose issues have a no-going-back quality. It is the house of **inheritance** but not just in a strictly financial sense, for it describes what we have inherited in a psychological sense from our childhood and our parents' relationship. Arguably, it describes the parental legacy, the legacy of their relationship. What they left to us as their child. What they got right, what they healed and what they didn't, what was left to be processed by their offspring. So it's not only what is bequeathed to us in a financial sense but in a psychological sense, too. The word 'bequeathed' literally means 'handed down by an ancestor or predecessor'.

The Eighth is a house of intimate relationship. Sex belongs here, although the Fifth House may be implicated too, because sex in modern times is about fun, playing, romance and having children. One can note though that when things break down for a couple in the bedroom, it is ownership of money and possessions that they argue about. The real source of pain and the nature of our own, often very uncivilized, feelings tend to be brushed under the carpet.

The Eighth concerns itself with where we unite with another. And we unite not only in a sexual sense, although perhaps all Eighth House relationships have sexual overtones. In a close relationship we have to somehow or other combine our values, our life experiences, all past and present circumstances with someone else who will, of necessity, have different values and experiences. This is the area of the chart where we have to **share**. In the Second House, we say it's mine, but in the Eighth, it's ours. Thus, this is the house where all our attitudes about life and, in particular, about intimate relationship and partnership in general have to be dealt with. Such attitudes we will have experienced consciously or unconsciously by being privy to our parents' values and attitudes. This is the place where we discover what the legacy from our parents' relationship actually was and we have to deal with it. Our first **intimate bonding** in life would have been with one or both parental figures. When as adults we enter into other intimate relationships, we are brought face-to-face with the legacy of that earlier bonding. Little wonder that the Eighth House is dubbed the house of karma; here the individual has to reap what was sown by the parents in their relationship, and what was sown in the person's own early relationships with them. Howard Sasportas, in his book *The Twelve Houses*, explains: 'The ruins and rubble from childhood are excavated in the Eighth House.' Intimate relationships necessitate that those ruins and rubble have to be cleaned up. As the house of intimate relationship the Eighth House is where our 'shadow' material is exposed; where it can't be hidden. This is the **area of relationship where we are exposed**. When closely involved with another, there is no hiding place. It is where we discover that, as well as being human, we are also animals, that we have strong, uncivilized, basic instinctual needs and desires (lust, jealousy, rage, for example). Instincts and desires that the civilized adult in us tends to shove under the carpet but which surface whenever the issue of survival presents itself.

One can say that the Seventh House describes our marriage or relationship as shown in the shop window. The Eighth reveals what goes on in the stockroom, well away from the shop floor. As described previously, it is what went on in the inner recesses of our parents' marriage, and in the recesses of our own early bonding with our parents.

The Eighth is also associated with **occult matters**. The word 'occult' simply means hidden. So planets in our Eighth, the sign on the cusp and its ruler will say something about our attitude to all that is hidden, dark and not easily accessible. **Depth psychology**, which concerns itself with digging around into **what is really going on**, is another example of an Eighth House preoccupation.

The Eighth famously also describes our attitude to death, indeed our **attitude to all transformative life experiences**, and perhaps our attitude to all major changes. The Eighth does sometimes describe something of the circumstances of our death and sometimes of our birth but it cannot be viewed in isolation. Our death, like our work, our health and our central relationships, is too huge to be described by one single house. More than being a house preoccupied with death, the concern of the Eighth is with **crisis**, a concern with the notion of **transformation**; transformations from one state to another. And again, we are brought back to the realm of intimate relationship because through close relationships we are transformed. A new person in our lives gives birth to all sorts of new things in us; we may dress differently, listen to different sorts of music, adopt new values and adjust old ones. The crisis link gives us a clue to the Eighth's rulership over **insurance**, because insurance is something we claim at times of crisis. Insurance policies provide a safety net so that when a crisis occurs we are given the resources of other people to enable us to transform ourselves from our present crisis state and be reborn.

Sun in the Eighth House

What is important for this individual is to live life to the heights and the depths, and thus the life may be characterized by crisis, colour, drama and intensity. The financial fortunes of the father and paternal side of the family will often be indicated by the aspects received by the Sun (e.g. wealth or bankruptcy). This placement often describes a strong psychic and sexual tie with the father. Inheritance will tend to come through the paternal line. Many with this placement will work in the banking industry. Others will have a particular interest in healing; this person can be turned on by feeling they are transforming another's life.

Moon in the Eighth House

This placement may describe someone who has an instinct for taking care of the resources of others. Thus, this is a good placement for the economist, stockbroker or treasurer. There is a strong need for close intimate relationship and a bonding with another, and also a sensitivity to undercurrents in the person's own relationships and in those with others. There's an awareness also of danger – this is not usually someone who takes life for granted. This placement can be descriptive of a person who is always there in times of crisis; the person who is emotionally clued-up and who manages to pull you through. The placement can indicate inheritance of property and inheritance through the mother, and sometimes financial benefits through women more generally. The inheritance from the mother doesn't have to be financial, although that can apply. Sometimes the inheritance from Mum can be of her culture, for instance in the case where someone's religion is passed on through the maternal line (e.g. Judaism).

Mercury in the Eighth House

This is a perfect placement for the tax inspector or stockbroker as there will often be an interest in the big world of corporate finance. There will also often be a curiosity about relationship and what goes on between people behind closed doors. An interest in psychological or occult matters is also common. For instance, this is the person who is especially curious about what happens after death. This is an ideal placement for those who work for the Samaritans organization. Here the counsellor talks people through their crises and, often, their inclination to commit suicide. Inevitably, many callers will also be 'heavy breathers'. Mercury here is perhaps the placement to associate with telephone sex! On occasion, Mercury here can describe sexual relationships with siblings or say something about a sibling's intimate relationships or death.

Venus in the Eighth House

This placement suggests financial gain through marriage or other personal relationships. Business partnerships may also work in the individual's financial favour. It is a good placement for all types of inheritance and for having benign relationships with insurance companies, tax inspectors and the like. It can also be found in the charts of those who work in the sex industry. In intimate relationships, it may describe an ability to put others at their ease. There can be an enjoyment of all that is erotic and mysterious.

Mars in the Eighth House

This placement can denote conflict over joint or shared resources. Beware, this individual may be impulsive about spending your money! Fights with insurance companies, the tax office or over matters of inheritance can be indicated. It is an excellent placement for a bailiff. More frequently, Eighth House arguments occur in the divorce courts. The anger may appear to be about money but in reality will often be about a breakdown in sexual relations. This can also be a very passionate, unsubtle, sexual placement and some with Mars here can be very concerned with conquest and will be upset if scorned. All else being equal, this individual doesn't shrink from the reality of death and will often exhibit courage in facing matters that others are too cowardly to contemplate. More reckless types (shown by the condition of Mars overall and also by other chart factors) may take risks with their personal safety. There can be an urgent need to understand and explore occult and psychological subjects.

Jupiter in the Eighth House

This placement has the potential for financial gain through inheritance or sometimes through speculation (e.g. winning money on a lottery). There are gains, too, from relationships and partnerships. Whatever the source, this is often a materially lucky position in which to have Jupiter. It can also be very generous. However, some with Jupiter here will get into hot water by over-extending themselves financially and through being greedy in financial matters. The prospect of death (their own and that of others) may hold few fears for this person who may view the ultimate exit as the final, and often exciting, journey. Life's other crises generally will often be viewed positively, too. Some will have a huge sexual appetite and an appetite generally for exploring the more hidden aspects of relationship, psychology, corporate finance and anything that happens behind closed doors. There will often be a sexual attraction to those from other cultures.

Saturn in the Eighth House

There can be a fear of intimacy and crises with this placement; some will do anything to avoid the pain of various types of trauma, and even the daily hurly-burly of being with someone can create anxiety. The fear may be of being controlled either in, or through, the sexual act. The individual will probably have inherited residual baggage from their parents in this respect. But through time, the individual may become an authority on intimate relationship and at home with crises of all kinds. In the bedroom, the person with this placement will often feel much better if they can be in control. There is a need for the person to define their deepest feelings with Saturn here. Fear of death may go with the territory too, with the individual potentially, through time and experience, becoming expert on that also. This is a good placement for those who are involved in the industries surrounding death, sex and money (especially insurance). On the financial front, there will often be responsibilities for joint resources, although some individuals will feel trapped and imprisoned by their responsibility for another's money. A feeling of obligation or vague guilt will have prompted them to take on this burden in the first place. Sometimes it will be ideal for those with Saturn in the Eighth to be the executor of a will or in charge of the household budget because they will be strict in such matters, firm on boundaries and therefore usually safe.

Uranus in the Eighth House

Unexpected changes of fortune are suggested with this placement. If Uranus is linked with Jupiter it can indicate fortunate wins (e.g. in a lottery) but it can also indicate unexpected losses, such as when the stock market suddenly crashes. Not that the experience of Uranus in the Eighth need be so passive; many with Uranus here 'plant bombs' in other people's lives by being agents of drastic change in some way. Uranus here may indicate a sudden death for the individual themselves, but only if borne out by other chart factors. Sometimes people with Uranus here have an urgent need to discover the truth about death as they see it, resulting in an interest in occult and psychological subjects. An open-minded attitude to sexual practices is also usual. This could be the individual who will not be frightened to befriend those who have had a sex-change, for instance. Less commonly, the individual themselves may live a transsexual life or be inclined to experiment in sexual matters. Frequently, this placement does indicate sudden, transformative, sexual encounters.

Neptune in the Eighth House

Neptune here can describe the seducer or the seduced, as this person can be very romantic and promiscuous in sexual matters and in intimate relationships generally. Some yearn to merge with another and may have few boundaries in such matters as a result. Really, the individual doesn't want to come down to earth in intimate relationships. For others, the sexual life may be what has to be sacrificed; platonic relationships are by no means uncommon with this placement, especially if borne out by other factors. For some, their sensitivity towards their partner and even psychic attunement with them precludes the more explicit physical act. A fantasy sex life may be preferred. Care needs to be taken by some with this placement when contemplating parting with their cash. The individual needs to check financial contracts very carefully as all may not be what it seems. Dreams of winning the lottery may also be the norm.

Pluto in the Eighth House

There can be suspicion of the corporate world with this placement and some with Pluto here choose to put their money under their mattress rather than trust a bank with it. Others will find the corporate world fascinating. It is a good placement for exploring the power of money, in various contexts. One of the family skeletons may be that of bankruptcy; albeit often long before the individual was born. In such circumstances, the person may become very street-wise in matters of high finance. Suicide, and even rape or murder, are potentially other skeletons that may be lurking in the family vaults (though this does also need to be shown elsewhere in order to be the case), and many with this placement will leave no stone unturned in probing these matters – even if they don't realize what has prompted them to do so. Owning their own more uncivilized feelings, and finding socially acceptable ways of expressing them, is essential for those born with this placement.

The Ninth House

Traditionally associated with **long journeys, higher education, philosophy, law, politics, religion, Church** and **State**, the essential concerns of the Ninth House are **exploration** and **meaning**. There is a 'reaching out' quality to this house which pertains to many matters which serve to stretch our understanding and consciousness. Geographical, metaphorical and metaphysical explorations belong in this house. As the Third House covers short-distance travel of the mind and of the body, the Ninth, which is directly opposite, is concerned with **long- distance travel of mind and body**. It is in this house that we discover that travel really does broaden the mind and does stretch our understanding as, ideally, does the pursuit of higher learning. Learning in this context takes us away from the mere acquisition of facts into the realm of Why and How. In the Ninth we ask what are the implications and ramifications of specific information – what does it all mean? Not only what does it mean for the individual but what does it mean for all of society? In the Ninth we are concerned with **the bigger picture**; we want to grasp the gist, the essence, the spirit of knowledge. Facts are not necessarily perceived as essential to this process.

Planets here will literally describe where we travel to and how we travel, as well as the purpose of that travelling, plus our attitude to **foreigners** and our experience of being a foreigner. As always, if the house is untenanted, look to the ruler of the house by sign, house and aspect for the relevant information.

Ninth House planets – and the ruler(s) of this house – will also describe our experience of higher education (what we study, where we study, how we study) and its importance or otherwise, as well as saying something about our moral code and general philosophy of life.

The Ninth is concerned with **society** and the ways in which society is structured. In natal astrology, the Ninth says much about how the individual views and, indeed, fits into society and into its legal framework. Society is kept cohesive by the values, ethics, morals and beliefs of a particular culture. Such beliefs both shape and are shaped by the Church, the government and the laws of the land. Thus, planets in the Ninth can do much to describe our relationship to society itself. More importantly perhaps, our Ninth also says something of **our personal morality**, our personal sense of right and wrong. This is not the same as the 'ought' and 'should' of Saturn (Saturn is concerned with the *policing* of morality), not the implementation of law or social constraint. The concern of the Ninth is of what the individual actually believes; the inner convictions which may motivate an individual and make a real difference to their actions.

Planets in the Ninth House (or the ruler of the Ninth if the house is untenanted) describe **what we project on to God** as well as our relationship to God. Also described is what we project on to a particular church or type of religious practice. The Ninth House is not alone in this regard; the planet Jupiter and any planets in Sagittarius can also have a bearing here. All three significators (planet, sign and house) may describe where, how and why we may 'play' God in various contexts. Any kind of advice-giving role might be described as a form of 'playing God'.

On a more superficial level perhaps, not only is the Ninth concerned with law, it is also associated with **in-laws**, and it is surprising how often planets based here do indeed describe these family members.

Sun in the Ninth House

This placement often describes an individual for whom the importance of education is supreme. For this person the hero is one who is well-travelled or well-educated or is perhaps one who educates. Many will excel in higher education or achieve recognition in a place far from their birth. Travel is usually important to those with the Sun in the Ninth. This is an ideal placement for an anthropologist as it can often describe someone who is illuminated by those from other cultures or beliefs.

Moon in the Ninth House

Instinctively of a philosophical turn of mind, this is also the person who is a knowledge-gatherer, the person who feels best fed if they are learning. The individual may live abroad or have a second home overseas. Others will have female partners, relatives or contacts in, or from, other countries. The individual will often feel comfortable with foreigners. Some with this placement end up in roles in which they take care of those from overseas. This can be anything from hotelier to the worker who finds homes for refugees. In short, many with this placement help others to protect their beliefs and culture.

Mercury in the Ninth House

This is an excellent placement for anyone involved in education, broadcasting or publishing, or any other occupation that involves 'spreading the word' in some way. The 'word' may be religious, but in secular societies it is less and less likely to be so. There is usually marked curiosity about other cultures and a huge curiosity concerning the big questions in life. Questions such as 'Who or what is God?' and 'What is right and wrong?' can be central to the individual. It is not a judgemental placement, quite the reverse – it is a questioning one.

Venus in the Ninth House

Relationships with people from other cultures are the norm with this placement. Some will attract this by virtue of being foreign themselves. Others will be attracted to those who live overseas. Lovers may be met on long journeys. Often there will be congenial relationships with in-laws. 'Diplomacy overseas' might be a key phrase and this is an ideal placement for anyone working in the diplomatic corps or working to bring people together who come from different religious or cultural perspectives. In educational matters, the sign placement will give more detail, but the individual will usually be drawn to the arts or human relations.

Mars in the Ninth House

At some time in the life, individuals with this placement will often be called upon to fight for their beliefs. This is an ideal placement for any kind of crusader. In matters of belief and education, this person doesn't believe in being passive. They will argue the toss at university and get impatient with religious, philosophical or moral teachings which seem, to them, to have outlived their usefulness. There is a strong urge to discover meaning in life and an impatience with anything that is too fusty and conventional. Mars in the Ninth can imply fighting with or against God and religion, or fighting *for* God. There may be an involvement with religions that have had to fight their corner or which have militancy built into their persona. Sikhism might be an example, as might the Salvation Army. In matters of travel, this is an adventurous individual. It is ideal for the camper, backpacker or Scout leader. Lying on a beach in Benidorm doesn't do it for those with Mars in the Ninth. Sexual adventures with foreigners or while overseas are also possible.

Jupiter in the Ninth House

Jupiter in its own house suggests a love of exploration and a life in which travel and education play a major role. This guru-prone individual tends to reach out to others and to reach out for meaning. Many will feel at home with the notion that the world is a global village. A life that involves questing and searching is to be expected. If ever at the receiving end of judicial decisions, those with Jupiter here will tend to come off advantageously. Many themselves will take on the role of judge in some way in their lives. Moralizing can be a feature for some but with others the inner image of a generous and liberal God will encourage a charitable, if potentially patronizing, view of most situations.

Saturn in the Ninth House

Some with this placement will have been brought up with a strict morality or religion. Whatever the circumstance, there will often be a tendency to see God (or at least, the Church) as punitive and strict. The individual with this placement may be quite strict themselves and have their own, quite tight, morality. Many with this placement have a strong conscience and can be frightened of doing something wrong. This is a person who has to find out about God for themselves and, if not God, then what constitutes right and wrong. This is a good placement for those who work in the law or politics. This is also a placement to associate with the teacher or preacher, and sometimes the eternal student or even the degree- or certificate-collector. Nevertheless, many will come late to higher education and may have been denied such opportunities when young. Potentially there is a fear of exploring, whether physically (as in travel) or intellectually but, as with other Saturn placements, over time the individual can become an authority in the very areas that hitherto had seemed so difficult.

Uranus in the Ninth House

This person might believe that individuals should be free to go wherever they want in the world and free to worship whichever god (or none) they want. Education might be seen as the great liberator and there might be strong, radical views on educational matters. A strong philosophy of truth can be expected, and a strong urge to bring the concept of truth together with that of faith. Frequently there will have been a break from the religious framework or moral code in which the person was raised. This can be seen as a way for the person to assert their independence from their family or even their culture. A preference for New Age subjects such as astrology may be indicated. Extreme political views are also possible with this placement. Unexpected journeys to exciting places may be favoured.

Neptune in the Ninth House

Neptune here is useful for the mystic and spiritual quester and also for the criminal! Activities concerned with drugs and alcohol in higher education are quite likely, for instance. Individuals with this placement are often very open to matters of 'right' and 'wrong' and some come to believe that these concepts are relative to the point of meaninglessness. The inner image of God tends to be forgiving rather than punitive.

Music can be the means for discovering, as well as expressing, their beliefs. There is a strong need to merge with something much more wondrous than that usually provided by everyday life, and some with this placement will be drawn to various mystical and religious lifestyles. Or to merely escaping overseas whenever it is possible to do so. Cruises may be particularly favoured with Neptune here. There can also be tremendous political idealism and a willingness to sacrifice themselves for their beliefs, whether these are religious, political or philosophical in nature. Some people may be overly idealistic and find themselves disappointed to discover that humans they have believed in, and to whom they have even devoted their lives, also have feet of clay.

Pluto in the Ninth House

The issues of survival and God often go together with this placement. For some, Pluto in the Ninth can be indicative of the deepest religious beliefs but, for others, it may describe a conviction that they have to eliminate 'all this God stuff' (in the words of one client) if they are to survive sensibly in the world. For most with this placement, there is a dislike of hypocrisy and a feeling that they must root it out. Those who go into, or become involved with, higher education are often drawn to archaeology or other subjects revolving around pre-history. This is also an excellent placement for those involved in psychology, research and anything of an investigative nature. Travel may be to places that have seen trauma in the past, perhaps due to nuclear fall-out or to volcanic eruption. Strong convictions are often held by those with this placement and some may be persecuted for their beliefs. Individuals who suffered at the hands of McCarthyism in the USA in the 1950s would be a good example. Persecution can also come about because of their culture. Those with Pluto in the Ninth may know something first-hand about racism, for instance.

The Tenth House and the MC

With most house systems, other than Equal, the Midheaven or MC marks the beginning of the Tenth House. The Medium Coeli (MC) translates from Latin as the 'upper heaven'. (See the opening paragraphs for discussion concerning the placing of the MC/IC axis in the Equal house system.)

The Tenth House and Midheaven describe our **aims** and **ambitions**. Whereas the metaphor of a tree's roots is appropriate for the opposite points of the IC and Fourth House, with the Tenth we are dealing with the top of the tree and with the area of fruit and foliage. This is the part of the chart that describes **what we aspire towards** ('aspire': to breathe towards). It may take a while to get there, but it is the direction in which we want to head. Thus, the Tenth/Fourth axis has a future/past orientation to it, rather as the Sun (future) and Moon (past) also do. The notion of aspiration is a valid one because the Tenth will often describe our **career** or **vocation** (the word 'vocation' literally means 'calling'). Certainly it will say something about the way we go about getting ourselves to where we want to be. As with the Ascendant, the MC/Tenth House must be viewed in terms of a complex (e.g. the sign and planets in that part of the chart, aspects and the ruling planets by sign, house and aspect). The whole complex will usually describe much about our profession (though the whole chart must be taken into account; one house is not large enough in scope to cover such a large area of life fully) but, more than that, it seems to show the way we live out **professional or public roles** and the way we get into them in the first place.

This area of the chart describes that for which we would like to be held in esteem, remembered, respected; what might be the summit of our contribution to the world. It also describes how we go about earning that respect. This in turn is linked to the ways in which we may seek to impress the world. And the manner and style we may adopt in order to impress others, in turn, says much about what impresses us. So, consider for a moment – what sort of person impresses you? Imagine you are at a party where you know very few people. A stranger starts chatting to you and asks the question 'What do you do?' The question is not merely about work (Sixth House); the question is loaded, for the answer you may give will be taken as an indicator of **prestige**, **rank**, **status** and **your role in society**. The answer you would like to give says something about **what impresses you**. So the Tenth says how we want the world to see us; **how we are in public**. The Midheaven as the highest point in the chart has much to say about our reputation because it describes us at our most elevated. Indeed, the planet closest to the Midheaven is known as the most elevated planet. In the opposite house (the Fourth), we are at our most private, hidden from view and in our old clothes, but here in the Tenth we are dressed up and on show. We are at our most professional and public.

The first people we ever sought to impress would have been **parental figures** and this house will describe both mother and father, albeit in different ways. It will describe the ambitions that one or both parents may have had for themselves (successfully lived out or not, conscious or not) and may have had for us. Very often, at least one parent will have pursued a career or been out in the world all day – this will be our experience of that person and the public's experience of that person. If you had a parent who was in the police, for example, you might have Pluto placed in this part of the chart. And then there is the parent who you were most seen in public with; the parent who told you about the big wide world and how to navigate yourself in it. He or she may have told you that the world is an exciting place or that it is hard or easy or scary. The possibilities are endless and the messages would have been implicit, rather than explicitly conveyed. The parental messages can be complicated but they will be there; this house has much to say about social conditioning.

The Tenth describes more than parents – it describes all **authority figures** in our lives and ourselves in the role of authority figure. So it will describe not only your boss but you in role of employer as opposed to employee (the Sixth House embraces employees). Once again, parental relationships are implied, for we have a strong tendency to extend our image of early authority figures on to the world at large. So in thinking that the Tenth describes your boss, remember it is more accurately describing what you project on to your boss. Similarly, the Tenth will describe what society and the world at large may project on to us. For instance, Diana, Princess of Wales, had Neptune in this house and was viewed by the public variously as a princess, a saint, a saviour, a victim and simply a glamorous woman. The Tenth will not only describe what society projects on to us but will also describe how we actually help to shape society. Diana, for instance, may have increased the feelings of compassion in society by being seen to draw attention to suffering and loss.

Sun in the Tenth House

Often denotes success and recognition in the person's field. People with the Sun here are often very ambitious, not only for success generally but sometimes for fame itself. And fame (or notoriety, depending on the sign and aspects to the Sun) is possible with this placement. The individual will tend to identify with the role they play out in the world at large; their career is what gives them a sense of 'I'. Being overly identified with their position in the world or career can be difficult if circumstances dictate that that position in society gets tarnished or lost, or quite simply they are made redundant. Often at least one of the parents was successful in worldly terms. Women with the Sun here need to ensure that they live out their ambitions for themselves wherever possible, as some with this placement will merely push men to the top. For both sexes, being the boss – the monarch of all we survey – feels much more comfortable than being in the role of employee.

Moon in the Tenth House

The Moon here can say that a person's true vocation is that of being a mother or that they seek to be publicly recognized for their nurturing and caring qualities. Sometimes the Moon in the Tenth can describe the person as being a professional mother, as in a carer in an orphanage, for example. Taking on the role of mother in the office, as in providing the shoulder that everyone cries on, could be another manifestation. And even where this is not the case, usually the career requires what might be called housekeeping skills. People with the Moon here are often particularly sensitive to their public reputations; any criticism can be felt rather as if a parent is disapproving of them. The sensitivity to the public can manifest in other ways, too; for instance, it can emerge as a sensitivity to the public's needs or to being able to respond well to an audience. Sometimes the circumstances of the public or vocational life fluctuate a good deal, especially if the Moon is placed in a mutable sign.

Mercury in the Tenth House

Usually denotes a career which involves an above-average degree of communicative activities: reading, writing, talking or driving. Some degree of public speaking is also possible at some point in the life. All forms of telecommunications, commerce, negotiation, transport and administration come within the seemingly endless vocational possibilities of this placement. This person will usually be ambitious to learn and happy to pursue whichever educational activities might be required to equip them for their trade. Often a chatty, curious, communicative or intellectual parent is indicated. Sometimes Mercury in the Tenth denotes a sibling who is renowned for their own communicative skills.

Venus in the Tenth House

Vocational activities involving the arts or beauty industries can be described by Venus here, as can a career utilizing diplomatic skills. More characteristically still, Venus here says that this person is keen to look good when in the public arena. This can mean looking good as in being viewed by the world as 'nice', or it can mean looking good, as in being attractive to look at. This is not someone who swears in public or goes out without thinking about what they are wearing. This person charms their way to the top. Sometimes a Tenth House Venus denotes a marriage for money or status, and frequently the activities of marriage and career are closely intertwined. Parental figures can manifest all the usual Venusian qualities; those of being lovable, sociable, pliable or just downright vain, to list only a few of the possibilities.

Mars in the Tenth House

Mars in the Tenth confers strength, ambition and usually denotes the individual having a career which involves fighting their way to the top or at least struggling to keep their head above the parapet. It may describe a career involving metals, heat (e.g. the welder, firefighter, mechanic, surgeon or butcher) or a profession that involves speed, daring, courage or danger. A career in the forces is another possibility as combat is a keyword. As a boss, those with Mars in the Tenth may lack the gentle touch; as an employee, the potential for clashes with the boss is high. Whatever the vocation, there is often a sub-text in the life that involves competing with an early parental figure and that situation can be extended into the professional arena. Mars here can also sometimes suggest fame or notoriety for the person's sexual prowess. Sexual attractiveness can be part of the picture of one or both parents, too.

Jupiter in the Tenth House

This will often denote lucky opportunities in vocational activities and success in one field. Frequently, those with Jupiter here want to do something big. Thus, it is helpful that people in authority tend to smile benevolently on those with Jupiter in the Tenth. This is particularly obvious in early life, when a young person may be viewed as being morally upstanding or ethical in some way. Playing God may be a facet of the chosen vocation and this applies to careers involving teaching, preaching, broadcasting and anything else where the person gives advice to others. One of the parents may have had a tendency towards social-climbing. An hysterical, over-the-top parent can also be indicated with this placement.

Saturn in the Tenth House

This denotes one who has a responsible attitude to their vocational activities. A feeling that they must achieve, must be respected, must be taken seriously can also go with the territory. Some people project the image of a strict parent on to the world at large, and thus feel that the world is watching them and ready to chastise them if they do something wrong. Sometimes a parent felt a failure in their career and the individual feels the burden of carrying out an unlived ambition. Sometimes the story involves a very successful parent in worldly terms, in which case the individual can feel pressured into living up to their parent's ambitions. The choice of career may come late and these people are often late developers. This can be because they are frightened to experiment with different types of work. The choices then can feel limited because it is through experimentation that we find out what is possible. A career involving structure, rules, regulations, time or the imposing of boundaries is implied. As with Saturn in the Sixth, anything from train driver or architect to leader of the country is possible. This placement can indicate hard, sometimes back-breaking work. Sometimes it accords with a vocation concerned with the elderly. Sometimes the job involves taking on huge responsibilities, and sometimes Saturn in the Tenth seems to limit or delay the prospects of promotion. Certainly those with Saturn here will achieve precisely according to their ability: luck will have nothing to do with it.

Uranus in the Tenth House

Uranus in the Tenth is ideal for vocational activities which involve technology, scientific apparatus and gadgetry, or for situations in which the individual is involved in an activity that is in some way anti-Establishment, progressive or offbeat. Some with Uranus in the Tenth will become known for their inventions, their genius or the innovative qualities that they bring to bear on situations. All need a vocation where they can act independently and many will feel much more comfortable being self-employed than when working in a large corporation. In more traditional set-ups, a feeling of rebellion against a bullying parent is sometimes repeated with the person's boss.

Neptune in the Tenth House

A career that involves rescuing others in some way, or in the arts, media or advertising, is very likely. Many fantasize about being in various public roles and are thus open to so many possibilities that it takes them some time to settle on a suitable vocation. The need to be idolized by the public can mean that many with this placement are seduced by the notion of being a celebrity or, if that is not possible, they can be addicted to following the lives of those who do have celebrity status. Others will get themselves into situations where people feel sorry for them. Often the individual feels pity for a parental figure; the mother may be viewed as a victim, for example, perhaps having sacrificed an artistic career to become a mother. And the desire to rescue Mum can be extended to the world at large.

Pluto in the Tenth House

Careers in refuse, sewage, psychology, undertaking, medicine, nuclear power and research are just some of the possibilities with Pluto in the Tenth. There can be a fear of being dominated by those in authority. Often this arises because of the experience of a dominating parent or some other threatening and scary authority figure in early life. For some, this can contribute to viewing the big wide world itself as a scary place and thus a vocation may be chosen in which the individual can hide from more public scrutiny. As always, where we find Pluto is where we can persecute or be persecuted, so some with Pluto here will gravitate to positions of power where they can feel invincible, while others may be merely crushed by the system. Sabotaging the boss, or being sabotaged by the boss (or by the public, if the person is famous), is a distinct theme. There is a likelihood of being made redundant at least once in the working life.

The Eleventh House

Traditionally the Eleventh House is associated with **friends, groups, hopes** and **wishes**. What we did in the Tenth we did for ourselves, for status, possibly in pursuit of a position in society, perhaps to live out the ambitions of our parents, whether or not these were realized or consciously understood. Basically, what we do in the Tenth (arguably) we do for self-aggrandizement but in the Eleventh House we can start thinking a bit about society. We have got our career together in the Tenth, so now we can go out and have a good time with friends, and we can join the Rotary Club, the Women's Institute, lend our support to an environmental group, hitch up to a protest group or join a band of musicians. Whether Freemason or in a group of gardeners, we can both be with friends and be concerned with progressing society in some way. In the Tenth House, we achieved some kind of position in society, perhaps even reached a position of authority, but in the Eleventh we can use that authority for some kind of social cause.

There is a **political flavour** to the Eleventh. In the opposite house (the Fifth) we may make pots but in the Eleventh we find ourselves in a group of people who are making pots. We make pots with others, perhaps contribute our pots to society. All the potters will tend to have the same zeal about the subject. There is a **common purpose**, a sense of shared values, a sense of kinship. The political quality comes into it because when individuals come together for a common purpose, they want others to join in their cause or they want that cause to be available to everyone. The hopes and wishes for the future are shared by all the members of the group, with respect to the subject or cause that unites them.

Planets in the Eleventh – or its ruler(s) – will describe the types of group we are drawn to and our roles within them. The Sun may earmark us as a leader, whereas Uranus may mark us out as too independent to function well in a group. The Moon here can describe communal living as well as the idea of mothering our friends. Robert Hand, in *Horoscope Symbols*, describes Eleventh House friends as being 'people who share our ideals'. And this is very true. Friends, especially close friends, may be described elsewhere in the chart – in the Seventh House, for instance. In the Eleventh, friends are basically **people who share our ideology** and/or share our recreational activities. Above all, a keyword for the Eleventh is **fraternity**, which means a body of people who associate with each other for a common purpose or interest.

The Eleventh describes how we are when we are in a group, how we are in situations which call for **relating to more than one person**. This can include work environments sometimes, because basically the Eleventh House applies to situations where we are a **member of a team**. Thus, the Eleventh will give clues as to what kind of team player a person is. In the Eleventh we are an equal among equals; neither boss nor underling. And here we are tied to the social norms and values of our peers – this is an area in the chart to associate with peer pressure.

In the same way that the Fifth House can be associated with entertainment, so too can the Eleventh, but here the emphasis is more towards **mass entertainment** as would be the case with a national sporting event or a concert. The Eleventh is always about the 'group' – it embraces both small groups and large ones. Activities are centred on the artist in the Fifth but in the Eleventh things become decentralized.

If the Fifth is about play, remembering that play is the way in which the child learns about socializing, then one concern of the Eleventh is **play-mates**. In the Fifth House the individual (as child or adult) is concerned with being special, important and unique, but the Eleventh carries the message that no one is more special than anyone else. Planets in the Eleventh show our individual contribution both to society and to smaller groups and teams with which we affiliate ourselves.

Sun in the Eleventh House

The group or 'gang' with whom the person runs around in early life (and beyond) often provides the route for defining their identity. The individual will often be a natural leader in any group. It is a good placement for the actor who, by definition, is often a member of a company of people. The image of the hero is of the person who puts society or their friends before themselves. The Sun here will often describe a father who was frequently out with his mates (in the pub if Neptune plugs into the placement!) or a father who belonged to some kind of team. Whoever first coined the expression 'team spirit' may have had the Sun in the Eleventh, as it very much conjures up the potential of this placement.

Moon in the Eleventh House

The Moon in the Eleventh House is a strong indicator that the individual will live in some kind of communal environment at least once in their life. Instinctively, those with this placement are good at 'making families'; there is usually an awareness that a 'family' can be created out of a variety of social relationships. The person may feel at home in a group and need the support of a strong network. They may also be good at supplying that support to others. The tendency to mother and care for friends is marked and friends, in turn, may provide emotional succour. Men will particularly favour women as friends and want relationships to be underpinned by the feeling of having a pal.

Mercury in the Eleventh House

Suggesting the bringing together of people for an exchange of ideas, Mercury here is ideal for membership of a book circle or something similar. Typically, those with this placement like talking to people and sharing ideas with all and sundry. It is classic for the spokesperson of any group. Ideas will often be progressive or political; this is not someone intent on discussing solely personal matters. Siblings can sometimes be the individual's best friend or friends can provide the sibling relationships that an individual may never have had.

Venus in the Eleventh House

Close female friends may be indicated by Venus in the Eleventh, along with a strong social life generally. Sometimes, there is a need to be seen with the right people and to have beautiful friends. For women, it is a good placement for girlie nights out but there can be female rivalry with Venus here. Lovers will often be found through friends. More seriously, Venus here is ideal for bringing people together for a common cause. Those with Venus in the Eleventh House can often foster co-operation between people and help them to find points of similarity.

Mars in the Eleventh House

This is an ideal placement for anyone in a sports team. It is good too for competing with friends and, again, sporting activities would provide a healthy outlet for this. Friends may well turn into sexual partners and vice versa. And for women, Mars here also implies male friends. Mars here can describe fighting for their friends (fighting their battles for them) or fighting with their friends. For those with difficulties in asserting themselves, it can describe choosing dynamic and assertive friends. More assertive souls may simply be overly dominant and bossy with friends or in groups. Mars here isn't necessarily a good team player. On a deeper level, Mars in the Eleventh suggests the fighting of battles for the group. It is ideal for a trade unionist, for instance. Some with Mars here will find it easier to get angry if they can do so on behalf of others and if they belong to a group that is sharing and fighting a perceived injustice.

Jupiter in the Eleventh House

Jupiter here may indicate a wide-ranging social life and involvement in many different groups. Preferred groups could include religious or philosophical groups or those concerned with 'good works' and the betterment of society. Equally possible is regularly meeting up with friends on the race course or in the betting shop! Some with this placement will favour travelling in a group while others will be known as the foreigner among their friends. Some will take on the role of teacher in the teams they find themselves in, and nearly all will benefit from having upright and generous friends. This placement usually describes the good fortune of having friends in high places. Being seen to be with the right crowd can be important to some with this placement.

Saturn in the Eleventh House

At times in their life, the individual may limit their friends and social contacts (e.g. when depressed). In earlier life especially, there can be a fear of not fitting into their peer group. Age gaps between the person and their friends are implied with this position. For a variety of different reasons, many with Saturn here have to learn to be more spontaneous with their friends and in groups. The blessing and the curse with Saturn here is of taking it all so seriously. Many with this placement will take responsibility in groups, perhaps by generally keeping the paperwork efficiently organized and ensuring that some kind of structure is set and maintained (it is an ideal placement for a company secretary), and this provides a feeling of safety and usefulness in the group.

Uranus in the Eleventh House

Individuals with Uranus here will not usually be drawn to mainstream groups, although they may be drawn to more radical political or New Age groups. While those with Uranus here often believe that it is important to break down the barriers that separate people, they may not have the appetite for all the compromising that is necessary to arrive at group consensus. Depending on the chart overall, they may not find it easy to toe the line or smooth over the cracks which inevitably arise when people come together. Uranus in the Eleventh can sometimes operate too independently to function well as part of a team. Nevertheless, many with Uranus here, in its own house, have an awareness of the notion of one world and can unite with others in pursuit of forwarding humanitarian, progressive or other ideals. Many with Uranus here will be attracted to more eccentric people or to those who are outsiders in some way.

Neptune in the Eleventh House

This placement implies the merging, indeed the losing, of the individual into some kind of group. This can be a band of musicians or an altruistic or spiritual group to which the individual belongs. Membership of the group can imply personal loss or sacrifice but also a feeling of being at one with something larger than themselves. Neptune here can indicate someone who is genuinely accepting of people from a wide variety of backgrounds. The openness and non-judgemental quality of Neptune in this house can give rise to tremendous idealism and a rare ability to be at one with others in friendships and in groups, but also sometimes to gullibility and deception. Getting in with the wrong crowd, and being deceived or duped by friends, can be more difficult manifestations.

Pluto in the Eleventh House

Some people with Pluto in the Eleventh may feel uncomfortable in a group; sometimes this is because they are more than usually aware of the negative, destroying energies that can arise in groups and, especially, in crowds. Equally, they can be aware of the good that can be done by a group of people with one voice, and some with Pluto here will display extraordinary zeal and commitment to a larger cause. Survival can be an issue here; either the individual belongs to a group which contributes greatly to their well-being or they feel that a group demands so much of them that their very survival is at stake. Some may sit on a variety of committees but will eschew power and the limelight, happy to get involved with doing the more lowly jobs for the team. Others will take on the mantle of power. As always, the whole chart has to be studied. Few but intense and complex friendships are implied, and the death or removal of friends can affect those with Pluto here very deeply.

The Twelfth House

'The opposition occupies the benches in front of you, but the enemy sits behind you.'
Sir Winston Churchill

As the house behind the First, this house has a strong **behind-the-scenes** quality. People who have packed Twelfth Houses often spend much of their lives in a behind-the-scenes capacity. Examples of this can include the person who works behind the scenes at the TV studio, such as the lighting person or costume designer. It may be the person who spends time in museums or libraries or other places where they don't have a voice themselves, but where they feed those who do have a voice. Activities in this house are often secret, or at least hidden from public view.

Opposite to the Sixth House, the Twelfth is also concerned with the notion of service, but here the service is of a less practical or mundane variety than its Sixth House counterpart. In the Twelfth the **service is free of rewards**. In the Sixth House, we pay what the astrologer Lindsay Radermacher terms 'the rent for life'. In the Twelfth we may be paying the rent for past lives. Many people associate this region of the horoscope with the notion of **karma**, interpreting it as being concerned with the paying of debts from previous incarnations.

Twelfth House matters are usually reckoned to be outside our control – they are certainly usually outside our easy, conscious realization. This house is known as the house of **self-undoing** or **bondage**, basically because this house shows **our hidden weaknesses** – qualities that we may have learned, possibly during our upbringing, are unacceptable. Paradoxically, our **hidden strengths** can also be found in this area of the chart. Qualities described by the planets in (and rulers of) this house will show not only **what we may hide from others, but what we also hide from ourselves**. And this is about the worst thing we can do with Twelfth House energies, which are really only a problem if we reject them. The house is supposed to be the house of **secret enemies** but the biggest enemy is always the unacknowledged aspects of ourselves. Unacknowledged aspects of ourselves always come to greet us in a projected form, and this is what is meant by the notion of secret enemies. An example might help. Mars in the Twelfth may suggest that the individual picked up clues in childhood that they shouldn't get angry, be overly competitive or be selfish. In adult life, asserting themselves in a straightforward manner might therefore be difficult. If there is an experience (which there needn't be) of a secret enemy, then it would be of someone – probably a man – attacking them from behind. This placement, however, suggests great inner strength and has the potential for a true understanding of Mars's energy. Research by Michel and Françoise Gauquelin has shown that this position occurs frequently in people who compete with themselves and with others – sportsmen and sportswomen at the top of their game. As always, anger can act as tremendous fuel. The research of the Gauquelins is interesting because it shows that planets in the Twelfth are strong indicators of both personality and subsequent profession. This is not a weak house.

The house embraces **institutions** where the individual is rendered powerless and removed from the maelstrom of everyday life. **Hospitals**, particularly psychiatric hospitals, and **prisons** belong in this part of the chart; when people are inmates in such places they are, at least to some extent, stripped of their individuality. Often they are 'put away' because they are viewed, rightly or wrongly, as being an enemy of the State. It may not be expressed that way but it is difficult to avoid coming to that conclusion. Sometimes the individual cannot even keep control of their personal clothing and will often be dealt with merely as a number or a case. They are disenfranchized from society. Traditionally, **slavery** belongs in this house and it is easy to see why, for the slave is also rendered powerless. Undoubtedly, this can be a house where the ego is meant to count for very little. Energies here are not necessarily denied expression, and neither are they necessarily difficult; the issue is more that they cannot be used so personally or selfishly. Energies here are sacrificed to the collective and often seem to be quite outside the individual's conscious control.

Planets in the Twelfth do not necessarily indicate namelessness, anonymity or obscurity. Consider the fact that Tony Blair, Margaret Thatcher (in some house systems), Henry Kissinger and many other world leaders have their Sun positioned here. This becomes more understandable when we realize that, in leading so public a life, the individual has to **sacrifice** a great deal of their personal life. Also, even though as leaders they may seem to be pulling the strings, the reality is that world leaders are like puppets; they are pulled hither and thither by circumstances much larger than they can possibly control. Additionally, by sending soldiers to the Falkland Islands, Margaret Thatcher was more or less saying to those soldiers, 'Be prepared to sacrifice your own lives.' Another way of thinking about this solar placement is to remember that the Twelfth is basically an area of **seclusion**. With the Sun placed here, there is a *spotlight* on the person's seclusion, so the individual is essentially denied their privacy.

We often feel vaguely **guilty** about the energies to be found in the Twelfth House (or, if untenanted, the sign on the Twelfth House cusp) and may be frightened of being found out. (Using this analogy, those with Sun in the Twelfth may feel guilty about being egocentric, seeking 'strokes' or needing recognition.) Whatever the nature of the planetary energy, becoming released from the guilt necessitates some kind of self-sacrifice.

In the Twelfth we have to surrender the energies of the planet placed there. If we do this willingly and consciously, doing so feels less like loss and more like spiritual advancement. As Tracy Marks reminds us in her excellent book, *Your Secret Soul*, the Twelfth is the **house of confinement**. This can be an involuntary event, such as being sent to prison or hospital, or it can be a voluntary decision, such as deciding to work in a hospital or prison. Or it can be devoting our energies to good works or maybe joining a monastery, convent or ashram. Above all else, the Twelfth is the house of sacrifice and indeed of **charity**; whether we view this house positively or not rather depends on how open we are to the notion of genuinely giving selflessly.

Sun in the Twelfth House

The giving of the self to the collective is the theme with this placement. While many may take on the role of being the power behind the throne, it should be noted (see above) that many world leaders were born with the Sun in the Twelfth House. However, being a leader in this way implies the sacrificing of at least certain aspects of their personal life; it implies giving themselves away. Others will work behind the scenes with this placement; the lighting engineer at the TV company would be a good example. Frequently there is a history of feeling overlooked, especially by the father. Often the individual is unaware of their need for acknowledgement and recognition, so the secret enemy can be their hidden ego. The secret enemy can be that inner voice which says that no one is going to see you, you are going to be overlooked, so either decide to stay behind the scenes or go all-out to be noticed. Some with this placement feel at their most alive during twilight hours.

Moon in the Twelfth House

The secret here is often how needy the individual feels. There can often be something of the 'trapped child' about this placement. Some will have had a mother who was hospitalized and the child will thus have learned to be self-reliant. Some will themselves have been hospitalized at a young age and may have felt vulnerable, lonely and unsupported as a result. I have also met people with the Moon here who have passed unhappy years in a boarding school. Some will live in an institution at some point in their lives but the Moon situated here doesn't necessarily imply that the experience will be an unhappy one, or one not consciously chosen. As always, the whole chart and the whole complex of the Moon have to be studied carefully. This placement can also describe situations where the individual takes care of and protects people who live behind the scenes (in a prison, hospital or another institution). It is also a good placement for museum curators and the like; for here the individual is caring for and protecting the particular institution.

Mercury in the Twelfth House

Often this individual is happy researching in libraries and archives. It can imply institutional learning, perhaps that the school they attended was an institution (e.g. a boarding school or children's home). In childhood, many with this placement were encouraged to keep quiet. In any event, many have learned to watch and listen and often have an ability to tap into the minds of others. There is certainly usually an interest in the motivations of others. This can be the hallmark of the person who is secretive about what they are thinking. The 'secret enemy' can be that inner voice that says 'no one will understand you, no one will listen, so you might as well shut up and talk to yourself'. This is a useful placement for those who help others to communicate or who help others to examine their motives.

Venus in the Twelfth House

Vanity is often discouraged at an early age with this placement; some people are taught to think of themselves as having missed out in the looks department. One woman I know won a scholarship to go to a prestigious school but felt very isolated because her family were poor and she believed that her clothes were vastly inferior to those of her peers. The secret with this placement can be a longing for money and for being worshipped for their beauty. While there may be an unconscious need for love and approbation from others, most with Venus positioned here also have a genuine love of peace, privacy and seclusion. The often unconscious need to be popular frequently makes those with Venus in the Twelfth behave in a markedly helpful manner.

Mars in the Twelfth House

Going for what they want in a direct manner is usually discouraged in childhood for those with this placement. Being selfish, assertive or angry will often be frowned upon. Perhaps because of this, the individual has a tendency to become victim to, or at least to encounter, Mars from the collective. Working with the mentally ill, or their carers, or with the abused is a common manifestation. One woman with this placement worked in a special educational unit with children who were too angry to fit into mainstream education. They had been sexually abused at a very young age and were discharging their rage on to whoever or whatever was available. For others, the secret can be sexual in some way. The early repression can take many forms but, whatever the story, those with Mars here have the capacity to tackle it with courage. Many will feel much better for physical exercise, whether this be some form of working out, sport or dancing.

Jupiter in the Twelfth House

This is often described as the 'guardian angel' placement because it is commonly associated with the cavalry coming over the hill just in the nick of time. But if Jupiter here affords a large amount of protection, the person often has to experience a crisis before their guardian angel comes to the rescue. Individuals are often brought up to believe they should not rely on their luck. For some, optimism, faith and sometimes religious practice is frowned upon and may be difficult to access. And having religious convictions, a faith that supports during the darkest hours, can be the secret that some with this placement carry. In a number of different ways, this placement can describe a closet gambler – a person who unconsciously pushes themselves into situations where they have to discover whether God will indeed provide. This can be a very charitable position for Jupiter and, for some, their secret is the extent to which their generosity is bestowed upon others.

Saturn in the Twelfth House

This placement has a variety of manifestations. There can be a tendency to feel responsible for all the suffering in society, for instance. Some with this placement take responsibility for the care of the mentally ill or others who are disenfranchized from society, while others simply assist those who are in need of a helping hand. Some will view others as being lonely and depressed, and the real secret (a secret they may even keep from themselves) can be their own feelings of isolation. There will often be a fear of chaos, of merging with another, of losing themselves, or of losing control, as in mental illness. However, as always with Saturn, the individual can, through time and personal experience, become expert in these areas. I have also known situations where there were few overt boundaries and rules set in childhood but the child was sensitive to covert 'oughts' and 'shoulds' floating around in the atmosphere. There is often quite a bit of free-floating guilt flying around with this placement. In those cases, some individuals find it difficult to enforce boundaries and seize their own authority. In other cases, the opposite is true; this can be an especially controlling placement for the reason that the individual is trying to keep chaos at bay. It is not necessarily conscious, but the father often pulls the individual's psychological strings, even if, as is often the case with this placement, he was missing or very much 'behind the scenes'.

Uranus in the Twelfth House

This placement is associated with an individual who was taught by their parents or by society to be conventional and to generally 'fit in'. So they tend to seem pretty conventional in public, but in private they can be much more radical in their views and much more unconventional in their behaviour. The closet can hold all sorts of unexpected secrets for those with Uranus in the Twelfth. The secret here may be that the individual is unconsciously in opposition to things to which they appear to acquiesce. Uranus here often equates to situations in which the person wants to be free and independent but feels trapped. This can be, for instance, the individual who complains of feeling trapped in their job or marriage yet won't make the changes necessary to become free. So they stay in the situation but do so while breathing the fire of rebellion inside.

Neptune in the Twelfth House

Individuals with Neptune here, in its own house, can be so open to what happens around them that this placement can give rise to the greatest insight and understanding or to considerable confusion. On the plus side, Neptune in the Twelfth contributes to a capacity to mirror everyone, but boundaries between the self and others can be very weak. There might be very little to prevent this individual plugging into all the suffering in the world, for instance, and many with this placement will have enormous compassion for society's victims. This can propel some into the role of saviour while others will simply wish to retreat from the maelstrom of a hard-nosed society. There can be strong escapist tendencies with Neptune here and sometimes an extraordinarily strong dream life.

Pluto in the Twelfth House

Some with Pluto in the Twelfth will be very attuned to all the pain and suffering in the world, and so can easily take a cynical view of even those things that are more obviously life-enhancing. Like a psychic refuse bin, some with Pluto here simply absorb all the negativity around them; all the unexpressed grief and fears that others conceal behind a happy face, and all the hidden reasons that are disguised by ulterior motives. A suspicion that their own life, or the life of others, is at stake in quite ordinary, everyday situations can make for a secret enemy that is plain paranoid, subversive or sabotaging. More positively, individuals with Pluto here rarely shrink from the true realities of life and often have a deep understanding of human motivation. Probing the mysteries of life and death will often form the backdrop to everything this person does. It is a common placement for those concerned with psychology, death or the occult.

The Importance of House Rulership

There is always a relationship between the house in which a planet is found and the house(s) that the planet rules. For example, imagine a person has the planet that rules their Fourth House situated in their Ninth House; this would suggest that the person would live (Fourth) abroad (Ninth) for at least part of their life. On its own this statement is a bit weak; as always, if something is true it will be written several times in the horoscope (what I think of as a three-legged stool), so imagine that the person also has the ruler of the Ninth House in their Fourth and maybe the Moon is in Sagittarius, too. In this case, the idea of living overseas is written three times and the astrologer can confidently predict that this would be a facet of this person's life. *This* is a three-legged stool!

House Rulership Examples

• The ruler of the Seventh House in the Ninth House could suggest marriage to a foreigner or relationships with people who are going to teach you about different cultures and beliefs.

• Ruler of the Tenth in the Seventh could suggest professional activities in partnership with a spouse, or that parental issues will be particularly evident in close relationships.
• Ruler of the Seventh in the Tenth might mean that the person's marriage or relationship is their 'career', or it could describe the meeting of their partner through professional activities.
• Ruler of the Second in the Fifth could translate as gaining money through the arts or possibly through children, or the person spending their money on their children.
• Ruler of the Sixth in the Third could suggest work of a secretarial or communicative nature, or possibly in transport.
• Ruler of the Sixth in the Ninth could suggest a job overseas or in education, law or religion.

The sign on the cusp of a house makes a general statement, while the house position of its ruler always gives more factual information and shows the direction in which the story goes. When embracing the signs involved, more detailed interpretation can follow. Imagine a woman has Pluto in the Eleventh House and Scorpio on her Third House cusp (so the ruler of the Third is in the Eleventh). This might suggest that she tends to be rather suspicious of groups and that she doesn't approach friendship in a superficial way (Pluto in the Eleventh). Possibly she felt betrayed (Pluto) by the friends (Eleventh) of her siblings (Third) at some point. Whatever the scenario, a good place for making friends or getting involved in group activities (Eleventh) might be through school (Third) or, later in life, through evening classes. The preferred areas of study might include genealogy, psychology, archaeology or occult subjects. For this woman, knowledge is power, and although it could be the case that some kind of educational situation fostered the suspicion of group situations in the first place, the greater knowledge and understanding gained through a classroom environment might offer an opportunity for transforming negative feelings.

Chapter 7

Non-Essential Bodies

This chapter touches on some of the myriad celestial bodies that can be included in the horoscope besides the planets. Since there are so many minor planets, for instance, students are strongly advised to get a thorough understanding of the horoscope basics – the planets, signs, houses and aspects – before venturing further afield. This is not to say that these other bodies are irrelevant, but what is known about them is at best limited and what they do describe is usually something very specific and small. Concentrating on the minor asteroids would, for example, be analogous to hunting for a dropped pin and ignoring the fact that the house is on fire.

Of all the non-planetary bodies that can be included in the horoscope, the two most commonly included by UK astrologers are the Moon's Nodes and Chiron, although various asteroids are also often included by astrologers in many European countries.

The message of the Moon's Nodes tends to manifest inwardly rather than outwardly. This, coupled with the fact that their meaning is so often described elsewhere, is one of the reasons why the beginner student, at least, should set their consideration of the Moon's Nodes aside until the rest of the horoscope has revealed some of its secrets.

Chiron's nature seems to be connected with the avoidance of mainstream classification, so much so that trying to arrive at hard and fast rules of how it will manifest in a chart doesn't seem to work all that well. The best advice might be to place Chiron in its appropriate position in the horoscope and simply to listen to the person who has it as they speak.

When placing the Moon's Nodes or Chiron in the horoscope, my advice would be to note the aspects to these bodies but not to draw in the aspect lines. This is simply because one wants to keep the chart as free of clutter as possible; that way the essentials can be more quickly located. For the same reason, if asteroids are included, they are probably better listed on the side of the chart rather than actually in it.

Part One: The Moon's Nodes

Known also as the Dragon's Head and Dragon's Tail, the precise meaning and importance of the Moon's Nodes is a matter of some debate in Western astrology. However, the axis has always been accorded tremendous significance in the Vedic system, where the North and South Node, named Rahu and Ketu respectively in Sanskrit, are given the status of planets.[1]

The Moon's Nodes are the points of intersection where the plane of the Earth's orbit around the Sun crosses the plane of the Moon's orbit around the Earth. Since the Moon's orbit has an inclination of 5 degrees 9 minutes to the plane of the ecliptic, there are two nodes in the Moon's orbit around the Earth. The point where the Moon in its orbit crosses from the south of the ecliptic plane to the north is called the ascending or North Node, and the point where it crosses from north to south is called the descending or South Node.

The sometimes fatalistic way of viewing the Nodes is due to the fact that eclipses can only ever occur on the nodal path, when the Sun, Moon and Earth are in a particular alignment. If the Sun and Moon are within 17 degrees of one of the Nodes then the New Moon will be a solar eclipse. A Full Moon is a lunar eclipse if it occurs within about 11 degrees of one of the Nodes. If either a New or Full Moon is within 5 degrees of the Nodes, there is a total eclipse.

- Cycle: 18.6 years regressing backwards (westwards) along the ecliptic.
- Approximately 18 months in each zodiac sign and moving at 3 minutes of arc a day and 1 degree 40 minutes a month.

Mean Versus True Nodes

As the Nodes precess, the complex gravitational interactions of the Moon and the Earth cause variations from the average or 'mean' value of the Nodes' motion. The position of the 'true' Node can vary by nearly 2 degrees from that of the 'mean' Node. And whereas the mean Node is always retrograde, the 'true' Node can also be seen to be stationary and in forward motion. It is a matter of some debate among astrologers as to which Node – true or mean – should be used. The mean Node has been employed for centuries and it is only comparatively recently that technology has enabled the 'true' Node to be plotted. There is also some debate as to whether, astronomically speaking, the true Node really is true.

Interpretation

Intersection points or nodes – where orbits meet – are always important in astrology (for example, the Ascendant and Midheaven are both intersection points) and are often associated in interpretation with the **principle of relationship** or at least with 'connection' either to groups of people or individuals.

To get a feeling for the meaning of the Nodes, imagine going out with some plan in mind and then unexpectedly bumping into someone (perhaps someone you haven't seen for 19 years) who is following their own particular path. The meeting may herald a change of direction for you. The conversation you have with each other could do that. There might be a **feeling of fate** about the fact that your paths have crossed. And literally, when you each move off, you are going north or south in reference to each other. Of course, this is not really an accurate analogy. At the place where the Moon's Nodes meet, there is nothing actually there, and it is not precisely the same as two people meeting. More accurately, it takes on the qualitative feeling of the film *Sliding Doors*. Each Node has stood in the same spot previously. The Earth has been there and will be again, and the Moon has been there and will be again. Hence the connotation of past and future with the Nodes; there is a **remembrance of a meeting and an expectation of another one in the future**. This could be a description of the notion of fate and it is little wonder that Nodes have been associated with the idea of karma and past lives. The sometimes fatalistic way of viewing the Nodes is also due to the fact that eclipses can only occur on the nodal path.

The word 'node' comes from the Latin *nodus* meaning 'knot'. In medicine, the word 'node' is sometimes used to describe a discrete mass of one kind of tissue enclosed in the tissue of a different kind. Two worlds are colliding, so to speak, in the body. In horticulture, a node is a point on a stem at which a leaf or leaves grow.

We talk about a knot in a piece of wood. In various contexts we use the word 'knot' to describe entanglement or complication, and that is probably an essential clue to the meaning of the Nodes. Reinhold Ebertin in *The Combination of Stellar Influences* makes no distinction between the North and South Node, but sees the nodal axis as being concerned with the principle of association. Certainly, this accords with my own experience and with the idea of a knot or entanglement. Indeed, a node is a place where things join. Thus, keywords for the axis might include **association**, **joining**, **entanglement, connection, meeting, remembrance**. Tight nodal contacts (or contacts to the nodal rulers) are very common in synastry and time after time one finds that transits to or from the Nodes describe whom one is interacting with, and in what way. For example, you may have transiting Node conjunct your natal Neptune and this might be the time when you mix with a group of musicians, mystics or alcoholics, and so forth.

More traditionally, the South Node is thought to describe the **areas of life which we may cling to**. And we cling because the South Node represents familiar territory and an area of life in which we have some experience. It is experience gained from our family, our upbringing, our heredity or from our past lives, depending on one's world view. Few would argue that it is easier to cope with and stay with whatever we are accustomed to, and so we can **get stuck** here. When cornered we may run back to this area. Describing what we have already taken in and **digested**, the material described at the South Node should be released or given back. When we remember that the South Node is the Dragon's Tail, the idea of evacuation is an easy one for us to grapple with.

The North Node is thought to describe territory which is largely unknown to us. We are able to do those things described by our North Node but doing so may require considerable effort. When we find ourselves in **unfamiliar territory** we need to be more alert, more conscious in order to negotiate our way through – we need to use our head. Thus, the North Node embodies the notion of **challenge** and higher development, an **area of potential** for us. It is the ascending Node (moving from south to north) so it is little wonder that it has become associated with the notion of 'going up', whether we view the idea of going up in the world from a material, social or spiritual perspective. Undoubtedly, the nodal axis has always been viewed as a spiritual axis and the idea of ascension conjures up the notion of becoming closer to God. The South Node, on the other hand, is descending and, being termed the Dragon's Tail, there is immediately an implication of something baser and more instinctual here. The Head implies the potential for conscious thought and decision-making whereas a Tail, without the benefit of the five senses and especially the eyes, will act instinctively.

Whatever the exact meaning of the nodal axis, the meaning of the Nodes is rarely obvious in worldly terms and this is because they are principally concerned with inner experience, perhaps indeed with our spiritual journey. The exception to this solely interior quality occurs when there are tight hard aspects, and in particular conjunctions, to one of the Nodes. These do sometimes yield obvious external manifestations in worldly terms. Certainly they describe the individuals and groups we are closely linked with. Many astrologers, for example, have tight aspects from Uranus (the planet of astrology) to the nodal axis in their natal chart.

Whether the manifestation is inward or outward, my own experience suggests that the Moon's Nodes will often encapsulate or summarize much of the essence of the chart as a whole. When attempting to understand the Nodes, it is essential that emphasis be placed on the nodal rulers. To view the Nodes merely by sign and house will almost always be misleading.

Part Two: Chiron and the Centaurs
Co-written with Melanie Reinhart

I was thrilled when Melanie agreed to contribute material on the Centaurs. Most of what follows is her work, and that on Pholus and Nessus entirely so. For the sake of brevity, some of her original text has had to be edited. Go to her website www.melaniereinhart.com to keep abreast of new material. Also see her books *Chiron and the Healing Journey* (Arkana, 1989) and *Saturn, Chiron and the Centaurs* (CPA Press, 1996).

Discovery and Astronomy

Chiron was discovered by Charles T. Kowal on 1 November 1977 at about 10 a.m. in Pasadena, California.[2] When discovered it didn't fit the existing categories of celestial objects and for this reason has been re-classified several times, having been defined variously as an asteroid, a comet and a 'planetoid'. Indeed, it still holds 'dual classification' as comet 95P and Minor Planet 2060. Most of the time it is positioned between Saturn and Uranus but, as a body that crosses the orbits of other bodies, it can at times be closer to the Sun than Saturn, and at others it can be further out than Uranus. It has a cometary tail which can reach 186,420 miles/300,000 kilometres in length and which appears to switch on and off – at times the tail can be seen, at others not. Once Chiron was discovered, its appearance was noted on photographic plates dating back as far as the late 1800s. It had been there all along but had not been noticed. Likewise, in the horoscope, Chiron symbolizes that which is 'hidden' by virtue of being so obvious that we don't actually see it. Very small, only 111 miles/180 kilometres in diameter, Chiron can also describe those things that, being so small, may seem insignificant but in reality are powerful. In keeping with its continual re-classification as a celestial body, Chiron's meaning in the horoscope resists categorization and defies description.

The Kuiper Belt

In 1992 the Kuiper Belt was discovered. It is a large zone of matter surrounding the solar system, comprising possibly billions of small celestial objects currently being discovered and classified. Named after the Dutch astronomer, Gerard Kuiper (1905-1973), who predicted its existence, the Kuiper Belt has yielded several new astronomical categories including the Centaurs. Some of the larger Kuiper Belt objects (KBOs) or trans-Neptunians such as Quaoar, Sedna, Ixion and Xena may prove to be of more than passing astrological interest but, so far, it is the Centaurs that have particularly caught the attention of astrologers. More than twenty Centaurs have been discovered, although to date only about twelve have been named.[3] Centaurs are 'born' when objects are drawn into the solar system from the icy wastes of space in the region around Pluto, pulled in by the gravitational field of Neptune. In Greek mythology, the Centaurs were a tribe of unruly creatures who were half-horse, half-human; only a few have names and an individual storyline. Similarly, while there may be countless Centaurs awaiting discovery in the depths of the Kuiper Belt, only a few have been named, thus demonstrating a neat parallel with the mythology. Chiron will probably remain the most well-known, the 'chief Centaur', just as Ceres is the 'queen of the asteroids'.[4] In mythology, it is mainly Chiron, Pholus and Nessus who have a substantial storyline, and so far these are the three Centaurs proving to be the most useful in astrological terms.

Astrologers and astronomers co-operated in the naming process of several of the Centaurs and this was the first time in recorded history that the divide between astrology and astronomy had been bridged. This rapprochement reflects Centaur themes: the bringing together of the scientific and the intuitive, the rational and inspirational, just as the half-horse, half-human image of the Centaur brings together disparate opposites, and challenges us to integrate that which seems alien.[5]

Orbital Features

The Centaurs are minor planets, which have some distinguishing features. They cross over the orbital paths of one or more of the other bodies between Jupiter and Pluto, and have very elliptical orbits. This means that they will seem to speed through some signs, astrologically, as they whizz around the narrower part of the ellipse while taking much longer to transit the signs on the long sides in between these points. Thus, Chiron spends about eight years in Pisces and Aries and only about two in Virgo and Libra. It takes Chiron about 50 years, Pholus about 90 years and Nessus about 124 years to complete an orbit. These elliptical orbits will mean a big difference in the distance from the Sun at different parts of the orbit. For example, Chiron's mean distance from the Sun is 13.73 AU.[6] At perihelion it is 8.453 AU, while at aphelion it is 18.899 AU. Its period of axial rotation is 5.9 hours, and its orbital inclination to the ecliptic is a steep 7 degrees.

Symbolism of Discovery

Chiron's discovery at this pivotal time in our history reflects a process of innovation and change by 'quantum leap', potential changes of consciousness, belief, behaviour and lifestyle, and also a time of technological changes. In this sense Chiron bridges the realms of Uranus (radical change, revolution and the overturning of old collective structures) and Saturn (lord of manifestation and preserver of existing forms). By weaving both impulses into a higher synthesis, more uniquely personal than either planet, Chiron's process may help us to individuate beyond the various pressures of the collective to which we are all subject. Commitment to the healing of ourselves, others and our environment is the price this minor planet seems to be asking us to pay.

In the Greek myth, Chiron was accidentally hit by an arrow, which had been dipped in the poisonous blood of the Hydra, and the theme of poisoning is an interesting one around Chiron and the Centaurs. They have been discovered during a period when the true extent of the toxic devastation of the environment is coming to light. Nuclear waste, chemical waste and pollutants, industrial accidents and toxic spills of one kind or another are very often in the news. We are daily flooded with toxic material – in our water, in the air we breathe, in the dental materials most of us have in our mouths. Arguably, it is the rings of Saturn that symbolically protect the immune system, and Chiron penetrating through Saturn's orbit may be a co-significator for some of the diseases of immune deficiency that have proliferated over the last few decades.

The Pluto Connection

Chiron may have a role in enabling us to integrate the powerful experiences signified by the outer planets, Uranus, Neptune and especially Pluto, which is in fact the largest inhabitant of the Kuiper Belt, and formerly the only 'orbit-crossing' planet. Certainly, Chiron seems to act as an emissary, agent or escapee of Pluto and can, to some extent, be interpreted in a similar way to a smaller, bite-sized version of that planet.

The Centaurs seem to preside over rites of passage and the processes of purification that accompany spiritual development. Their discovery may enable consciousness and awareness to be brought into areas of the soul previously inaccessible except perhaps to hermits, mystics, shamans and others dedicated to the inner journey.

Mythology

Chiron is often associated with the archetypal theme of the Wounded Healer. He was the son of Kronos (Saturn) and a sea-nymph called Philyra. Because both parents were in their horse-form when he was conceived, Chiron emerged as a Centaur: half-horse and half-human. When she saw him, Philyra was so horrified that she prayed to be turned into anything other than what she was – the mother of a monster. Chiron was abandoned and then rescued by a shepherd who took him to the Sun god Apollo. Chiron's mother Philyra demonstrates the primary state of mind that creates our suffering – the inability to accept things as they are and instead to react in a rejecting and negative way. The astronomy is reflected in the mythology, in that Chiron is taken to Apollo, and fostered by the Sun god. In their elliptical orbits, Chiron and the Centaurs appear to be moving inwards to the Sun just as Chiron was taken to Apollo. This detail also reminds us that our suffering and our compulsions need to be brought into the light of compassionate awareness, for Apollo was the god of healing, music and prophecy and other skills.

In the episode which earned Chiron the title of Wounded Healer, Hercules, one of his students, accidentally wounded him. Because Chiron was a demi-god, he could not die, but neither could he heal himself because the wound was poisoned. Chiron in astrology often represents that which we can do for others but we cannot do for ourselves. After existing in agony for a long time, trying unsuccessfully to heal himself, Chiron changed places with Prometheus, who was chained to a rock as a punishment for tricking Zeus (Jupiter). Thus, both Chiron and Prometheus were released from their suffering. Chiron was finally able to die and was immortalized in the constellation of Centaurus, which flanks the Southern Cross. This is a powerful description of the process whereby our suffering is resolved – by full empathy and acceptance of it and/or empathy with the suffering of another.

Chiron and Exile

In keeping with the mythology, a theme of exile is often felt around Chiron. We find Chiron in the horoscope where we may feel different, not understood and outside life in some way. In this respect, Chiron seems to operate like a weak version of Uranus. Whereas we can associate Uranus with rebellion and revolution, and perhaps the awakening of rebellious feelings in others, with Chiron the experience is more that of sitting outside the herd.

Chiron, Death and Transition

Matters pertaining to death in the horoscope are of course signified by Saturn, Pluto, the Eighth House and Scorpio, but Chiron undoubtedly joins this team of significators. Themes like voluntary euthanasia, assisted suicide, living wills and the rights of the dying are specifically symbolized by Chiron, whose role seems to come under the umbrella of the conscious acceptance of death. Such acceptance can play an important part in the process of healing. By transit, Chiron can signify the deaths of significant others in our lives, although there will always be other indicators pointing the same way as well. It is often active at times of illness, too, when we may be forced to face the fact that we are mortal. In mythology, Chiron was accidentally wounded by Hercules and Chiron often seems to be at work when people get caught up in some kind of larger crossfire. For instance, it is often prominent in the charts of major disasters, especially when in opposition to Saturn for some reason.

Chiron and Disability

The American astrologer Kim Rogers-Gallagher has noted how similar the glyph for Chiron is to the symbol for wheelchair access.[7] She points out that the wheelchair disability symbol was adopted in 1968 when Chiron was at 0 degrees Aries, a potent point which often signifies the birth of something. Chiron, in common with Pluto, certainly seems to be a co-significator of at least some forms of disability and its discovery 'coincided' with the time when disability was finally becoming something that could be acknowledged and discussed. The campaign for equal rights for people with disabilities was at a height in 1977 in the USA, pre-empted by Edward Roberts who was the first person with a severe disability to be a student living on campus. In the same way that the whole subject of death was largely a matter of denial in the West until the 1970s, so were all matters pertaining to disability. The vast majority of the American public, for instance, never knew that President Roosevelt, who was in power from 1933 to his death in 1945, was totally paralysed from the waist down (due either to polio or Guillain-Barre syndrome which he contracted in 1921). To this day, most pictures of him omit his wheelchair. In Roosevelt's horoscope,[8] Mercury, the ruler of his chart in the Sixth House exactly square Pluto, is a potent signature of his disability but Chiron falling in the Eighth House describes the fact that, in terms of the general public at any rate, his disability was a secret; he 'suffered in silence'. Presumably, with a paralysed lower body, to some extent he would have been disabled sexually, too; another wound to grin, bear and learn to accept.

Alongside Pluto, Chiron sometimes certainly does appear to be a significator of disabilities that warrant the use of wheelchairs or might require one in the future, especially if the individual is coy about the fact. For example, a client with Sun tightly conjunct Chiron in Sagittarius in her Seventh House had a husband (Sun and Seventh House) who suffered from multiple sclerosis. The sign Sagittarius and its rulership over the hip area of the body is undoubtedly relevant here, too. As well as being a significator of wounds in the psychological or spiritual sense, Chiron sometimes literally describes inherited physical weaknesses. Indeed, even though they may manifest in different forms, diseases are seldom eradicated according to the homœopathic world view. Instead, they are passed down through the generations, appearing like a new head on the body of the Hydra.

Chiron, Medicine and Music

Eve Jackson has noted that chiropody, chiropractice and chiromancy (palmistry) all share with Chiron the Greek root *cheir* meaning 'hand'.[9] In the context of Chiron, we might also think of the word 'handicap'. Since the discovery of Chiron, there have been significant advances in orthodox medical/surgical practices which require skill with the hands (e.g. keyhole surgery) or hand/eye co-ordination, as well as a huge increase in the use of alternative therapies. In mythological terms, Chiron taught not only healing but warfare, hunting and music, too. His mastery of warfare (teaching others how to kill) is reminiscent of assisted suicide, but Chiron may also be a significator of music or, at least, recorded music. The key may be in the word 'recorded', in line with Chiron's tendency to retrace something.

Rites of Passage – the Chiron Return

Because Chiron's orbit is so elliptical, its cycle is irregular and can only be tracked through the use of an ephemeris. For example, Chiron's first square to its own natal position may occur any time from about the age of five to the age of twenty-three, depending on the sign in which it is found. However, it returns to its natal position approximately every fifty years, and this age is an important threshold crossing for both men and women. For a few years after its return, Chiron retraces all the aspects by transit that occurred in the formative years of our lives. Thus, we have the opportunity to revisit and bring healing to those areas, and very likely life will provide experiences that open them up. Understanding this process can make a big difference, as it helps us to move beyond what is happening in the present by understanding the elements of past experience which are being recapitulated.

Studying Chiron in Your Horoscope

Do not expect to equate Chiron with healing/suffering or any other themes in the way that you can equate Mercury with communication issues, for example. It is best not to try to interpret Chiron as one might a traditional planet. Rather, you should wait, look, listen, sense and feel, keeping a questioning and open mind. This will allow the contemplative space for the obvious to reveal itself, which will connect with Chiron's symbolism, by house, sign and aspect. Using the analogy of a radio, if you are not tuned to the right frequency you cannot find the station to hear the music playing! The best way to understand Chiron in your horoscope is to track its transits over time, particularly the conjunction, square and opposition.

Some Classic Chiron Themes

In some horoscopes, inserting Chiron will have the effect of highlighting a pattern, creating a new emphasis or serving to explain something really prominent about a person that is not otherwise reflected in the chart. Studying Chiron often makes for an 'aha' effect, where suddenly things click into place. People who cannot relate to Chiron fall into one of two categories. There are those who are so busy blocking out the deeper dimensions of their soul that they cannot resonate with Chiron, out of fear. Then there are those who are living so close to the archetype that they cannot see it!

There can be an obvious 'unhealable wound' depicted by Chiron's placement, a situation that we cannot escape from although we may try to, and which provides grist to the mill of our 'soul-work' for many years. Just as in the myth, however, there is potential resolution and release. Very often this revolves around accepting the unacceptable, the unfair, the incomprehensible; it may mean no longer trying to figure things out and fix them but instead simply to allow ourselves to be with the experience. Chiron can also depict a brilliance, something which stands out and defines a person. It can show where we behave or feel like an outsider, a maverick or wanderer, where we resist being tied down, where the constraints of society weigh heavily. There is a wildness, a freshness, a volatility of energy, a certain instability where we can go to extremes. It can also be like a blind spot where something is obvious to everyone but ourselves. Psychologically, it could be said that Chiron symbolizes part of us that has been split off. It has become dissociated because of trauma or suffering, or simply through a lack of understanding or language to process an experience. Transits act like the classic shamanic process of 'soul retrieval', where that which has been outcast seeks to return.

Pholus – the Lid Comes Off

Pholus was discovered in 1992. Its process seems to be one where a small event sets off a chain reaction, either inwardly or externally, in terms of the consequences. In the Greek mythology, Pholus was the keeper of the sacred jar of wine of Dionysus. Dionysus was the god of ecstasy, whose rites were often characterized by drunkenness and chaos, and sometimes they culminated in violence. Similarly, Pholus-related events often involve things getting out of control. The way to deal with Pholus is to take only essential actions until the floods subside and things settle down. The jar of Pholus was not supposed to be opened for four generations, and so the astrological Pholus often highlights the releasing of ancestral processes, whether these are known or unknown to us. In some way, bearing witness to the past can be important as we are called upon to clarify our own ancestral lineage. Sometimes there are specific things to do, such as forgiveness work or putting flowers on a grave. But often it is simply to inwardly acknowledge the suffering of those who went before us, and to recognize the tragedy of it.

Nessus – the Buck Stops Here

The third Centaur to be discovered is one that seems to address issues to do with the abuse of power, and it too has ancestral implications. It seems that Nessus brings opportunities to understand and release deep patterns of helplessness, being taken advantage of, and of being oppressed. This is particularly relevant for people raised in a culture where they are in a minority group. The processes of Nessus really do seem to bring to an end the unfathomable ties that bind us to people, places and situations. We can psychoanalyse our bonds, do tie-cutting exercises, sweat and strain to be free of situations which burn with relentless continuity, but only when such endeavours are in harmony with the deeper timing of the soul will they result in deep release. And when they do, the healing is unmistakable. Nessus activations correspond with times when things really do end, finish and transcend to another level, when release occurs and when the turning point is reached. This sometimes happens through an intensification of suffering. The end of falsely hopeful innocence, and the opening of a deeper wisdom, is signalled by Nessus transits. Nessus (and transiting Nessus) sometimes correlates with itching and burning skin, as occurs in cases of eczema, nettle rash and allergies, for instance. This accords neatly with the Greek myth in which Nessus attempted to abduct and take advantage of Heracles' wife, Deianeira. Heracles saw that the rape was about to happen and shot Nessus. As he lay dying, Nessus gave Deianeira a potion containing his heart's blood and his semen, saying that the potion would ensure that Heracles would be faithful to her. When Deianeira became unsure of Heracles' fidelity, she smeared the potion on his shirt but Nessus had lied; the mixture, impregnated with his toxic blood, was poisonous and it burned Heracles terribly. To escape the pain Heracles threw himself on to a funeral pyre. Appalled by what had happened, Deianeira committed suicide.

Part Three: Asteroids

The asteroid belt is found in the 20 million miles/32 million kilometres of space between Mars and Jupiter, and within this belt there are perhaps millions of small rocky objects orbiting the Sun. These bodies vary greatly in size and can range from the size of a pebble upwards. Some even have moons orbiting around them. The vast majority are very small, however, and only about thirty are thought to have a diameter in excess of 124 miles/200 kilometres. About 130,000 have been classified and about 13,000 have been named. The four asteroids Ceres, Pallas, Vesta and Juno, which were the ones to be first discovered (between 1801 and 1807), have particularly interested astrologers. Size may not be everything but six of the more recently discovered asteroids are larger than Juno, the smallest of the original four. Ceres was the first to be discovered and, with a diameter of about 580 miles/930 kilometres, is overwhelmingly the largest asteroid. On 24 August 2006 it was re-classified as a 'dwarf planet'. If astrologers consider that Chiron is worthy of consideration, then perhaps, at the very least, Ceres should also be, especially given that Chiron, with a diameter of a mere 112 miles/180 kilometres, is five times smaller than Ceres and about sixty times more distant. The four main asteroids Ceres, Pallas, Vesta and Juno are said to describe different aspects of the feminine, and particular 'feminine' skills, which if not exclusive to the female sex, certainly tend that way. Ceres is usually associated with Mother Earth and, with the growing awareness of how humanity is killing off the planet, it is perhaps not surprising that the asteroid has recently been promoted to 'dwarf planet' status and into the public consciousness. Ceres has much in common with the Moon in that it also describes how we nurture, care for and nurse others. More specifically, Ceres has been linked to that inevitable and often painful separation between mother and child. It is said to describe all situations that involve separation, including those which happen at death. It is also associated with agriculture, and the word 'cereal' is derived from Ceres.

As perhaps is the case with all minor planets, it seems that individual asteroids are significators for very specific areas of life and a great deal of research would be required to ascertain what those specific areas might be.

An example of a minor asteroid at work happened last year when I was staying in a cottage which had an outside toilet. With me was a friend who was very frightened of spiders. As soon as either of us opened the toilet door, we were greeted by two huge spiders hanging from their webs. My friend was unable to use the facilities but fortunately I have no particular fear of spiders and was able to move them to a less prominent position. My Saturn in Scorpio is exactly conjunct my friend's *Arachne* (surely an asteroid to associate with spiders?), which seems to symbolize the fact that I took responsibility for moving the critters. Scorpio is, of course, the sign to associate with toilets and perhaps also, in a very general sense, with spiders. Transiting Arachne at the time was exactly conjunct my Sun and square my Saturn, and therefore also square my friend's Arachne. More interesting still, the release date for the video version of the film *Arachnophobia* (1 October 1999) in the UK occurred when the Sun and Arachne were exactly conjunct. Note that one probably needs to use tight orbs (1 degree), especially with these minor asteroids.

Recommended reading: *Asteroid Goddesses*, Demetra George with Douglas Bloch, ACS Publications, 1986.

Chapter 8

Steps Towards Chart Interpretation and Synthesis

What follows are various points to consider when interpreting birth charts, as well as profiles of astrology in action.

Move Away from Such Concepts as 'Good' and 'Bad'

Arguably, there is no such thing as 'good' or 'bad' in a horoscope. There aren't good planets or bad planets, nice signs or nasty signs. Human beings moralize and decide what they think is right or wrong, acceptable or unacceptable behaviour, but, as far as astrology is concerned, such terms are meaningless. In any case, the very virtues or character traits that one person loves about another will be the very traits that someone else would either find abhorrent or interpret quite differently. Every human has their place in the overall scheme of things. Saint or sinner, each of our actions presents others with challenges and opportunities. Every horoscopic symbol also has its purpose and yet all can present difficulties if over-used or under-used.

Consider the Time, the Place, Context and Culture of the Chart

Given that the birth chart is merely a map for a particular time, it cannot, by itself, say what it refers to. A chart may be set up, for instance, for the moment an insect is born, for the time a thought springs to one's mind or for the moment when hands are shaken on a business deal. It can be set up for absolutely any moment at all. On page 325 is the horoscope for Henry VIII of England. There is nothing in it to say that he was a king, a man or even a human being. However, once the context of the chart is placed (15th-century England, white, male, royalty), then the life and character of the man can be deduced. Culture and context are important and must be borne in mind when looking at a horoscope. Also fundamental is the reason *why* one is looking at it. The astrologer is never separate from the chart and the life under consideration, for in some way the horoscope under review is part of their own growth process at that particular moment. There is also the question of *when* one is studying a chart – that is not coincidental, either. For example, at the time of writing and for the last few months, Jupiter has been square Neptune in the sky and client after client who has consulted me has had tight aspects between these two planets in their natal chart. In April 2006, when the Sun was in Aries, Mars in Gemini and Jupiter in Scorpio, I started to work on the chart of the Olympic athlete Kelly Holmes who, 'coincidentally', I soon discovered, also happens to have the Sun in Aries, Mars in Gemini and Jupiter in Scorpio! She also has aspects, which if taken together, have something of a Jupiter-Neptune flavour.

Remember the Three-Legged Stool Rule

There are themes in every chart which will describe the person and their life story. These themes can be viewed as stories, personal myths, psychological complexes or sub-personalities. However one thinks of them, the astrologer's job is to try to discover, understand and describe them. To this end, when working one's way around a chart, it is a good idea to adopt a 'three-legged-stool' approach, so-named because if a stool has less than three legs it will collapse! In other words, if something is true, it will be repeated at least three times in the chart and more usually five or more times.

Be Methodical
The experienced astrologer may decide to start anywhere, but for the beginner the best strategy in starting to work on a chart is to go through it in a methodical way and to make notes as one does so. It is usually a good idea to complete some kind of interpretation checklist (see below) and to then start one's note-taking at the Ascendant and then move on to the planet that rules the Ascendant. Frequently, the chart ruler can be taken as the front door to the chart, leading the interpreter into the main storylines. Working one's way around at least two-thirds of the chart ensures that the repeated statements, and therefore main themes of the horoscope, will emerge. Seeing only one factor and interpreting it in isolation inevitably leads to inaccurate observations. Viewed singly, a planet in a sign, for instance, will yield very little information beyond vague descriptions about personality.

Don't Feel You Have to Understand Everything
Inevitably, when working one's way around the chart and making notes as one goes, one will hit symbolism that seems incomprehensible at first. It is perfectly 'normal' for even experienced astrologers to find symbolism that doesn't really 'speak' to them initially. Simply note the relevant significator and consider what it might actually mean later on. Making sense of a horoscope can be rather like doing a crossword: as one solves some clues, other clues which previously seemed too difficult become solvable. However, unlike a crossword, one can never fully get to the bottom of an astrological symbol, any more than one can get to the bottom of a human being. In any case, while it is perfectly possible to do 'blind' work (to interpret the chart for a person and know nothing about them), there can be many ways in which an astrological significator may manifest itself and so, to an extent, some input from the owner of the horoscope will make any reading much richer.

Remember That ...
• The main life storylines will be shown by **T-squares**, **Grand Crosses** and other tight aspect formations.
• The main themes will also be shown by **tight major aspects** and also by the tightest aspects overall. Looking for the tightest aspects in a chart (all aspects) will often help one to notice important things that might otherwise be missed.
• If an accurate birth time is known, the main life storylines will also be shown by **planets conjunct any of the four angles** and tight, especially hard, aspects to the angles.
• The main themes will be shown by **clusters of planets in signs and houses**.
• The main themes will often be backed up by **marked imbalances**, such as a predominance or lack of an element, mode, or type of aspect. An imbalance may manifest in a variety of ways; how it will do so usually becomes clear as one works one's way around the chart. There is never only one marked imbalance: if one has a lot of one thing, then it follows that there must be a lack of something else. Each imbalance has to be viewed in the light of all others. A marked imbalance will always be important; it's like the background wash of an oil painting, where the colour has to be just right because it sets the tone for the whole canvas.

Follow the Rulership Trail

• The Ascendant sign usually makes a general statement. The Ascendant ruler usually makes that statement more specific. For example, perhaps you have Cancer rising. Among many other things, this might suggest that you go out into the world wanting to protect (general statement). If the Moon were to be found in Gemini in the Twelfth House, maybe your dominant urge would be to protect books in a library, documents in a museum or a sibling housed in a school, prison, hospital or other institution.

• If a house is empty, look to the ruler(s) – by sign, house and aspect – of the house cusp for information about that house. There is always a relationship between a planet and the house it rules. For instance, the ruler of the Seventh in the Ninth might imply marriage to a foreigner. More about on this can be found on pages 300-1.

Watch Out For ...

• **Planets in their own sign**. Here is something analogous to a double dose of a planetary energy, a kind of built-in double whammy.

• **Planets in their own house**; they too gain strength.

• Any planet that sticks out for any reason – perhaps by receiving the most aspects, or by being the most elevated planet (the one nearest the MC). Such factors may give additional weight to the planet.

Ignore

• **Wide trines and sextiles**.

• The **Part of Fortune** (and all other Arabic parts). They may have some relevance but come very low down in the pecking order of what is important.

• **Retrograde planets**. While this can be important in forecasting work when dealing with progressions, and is very important in horary technique, retrogradation is usually best ignored in natal work. Consider the fact that Mercury is retrograde for about two months of every year, Jupiter for about four months and Saturn and the outer planets each for five months; with such long time spans, retrograde planets are not going to contribute any very personal or specific pieces of information.

Horoscope Checklist

Design some kind of checklist, so that when working your way around a chart you are assured of noticing all the important points. An example is presented on the next page:

Interpretation Checklist

The Whole Chart

Is there a heavy emphasis on either the positive (fire and air) or negative (water and earth) signs, implying an extrovert or introvert personality?

What are the strongest and weakest elements?

Which mode, if any, is the strongest and which is the weakest?

Is there an aspect pattern (such as a T-square, Grand Cross, Grand Trine, Kite, etc.)?

Strongest Planets/Signs/Houses

Is there a rising planet (e.g. a planet conjunct the Ascendant)? If so, this planet will exert a powerful influence.

Are there any planets conjuncting the MC, Descendant, or IC? Less powerful than a planet on the Ascendant, nevertheless any angular planet should be given weight.

Are there any unaspected planets? Are there any mutual receptions?

Are any planets strengthened by virtue of falling in their own sign?

Are any planets strengthened by virtue of falling in their own house?

Is any planet dignified or debilitated for any other reason (see pages 216-18)?

Are certain signs particularly dominant in the chart?

Are certain houses heavily tenanted?

Is there an emphasis/under-emphasis on the first three, second three, third three or final three signs or houses?

Is any planet at the Sun/Moon midpoint or, if the birth time can be relied upon, at the Ascendant/MC midpoint?

Strongest Aspects

Is there a predominant type of aspect in the chart (e.g. numerous trines) or a type of aspect which is missing (e.g. the square)?

List the tightest aspects (use all aspects).

List all major aspects (conjunction, opposition, square, trine and sextile) that have less than a 2-degree orb.

For the Would-Be Professional

The wonder of astrology is that everyone, with a little effort, can use it for themselves in myriad ways in their daily lives. A few individuals choose to take it further, to learn the craft thoroughly, to take exams, and to make a career of it. Although it is outside the remit of this book to touch on even half the issues that the would-be professional has to explore, the following paragraphs are intended for individuals bent on that path, and may also be of some interest to the beginner.

As well as attending courses and reading books, everyone can use the world around them to learn their astrology. If one is familiar with the charts of loved ones, listening carefully to friends and relatives and considering what they have done and are doing with their lives is perhaps the best way of learning. Reading autobiographies of people when their horoscope is in your hand is almost as revealing. Note that autobiographies are infinitely better than biographies because in an autobiography one is hearing the subject's own words, their own interpretation of their life.

Remember the Importance of Process

All students of the art cut their teeth on learning to describe. All readers will recognize this kind of astrology: a person may have three planets in Taurus and will therefore be described as reliable, stoic, stubborn, and so on. In truth, none of us fully gets away from astrological description and perhaps we shouldn't. When it comes to having conversations with people about their chart, though, it has to be said that descriptions can be overly general and are only of limited help (most mature adults can accurately ascribe basic words to their character) unless one can also say *why* the individual acts in a certain way and in which circumstances they do so. Some differentiation is required. What is the motivation underpinning the behaviour? It is in understanding our motives that the potential to increase our free will can occur. If we become conscious of our behaviour and come to understand why we behave in the ways we do, then we can start to exercise choice the next time we are presented with the same stimulus: we can choose to behave as we usually do, or we can decide to adopt a different strategy. True, the choices of our behaviour and our life will always be circumscribed by the potential of our birth chart, but there seems to be quite a bit of leeway within those perimeters. People are not static. How they inhabit their chart at the ages of five, twenty-five and fifty may be very different. Thus, our astrology needs to reflect the fact that we are all coming from somewhere and going somewhere. There is movement. Arguably, we are on a journey, changing, developing and unfolding. Even periods of seeming regression in the life may happen in the service of some future development.

Family Inheritance or the Pull of the Soul or Spirit?

A major subject of psychological debate is that regarding nature and nurture. Is the individual the way they are because of their genetic inheritance or because they were raised in a certain way and exposed to all the various experiences of childhood? The horoscope, reflecting both nature and nurture as it does, suggests that a better question might be: In what way does nurture combine with nature to produce the individual in question? Given that a person's fate is reflected in their birth chart, could it be the case that, on some level, the individual 'chooses' their body, family, environment and everything else in which to be born and raised, in order to live out that fate and become the person they are supposed to become?

In his excellent book, *The Soul's Code*, James Hillman explains that each of us is given what he calls a 'daimon' before we are born which accompanies us throughout our lives. When using the word 'daimon', Hillman is referring to something that has variously been called a person's soul, spirit or guardian angel. Neither is it so far from the image of the unconscious held by some psychologists, even if this is a more reductive concept.

If we choose to avoid the 'upbringing equals the person we become' equation, this does not mean that we should avoid the story of an individual's childhood. As Hillman says, we should watch the daimon in action during childhood so we understand its intentions and do not stand in its way. There are so many ways to view a life and to view a horoscope but, in my opinion, a peek into childhood and even into the birth moment itself (if information about that is known) can have a stunning capacity to shed light on an individual's underlying, and usually not very conscious, motivations. Obviously this is not possible, or only partially so, when studying the charts of celebrities.

Know Thyself

Self-discovery is a lifetime's journey; for all of us, self-knowledge is never going to be a destination that can be fully attained. Nevertheless, the astrologer who sees clients, or has ambitions to do so, should be actively travelling on this journey. The better we know ourselves, the higher our chance of recognizing the reality of another person. Otherwise, we assume that our own experiences are the same as everyone else's. This is perhaps the most common example of the mechanism of projection.

Prior to the appointment, the astrologer needs to study the chart so that even though they may not understand what much of its contents actually may mean, they do know where everything is and which aspects, etc., are being made. The astrologer should basically be capable of drawing the chart from memory by the time the doorbell rings. In addition, all the various imbalances would have been noted and, assuming some degree of forecasting work is involved, the various transiting, progressed and/or directed planets and aspects would also be imprinted in the astrologer's mind. The student may feel daunted at this point but there is no need; with some experience, an astrologer can prepare for a client in quite a short space of time.

Projection – the Art of Throwing Oneself Away!

The word 'project' literally means 'to throw'. For example, an overhead projector is a device that throws an image, placed on a transparency, on to the facing wall. Psychological projection is a process whereby an unconscious quality or characteristic of one's own is attributed (thrown on to) the external world, and on to individuals and groups within that world. In other words, the particular characteristic is perceived and reacted to in an outer object, person or group. Projection is a fact of life – all humans do it, which is why struggling to know themselves has to be the aim of every astrologer. Otherwise, we run the risk of inappropriately attributing characteristics, motives and life stories on to others; the reality of the other person can be missed entirely. The most common form of projection that we all encounter occurs when a person assumes that another person will feel or behave exactly as they themselves do.

Projection is also an inbuilt feature of the horoscope. While everything in the chart relates to the 'owner' of the chart, all the planets, signs and houses are also representative of all the other people in that person's life and also of all the situations that they might encounter: friends, parents, children, partners, pets, work, school, church, and so on.

Your Client is More Important than Their Chart

The word 'interpret' means to explain, to translate, to make something clear, to make out the meaning of. The prefix 'inter' means between, among, amid, in between. Basically, the astrologer is an interpreter, an agent, a go-between between the client and their horoscope. Or, as discussed in the first chapter, quite simply a map-reader. The richer the astrologer's understanding of the symbolism and the greater their capacity to articulate it, the more meaningful the translation will be for the client. The student in training will inevitably be nervous and too unsure of their grasp of the symbolism to be able to be completely flexible during a consultation, but after a few sessions confidence will increase and, with it, an ability to be flexible and responsive. At that point, when the astrologer is actually working with someone and discussing that person's chart – whether they are being paid for this service or not – the astrologer needs to be able to concentrate on their client, not on their client's chart. Knowing the chart well, it is often nicer for the astrologer to ask appropriate questions and reflect back the client's answers, rather than to spend the entire session giving a pre-digested interpretation. Chart interpretations can go in a variety of different directions, all no doubt described by the client's chart, the astrologer's chart, their synastry and the chart for the moment. It has to be said that there are clients who, for a variety of reasons (shyness, wanting to prove or disprove astrology, wanting to test the astrologer, etc.) will want to keep quiet, reveal nothing and just listen to the astrologer speak. However, the vast majority of people will want to become involved at some point during the proceedings and things can loosen up then. No matter how quiet the client is, at some point they will feel safe and the astrologer will inevitably say some things that the client finds interesting and wants to discuss further. What tends to get a person talking is the sense that they are being understood – that the astrologer recognizes them and is mirroring their experiences accurately. This in itself can be a very healing experience. A chart reading is a two-way process where both parties can learn from each other. However, this can only happen when the astrologer concentrates on listening to their client, rather than trying to 'prove' astrology or show off their skills.

Supervision

Even the most experienced astrologer can learn something from every astrological conversation. Having someone practised in the art as a back-up resource can help us to see things we might otherwise miss. A supervisor is there to enlarge our view, to offer *super vision*. They can help the practitioner not only to learn from their mistakes but also to gain confidence and greater self-awareness.

Chapter 9

Profile: Henry VIII
and an Illustration of T-Squares

As discussed in Chapter 5, tight conjunctions and tight hard aspects *always* need to be weighted heavily in chart interpretation as they will be descriptive not only of character and motivation but will also be indicative of the main life stories. If a planet is receiving two or more tight hard aspects, as is the case with T-squares and Grand Crosses, then the planets involved are doubly worthy of attention. Depending on the orbs one uses or how one defines such aspect patterns, roughly 40% of charts have at least one T-square and roughly 5% have a Grand Cross.

I don't know the statistical likelihood of having two T-squares, but Henry VIII of England had two. One involved Jupiter, Neptune and Mars, and the other involved Mercury, Saturn and Pluto.

Henry VIII[1] is a well-known figure even to those with little interest in English history. He is most famous for his six wives and for having two of them beheaded. He is famous, too, for creating the Church of England and placing himself at its head, having first separated himself from the Pope and dissolved the monasteries. He was a colourful man with gargantuan appetites and a terrible temper. In youth, he was physically very powerful and given to war, to hunting, to jousting and many other sports. But he was also a scholar, a musician, a gambler, a great patron of the arts and given to feasting, dancing and other forms of entertainment. It is not my aim to interpret Henry's chart from a particularly psychological point of view, given that I know so little of the mindset of 16th-century England or of Henry's early home life. The aim here is to show how the hard aspects in his chart graphically describe his character and the events of his life.

I will start with the Jupiter, Neptune and Mars mutable T-square falling in angular houses. The way to begin thinking about this T-square, as with all others, is to notice any repeated energies. Here we have a triple Jupiterian flavour because: Jupiter is one of the planets involved; Neptune is placed in Sagittarius, which is traditionally ruled by Jupiter; and Mars is the ruler of Henry's Ninth House. With Mars in the Mercurially-ruled sign of Virgo, and Jupiter in the Mercurially-ruled sign of Gemini, there is a double Mercurial feel, too. Mercury, Jupiter and mutability give this configuration a decidedly restless, explorative, roving quality. It describes someone who wants to cover a lot of ground both mentally and physically. As the sign Pisces is on the cusp of the Seventh, Jupiter and Neptune are the co-rulers of this house, showing that whichever stories this aspect pattern describes, Henry's marriage(s) are implicated, too. This is also hinted at by the fact that the 'empty leg' of this T-square falls in the Seventh.

Henry VIII built up a huge naval fleet and it is easy to see that here. The T-square suggests fighting (Mars) abroad (Jupiter) and on the seas (Neptune). The potential for war overseas is also underscored by the fact that Mars is the ruler of the Ninth House. Henry saw his main job as king as being about protecting the country and being able to fight off foreign invaders.

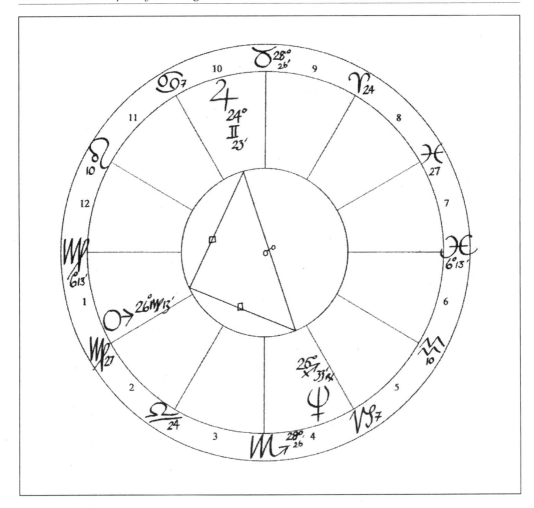

Brought up a Catholic, Henry severed his ties with the Catholic Church, destroyed monasteries and created the Church of England. This was largely because he wanted a male heir and had to be free to divorce and marry in order to obtain one. Put into simple astrological language, one might say that Henry was angry (Mars) with the Church (Jupiter) and thus dissolved it (Neptune). Neptune is in the Fourth – Henry dissolved the *houses* of the Church: the monasteries. The T-square shows the potential for tremendous religious idealism, it describes someone who will be willing to fight (Mars) for what he believes (Jupiter). Potentially we have a man who will fight to make his dreams (Neptune) come true. The T-square is suggestive of someone with a huge vision of an ideal State, an ideal Church and an ideal country. Mars in Virgo square Jupiter suggests a tendency to blow small things out of proportion and to get angry over quite trivial matters. This combination of planets suggests the potential for great rage as angry feelings can become both diffused (Neptune diffuses what it touches) and exaggerated (Jupiter). Henry's rage might alight anywhere and far from the source of his initial irritation. Mars-Jupiter-Neptune can be associated with an idealization and exaggeration of the masculine principle. An individual with merely Mars and Neptune in aspect will inevitably dream of sporting prowess, success on the battlefield or in the bedroom. In Henry's case, this was not mere fantasy; he sired many children (even if few survived) and he excelled at many sports. This Jupiterian T-square also describes his enthusiasm for gambling. The Mars-Jupiter part of the equation suggests a large sexual appetite, though with Mars in Virgo there was possibly a certain fastidiousness (and no doubt the usual royal penchant for virgins!). However, with Mars squaring Neptune, Henry could well feel impotent both sexually and in other ways. With the square aspect we are often uncertain about our capacity to perform with respect to what the relevant planets are concerned with. We can then go overboard, proving that we can do whatever they refer to. In Henry's case he would seek to prove that he was strong, vigorous (sexually and otherwise) and able to win any contest. The combination confirms his reputation for bullying behaviour, given that a bully is someone who chooses to attack those who are weaker.

Henry's Mars-Jupiter bent towards sexual exploration is helped along even further by the input of Neptune, as this planet will remove any boundaries in this area – he might be open to anything, so could easily be the seducer and the seduced. Indeed, he probably seduced the majority of his citizens into accepting war and also into accepting the Dissolution of the Monasteries, for as Ridley tells us, the '50,000 inhabitants of London hated foreigners' and the ordinary Englishman of the time was ever ready to see the Church as corrupt.[2] The bloodthirsty English of the time loved a good fight and no doubt Henry perfectly fitted the image of what an ideal male and an ideal monarch should be like. Arguably, Henry's tremendous naval fleet came out of both his and the nation's hugely idealized and inflated image of masculinity. In all matters it seems (and might be expected from this combination of planets), Henry tended to over-reach himself; for instance, he spent huge amounts of money and he ate and drank in enormous quantities.

Given that Sagittarius is linked with the thigh area of the body and Mars with wounds and inflammation, Henry's T-square is also one of the significators for the fact that a wound he acquired in a jousting accident in 1536 became ulcerated, putting paid not only to his sporting life but to exercise in general. All of this led to vast weight gain and diminishing health. Historians know from his suit of armour in the Tower of London that his waist later measured 54 inches/137 centimetres. His gluttony wasn't a problem when he had been leading an active life but became one when that activity ceased. The configuration also has huge potential for acquiring sexually transmitted diseases and historians often suggest that Henry contracted syphilis.

Henry's second T-square involves Mercury, Saturn and Pluto, and once again there are several double whammies. Children crop up as a subject area not only because the Fifth House (the house of children) is tenanted, but also because Mercury, the planet to associate with children, is in Leo. Leo and the Fifth House also share the topic of creativity. Another theme in this T-square is death, of which Saturn and Pluto are both significators. Education and communication (because of Mercury and the Third House involvement) are the key areas to be described in yet another double whammy. Note that, if one includes Chiron at 2 degrees of Taurus, this T-square becomes a Grand Cross.

As the second son of Henry VII, Henry was not expected to become king and was educated to go into the Church. He became heir to the throne when his older brother, Arthur (1486-1502), contracted an infection and died. The death of the brother (other siblings also died) is clearly shown in the chart: Mercury (siblings) is opposing Saturn and square Pluto (Mercury also gains prominence by being the chart ruler, and Saturn is quincunx the Ascendant); Pluto is in the Third House (the house of siblings).

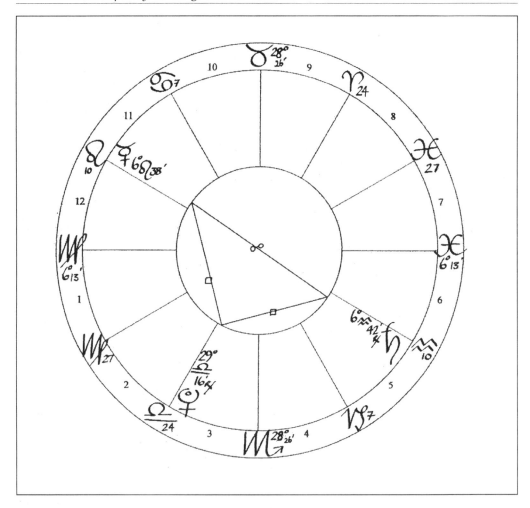

The same significators also describe the fact that so many of Henry's own children died. Nowadays, Saturn in the Fifth would not on its own describe the death of children, but it would have been a strong significator in 16th-century horoscopes when infant mortality was high anyway. Added to which, Saturn is also the ruler of the Fifth. Mercury is also making hard aspects to Saturn and Pluto and, in addition, Uranus is in the Fifth squaring Pluto. While this latter aspect was generational, it also shows the potential for unexpected (Uranus) death (Pluto) – both that of Henry's brother (as Pluto is in the Third) and of so many of his own children.

The T-square is consistent with Henry's obsession with having children but also goes some way to accounting for his dislike of paperwork and his formidable intellect, for both Saturn and Pluto will work to strip the mental faculties of needless clutter and aid concentration. Saturn opposes Mercury very precisely and gives the potential for extraordinary mental self-control and discipline, while the link with Pluto gives a compulsive need to know, to analyse and to ferret out information. Falling in Leo, Henry's Mercury suggests that he would take pride in his knowledge, and certainly would not want to be thought ignorant. It shows, along with Saturn falling in the Fifth, his interest in drama and in the arts generally. The T-square can also be associated with a penchant for negative thinking, for exacting standards, and for smelling rats even when they may not exist. As he got older Henry became suspicious to the point of being paranoid, helped along no doubt by the genuine intrigue and treachery of the times. The T-square would have also favoured all sports and other activities that required hand/eye co-ordination.

Although it is not my intention to comment on the entirety of Henry's chart, it is worth commenting on one or two other chart factors. Firstly, Venus tightly conjunct the MC (and South Node): Henry is famous (MC) for his many (Gemini) love affairs with women (Venus). He is famous for his love of pleasure generally and also for writing and performing many songs, both secular and religious, including 'Greensleeves', which apparently he didn't write. The conjunction is indicative of his popularity with the public; he was mostly well-loved throughout his reign. I know little about Henry's father beyond the fact that, unlike his son, Henry VII was a strongly peace-loving man. He loved money and his urge towards peace may have been partly because he didn't want to waste money on war; all of this is suggested by Venus conjunct Henry's MC.

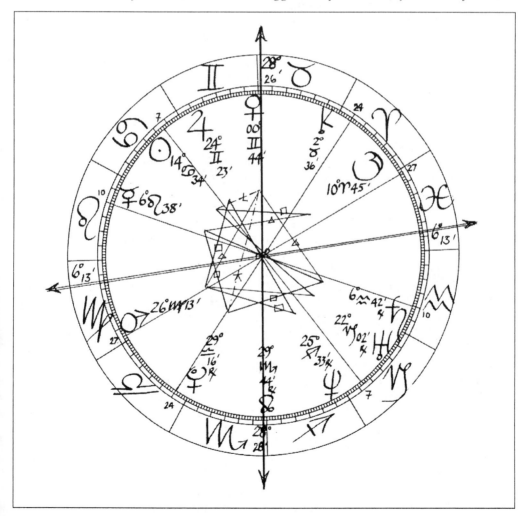

Henry VIII: 28 June 1491, 8.45 a.m. LMT, Greenwich, England (51N29, 0W00)

Henry VIII's mother, Elizabeth of York, had more claim to the throne than her husband but female monarchs were not in favour at the time (so it's little wonder that Henry was obsessed with producing male heirs). According to Ridley, Elizabeth was beautiful and docile, a loving mother and a much-loved woman – all indicative of Venus conjunct MC.

Henry is well-known for his six wives and for having two of them (and quite a few other people) beheaded, and his natal Moon is in keeping with the death (Eighth House) of women (Moon) by their heads (Aries!). This would have been fairly common practice for a sovereign at the time. Falling in the Eighth, his Moon describes a tremendous need for emotional closeness and intimacy (as well as the need for an heir), but in Aries it seems he was impatient to start relationships but not so good at keeping them! However, his first marriage to Catherine of Aragon, his late brother's widow, did last for 24 years, although it was punctuated by affairs. Henry's Moon in the Eighth describes a sensitivity to the possibility of death and is in keeping with a family history where death has been commonplace. The Moon in Aries can be interpreted in a similar way to the Moon in aspect to Mars and, given that Henry's Moon is also square to his Sun in Cancer, there is a doubly Moon-Mars feeling to it. It surely therefore describes Henry as being touchy, over-sensitive, easily offended, prone to flying off the handle, quick to respond in battle and slow to consider more peaceable means of settling disputes. It is also an aspect to associate with over-eating and also with miscarriages and premature births.[3] In the Scorpio house, it has a particularly smouldering, brooding feeling to it.

Along with Henry's over-the-top Jupiter T-square, the Sun in the Eleventh in Cancer is a major significator for Henry's famous banqueting (celebrated for both the size of his banquets and for their frequency), because surely someone with this placement might say: 'Treat your friends like royalty, protect them and care for them and, above all, feed them!' In mundane astrology, the Eleventh House is associated with Parliament, and having the Sun here is appropriate for Henry who, being a Tudor king, led what might be described as a totalitarian state. In other words he was the leader of the group and the group here can be interpreted as his friends, the nobility he knocked around with, or the nation as a whole. His Sun square Moon perhaps points to the struggles between the past he inherited and the future he wanted to create. In other words, doing his own thing would feel at odds with the history of his family. With its strong Mars overtone, this square hints at the domestic unrest Henry experienced both in his home and in the country at large. His father's dislike of him, and also Henry's resultant insecurity, can be deduced from this square.

History Matters

Given that the outer planets hadn't yet been discovered, astrologers during Henry's reign would have been looking at a very different chart and one without T-squares. Even today, a few astrologers would omit the outer planets. The fact of the matter is that, provided one uses house rulerships, not a lot changes without the outer planets. We can still see most aspects of Henry's life, including overseas wars, his fight with the Church and his many wives. Nothing describes the Dissolution of the Monasteries as beautifully as Neptune in Sagittarius in the Fourth, but Mars square Jupiter is consistent with the vandalism of Church property. And given that infant mortality was so high at the time, an aspect like Mercury opposing Saturn in the Fifth House would be more than enough to suggest the likely deaths of both his children and his siblings. However, in Western society today, the Mercury-Saturn opposition wouldn't be a strong enough significator to describe what we would now consider to be a terrible fate; the likely deaths of the children and siblings are only described because Pluto, as well as Saturn, is part of the equation. The Mercury-Saturn opposition could be used to describe both Henry the scholar and a Henry prone to negative thinking. However, that aspect doesn't quite carry the idea of paranoia (arguably only Pluto can do that) from which Henry definitely suffered in later years, but then the word didn't exist in Henry's time. So the decision about whether to include the outer planets rather depends of the vantage point from which one wants to view the horoscope. If one was well-versed in the history of 16th-century England and wished to interpret horoscopes from that perspective, then the outer planets could be omitted. However, if one is looking at history from even a slightly contemporary or psychological point of view, then arguably the outer planets must be included.

Profile: Kelly Holmes
and an Illustration of the Sun/Moon Midpoint

Kelly Holmes[1] is famous for winning gold medals in both the 800 metres and the 1500 metres at the 2004 Olympic Games in Athens; the first-ever British woman to become a double Olympic champion. Her list of other sporting achievements includes winning two Commonwealth Games gold medals, half a dozen silver medals and three bronze medals in various championships. She has had numerous other honours bestowed upon her including being made a Dame and named the BBC Sports Personality of the Year and, unconnected to her Olympic success, an MBE in 1998 as Sergeant Holmes for services to the British Army. Although she won the English Schools 1500 metres in only her second season of running, Kelly gave up athletics to pursue a career in the army. She became an HGV driver before she was able to train for the role she had hankered after in the first place, that of a PT instructor. She was persuaded back to the track about four years into her nine-year army career.

Kelly's autobiography starts with the following words:

> *My mother was seventeen when I was born ... the fact that she had me at all must mean something, given the odds she faced. She was involved with a Jamaican guy, something that in the 1970s was not the done thing – at least not by white girls in the whiter than white county of Kent. I was an accident that no one wanted to happen.*

Only a Sun-Jupiter person (or someone strongly Sagittarian) might make a gambling allusion so soon in their autobiography, and maybe Jupiter in Scorpio might talk about something being *against* the odds! In any event, to some extent these words sum up Kelly's sporting life – she won her gold medals against all odds. The odds were stacked against her, not because she wasn't a natural runner (she most certainly was and, I daresay, still is). The odds were stacked against her because it seems that, time and time again, there were accidents waiting to happen. She battled with a host of sports injuries (including a pulled hamstring, a stress fracture in her leg, a ruptured Achilles tendon, and torn calf muscles) and periodic severe abdominal pains which turned out to be caused by ovarian cysts and complications arising from them. Despite all adversity, Kelly battled through to achieve her childhood dream of becoming an Olympic champion.

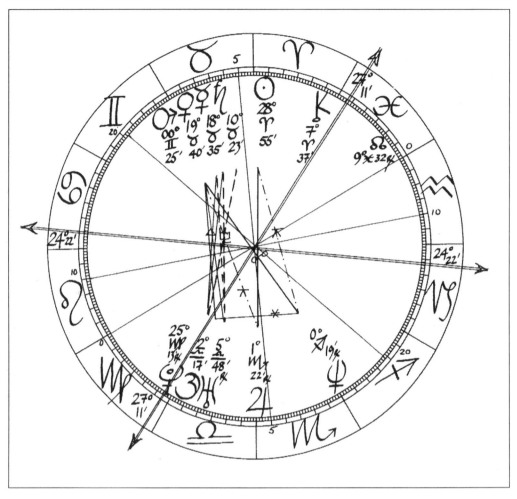

Kelly Holmes: 19 April 1970, 11.00 a.m. CET, Pembury, England (51N09, 0E20)

Much of Kelly's childhood is described by her Fourth House planets. Kelly's mother was told by her parents either to have Kelly adopted or to leave home. So she fled to London to be with Kelly's father but the relationship foundered within a year or so. Kelly was then temporarily placed in a children's home while economic necessity and homelessness drove her mother to return to Kent to sort herself out. Kelly's mother was eventually persuaded by her family to have Kelly adopted. However, when a woman from Social Services arrived to take Kelly away, her mother became distraught and couldn't bring herself to let Kelly go. Kelly was to return to the children's home for a time when she was four but her life settled down when she was seven when, in the typical style of Uranus in the Fourth, Kelly acquired a step-father when her mother married an old school-friend. She describes Mick as being a real father to her throughout.

Interpretation Checklist

The Whole Chart

• Is there a heavy emphasis on either the positive (fire and air) or negative (water and earth) signs, implying an extrovert or introvert personality? *No.*
• What are the strongest and weakest elements? *No clear dominating element or lack.*
• Which mode, if any, is the strongest and which is the weakest? *Cardinality is the strongest (the Sun, Moon and Ascendant are in cardinal signs).*
• Is there an aspect pattern (such as a T-square, Grand Cross, Grand Trine, Kite, etc.)? *If one uses the angles, there is a Grand Trine between the Ascendant, MC and Neptune.*

Strongest Planets/Signs/Houses

• Is there a rising planet (e.g. a planet conjunct the Ascendant)? *No.*
• Are there any planets conjuncting the MC, Descendant, or IC? *Yes, Pluto conjuncts the IC.*
• Are there any unaspected planets? Are there any mutual receptions? *No.*
• Are any planets strengthened by virtue of falling in their own sign? *Yes, Venus.*
• Are any planets strengthened by virtue of falling in their own house? *In the Placidus house system, there are two: the Moon is in the Fourth House and Saturn is in the Eleventh.*
• Is any planet dignified or debilitated for any other reason? *The Sun is exalted in Aries.*
• Are certain signs particularly dominant in the chart? *None especially. Five planets (three of them personal) are placed in the Venus-ruled signs of Taurus and Libra.*
• Are certain houses heavily tenanted? *In Placidus, the Fourth, Tenth and Eleventh contain the most planets.*
• Is there an emphasis/under-emphasis on the first three, second three, third three or final three signs or houses? *The Third Quadrant is empty.*
• Is any planet at the Sun/Moon midpoint or, if the birth time can be relied upon, at the Ascendant/MC midpoint? *Mars and Neptune are at the Sun/Moon midpoint.*

Strongest Aspects

• Is there a predominant type of aspect in the chart (e.g. numerous trines) or a type of aspect which is missing (e.g. the square)? *Oppositions and sesquiquadrates predominate. There are no squares involving the planets.*
• List the tightest aspects (use all aspects). *The tightest aspects are Mars opposite Neptune (6 minutes only) and Saturn sesquiquadrate Pluto (10 minutes only).*
• List all major aspects (conjunction, opposition, square, trine and sextile) that have less than a 2-degree orb. *Sun opposite Jupiter; Moon trine Mars; Moon sextile Neptune; Mercury conjunct Venus; and if the birth time is accurate, Pluto sextile the Ascendant.*

Kelly's Cancer Ascendant suggests that she goes out into the world wanting to protect others. With the Moon falling in the Fourth, no doubt she is keen to protect her family, her privacy, her home and her roots. In her autobiography, she describes herself as 'fiercely protective' at one point – a phrase I associate with Moon-Mars contacts. Here we see a version of that: the Sun in Mars-ruled Aries is square to the Cancer Ascendant. Cancer rising is also descriptive of the strong bond that Kelly has with her mother.

The Moon-Uranus conjunction increases the touchiness and sensitivity already shown by the Cancer Ascendant and suggests a tendency to feel rejected very easily. This sensitivity to rejection could incline towards a reluctance to ask for help. Moon-Uranus contacts can be associated with inconsistent parenting (though not necessarily through any 'fault' of the parent), emotional cut-outs and shocks in one's early life, coupled understandably enough with feelings of rejection. Falling in the Fourth, these possibilities become even more probable as does the likelihood of frequent house moves.

For Kelly the Moon-Uranus conjunction suggests that she dislikes feeling hemmed in. Used to being independent and emotionally self-sufficient, she is a woman who needs space – space to live where and how she pleases. She needs to know that she can change where she lives, or who she lives with, at the drop of a hat. The Moon in the Fourth might suggest a patriotic streak; it certainly suggests that wherever she lives, her home needs to be a place of refuge. Pluto falling on the IC also describes the early experience of being uprooted and, given that Pluto (and sometimes planets in Scorpio) can be taken as a significator for the colour black, it very much describes her biological Jamaican father and her maternal grandfather who was a blacksmith. As does the Fourth House Jupiter in Scorpio.

If one chooses to view the chart from an Equal house perspective, then the Moon/Uranus conjunction moves to the Third House and describes her mother as marrying (Libra) an old school friend and also of becoming a mother when virtually a schoolgirl herself. It is also a perfect significator to describe the surprise of acquiring step-siblings – those by her mother when she married and those of her biological father, with whom Kelly briefly met up years later. The Moon falling in Libra also describes the fact that Kelly's mother insisted upon politeness and good manners and that things were always tidy (Libra does like order!). With its sweet Venusian rulership, the Moon also signifies her mother's name, *Pamela*, which means 'honey'.

Kelly's Sun in Aries in her Tenth House describes her as being ambitious to win, to compete, to come first and, of course, she did so in Athens, where the Olympics were first held. With the Sun in the Tenth, success in her career does much to strengthen her identity; it gives a sense of 'I'. One associates the Sun with gold and she is the first and only British woman to win two gold medals, described perhaps by the fact that Mars, the Sun ruler, is in Gemini, the sign of twins! The (dissociate) opposition to Jupiter increases the ambition of the Tenth House Sun and describes Kelly as being something of a visionary, able to glimpse future possibilities and probably tending to live in the future generally. Perhaps it is not surprising, therefore, that when she was only fourteen she fantasized about winning an Olympic gold medal. Sun-Jupiter people tend to have big goals and high expectations of fulfilling them. The contact adds a certain buoyancy and exuberance to the chart and lends a degree of self-belief and optimism. It is often descriptive of the person who can at least appear to be confident. There could be a tendency to over-reach oneself, however, and one might suspect that some of Kelly's injuries came about because she gambled on her luck and pushed herself too far (aided by the Saturn-Pluto sesquiquadrate). Sun in Aries opposing Jupiter is not only a highly competitive combination but a highly adventurous one, too; little wonder that Kelly felt so at home during the nine or so years she spent in the army. Like the Moon-Uranus conjunction, the restless, not easily satisfied Sun-Jupiter opposition again suggests that Kelly needs a lot of space: space to grow and room to explore. Jupiter falling in the Fourth suggests she will live abroad at various times. This possibility is underscored by the ruler of the Ninth House (Neptune) falling in Sagittarius. As Neptune falls in the Fifth House of children, there is also the possibility that she might adopt children from other countries.

The interesting and unusual feature of Kelly's Sun-Jupiter opposition is that Mars happens to be the ruler of both the Sun and Jupiter. The Mars-Neptune opposition is the tightest aspect in her chart and is important for another reason: it falls at her Sun-Moon midpoint (see later).

Having such a strongly tenanted Eleventh House indicates the likelihood of being part of a group of people with shared interests (Mercury) and values (Venus), but with Venus and Mars there it also describes the rivalry and competition among those friends, which is the lot of every athlete.

Mars in Gemini neatly describes competing (Mars) over short distances (Gemini) in a team (Eleventh). From the point of view of astrology, 1800 metres would be classed as a short distance! If Mars in the Eleventh is ideally placed for being in a sports team, its opposition to Neptune is consistent with Kelly's *twin* childhood dreams of becoming a PT instructor in the army and a winning athlete. Mars in Gemini is a particularly resourceful placement and, with the input from Neptune especially, it is imaginative at finding solutions to tricky problems. In the Eleventh, as well as in Gemini, it is also an excellent placement for all manner of networking within the sporting community. The opposition also describes a capacity to encourage – nay, seduce – others (especially children, since Neptune is in the Fifth) into supporting Kelly's sporting vision and also into pursuing their own sporting (and other) dreams. Mars in the Eleventh suggests that Kelly will tend to find it easier to fight battles for the group than solely for herself, and in the same way that the soldier, however much bent on personal glory, is fundamentally fighting for his or her country, so Kelly too was running for Great Britain. As always, in the Eleventh House, we do things for ourselves and also for others.

When studying a horoscope one needs to see which planetary energies (planets, signs and aspects) predominate and which take a back seat. In aspect terms, this is a chart dominated by oppositions and sesquiquadrates. The oppositions perhaps point to a life of extremes: a rollercoaster of ups and downs. With no hard aspects from Saturn to personal planets and no squares, for good and ill, there is little in this chart to slow Kelly down. Sun in Aries opposition to Jupiter and the strong Mars may add a degree of recklessness and incline towards accidents but they also give rise to qualities that are essential for any athlete; namely, speed, courage and daring. Qualities that have been aided by the tenacity of a Cancer Ascendant, the steadiness of purpose of Saturn in Taurus, the abiding faith of Jupiter in Scorpio and the will-power and determination provided by four planets across the Taurus/Scorpio polarity. Saturn is very widely conjunct the Sun and, more to the point, is sesquiquadrate Pluto with an orb of only 10 minutes, making it one of the tightest aspects in this chart and therefore extremely important. This is an indefatigable, almost masochistic, combination, renowned for its endurance and ability to keep slogging away through rigid self-discipline. Reinhold

Ebertin describes it as: 'The capacity to make record efforts of the highest possible order.'[5] Given that Pluto is on Kelly's IC, no doubt the aspect will describe something of her parents and grandparents. The strength required of the blacksmith, her maternal grandfather, is certainly shown here.

As the ruler of five planets and in its own sign, Venus is also a strong planet in this chart, boding well for popularity and, in the Eleventh, for good friends. The prominence of Venus is in keeping with Kelly's popularity in the country and no doubt with many of her fellow competitors; however, the sesquiquadrate to Uranus might describe some severed ties and crossed wires in relationship terms. With Pisces on the MC and its ruler in the Fifth, Kelly's single-minded devotion to her sport has meant some sacrifice with respect to her social life. Saturn in the Eleventh also suggests that time spent with friends might be limited. Saturn here often has difficulty forming the more superficial friendships (in early life, at any rate) and any awkwardness in this area in childhood may even have inclined Kelly towards pursuing athletics in the first place. In the world that children inhabit, kids do whatever is required to compete for attention and affection. My interpretation of this is that winning races gave Kelly an edge that her siblings and schoolmates didn't have: she could come first in something. Additionally, in transporting her to various places to train and to compete, her parents would have temporarily had to put all other activities and responsibilities on hold during the times they were with her. And being strong and able to run is useful in other ways, too; from the point of view of a child, one knows one can defend oneself or run away entirely. Perhaps the Moon-Uranus is key also. Kelly's mother attributes Kelly's success to the fact that she was different: black in a otherwise white environment. Perhaps on some level she felt she had to prove herself.

Chiron (see pages 306-10) in the Tenth House in Aries is also descriptive of Kelly using her talent for coming first, and being way ahead, in a professional capacity. It may also describe the quality of being different by virtue of coming from mixed-race stock at a time and in a place where this was unusual, particularly since it opposes the Moon/Uranus conjunction.

A relatively young woman, doubtless there will be many opportunities for Kelly to be true to her Aries self, to be first to accomplish many things in the future. For example, given that Neptune falls in the Fifth and rules her MC, she might well become an ambassador for young people, perhaps in encouraging them to take up sport or to follow their dreams in other ways.

What is a Midpoint?

A midpoint is the halfway point between any two factors in the horoscope, measured in longitude. For instance, if the Sun is 13 degrees Aries and the Moon is 13 degrees Gemini, the halfway point between the Sun and Moon is 13 degrees Taurus. This is *one* of the Sun/Moon midpoints because, as with all midpoint possibilities, the Sun and Moon actually have 8 midpoints and these are made up of any point in the chart which is directly opposite 13 Taurus, or square to it, or sesquiquadrate or semi-square to it – basically any multiple of 45 degrees to the midpoint. So in the example above, 13 degrees of *all* the fixed signs and 28 degrees of *all* the mutable signs fall at the Sun/Moon midpoint.

If using the 10 basic planets plus the Ascendant, Midheaven, Node and Chiron (14 points in all), there are 91 midpoint combinations in every horoscope. At their midpoint, two factors in a chart will powerfully interact and cause their specific principles to combine. If there happens to be a third factor falling on the midpoint, this third energy will activate and combine with the other two. So if Pluto happened to be placed at 28 degrees Sagittarius in the example of Kelly Holmes, below, it would be said to be 'at' the Sun/Moon midpoint and would be written: PL=SO/MO. Most midpoints are not being touched by another factor and are therefore said to be 'empty'. However, they can become temporarily activated by transit, progression or direction. Note that only tight orbs are used – usually 1 degree. In our example below, 13 degrees Taurus (the shortest arc) and the point exactly opposite, 13 degrees Scorpio, are known as 'direct' midpoints and all others as indirect ones. In practice, all the midpoints have been found to be equally powerful, whether direct or indirect.

The discussion of midpoints in any detail is outside the scope of this book,[6] but the subject is included simply to show that that it is always worth checking the Sun/Moon midpoint because, when a planet falls at this point, the effects can be very striking. The ASC/MC midpoint is also important but, because the angles are moving very quickly, being able to calculate it is dependent on the birth time being very accurate.

How to Calculate a Midpoint

The best thing to do is to convert the planets you are interested in into absolute longitude. Imagine that you want to convert a planet at 18 degrees Aquarius into absolute longitude. The first degree of Aquarius (0 degrees) is 300 degrees so 18 degrees of Aquarius will be 318 degrees.

Table of Absolute Longitude			
0	Aries	180	Libra
30	Taurus	210	Scorpio
60	Gemini	240	Sagittarius
90	Cancer	270	Capricorn
120	Leo	300	Aquarius
150	Virgo	330	Pisces

So Kelly Holmes' Sun converts to 28 degrees 55 minutes and her Moon to 182 degrees 17 minutes. Add these two together (211 degrees and 12 minutes) and divide your answer by two to yield 105 degrees 36 minutes.

When doing your sum, remember that there are 60 minutes in a degree and 30 degrees in a sign. If your final answer is more than 360 degrees, subtract 360. Convert your answer expressed in absolute longitude to its corresponding sign and degree. In this case, 105 degrees and 36 minutes converts to 15 degrees 36 minutes of Cancer. Given that Kelly's Sun and Moon actually have eight midpoints and that these will be made up of any point in the chart which is directly opposite 15 degrees 36 minutes Cancer, or square to it, or sesquiquadrate or semi-square to it, this means that 15 degrees 36 minutes of *every* cardinal sign falls at her Sun/Moon midpoint, as does 0 degrees and 36 minutes of every mutable sign. As Mars in her natal chart is at 0 degrees 25 minutes Gemini and Neptune is at 00 degrees 19 minutes Sagittarius, one can see that both these planets fall at her Sun/Moon midpoint.

What Does the Sun/Moon Midpoint Describe?

The Sun and Moon are two extremely important points in any horoscope. They represent opposing but complementary principles; masculine and feminine, conscious and unconscious, the future and the past, what one wants and what one needs and, according to Mike Harding,[7] left-brain and right-brain activity. The Sun-Moon midpoint represents a fusion point between these two fundamental principles and, as such, is an extremely creative point, describing often what a person creates and how they do so. This is a point in the chart where they can relate wholeheartedly, body and soul, heart and mind, and how they get themselves together. Kelly has 'got herself together' through sport, a frequent Mars-Neptune activity.

Midpoint interpretation is not necessarily an easy exercise, but one way into trying to get to grips with what SO/MO=MARS/NEPTUNE might mean would be to initially consider Mars-Neptune aspects in general terms. Frequently, individuals with these aspects do something with their lives that creates an illusion of invincibility and super-human strength. Perhaps frightened of seeming weak, they don't like backing down or copping out on a challenge. This would certainly appear to be the way that Kelly has dealt with her opposition. The competitive spirit is also often viewed in the best possible light, almost as something spiritual. Basically, many of the traditional male attributes are glamorized and idealized in a multitude of different ways with this combination. Given that Neptune has much to do with the yearning and fantasies of the collective as a whole, the Mars-Neptune person often embodies the sexual or sporting dreams and fantasies of all of society, as is the case here. Joe and Josephine Bloggs may yearn to win races and score goals but in all likelihood they are never going to do so. The Mars-Neptune person may well do it for them and in so doing provides a role model for doing one's best. Of course Mars-Neptune aspects can manifest in many different ways depending on the chart overall; they could, for example, suggest a sensitivity towards or even a craving for drugs (it is indeed the combination to associate with injected drugs – prescribed or otherwise), they might be good for music and dancing and, in terms of sport, one also imagines a leaning towards swimming or water sports. Far from strength and courage, Mars-Neptune can also be associated with weakness either in psychological terms or physically, as where the muscles (Mars) are weak for some reason. In a woman's chart, it can also be descriptive of the kind of men she hooks up with. As always an individual can use their aspects or be used by them.

When Mars and Neptune are at the Sun-Moon midpoint, the manifestation of the two planets will be central to the life, describing both what the individual needs (Moon) to do and wants (Sun) to do. Mars-Neptune will no longer describe one facet of the individual among many other facets of their character, as would be the case with an ordinary aspect. Now Mars-Neptune psychology may become nothing short of the individual's reason for being. This is because the Sun and Moon are so important in the horoscope, perhaps especially so at the place where they come together. The combination also suggests an image of a hero (Sun) and perhaps of one's mother (Moon) and father (Sun) as someone who can rise above their sufferings. A person who will fight off any hint of being a victim. Perhaps someone who can rescue others from difficult situations. Kelly's dream of winning an Olympic gold medal has been central to her life and making that vision a reality has involved great strength and courage – all very descriptive of her SO/MO=MARS/NEPTUNE.

Profile: Agatha Christie

'Agatha Christie has given more pleasure in bed than any other woman.'
Nancy Banks-Smith

Astrology students sometimes like to divide a horoscope interpretation into areas such as work, relationships, money, health, etc. While this can be done, the reality is that a particular characteristic of a person will not be confined to only one area of life. A theme will work through the life on many levels and each will inform upon the other. Also, anything major concerning the person's life (and their relationships, health and work are usually major life areas) usually encapsulates the psychology of the whole chart and is not merely contained within a few houses. Concentrating on the area of work or vocation, let's take an example of someone whose work is pretty well known, the late writer Agatha Christie, to see the extent to which the whole chart is implicated.

Agatha[8] was the author of 77 detective novels, several books of short stories, six romantic stories under the pseudonym Mary Westmacott, several plays (including *The Mousetrap*, which is the world's longest-running play), an autobiography and a book of poems. She is outstanding not for what she wrote, or even for the amount that she wrote, but for the fact that she has outsold every other novelist – ever. Creator of such characters as Hercule Poirot and Miss Marple, her books have literally sold in their billions and countless film and TV adaptations have been made from them. Agatha was not a thriller-writer; her main genre, and the one in which she excelled, was cosy crime. The cosy mystery has no blood, no gore, no gruesome details. The characters tend to be stereotypical and thus comfortingly familiar. The morality is old-fashioned – there are goodies and baddies and justice always conquers in the end. The success of the cosy crime novel surely lies in its capacity to paint a comforting and reassuring (albeit quite false) world of order and fairness. Precisely the kind of world that someone with the Moon in Libra might need to believe in.

Given the popularity and abundance of Agatha's output, the fact that she was a writer should be overwhelmingly obvious from her whole chart, and it is. While Agatha's detective stories were surely much more than 'work' for her (perhaps a soul's purpose, a personal form of therapy, an outlet for her unconscious and other issues), let's remind ourselves of the usual significators we might be looking for in terms of work and writing. The houses to associate with work are the Second, Sixth and Tenth, and the house to associate with writing is the Third House. The planets most associated with writing are Mercury and the Moon. The sign to associate with writing is principally Gemini. The Ninth House and Jupiter are also associated with publishing. And the significators for the fact that the bulk of her work dealt with crime of one sort or another? Criminal activities, notably theft, come mostly under the umbrella of Mercury. Mars can be associated with violence and the thief also tends to have a prominent Mars because speed and daring are always a requirement in any theft. Pluto can be associated with murder. Scorpio is the sign, and Neptune and Pluto the planets, that are associated with mystery. Turning to Agatha's chart we find:

• With Virgo rising, Mercury is the chart ruler and it also gains prominence by being the Sun ruler as well. The planet is placed in the Second House, which describes the source of an individual's income. Note that, while Mercury is a planet to associate with writing, it also embraces all other communicative activities and so, on its own, Mercury here might describe some other more common Mercurial occupation such as secretarial duties, commerce or work in transport. It probably is descriptive of someone who values education, reading, communicating and corresponding with others, provided that such communication is harmonious (Libra), but the occupational possibilities are many. Because Mercury is placed in Libra, Agatha might have earned her wages through 'balancing the books'; she might have become a book-keeper. The abundance of possibilities explains why the whole chart has to be studied.

• Venus, ruler of the MC (one's vocation), is placed in the Third House of writing in Scorpio – the sign to associate with mystery, detection and, arguably, murder. Venus is also semi-square Mars. As Libra is on the Third House cusp, Venus is also the ruler of the Third House.

• There are two planets (Neptune conjunct Pluto) and the North Node in the Tenth House of vocation and they are all placed in Gemini, which is the zodiac sign most associated with writing. Pluto is the significator of the biggest taboo – murder – and thus a career about imaginary murder (with the input of Neptune) and, it has to be said, idealizing murder (refining it, taking the act very far from its hideous reality), is well-shown. Indeed Agatha's murder stories have become a source of escapism for the public through film and TV. Neptune and Pluto were conjunct in Gemini for decades but will not routinely appear in the Tenth House of vocation for the majority of people born during the period. One might argue that Agatha's work has endured so well because she 'spoke' for her generation and because her work embodies a particular time in English history.

• The Sixth House is the house most associated with work. A ruler of the Sixth House (Uranus) is in Agatha's Third House of writing. (The Third House is also the house of siblings and it was Agatha's sister who first persuaded her to have a go at writing.)

• Mercury gains further prominence by the tight semi-square aspect it makes to the Ascendant. Had Agatha been born many minutes earlier or later in the day, this aspect would not be present; it is very personal to her. Mercury is also worthy of interest because, other than this semi-square, it is unaspected.

• The Sun in Virgo is tightly square Mars and the Moon is widely so. Therefore, Agatha's writing would provide a socially acceptable way of expressing the potential violence of these aspects. It is a great aspect for a criminal, although of course most people with it are not criminals.

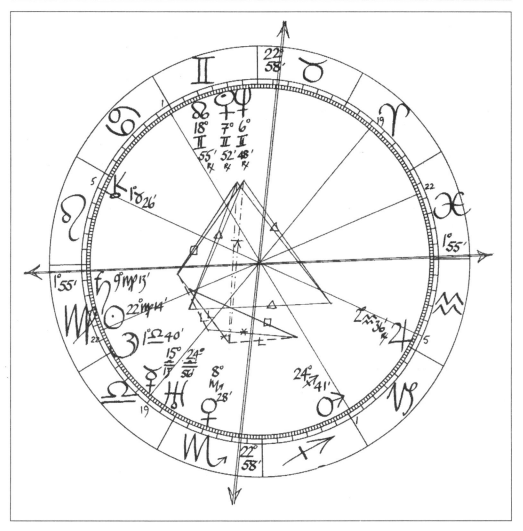

Agatha Christie: 15 September 1890, 4 a.m. GMT, Torquay, England (50N28, 3W30)

The same significators that have described Agatha's fiction will also be descriptive of other aspects of her character and life. And chart factors that have seemingly nothing to do with work or writing will plug into her style of writing and the motives for doing it. For instance, the earth/air quality of Agatha's chart describes the dryness of her work. She is not a writer to indulge in passion or emotion. The earthy quality, combined with the rising Saturn, gives a clue to the fact that she seems to be so controlled. Even her autobiography, although lengthy, gives little away in terms of her feelings and scarcely mentions her much publicized disappearance in 1926. The earth/air combination, coupled with a Fourth House Mars in Sagittarius, also point to the fact that she felt at home in the desert, for surely air combined with earth, and even Virgo on its own, is reminiscent of sand.

Venus in Scorpio in the Third describes a love of communicating mysteriously, and even when talking about herself it's clear that when she wants privacy she will insist upon it – leaving out or glossing over, one suspects, the less palatable parts of her life, in the same way that she glosses over much of the horror of murder in her fiction.

Her Saturn rising in Virgo suggests that Agatha approached the world with a certain amount of fear and trepidation, especially when young. It suggests that she was hard on herself, forever self-critical, and expected to be admonished by others. In turn she'd want to present an efficient, responsible and controlled image to the world. Above all, she would want to be useful and of service to others. The two most well-known characters created by Agatha – Hercule Poirot and Miss Marple – are surely caricatures of Virgo and therefore inflated sub-personalities of Agatha herself. In true Virgo style, both are confirmed singletons and both have an extraordinary eye for detail. Miss Marple, a stereotypical maiden aunt, knits for her nephews and is a useful member of the community. She is portrayed as the kind of person whom, seeming so ordinary, might easily be overlooked, and yet the reader and the fictional police all come to view this creature with awe and respect. Hercule Poirot is fastidious to the extreme in his appearance, observant, analytical, rational and highly critical of the police service.

If Virgo is the most prominent sign in the chart, one of the most prominent aspects has to be Saturn square Neptune/Pluto, both because it is tight and because the planets involved all fall in angular houses. Saturn/Neptune is a combination to potentially describe a fear of poisoning or someone who becomes an authority on poisons or other chemicals. With so much Virgo in her chart, it is not surprising that Agatha worked as a nurse during the First World War. She also trained and worked as a dispenser (something akin to an assistant pharmacist) in both wars. This was where she acquired the knowledge of poisons that was to prove so useful to her in her detective novels. Saturn square Neptune/Pluto is also an aspect to associate with guilt. Falling in the First House, Saturn suggests that Agatha had a strong sense of responsibility; that she felt responsible for other people's health (hence the nursing) and also for their sickness.

To pursue this last point further, let's consider Agatha's childhood and parents. Charts yield many significators to describe our parents and siblings, and this is hardly surprising since these figures dominate our early lives. The messages we extract from our early years don't easily go away. Instead, they usually fuel everything we say and do for evermore. Nevertheless, it is too simplistic to say that what happens in childhood causes what happens thereafter. Astrologically speaking, it is more accurate to say that we come into the world with a horoscope which describes certain themes, myths and stories. Our whole life is but a series of different manifestations of those stories which we extract from the world, experience and deal with according to our age, resources and experience. Whether the Tenth House should be accorded to the mother or father is a matter of some debate (see pages 287-8). My own view, followed here, is that both the Fourth and Tenth Houses, and the MC/IC signs and rulers, describe both parents. This means that both parents will share many of the same significators. Any planet falling in the sign of Cancer usually says something specifically about the mother and any planet found in Capricorn also in some ways describes the father. Agatha had no planets falling in these signs.

In Agatha Christie's case the significators for both parents are:
- Neptune in Gemini because it falls in the Tenth House.
- Pluto in Gemini because it falls in the Tenth House and is the ruler of the Fourth House.
- Mars in Sagittarius because it is in the Fourth House and is the ruler of the Fourth House.

- Venus in Scorpio because it is the ruler of the MC.
- The signs Taurus and Scorpio because they fall on the MC/IC axis.

An additional significator for her mother is:
- The Moon in Libra in the Second because the Moon specifically relates to the mother.

As for her father, the additional significators are:
- The Sun, which is a traditional significator. Note its square to Mars and semi-square to Venus.
- Saturn, which is another traditional significator and, as we have seen, is square Neptune/Pluto.

Agatha's father, Fred, is described by her as a 'very agreeable man', popular, with an 'enormous number of friends whom he enjoyed entertaining'. And rather lazy: in other words, Venusian (Taurus on the MC and Sun semi-square Venus). We are told that 'he had no outstanding characteristics', had been trained for nothing and was not particularly intelligent. She thought he had a 'simple and loving heart'. It seems that he didn't do very much with his life; he had an independent income and spent his days at his cricket club (where he was president), coming home at mealtimes. The Sun square Mars, with Mars falling in the Fourth and being the ruler of the IC, shows the interest he had in sport. Perhaps Mars falling in Sagittarius describes the fact that he was foreign (American), he had a good sense of humour, was generous to a fault and easy-going.

Significantly, Fred died when Agatha was eleven years old. This is described by the Saturn square Neptune/Pluto: she lost her father through death. But even before he died, Fred was a weak father figure (Saturn/Neptune), a man who, arguably, wanted to escape from his responsibilities, perhaps because he had distorted the notion of responsibilities in the first place by experiencing them as more onerous than they need be. What Fred died of is not clear (Saturn square Neptune/Pluto is in keeping with the fact that his illness was apparently never properly diagnosed). With Sun square Mars, perhaps he had a heart attack. Whatever happened, Agatha believed that his health was worn down by his continual financial worries. Again, all very Saturn/Neptune: the father who feels weak and unable to cope. A 'nice' man who wants to avoid confrontation and anything disagreeable. In her early childhood, Agatha's family was quite well off but gradually, through the mismanagement of trustees, bad luck, bad advice or poor investments, their financial circumstances deteriorated so that, after Fred's death, they had become comparatively poor.

When a child loses a significant person in their life, or something else goes very wrong in childhood, on some level the youngster often feels as if it is their fault, even though they may not always be fully conscious of this feeling. Agatha was too young and too powerless to be able to do anything about her father's illness, his death, their poverty or her mother's subsequent illness, but with Saturn rising she almost definitely would have felt responsible. And surely that is the crux of detective fiction and an unconscious reason for Agatha writing it, because the detective is always trying to find out who has an alibi, and therefore who is guilty and who is not. It's as if she spent her life trying to work out who was responsible for her father's death and trying to establish that she wasn't. Perhaps in her mind, as a child, she vaguely thought he had been poisoned. In any event, it's easy to argue that, by dying, her father left the scene of the crime; he didn't have to deal with the impoverishment of his family, or his feelings of guilt about it.

Clara, Agatha's mother, was easily bored. She liked to flit from one subject to the next and was able to think of several different things at once. Everything she talked about sounded exciting. How Neptune/Pluto in Gemini this sounds! Further, we are told that Clara was of 'a naturally mystic turn of mind', that she was very intuitive and possibly clairvoyant. Still in keeping with this Gemini conjunction, when she died at the age of 72 it was from bronchial problems. As always, planets in the Fourth and Tenth describe both parents. Mars is in the 4th and its square to the Sun is descriptive of the fact that, after Fred's death, Clara started having heart attacks. These attacks would come on so suddenly that Agatha often woke in the middle of the night, convinced that her mother had died. Saturn rising in Virgo is descriptive of someone who approaches the world and those within it with considerable anxiety. Her early exposure to other people's anxieties and her worries about her mother's health are well described in her autobiography. Agatha's writing perhaps became her means of escape, her way of controlling her anxiety.

Agatha's Moon in Libra describes that aspect of both her and her mother that wanted to keep things nice and harmonious. Although by no means unusual in middle-class Victorian families, it's clear that they were both allergic to any kind of public embarrassment; both took pains to behave appropriately in all social situations. This describes her mother when Agatha was a child, and this is Agatha herself as an adult. In fact, in keeping with lunar psychology, the need for social approval is probably descriptive of a large part of the family dynamic in which she was raised. Her father also probably took pains to put on a good front. It's clear from Agatha's autobiography that she experienced her mother, in true Moon in Libra style, as someone who wanted to please people and to see things from their point of view. For instance, following on from Fred's death, Clara knew that the sensible thing to do would be to sell the large, crumbling and expensive-to-maintain family house and buy something smaller, but the children didn't want this and so Clara kept the big house. Agatha's Moon is in her Second House, in keeping with the fact that it was her mother who looked after the finances. It is also in a Grand Trine with Jupiter and Neptune/Pluto – aspects that I would probably ignore except that the trine between the Moon and Jupiter is tight, describing perhaps Agatha's ability to stay upbeat and positive, and her need to believe in some kind of natural justice. In Agatha's whodunits, the scales are always balanced towards the good in the end. The goodies live happily ever after and the baddies get caught, though usually in the nicest possible way. Although there are crimes, nothing crass, ugly or violent gets an upper hand. And although the thrust of her work revolves around mystery, there is often a secondary story of a love affair, and this is described by the habitually match-making Moon in Libra, Mercury (which is also in Libra), plus Venus falling in the Third House of writing.

Agatha's first husband is shown by her Mars in Sagittarius (his name was Archie!) square her Sun. He was clever, daring and resourceful, a decisive man who was single-minded in getting what he wanted. Reminiscent of her father in his ability to go his own way, Archie was certainly like her father in his devotion to sport – in his case, the passion was for golf. In keeping with the Mars square, Archie was one of the first pilots to fly. Very daringly and courageously (Sun square Mars) for the time, when planes were unsafe and unreliable, Agatha also took to the air: she had a short spin for £5 on 10 May 1911.

Agatha's second husband was Max Mallowan, an archaeologist to whom she was married for 35 years. He is mostly shown by her Seventh House and the ruler Neptune being conjunct Pluto (the planet to associate with archaeology). Max was fourteen years younger than Agatha (Neptune is in the youthful sign of Gemini), he wrote papers and books and was successful in his field. He is described sketchily but in a fairly Piscean kind of way; he was kind, tactful and sympathetic. After they married Agatha became interested in archaeology herself and would join Max on his digs, sometimes spending six months of the year in Syria and other parts of the Middle East. The ruler of the Seventh falling in the Tenth brings the two houses together and conjoins marriage with career in various ways. One way is that both the detective and the archaeologist spend their time digging in order to expose that which is dead and buried. As has been noted, the desert is a dry place and it is not surprising that Agatha with her earth/air chart would be at home there. Mars in Sagittarius square her Sun shows she was an adventurous traveller; even now, few women will travel on their own to exotic locations, far less in the 1940s. Indeed, it was while she was travelling in the Middle East that she met Max. Mars in the Fourth in Sagittarius also describes her as potentially making a home overseas and possibly in a religious, war-torn, hot, dry region. Mars in the Fourth also describes the fact that Agatha had a London home bombed in the war and a Devon home used at one time for war purposes by the US Navy.

Agatha disappeared for ten days in December 1926 following the death of her mother and Archie's announcement that he had fallen in love with someone else and wanted a divorce. What happened to Agatha during this time, and her motives for her disappearance, are far from clear. Entire books and a film have focused on it, all in keeping with Neptune/Pluto in the Tenth – Agatha is famous for mystery! She says she was suffering from amnesia brought about by stress and grief. Others have suggested that she wanted (in Venus in Scorpio fashion) to get her revenge on Archie by making him worried that she had committed suicide. Uranus in Libra in the Third House may also be relevant; the notion that her marriage (Libra) had broken down (Uranus) came as a great shock and put her mental equilibrium out of balance, particularly considering that few people did divorce in those days. With her Moon in Libra, Agatha needed to think of herself as happily married. Whatever actually happened, one might conjecture that she experienced a huge anxiety attack and wanted to avoid reality for a while.

Profile: On Integration: the Case of 'Amanda'

When studying a chart, students of astrology are often faced with a variation of the following question: Does the fact that Joe Bloggs has X in his chart cancel out his also having Y there? When one gets down to it, the answer is always 'No'. Joe Bloggs has X and Y in his chart and, while there may be tension between X and Y, they are never going to be mutually exclusive; at best they will work together in the life and each will become reliant on the other.

The chart for Amanda[9] is a case in point. On the one hand, her chart has a strong Saturnian feeling to it and yet there are also major Leo/Jupiter features. The Moon in Capricorn quite closely square Saturn is suggestive of an Amanda who is serious, controlled, fearful of not being good enough and shy about expressing her feelings. While potentially ambitious, this is a non-pushy, non-flashy, realistic, down-to-earth, hard-working Moon. The Sun in the Fifth House conjunct Jupiter in Leo square Neptune, on the other hand, is descriptive of a much more buoyant, exuberant, enthusiastic, risk-taking, full-on, 'out there' energy. It is suggestive of someone who appreciates pomp, ceremony and pageantry. The squares to Neptune are descriptive of someone who appreciates glamour, longs for an escape route and yearns to be in some way special. What follows is the story of how all the various strands of her chart have worked together.

Amanda's father was an academic musician and conductor, and her mother might have been a professional singer had family responsibilities not interceded. Following the family musical tradition, Amanda was blessed with a beautiful voice and went to Cambridge to study music. Unfortunately she received unsuitable voice training while she was there and, although she didn't realize it at the time, damaged her vocal cords. She left university and went to work in advertising. However, her true vocation, as indeed her chart suggests, was to be an opera singer and for some years she made strenuous efforts to turn this dream into reality. These efforts included surgery to her vocal cords and a great deal of voice training, all of which she funded herself through

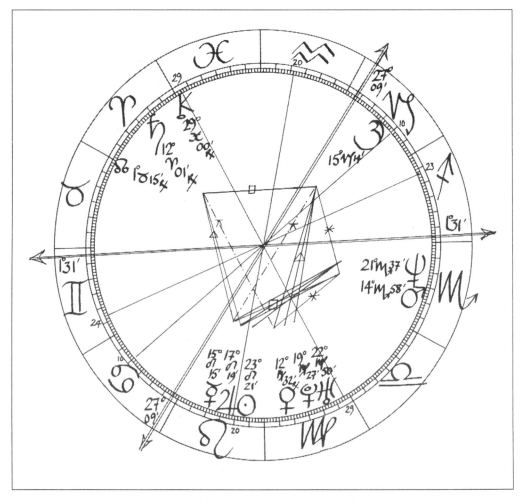

'*Amanda*': 16 August 1967, 11.30 p.m. GDT, Liverpool, England (53N25, 2W55)

her non-singing work, which she continued alongside her training. Now she is a successful freelance singer working in the UK and abroad and, at the time of our meeting, a permanent member of the Royal Opera House for that particular season.

The classic zodiac combination associated with opera is Leo and Scorpio. Most people with an emphasis of personal planets in these two signs really love opera if they are exposed to it. Leo suggests drama and colour, and Scorpio indicates passion, tragedy and revenge (favourite storylines of many operatic scores). The input of Jupiter describes the exaggerated drama and tragedy which can only be found in the operatic arena. Neptune, a planet to associate with music, is in the Sixth House of work and made more important by its square to the Sun. Venus, the other planet to associate with music, is in Virgo, suggesting musical craft and technique, and it is in the Fifth House (the Leo house) of creativity. Mercury is conjunct Jupiter squaring Mars in the Sixth, suggesting work that involves the telling of dramatic and potentially angry and violent stories. Even the Uranus/Pluto conjunction in the Fifth can be descriptive of some kind of explosive, creative technique. Much more could be said about all this but the reader should have no difficulty in seeing the potential opera singer in the Fourth, Fifth and Sixth House planets and aspects, but what about the rest of the chart?

Amanda has Gemini rising, suggesting that she goes out into the world wanting to learn and to communicate. The ruler, Mercury, is in the Fourth House conjunct Jupiter. This suggests that her parents (Fourth) had huge (Jupiter) ideas (Mercury) about her education. They were ambitious for her; they wanted a superior (Jupiter) education, nay, the best (Leo) education for her. Or she wanted it for herself. Little wonder that she attended Cambridge University, for centuries considered to be one of the seats of learning in the UK. Cambridge started out as a centre of religious observance (Jupiter) and is a place where royalty (Leo) go to to study. Many of the colleges were founded by the 15th-century monarchs. As the ruler of the chart, the importance of Mercury cannot be denied and here it falls in the Fourth House of home while falling in Leo, the sign we associate with royalty. Amanda sings in the Royal Opera House, which is often referred to, quite simply, as The House. The idea of communicating (Mercury) dramatically (Leo) in an opera house (Fourth) couldn't be more explicit.

Is it any surprise with the Moon falling in Capricorn (and not forgetting the square to Saturn) and in the Ninth House of further education that Amanda went to one of the oldest universities in the English-speaking world? A circumstance that required tremendous hard work and academic rigour, a rigour that only Saturn can deliver. This isn't any old university: Cambridge University is an institution (Capricorn) that commands respect (Capricorn) throughout the world (Ninth). Returning for a minute to the chart ruler, Mercury conjunct Jupiter in Leo, Cambridge University is *hugely prestigious* in the same way as the Royal Opera House. The town itself is very old, full of medieval and Tudor stone buildings. As for the Opera House, this, too, is shown here, for it is also something of an institution. In other words, everything in the chart, when put together, points to a university such as Cambridge and also to the Royal Opera House. One thinks of the Moon in Capricorn as being potentially descriptive of some kind of professional mother or caretaker, but here it is descriptive of a professional house! Falling in the Ninth House, there is the suggestion that Amanda will sing in opera houses abroad. The Moon in the Ninth, and the ruler of the Fourth in the Ninth, suggests that she will live overseas or at least, at some point, have a second home in another country. That country is likely to have a strong Saturnian flavour, as will many of the cities in which she gives concerts.

As for Amanda herself, the Sun, Jupiter and Mercury in Leo suggest that she can bluff confidence. The squares to Neptune also indicate that she can be a great deceiver! She is good at appearances (in both meanings of the word); good at show. As a singer and in real life, she is a great actor. One is reminded here that the Sun in the chart, far from describing how one actually is, indicates what one is striving to become. In other words, the more Amanda achieves and the more recognition and acknowledgement she receives for that achievement, the more genuinely confident she will become.

Her life in music allows her to escape from much of the harshness of the world, a harshness that her Saturnian side is all too aware of and (Sun square Neptune) to which she is sensitive, too. As an opera singer, Amanda gives voice to the Scorpio themes of betrayal, revenge, death and tragedy while avoiding or, if you like, transcending them in the real world. There would have been many times when she would have doubted her abilities (the Moon in Capricorn square Saturn) and, on occasion, no doubt she will continue to do so. However, the Leo planets with that buoyant Jupiter will hopefully prevent her from feeling completely crushed and defeated, and enable her to rise above such feelings.

Holistic Astrology – Peter and the Indian Cobra

This case is shown with a triple purpose. First, to show how exciting and holistic even very simple astrology can be. Second, to show similarities between homœopathy and astrology and to introduce the reader to homœopathy. Third, to illustrate some of the philosophy put forward in Chapter 1, but, in particular, the idea that all manifestations in and by the universe (macrocosm) are also reflected inside every individual (microcosm). This means that all the plants, animals, geology, geography and everything else in the universe can also be seen in the horoscope. Charles Carter tells us that 'every kind of life may be classed astrologically'[10] and I agree with him. Let's use the example of birds and assign to them the rulership of the sign Aquarius. For individual species, we need to think in terms of sub-divisions (and even sub-sub-divisions): robins would come under the sub-division of Aries; poultry would come under Cancer; swans under Leo; sparrows under Virgo; many birds of prey under Scorpio, and so on. This sub-division idea is very similar to techniques employed by Vedic astrologers. In previous chapters, I have attempted the classification of various things, such as countries and animals, to the signs. What follows is an illustration of some of the correspondences put forward, based on my personal observations, some of which agree with and some of which significantly depart from traditional correspondences.

Homœopathy is a system of medicine based on the idea that a disease with a particular set of symptoms can be cured by a medicine made of a substance which, if it were given to a healthy person, would produce similar symptoms. For example, the humble onion (*Allium cepa*) makes our eyes water when we slice it and is used homœopathically for those with hay fever, largely characterized by watering eyes. Hippocrates (c.460-c.370 BC), a great physician and astrologer of his day, is usually credited with having laid the foundations of modern medicine in the West. He is also credited with the phrase 'Similia similibus curantur' – like must be treated with like. However, others – in Greece and India for instance – said the same many centuries before.

About Homœopathic Remedies

Homœopathic remedies can be made from many things: plants, minerals, animals, even disease substances, are all common source materials. Such minute amounts of the relevant material (too small to be detectable by scientific analysis) are used that plants or other substances considered poisonous in their crude state can now be safely employed. Where animals are used, one bee that has died naturally could probably supply the whole world with the remedy *Apis* for generations. Making the remedy is a complex business but, simplistically speaking, the substance is diluted greatly and then succussed (shaken), or ground, to harness its curative properties. The amount of dilution and shaking varies according to the potency (strength) of the remedy being made; the higher the potency the more the substance is diluted and the more it is succussed or ground. With homœopathy, less is certainly more. While not even a single molecule may remain of the original source material in even a low potency of the remedy, homœopathic remedies do work, or at least they work if the patient is given the correct remedy (what is known as the simillimum). Homœopaths, in keeping with the findings of modern physics, suggest that what does remain in the medicine is some kind of pattern, essence or 'memory' of the original substance. It is this essence that is thought to ignite the healing process.

As astrologers we tend to say that what is going on in the sky is 'similar' or mirrors what is happening on earth. We might say that the horoscope is a map, a mirror of the psyche or indeed of a situation. It is part of the astrologer's role to hold up that mirror, so that the situation can be seen more clearly and thus, hopefully, appropriate choices can be made. At the very least, a greater understanding of the matter in hand can be reached. In that sense, the consultant astrologer too is 'treating like with like' and arguably, therefore, practising a form of homœopathy.

A routine medical examination in 1998 revealed that Peter,[11] then 44 years old, was born with a missing cusp in the aortic valve of his heart. He had bronchial pneumonia as a child and a collapsed lung as an adult and, while both conditions would have been related to his congenital heart abnormality, his valvular problem had not been diagnosed. Throughout his life, Peter's only real symptom had been breathlessness on exertion; this was mild in his early life but noticeable by 1998 and markedly so by 2000 when I first saw him. Peter had never been athletic and as a boy was not really able to get actively involved in sport, even though sport is something he has always followed as an armchair spectator. However, if Peter felt less physically able than other boys, it was not so huge an issue that he thought anything of it, nor did anyone else appear to notice.

By the spring of 2000, Peter was presenting with aortic regurgitation and high blood pressure. Unable by this time to take a deep breath at all, he was quite poorly. He had been told that he had to have a bypass, and to have this surgery sooner rather than later. His licence to work with radar had been taken away from him because of his acute physical and emotional distress.

Peter was (and is) in a stable marriage with a young daughter and very much enjoyed his work as an air-traffic controller. As well as being worried about his health and the repercussions it might have upon his family, he was concerned about money and losing his lucrative job. He had been told that he would be found alternative employment but it would be 'on the ground', which might mean less status and would probably mean less pay.

Peter had no particular belief in homœopathy and scarcely knew what it was. But he was somewhat desperate and, more than that, wanted to pacify his sister (a friend of mine), who was insisting that he should try it. Anyway, it transpired that our consultation happened in Peter's living room. I got very little information out of him and I left the house without a clue as to what to do. What I did discover was that although Peter was an air-traffic controller with a fear of heights, his favourite dream was of flying. Surely this was significant? He said that his only other health problem was a persistent skin eruption on his face.

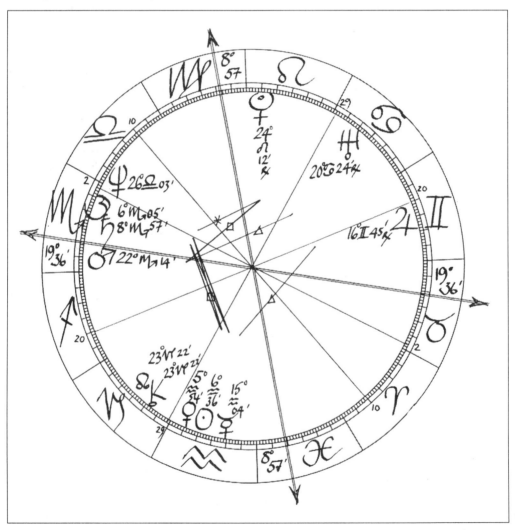

Peter: 27 January 1954, 2.20 a.m. GMT, Epsom, England (51N20, 0W16)

Peter's chart is dominated by squares between Aquarius and Scorpio. Mars is rising in Scorpio, describing perhaps a man who goes out into the world competing and perhaps feeling attacked, so he has to defend himself. With Mars falling in Scorpio, he would be particularly keen to defend his privacy. The Mars and Ascendant are also in tight square to Pluto, intensifying this feeling to the point where his very survival is at stake. He easily feels threatened. Pluto is in Leo, the sign to associate with the heart, and of course he has a literal survival issue (hidden for so many years, in true Plutonic fashion) with his cardiac problems. The theme of the *survival of the fittest* holds true for all living things but the theme of competition is particularly evident in the animal kingdom, and the rising Mars square Pluto gives a clue that the required remedy may come from the animal kingdom. Perhaps an animal that easily feels threatened and whom others, in turn, may find menacing.

The Sun has always been associated with the heart, and the Leo/Aquarius axis with the heart and circulatory system. We can also see that Peter has the Sun conjunct Venus and square Saturn, implying lessons and difficulties with his heart in various contexts, including emotional ones. Saturn is the co-ruler of his three personal planets in Aquarius and, much more significantly, his chart has tight aspects with Sun/Saturn, Moon/Saturn and Venus/Saturn. Together, these speak of someone who needs to feel in control, someone who is dutiful and responsible. Indeed, he may feel he is responsible for everything, but probably without the necessary confidence (or the physical strength) to feel equal to those responsibilities. With Saturn falling in Scorpio, the suggestion is that Peter is responsible for averting death and crisis and, with the Sun/Moon involvement, potentially responsible for his parents (whose own health was failing). With responsibility being such a huge issue, it is little wonder that he needs to feel in control. The Aquarian planets show he wants space and freedom, but surely responsibility issues don't sit easily with the enjoyment of personal liberty? As an air-traffic controller, Peter is faced daily with the huge responsibility for the survival of others;·his job is all about averting crisis.

The curative remedy for Peter was *Naja*: a remedy made from the venom of the Indian cobra. It is not a remedy that is commonly prescribed but it does crop up frequently in patients presenting with valvular disorders. By 'curative', I don't mean that his missing valve could ever be replaced or that his health is, or might be, the same as others who do not have this congenital problem. But his condition did materially improve after some weeks on the remedy. His need for surgery diminished greatly so that now, some five years later, his condition is merely being monitored; he no longer needed an operation. His doctors were flummoxed by his improvement and each implied that the other had exaggerated his condition. His breathlessness and sleep improved substantially, as did his anxiety. He also very quickly felt better in himself and could return to his old job because he was given his licence back. In the end, he took the decision to work in the less stressful air-traffic control training centre, where he reports being happy.

Returning to Peter's breathlessness, three personal planets in Aquarius certainly describe someone who wants space, wants to breathe: the squares from Scorpio, and specifically from Saturn in that sign, imply the sense of being suffocated. One imagines (with the input of the Moon and Venus) that he might feel that women suffocate him. Often no doubt his strong sense of responsibility, and fear generally, prevents him doing what he really wants; hence the feeling of not being able to breathe. Snake remedies come up a lot in cardiac problems: the feeling of suffocation is common to many people with coronary problems and, of course, many snakes kill their prey by suffocation.

Of the remedy *Naja*, the much respected Indian homœopath Rajan Sankaran says that it is similar in many ways to other snake remedies but that what singles it out is the strong sense of *duty* connected with it.[12] He says the behaviour of *Naja* people is similar to that of the cobra: they may threaten to strike but will only do so under immense provocation. One might add that it is also rather like the behaviour of Mars-Pluto for whom violence is a real taboo and, falling in Scorpio-Leo, beneath one's dignity. When asked what his fears were, Peter said: 'I don't like to get into a situation where I have to argue the point.'

Peter was very slim but told me that he had been overweight in the past. As a youth his weight in stones matched his age in years; at 17 he weighed about 17 stone (238 pounds/108 kilos). His sister reported that he could be slightly anorexic; he said he was simply careful about what he ate, as he could easily binge. I asked him how he had managed to lose weight when obesity had been a problem. He said he just fasted for a week and then went on periodic long fasts. Surely this is very snake-like behaviour? Snakes don't have to eat that often but, when they do, their whole shape swells magnificently to the size of their prey!

Peter reported a fear of heights and yet in his favourite dream he is flying. Like many snakes, the cobra's main enemies (other than humans) are birds. If we look at the signs of the zodiac from the point of view of the animal kingdom, snakes can be ascribed to Scorpio and birds to Aquarius. Peter's chart can be viewed as Aquarius versus Scorpio but equally it can be viewed as bird versus snake. Flying is the huge advantage that a bird has over a snake. As an air-traffic controller, Peter is in control of the big birds in the sky! Incidentally, *Naja* is one of a handful of remedies that has dreams of flying as part of its symptomatology – a fact that led to the choice of remedy in the first place. His favourite dream of flying perhaps symbolizes the cherished wish to be looked up to and of being in a position where one has no enemies (flying birds have no enemies except, in some cases, other birds); a nice place to be if one feels easily threatened.

There is nothing unusual about the fact that Peter likes 'consistently hot weather' (day after day, unchanging hot weather), nor is there anything unusual in his liking for rock music. Nevertheless, it is interesting to note that snakes – which are cold-blooded creatures – can often be found on rocks, basking in the hot sun. And one notes the particularly cool persona adopted by many with a Scorpio/Aquarius mix. Additionally, people with cardiac disorders often feel the cold.

Sankaran says that the physical appearance of the face of the person requiring *Naja* can often look rather like the hood of the cobra, with perhaps glasses creating that impression. In Peter's case, his facial skin was very dry. It peeled along the hairline, eyebrows and down the side of his nose, in a cobra shape. At times he reported that it was red and felt raw and itchy. The planet associated with skin (Saturn) in Scorpio (snake), picking up Venus, perhaps describes doubts Peter may have harboured (as one does with skin problems) about his attractiveness. The remedy cured this eczema-like skin eruption completely. In a variety of ways, he felt able to face the world.

As a child, Peter kept snakes and he also brought home injured birds. Interestingly, his sister is frightened of birds (the Aquarius planets fall in his Third/sister House). Should we read anything into the fact that he had a gerbil (snake food?) in his living room?! The final icing on the cake is the fact that, in Chinese astrology, Peter is born in the year of the snake!

A version of this article has appeared in the Astrological Association's Journal *and also in the Astrological Lodge of London's* Quarterly. *Thanks to the editors of both publications for agreeing to its inclusion here.*

Profile: The Chart for a Country – Indonesia

Astrology can be applied to many subjects. While some specialist knowledge of the relevant subject is useful and specific astrological techniques are required for mundane astrology (the application of astrology to world events), nevertheless the basic way of

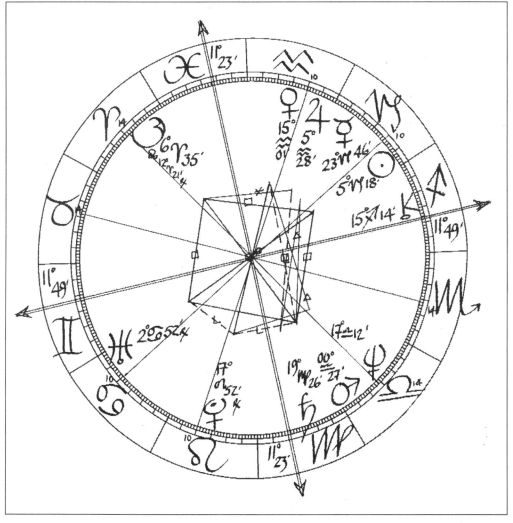

Indonesia: 27 December 1949, 5.22 p.m. (-8), Jakarta, Indonesia (6S10, 106E48)

viewing horoscopes that I have already outlined works pretty well, whatever the subject matter. Here are some keep-it-simple snapshots of a couple of non-personal charts.

As with most countries, there are many charts that might be used for Indonesia. The one shown here is for the official start of the country's independence; the time when Queen Juliana of the Netherlands signed an Act formerly severing the connection between Indonesia and the Netherlands.[13]

This large country,[14] formerly the Dutch East Indies, has a population in the region of 200-250 million people. It embraces about 18,000 islands – the largest archipelago in the world – of which about 6,000 are inhabited, the largest or most well-known being Sumatra, Java, Kalimantan (two-thirds of Borneo), Bali and Sulawesi. The Gemini Ascendant is surely reflective of the scattered, variable quality of the country and its national motto which is 'Unity in Diversity'. Resting as it does on the edge of various tectonic plates, Indonesia is frequently hit by earthquakes. The islands are also home to about sixty active volcanoes including the legendary Krakatoa which, when it erupted in 1833, created the largest explosion ever recorded.

Among other things, Indonesia's chart has a Grand Cross involving the Sun, Moon, Mars and Uranus. Added to this is Pluto, which contacts both Mars and Uranus by semi-square aspects. In fact, Uranus semi-square Pluto is exact to the minute. Pluto also opposes Venus. This combination of the Sun, Moon, Mars, Uranus and Pluto is spicy and exciting but, with a strong flavour of fireworks, could hardly be called safe. There is considerable potential for inflammatory, violent situations and unexpected deaths on a grand scale, all reflecting Indonesia's aforementioned vulnerability to earthquakes, tsunamis and volcanoes. Ethnic tensions and political unrest have tended to complete the general picture of instability. The Grand Cross also hints at some of the things Indonesia is famous for – its spices, for example, and its oil.

Judging by this chart (and doubtless consideration should be paid to its other charts, too), good government will be particularly needed between 2008 and 2012, when Uranus in Aries and Pluto in Capricorn in the sky will trigger this powder keg of a Grand Cross.

Profile: The Chart for an Accident

The following example illustrates how, in looking at a chart for an event, it can be fruitful to imagine that the chart belongs to a person. Even without meaning to, one ends up using language that is pertinent to the matter in hand. This example[15] also illustrates the potency of a rising planet. It also raises the issue of meaning.

Picture a narrow, not very long, residential road in North London with Victorian houses on either side, some small and some large. The only blot on the landscape is the heavy traffic and, in particular, the lorries that hurtle up and down the road. Against this backdrop, shortly after 4 o'clock on a June morning in 1983, a 38-ton juggernaut drove into a couple of houses. The occupants of those houses were unharmed as they were sleeping at the back but the driver and co-driver of the juggernaut were killed.

Turning to the chart, the first thing one notices is a lack of earth. It's almost as if the vehicle wasn't grounded, and the rest of the chart points much the same way. There are three close conjunctions and several oppositions, but no squares. If this were the chart

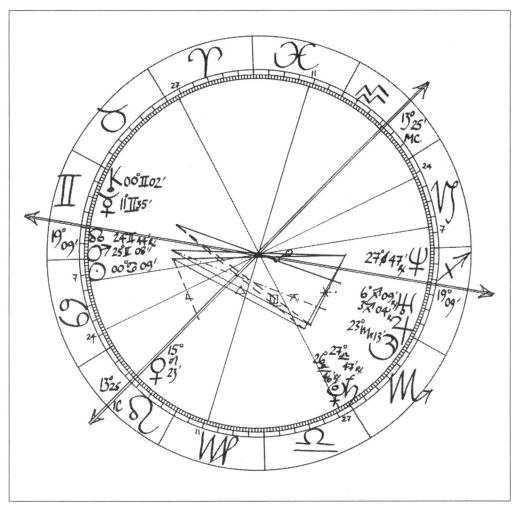

Accident: 22 June 1983, 4.05 a.m. GDT, (51N33, 0W06)

of a person, one might wonder if they were somewhat prone to extremism and whether there was sufficient strength for getting themselves out of tight corners. The Ascendant falls in Gemini, the sign of short-distance travel, and Mars is there conjunct the Node, implying energetic and forceful communication with the immediate environment and those within it, perhaps descriptive of an overwhelming 'drive' to come first (although apparently the vehicle wasn't speeding). The Mars/Node/Sun conjunction opposes Neptune, suggesting that although there is a lot of energy, it is not only scattered (Gemini) but dispersed, diffused and lacking direction. Mercury, the ruler of the Ascendant, is in the Twelfth House and opposes Uranus but doesn't do much else. If this were a small boy, one might expect a lad who'd have a mind of his own. Perhaps he'd have learning difficulties, maybe he'd communicate in fits and starts; one would expect his mind to be going very fast but perhaps somewhat erratically. Although he might be good at grasping the main issues, one wouldn't expect much precision or accuracy. As a parent or teacher, one might think this boy needs brakes!

Prior to the accident, many residents were already distressed and angry about the traffic in their road and one woman could even tell the tonnage of lorries, and whether they were full or not, simply by listening to the sound the trucks were making as they sped past her top-floor flat. However, before the accident people hadn't started talking to their neighbours about their disquiet to any marked degree. The lorry was carrying carcasses of meat; symbolically, as well as literally, it was carrying meat for the local people because finally they had something to get their teeth into. In true Mars in Gemini fashion, angry neighbour talked to angry neighbour and a Traffic Action Group was formed to put their ideas into action. Over the months following the accident, the group successfully petitioned the local council for various measures to be taken. The Saturn/Pluto conjunction in Libra plugs into Sun/Mars opposition Neptune by soft aspect; the message being that the heavy tonnage (Saturn/Pluto) wasn't fair (Libra) and was seriously undermining everyone's health (Sixth House). The Traffic Action Group wouldn't have been formed had the accident not occurred where it did; a mere couple of minutes earlier or later, the lorry would have been travelling down a different road entirely. All of which raises philosophical questions that the reader can consider at leisure. One final point – the meat was carried as hung-up carcasses. Looking at the shape of the chart, does it not resemble the back of an open lorry with goods hanging down on the right-hand side and goods hanging down on the left? In our mind's eye, can we not see the lorry going around a corner and the meat on one side hurtling over to the other side and unbalancing the vehicle altogether? And should we attribute any meaning to the fact that the lorry was carrying its meat from *Kil*bride to *Mar*seilles?

NB: If you want to find out the latitude and longitude of a street in order to set up a super accurate horoscope (assuming you have a super accurate birth time too of course), simply go to www.multimap.com or www.streetmap.co.uk

Notes and References

Chapter 1: First Things First – Philosophical Underpinnings

1. The reader wishing to know about the practice of astrology and touch on some philosophy from a contemporary and practical 'hands on' viewpoint would do well to read Dennis Elwell's excellent book *Cosmic Loom*, The Urania Trust, 1999.
2. The word 'karma' is usually translated as meaning 'action', and comes from the Sanskrit word *kri* meaning 'to do'.
3. Much of our understanding of karma and reincarnation is derived from the Hindu teachings of about 3500 BC, which are enshrined in the ancient scriptures known as The Vedas.
4. According to Matthew Wood, *The Magical Staff – The Vitalist Tradition in Western Medicine*, North Atlantic Books, 1992.

Chapter 2: Elements and Modes

1. Suggested further reading: *Astrology, Psychology and the Four Elements*, Stephen Arroyo, CRCS Publications, 1975.
2. Marilyn Monroe: 1 June 1926, 9:30 a.m. PST, Los Angeles, California (34N03, 118W15). Source: Birth certificate.
3. Dean, Geoffrey, and Mather, Arthur, *Recent Advances in Natal Astrology*, The Astrological Association, 1977.

Chapter 4: The Planets and Other Essential Bodies

Astronomical data have been taken from www.nasa.gov and *Teach Yourself Planets* by David Rothery, Teach Yourself, 2003.

1. Robert F. Kennedy: 20 November 1925, 3.11 p.m. EST, Brookline, Massachusetts, USA (42N20, 71W07). Source: Data from Kennedy's office.
2. Tyler, Pam, *Mercury: The Astrological Anatomy of a Planet*, Aquarian Press, 1985.
3. Graves, Robert, *The Greek Myths*, Penguin Books, 1960.
4. Bolen, Jean Shinoda, *Goddesses in Everywoman*, Harper Perennial, 1984.
5. Wilkinson, Richard G., *The Impact of Inequality: How to Make Sick Societies Healthier*, New Press, 2005.
6. *The New York Times*, 7 August 2002.
7. Arroyo, Stephen, *Relationships and Life Cycles: Modern Dimensions of Astrology*, CRCS, 1979.
8. ibid.
9. Jackson, Eve, *Jupiter, an Astrologer's Guide*, Aquarian Press, 1987. Unfortunately, this excellent book is no longer in print.
10. Gauquelin, Michel, *Written in the Stars*, Aquarian Press, 1988.
11. Gustave Flaubert: 12 December 1821, 4 a.m. LMT, Rouen, France (49N26, 1E05). Source: Birth certificate. N.B. 13 December is also a possibility.
12. Construction of the Berlin Wall started on 13 August 1961 and its destruction began on 9 November 1989.
13. For more information on the discovery of Uranus, read Dava Sobel's book *The Planets*, HarperPerennial, 2006 edition. This includes a lengthy letter written in 1847 by William Herschel's sister, Caroline, in which she tells the story of the discovery of both Uranus and Neptune.

14. William Herschel: 15 November 1738, Hanover, Germany. He was born with Uranus at 3 degrees Capricorn opposing Neptune at 2 degrees Cancer. He died on 25 August 1822 at the age of 84. His Uranus return was very tight at the time – the planet was at 3 degrees Capricorn. Even more spooky was the fact that Neptune, which would never have been discovered if Uranus hadn't already been found, was now conjunct Uranus at 2 degrees Capricorn.

15. Kollerstrom, Nick, *Astrochemistry – A Study of Metal-Planet Affinities*, Emergence Press, 1984.

16. See www.uic.au/ura.htm

17. An apothecary turned chemist, Klaproth was born in Wernigerode, in the Harz region of Northern Germany, on 1 December 1743 and died on 1 January 1817. More can be found out about him at:
www.genchem.chem.wisc.edu/lab/PTL/PTL/BIOS/klapoth.htm

18. John Couch Adams was born on 5 June 1819 and died in 1892. According to Wikipedia, Urbain Le Verrier was born on 11 March 1811 and died on 23 September 1877.

19. See an article written by Nick Kollerstrom at
www.ucl.ac.uk/sts/nk/neptune/chron.htm

20. Mayo, Jeff, *The Planets and Human Behaviour*, CRCS Publications, 1997.

21. Greene, Liz, *The Astrological Neptune and the Quest for Redemption*, Red Wheel/Weiser, 2000.

22. For more information, go to http://education.jlab.org/itselemental/ele093.html

23. This is according to Robert Leggat at http://www.rleggat.com/photohistory who goes on to say that Herschel used the word 'photography' in a lecture given to the Royal Society on 14 March 1839 and undoubtedly was the person who made the term known to the world. However, it seems that an anonymous writer with the initials 'J.M.' had actually used the word a few weeks earlier on 25 February.

24. See http://amblesideonline.homestead.com/PRPlanetPluto.html for more details on the naming of Pluto.

25. Honor Blackman: 22 August 1925, 6 a.m. BST, Plaistow, London, England (51N32, 0E03). Source: From her to Frank Clifford, as quoted in *British Entertainers: The Astrological Profiles*, Flare Publications, 2003.

26. See http://www.bbc.co.uk/dna/h2g2/alabaster/A703199

27. Homœopathic proving is the process whereby new homœopathic remedies are discovered. Provers are healthy individuals who take a newly prepared homœopathic remedy (which is a much diluted and shaken version of the crude substance) without knowing what that substance is. When a healthy person takes a remedy, they manifest the same signs, sensations and symptoms (albeit in a weaker form) which the substance would cure in sick individuals. Plutonium was proved by homœopath Jeremy Sherr in 1995/6.

Chapter 5: Aspects and Planetary Combinations

1. Tierney, Bil, *The Dynamics of Aspect Analysis*, CRCS, 1993.

2. Carter, Charles, *The Astrological Aspects*, L.N. Fowler, 1967 edition.

3. Addey, John, *Harmonics in Astrology*, Cambridge Circle, 1977, and Hamblin, David, *Harmonic Charts*, Harper Collins, 1987.

4. Kollerstrom, Nick, and O'Neill, Mike, *The Eureka Effect: Astrology of Scientific Discovery*, The Urania Trust, 1996.

5. Dean, Geoffrey, and Mather, Arthur, *Recent Advances in Natal Astrology*, The Astrological Association, 1977.

6. Carter, Charles, *The Astrological Aspects*, L.N. Fowler, 1967 Edition.

7. Baigent, Michael, Campion, Nicholas, and Harvey, Charles, *Mundane Astrology*, The Aquarian Press, 1984.

8. Carter, Charles, *The Astrological Aspects*, L.N. Fowler, 1967 edition.

Chapter 6: The Houses

Works quoted in the text/recommended reading:

Sasportas, Howard, *The Twelve Houses*, Flare/LSA, 2007.

Marks, Tracy, *Your Secret Self: Illuminating the Mysteries of the Twelfth House*, CRCS, 1989.

Hand, Robert, *Horoscope Symbols*, Schiffer, 1987.

1. In Western culture, the Sun can be associated with our surnames – the one we are born with and those we may acquire through marriage.

Chapter 7: Non-Essential Bodies

1. For consideration of the Nodes from the Vedic perspective, see *The Lunar Nodes: Crisis and Redemption*, Komilla Sutton, Wessex Astrologer, 2001.

2. Date of photographic plate showing Chiron: 18 October 1977, 9.08 a.m. UT, Palomar (33N19, 116W53). Discovery date: 1 November 1977, 10.00 a.m. PST, Pasadena, California (34N09, 118W09).

3. See the website http://cfa-www.harvard.edu/iau/lists/Centaurs.html (updated daily).

4. This parallel was suggested by Robert von Heeren in his book, co-authored with Dieter Koch, *Pholus – Wandler zwischen Saturn und Neptun* (German language only), Chiron Verlag, Tubingen, Germany, 1995.

5. For further details see the following websites:
www.robertvonheeren.de
www.expreso.co.cr/centaurs
www.zanestein.com/chiron

6. One AU (astronomical unit) = 93 million miles/150 million kilometres = mean distance from the Earth to the Sun.

7. Personal communication at a conference in Lucerne in 1993 or 1994.

8. President Franklin D. Roosevelt: 30 January 1882, 8.45 p.m. LMT, Hyde Park, New York, 41N47 73W56. Source: His father's diary.
A Democrat, he held office for four terms, the only President to serve for more than two. His Aquarian planets go some way to explaining his humanitarian bent but his Chiron in Taurus in the Eighth House conjunct Jupiter and Neptune augments the liberal, charitable impulse of that conjunction, describing the strenuous and perhaps brilliant efforts he made during the Great Depression to make viable economic reforms and alleviate the suffering of the unemployed.

9. From a lecture given at the Astrological Association's Conference, York, 1983.

Chapter 9: Profiles

1. Henry VIII: 28 June 1491, 8.45 a.m. LMT, Greenwich, England (51N29, 0W00). Source: Martin Harvey quotes the British royal archives.
Henry's Wives:

Catherine of Aragon: married in 1509, divorced in 1533.

Anne Boleyn: married in 1533, beheaded in 1536.

Jane Seymour: married in 1536, died in 1537.

Anne of Cleves: married in January 1540, divorced in July 1540.

Katherine Howard: married in July 1540, beheaded in 1542.

Katherine Parr: married in 1543, outlived Henry, and died in 1548.

2. Ridley, Jasper, *Henry VIII*, Penguin, 1984.

3. For more detailed explanations of Moon-Mars and other aspects, see Tompkins, Sue, *Aspects in Astrology*, Element, 1989 (Rider, 2001).

4. Kelly Holmes: 19 April 1970, 11 a.m. CET, Pembury, England (51N09, 0E20). Source: Sue Tompkins quotes her, via her manager.

All information regarding Kelly is taken from her autobiography *Black, White and Gold*, Virgin Books, 2005. I would speculate that Kelly was born closer to 10.53 or 10.54 a.m. One reason for suspecting this earlier time is that her progressed MC would then have been tightly conjunct her Sun when she won her Olympic gold medals. The data for those races are as follows:

800 metres: 23 August 2004. Start time: 8.55 p.m. local time, Athens (37N58, 23E43). 1500 metres 28 August 2004. Start time: 8.30 p.m. local time, Athens (37N58, 23E43).

Note that while this is not, by any means, a major significator for her winning the race, during the 800-metre race, the Sun and Mercury in the sky fell at Kelly's Sun/Moon midpoint. This is an occurrence that, for the Sun alone, will happen eight times every year, but not, of course, every time Kelly has run a major race.

5. Ebertin, Reinhold, *The Combination of Stellar Influences*, AFA, 1994.

6. For further reading about midpoints as well as other techniques see: Harvey, Charles, and Harding, Mike, *Working with Astrology*, Consider, 1998.

7. ibid.

8. Agatha Christie: 15 September 1890, 4 a.m. GMT, Torquay, England (50N28, 3W30). Source: From her.

All information concerning Agatha Christie has been taken from *Agatha Christie – An Autobiography*, William Collins, 1977.

9. 'Amanda': 16 August 1967, 11.30 p.m. GDT, Liverpool, England (53N25, 2W55).

10. Carter, Charles, *The Zodiac and the Soul*, Theosophical Publishing House, 1968 edition.

11. Peter: 27 January 1954, 2.20 a.m. GMT, Epsom, England (51N20, 0W16).

12. Sankaran, Rajan, *The Soul of Remedies*, Homoeopathic Medical Publishers, 1997.

13. This data is taken from *The Book of World Horoscopes* by Nicholas Campion, a meticulously researched and indispensable reference book for anyone interested in the horoscopes of countries or world events. As Campion says, Indonesian independence was first proclaimed on 17 August 1945 but the Dutch refused to recognize it. Judging by events such as the Bali bombing, and the earthquake and tsunami on 26 December 2004, the 1945 chart would seem to be a relevant one for additional consideration.

14. Statistics concerning the country vary hugely. The main source used here is *The Times Atlas of the World*, Eleventh edition, Times Books, 2003, and www.wikipedia.com

15. Accident: 22 June 1983, 4.05 a.m. GDT, 51N33, 0W06.

Other titles from Flare Publications

For books, discounted titles as well as consultations, events and giveaways, check out our websites at www.flareuk.com and www.londonschoolofastrology.co.uk

Our titles can also be bought online at various sites, and we encourage readers to support these two landmark London-based bookshops:

The Astrology Shop, 78 Neal Street, Covent Garden, London WC2H 9PA, tel: 020 7813 3051, www.londonastrology.com

The Midheaven Bookshop, tel: 020 7607 4133, www.midheavenbooks.com

If you wish to keep informed of our special offers and new books as they become available, please write to us at Flare/LSA, BCM Planets, London WC1N 3XX, England or email: admin@londonschoolofastrology.co.uk

Currently available:

Aspects in Astrology by Sue Tompkins (0-7126-1104-5, 310pp, Rider, 2001)
The essential and informative guide to astrological aspects and planetary combinations. A modern classic.

Astrology in the Year Zero by Garry Phillipson (978-0-9530261-9-7, 272pp)
The inside track on what astrologers actually do and the criticisms they face – based on over 30 interviews with contemporary astrologers and scientific researchers. Including insights into business, psychological and predictive astrology, this is the most thought-provoking, pertinent and controversial critique on the subject ever written.

British Entertainers: the Astrological Profiles by Frank C. Clifford (978-1-903353-01-1, 320pp)
Develop your understanding of astrology by studying the charts and biographies of over 800 celebrities from film, theatre, television, comedy and music. This third edition includes hundreds of new data from the author's files, thousands of dated events, transits, and biographical quotes, plus the astrological signs of entertainment success.

The Draconic Chart by Rev. Pamela Crane (978-0-9530261-4-2, 278pp, comb-bound)
This pioneering work reveals the history and importance of the Draconic Zodiac, which offers deep insights into your life meaning, driving principles, spiritual purpose, vocation and karma. Plus Reverend Crane's own impassioned journey from her first apprenticeship to the discovery of the horoscope of Christ's Nativity.

Jupiter and Mercury: An A to Z by Paul Wright (978-1-903353-00-4, 86pp, limited comb-bound student edition)
Covering a wide range of topics – from creativity, celebrity and luck, to evangelism, morality and murder – this is an important work that will challenge, expand and refine your astrological understanding of both planets.

Mars: Your Burning Desires by Frank C. Clifford and Anna Stuart (978-0-9530261-6-6, 32pp)
Discover what your Mars placement reveals about your desires, attitudes to love, sexual turn-ons and turn-offs.

Shorthand of the Soul: the Quotable Horoscope by David Hayward
(978-0-9530261-2-8, 256pp)
An inspirational collection of over 2000 quotations (with astrological significators)
embracing every aspect of life. The wit and wisdom of poets, philosophers, authors
and celebrities bridges the gap between the symbolic worlds of literature and
astrology. With full index.
The Sun Sign Reader by Joan Revill (978-0-9530261-3-5, 224pp)
Drawing from literature, radio and television, this astrological birthday book is an
entertaining cocktail of fictional birth and event dates. A stimulating introduction to
hundreds of authors and their works.
Venus: Your Key to Love by Frank C. Clifford and Anna Stuart (978-0-9530261-5-9,
36pp)
Discover what your individual Venus placement has to say about your relationships
and attitudes to love and sex.

Also available:

Palmistry 4 Today by Frank C. Clifford
A truly original 4-step guide to understanding your relationships, career, health and
future. Play 'palm detective', learn timing techniques, discover what the hands reveal
about love, health and career, and practise by studying real examples and palm prints.
Originally published by Rider in 2002, the revised US edition (Flare, 2007) includes a
full certificate course of assignments.
Palm Reading by Frank C. Clifford
A fully illustrated Hamlyn guide to your personality, work and relationships, as
revealed by the lines and shape of your hands.

Coming soon from Flare:

The Midheaven: Spotlight on Success by Frank C. Clifford
Birth Charts: Horoscopes of the Famous by Frank C. Clifford
The Twelve Houses by Howard Sasportas

The London School of Astrology
– a holistic approach to astrology –

- Accredited Foundation courses for beginners in central London
- Accredited Diploma courses for those with more experience
- Saturday seminars, residential courses and other events
- New short courses in palmistry (modern hand analysis)

- Learn astrology in a fun, supportive environment
with the UK's most experienced astrologers/tutors
- Fun, self-knowledge, spiritual development, vocational training

To find out more
Visit our website: www.londonschoolofastrology.co.uk
Email: admin@londonschoolofastrology.co.uk

Telephone: 0700 2 33 44 55

London School of Astrology
BCM Planets
London WC1N 3XX